THE TUMULTUOUS HISTORY OF
THE BANK
OF AMERICA

THE TUMULTUOUS HISTORY OF
THE BANK OF AMERICA

MOIRA JOHNSTON

BeardBooks
Washington, D.C.

Library of Congress Cataloging-in-Publication Data

Johnston, Moira, 1934-
    The tumultuous history of the Bank of America / by Moira Johnston.
        p. cm.
    Rev. ed. of: Roller coaster. c1990.
    Includes bibliographical references and index.
    ISBN 1-58798-020-7 (paper)
    1. Bank of America--History. 2. Banks and banking--United States--History.
I. Johnston, Moira, 1934--Roller coaster. II. Title.

HG2613.S54 B275 2000
332.1'23'0973--dc21   00-034290

To my precious friends,
whose love and encouragement
keep me writing

I wish to pay special tribute to Sheilagh Simpson, my editorial and research associate throughout this long and daunting project. Her professionalism, dedication, creative initiative, sound editorial judgment, and extraordinary breadth of skills make her an incomparable one-woman support system for a writer of big and complex works of nonfiction.

We used to call her MotherBank, or the University of America because so many people trained there and left. After a few years, your pay just would not stay competitive. But while you were there you always knew you were with the best. The biggest bank in the world. You carried the $100 billion business card, and every door opened to you.

—JONATHAN SAIGER, former officer
trainee at the Bank of America

A lot of analysts look at the numbers, and they think the numbers are revealing when, in fact, the numbers are very much after the fact. It's the personalities that mold the institution. And a lot of times the personalities tell you more about where that institution is going, what kind of mistakes might be made . . . the troubles.

—DONALD K. CROWLEY, financial analyst
and former BankAmerican

Prologue

I

ON MAY 19, 1987, John S. Reed, CEO of Citicorp, the most powerful bank in the United States, ordered a computer entry in his bank's accounting department that shifted $3 billion from the "retained earnings" column to "reserves for credit losses." An institution whose corporate purpose was profit had voluntarily stripped $3 billion—more than the total assets of most American banks—from the profits side and put it into the store of money held in reserve as a buffer against bad loans. With the stroke of a computer key, Reed had inflicted ravaging damage to his balance sheet.

The act was a raw display of power, a declaration to its peers and to debtor nations that Citicorp played from strength—that it could afford massive losses. But it also said the unthinkable: It *expected* losses. It was a daring unilateral act that could draw the market's fire, drive its own stock down, earn the wrath of the international banking community, and invite attacks of "predator" if trying to keep up with Citicorp—as all big banks would feel forced to do—brought any of America's weakened behemoths to their knees.

But "something had to be done," said Citicorp's William R. Rhodes, principal choreographer of the debt-restructuring ritual that had kept the specter of default at bay since 1982. Brazil had become a rogue debtor, refusing, since

February, to pay a cent of interest on its $111 billion of foreign debt, $67 billion of that owed to commercial banks. If Brazil did not resume payments soon or reach some emergency accommodation with the banks, the world's eighth-largest nation would be formally branded "value-impaired" by American regulators, forcing all banks that had lent it money to strip hundreds of millions, even billions, directly from their precious capital and pledge them against possible losses.

Brazil must be brought swiftly to the bargaining table. But so must bankers be brought, at last, to reality—to the fact that they would never get all their money back. Bankers must be made to face "the thing we all know in our hearts: The debt burden is too large for the countries," as Bank of America's chief foreign credit officer, Lewis W. Coleman, summed up the situation.

"John did something big, dramatic, useful . . . and he changed the world," Walter B. Wriston, Reed's legendary predecessor, said exultantly, as news of the hit spread like an electric shock.

ACROSS THE STREET from Citicorp Center, Louis G. Schirano, First Interstate Bancorp's specialist in international debt restructuring, had been leaving his Third Avenue office, furled umbrella under his arm, as the green digitized words ran across his computer screen. In disbelief, he repeated them. "Citicorp says they'll, ah, add three billion dollars . . . repeat, says Reuters, *three billion dollars* . . . for loan loss reserves. . . ." Schirano ripped off his jacket, eyes riveted to the screen. "Citicorp says it sees . . . a loss of $2.5 billion for the second quarter and one billion for '87. . . ." Within nanoseconds his phone had gone wild. He called the New York Federal Reserve to make sure the Fed "window" was open with emergency funds for any bank that might need them, and was told, "Absolutely." Colleagues rushed to his office door in the need to cling together in the first wave of shock and uncertainty.

What would happen? Would bank stocks plunge? Would all the banks be forced to follow the leader and plunder their precious earnings to set up bigger reserves than the giant elite banks had ever before been asked to pledge? It could be the coup de grace to Bank of America, the floundering giant that had once been the largest bank in the world.

Schirano reminded all bankers: "It is nowhere written that banks cannot fail." His own bank, First Interstate, had just been thwarted in an audacious effort to take over the troubled California giant. "I'm sure that Citicorp didn't mean it explicitly as a threat to B of A," said First Boston's William B. Weaver, the investment banker who had just helped BankAmerica sell its big Italian bank as part of a fire sale of assets to raise desperately needed capital. "But I think Citicorp has raised the hurdles for everybody else."

"I DON'T BELIEVE IT, I don't believe it, I don't believe it," George M. Salem said in catatonic repetition, creating such a commotion that "people thought I needed a hospital or an ambulance." One of Wall Street's best-known bank analysts, he had been in Dallas at the desk of the treasurer of American Airlines. "It was three-twenty . . . three twenty-five—an hour earlier than New York. I'm sitting here talking to him, and sliding across this large Quotron screen right next to his shoulder, looking right at me, was 'Citicorp to have $2.5 billion loss in second quarter.' " It was, Salem thought, "the biggest news since the depression. Citicorp is the most important stock in the industry—a powerful, proud, always profitable bank—and it's starting to look like one of the wounded. Not in B of A's condition, but . . . this could be a world financial crisis."

He had been running the numbers on this for months: what it would do to equity, the balance sheet, financial health. What could not be quantified was the impact on the market. "My number one role is what's going to happen to the stock and what do we tell our clients." His recommendations to buy or sell Citicorp and other bank stocks could make or lose many millions for his customers. "I *have* to be in New York," he knew. Feeling "just enormous mental pressure," he caught a five-fifteen flight out of Dallas for New York.

AT FOUR-THIRTY, while Salem was in the air, in a large dining room within the two-square-block headquarters whose beveled roofline has become Citicorp's international landmark, John Reed dropped his bombshell. Reed, a slight and boyish-looking forty-eight-year-old with the style more of an Ivy rowing crew cox than of the most powerful commercial banker in the Western world, faced a press conference called on the thirty-ninth floor of 399 Park Avenue—an event described by Salem's assistant as "one gigantic mishmash" of media and analysts. "To cushion the bank against bad loans," he was, indeed, placing a $3 billion reserve.

It had already been an epic day for Citicorp. The board had met and given its approval. Reed and his senior team had notified key people—the Federal Reserve, Treasury, the Comptroller of the Currency—trying to maintain secrecy as Citicorp's own foreign currency traders got wind of the rumor and pulsed it through their electronic network. Bill Rhodes had called Michel Camdessus and Barber B. Conable, Jr., chiefs of the International Monetary

Fund (IMF) and the World Bank. Reed had consulted with Wriston, retired but still keeping an office in Citicorp Center across the street, and Wriston told him, "That's the finest thing you've ever done. You have my hundred percent support." Just before the press conference Reed had personally called the CEOs of the two banks that would be hit the hardest by his act: Manufacturers Hanover and Bank of America.

A FULL-JOWLED AND BESPECTACLED MAN with the same granitic facade as the mighty bank that has been his mistress for all but five of the last thirty-eight years, A. W. Clausen took Reed's call from his ice blue velvet chair in his fortieth-floor office in BankAmerica's headquarters tower in San Francisco. It was the sharpest, most humiliating blow B of A had taken from Citicorp in five decades of rivalry.

Citicorp had more at risk in Brazil than Bank of America: $4.7 billion in loans and a golden business relationship that went back to 1915. But no one was at greater personal risk than Tom Clausen. Through the 1970s he had been lord of the world's largest, most profitable bank. His earnest gray management style had been celebrated in *Forbes* as the reason "this big, slow-moving tortoise seems perfectly able to keep up with the flashier, more dynamic hares," as California's Bank of America overtook its New York rival, Citibank, in profitability and smugly avoided the eastern giant's huge loan losses. Having reached this corporate apex, Clausen had left in 1981 to take up the role of banker-statesman as president, for five years, of the World Bank—just as the seeds he had helped plant blossomed into a devil's patch of disasters.

The proud image now lay in shambles. Humiliation had become a global media event for the bank that, just a few years earlier, had commanded the largest concentration of wealth of any private financial institution in history— more than the Medici, Fuggers, Rothschilds, or J. P. Morgan. Now, by any of the bloodless numbers and ratios used by financial analysts to measure corporate health, the Bank of America was very sick indeed.

And it was being run by men from Wells Fargo, founder A. P. Giannini's longtime banking rival—a blow to make A.P. bellow from his grave.

In banker's blue flannel, his thinning hair combed with measured precision into strands across the top of his forehead, Clausen had been commandeered out of retirement from the World Bank to lead the crumbling colossus through the daunting job of its "recovery." With the determination of a stubborn Norwegian from Illinois, the born-again banker had returned, to the shock of the financial community, to "make B of A . . . the preeminent institution it was for so many years. That's a guarantee."

Clausen had returned to a financial world that was transforming the centuries-old image of "banker" and redefining the very word *bank*. Most of the change had happened since he left commercial banking in 1981, and now he must move without a false step through a fiercely competitive marketplace wrenched by the accelerating forces of deregulation, by a powerful internationalizing trend that tied the fortunes of every American bank to the global marketplace, and, above all, by the electronic revolution—a revolution that moved even Clausen's rock-stolid style to lyricism as, aided by speech writers, he saw "a metaphysical world in which economic value dances on a silicon chip."

In this crucible of change, Clausen must call up qualities he had never shown—the fleet-footed responsiveness and visionary strategies that were now the most rudimentary tools for survival. If he pulled it off, if he returned the bank not just to regional mediocrity but to international preeminence, he would be a corporate hero to surpass Lee Iacocca; he would stand beside A. P. Giannini. If he failed, the vestigial remains of the world's biggest bank might well languish, by the year 2000, as a provincial satrap in Japan's financial empire—or as a satellite of Citicorp, which, as Reed called Clausen, had reportedly accumulated 2 percent of BankAmerica's stock.

He had taken the helm of a bank undergoing a full, rolling restructuring that had been launched by Samuel H. Armacost, the president who, after struggling for five years to exorcize the problems built up since the fifties, had been ousted by the board, sacrificed to the angry gods of profit who seemed to have turned their backs on Bank of America. Clausen was riding the momentum, whipping it with a tougher and more austere hand. He had successfully fought off a takeover attempt, and he and his inside team were glimpsing improvements in the underlying trends. Still losing money, but losing *less* money. They believed that under the surface disasters, recovery was beginning. Mother-Bank, as its employees lovingly called the institution, was still sustained by that incomparable resource, the deposits in her 850 branches in California, the richest banking market in the country.

But Bank of America was so weak, so short of capital that it could withstand few more shocks. There were rumors in the street that B of A was close to bankruptcy, that the Comptroller of the Currency and the Federal Deposit Insurance Corporation (FDIC) were preparing to swoop down and bail out or sell off "capitalism's greatest prize." Clausen had been hoping, within months, to toss his first tiny scrap of good news to the hungry business press, a modest increase in operating earnings that might—if Brazil did not sabotage his plans—bring the bank back to the cusp of profitability after three years of staggering losses. And now Reed's act was, as a banker termed it, "a stake in the heart" to Clausen's infant recovery. If the market liked Reed's move, if the stock went up, the pressure on all the big banks to fall into line would be irresistible.

AT EIGHT the morning after Reed's announcement, analyst George Salem declared that Citicorp stock would fall. Citi's stock had closed at 50⅝. As he lowered Citicorp's rating, Salem predicted, "Today it will close in the forty-eight to forty-nine dollar range." Within minutes his predictions had been beamed out to Dallas, San Francisco, Chicago, Europe. They were on the screens at the desks of more than four hundred institutional investors, the professional investors who move great blocks of stock and largely control the market.

As Salem raced uptown for Citi's 11:00 A.M. analysts' meeting, the market opened. Citicorp was up. It moved up all day and closed up 2½, at $53—while B of A's fell ¼ to $11. "The market likes it," said Wriston, elated. "I told John this would give the stock twenty points!" Said Salem: "I looked like a horse's rear end." But the next day, and the next, he went back and argued that Citicorp stock would fall. "You think it's glamorous to go before this cynical group for the third time and tell them, 'It's irrational. It's hysteria'?" Citicorp stock continued to climb. "People thought the third world debt problem was over."

THE BIG BANKS sat tight for a week. Then, the day before B of A's annual meeting on May 26, the first of the major banks marched into line behind Citicorp. Chase Manhattan pledged a $1.6 billion reserve. At the press conference before his annual meeting the next day, Clausen kept up his bluster. "Let me repeat it. . . . We are looking at our mix of assets and are saying that our reserves are adequate." But Chase had forced his hand.

On June 8 Clausen made his announcement: Bank of America would add a $1.1 billion allowance for credit losses. He was taking the hit. The man who "could not tolerate a down quarter," as his predecessor had observed, would take a near-billion-dollar loss for the year. Far worse than Armacost's worst year. Three times larger than 1986. Deep inside the corporate organism, recovery might be under way. But the perception was that the Bank of America was still a very sick bank. Everyone knew that perceptions could kill more surely than fact.

II

BRAZIL WAS NOT the only rogue debtor bedeviling the Bank of America. A continent away two octogenarians in cotton aprons struck back from a California tomato farm, baring a mismatch of corporate priorities that may underlie the bank's decline far more than the imprudent loan practices that triggered the Brazilian crisis.

WITH THE PARLOR curtains drawn against the midday heat, the two old women sat in their armchairs. Gnarled hands gripped the arms as they waited for the call that would come soon from the courthouse in Yuba City. The depression-style calico print housedresses they wore did not even hint at the size and importance of the money and issues that were at stake. Elide Stanghellini and her sister, Angelina Fava, eighty-three and eighty-one, with Elide's son, Bob, had sued the Bank of America. They were caught up in an event that, to Americans largely removed from the land, was charged with unbearable poignancy: a family losing its farm. Fighting back, they had challenged a bank perceived as so mighty and prestigious that many, especially abroad, believe it to be the United States' national bank. They had sued in a desperate attempt to reclaim the near-million-dollar savings the bank had already claimed and to stave off foreclosure on every acre, tractor, house, shed, and asset built up over three generations of farming California's Sutter Basin. They had sued for $50 million. For the women, the jury's verdict would determine if they must pack up and leave their home of sixty-five years.

A year and a half earlier Elide and Angelina had been feisty elders able to drive themselves into Knights Landing in their old Chrysler to shop and bank and able to keep house without help. In the picture taken for the cover of *California Farmer* with the news of their lawsuit, they stand staunch in their aprons, models for the classic American Gothic image of farm women. Now they were spare wisps being cared for by a housekeeper. Framed by white hair pulled back into austere knots, the aged skin was suspended over strong Italian armatures, but the faces were drained of spunk and expression.

The sisters' visible decline had been swift and sudden and seemed to parallel, almost to the day and hour, the visible decline of the bank. As the stress from the lawsuit sapped them, Elide and Angelina fingered their blue Bank of America passbooks like prayer beads. Confiscated by the bank, but now returned, the little books—thirty of them—recorded more than sixty years of savings.

The passbooks were family mementos. Their father's cousin Lorenzo Scatena had raised A. P. Giannini, the bank's founder, as his son. The women had been weaned on the lore: Lorenzo, who hauled fruit and vegetables from ranch to railway with his team and wagon in the San Jose area in the 1880s, had married the twenty-two-year-old widow Giannini after her husband had been shot and killed in a fight over a $10 debt. He had adopted the ten-year-old boy, Amadeo, and his siblings. Elide and Angelina's own father, Mansueta Fava, had come to this region to farm beans the very same year, 1887, that young Amadeo Peter Giannini started cruising the farmlands of the San Joaquin, Sacramento, and San Fernando valleys, a teenaged entrepreneur buying produce for his stepfather's L. Scatena & Company, by then flourishing as a wholesale marketer of produce in San Francisco. Only three years apart in age, the two young men became good friends and did business together; Amadeo brokered Fava's fruits and vegetables in San Francisco. The family's proudest story is that A.P., as he was known to the world at large, invited their father to found the bank with him, the bank, born as the Bank of Italy in 1904, that had become, by 1945, the largest bank in the world and that was still, in 1987, the world's largest private lender to agriculture. The women still argued over why their father said no, while his cousin Scatena became a founder and board member of the future Bank of America.

The numbers in the passbooks had meaning to the women as a measure of the presence of the Fava family on the acres their father had farmed from 1914; he had moved the family then to the banks of the Sacramento River, where the higher rim lands could be farmed as the swamp and tule could not before the levees and reclamation projects. As girls they had met the barges that docked at China Ferry Landing, bringing their dad plows, oil, and seed. "We helped our mother cook, jam, things like that," Elide recalled. They had brought food to the fields during harvest. They had sewed the burlap sacks that were filled with grain and rice in the field, loaded on wagons, and stacked on the decks of the paddle steamers that carried them to San Francisco. They had watched the Sutter Basin—a one hundred thousand-acre patch of green in the heart of the great Central Valley, which stretches from Red Bluff in the north to Bakersfield in the south—become one of the world's most luxuriant food producers. These savings in the Bank of America were their legacy of that bounty, a legacy that had swelled, at times, to $5 million. The market value of the land they could lose today was over $3 million; the loans at issue were over $3 million. At issue, for the women, was holding their home.

Until 1980 the family had never borrowed from the bank. The Favas and Giulio Stanghellini, the Italian immigrant Elide married, had been such good and frugal farmers that they had managed to show a profit—$400,000 net one year after Bob took over at Angelo's death—without ever taking a loan. But the bank had always been their friend. Bank officers in the local Knights Landing branch had dropped by over the years to talk and drink coffee.

Persuaded by the local branch to expand the farming operation to make more efficient use of his fleet of expensive mechanized equipment, Bob had borrowed his first half million–plus just as the first signs of a break in a decade of strong agricultural prices began to appear. He had watched the agricultural depression move toward Sutter Basin like a twister. "The Midwest got it first. . . . It hit us slower here because we're diversified." But in 1980 rains hit just as the first fingers of recession reached into the basin. The bank had urged Bob to borrow again to expand production and make up the losses. And to borrow, like Brazil, to pay the interest that was escalating the debt out of control. Once the loans began, the women had passively signed, again and again, putting up the land and cash they owned as collateral. "If Bobbie needs the money, we'll do it," they'd say. The bank was behind them. Trust was total. "And farmers don't read the small print," says Bob. "That's why we have bankers." It was only after the shock of the bank's turning its back on any further financing of the farm in 1985—once the farm and family were hopelessly snared in a web of debt—and threatening foreclosure that Elide and Angelina stopped blaming Bob for mismanagement and permitted him to hunt for a lawyer who might help them make sense of the inexplicable disasters that had struck harder than any flood or crop failure.

Bob had found Richard R. Murphy in Lodi, in an upstairs one-lawyer office he ran with a staff that included his wife and several of his nine children. Raised on a farm in South Dakota, Murphy was a crusading small-town lawyer committed since 1967 to the fight for the American farmer—a fight that had often pitted him against the banks. Now, he found himself at the heart of California's Farm Belt as bankrupt farmers unleashed a barrage of angry lawsuits against their banks. The suits were partly a release for fifty years of farmers' pent-up resentment, for Bank of America has carried the stigma of land grabber since it bought up defaulted and abandoned farm properties in the depression. An apple grower in Sebastapol, 100 miles west of Sutter Basin, won a $26 million court award against Bank of America just as the Stanghellini case was filed. It was Murphy's moment.

The two men had spent weeks stripping off the layers and years of events, trying to figure out what had happened. Bob had run into his old banker, Michael Peterson, on the high school steps at his daughter's graduation in Sacramento. Bob had been shocked as Peterson, the man who'd made him the loans, told him about some of the bank's actions on the loans. If true, they were, at best, callous betrayal of his aunt's and mother's trust. At worst, conspiracy. Gradually Murphy and Stanghellini became convinced of a grand plot: The bank, desperate to raise capital to bail out the multibillion-dollar loan losses beginning to surface in Latin America, had forced farms into default so that they could grab them up and sell them to raise capital. Even if their theory stretched motives to the edge, the two were gathering evidence that the

abandonment of the Stanghellinis was part of a new bank strategy to remove
itself from agricultural lending, a strategy never revealed to the farmers.

To win the massive lawsuit shaping in their minds, they would have to
convince the jury that the bank had gone beyond imprudence and ineptness to
willful fraud—that it had orchestrated the fugue of loans with the intent of
having the Stanghellini farm fail. The jury would have to believe that the bank
had perverted the basic banking mission: to serve society's needs by providing
credit and a safe home for savings—a mission, in specific terms, to take
deposits in with one hand and lend them out with the other, making a fair profit
in the spread between the interest rates it paid for the deposits and the
somewhat higher one it received for the loans. Murphy would argue that the
bank had failed on both counts, paying the two sisters coercively low interest
on their savings, while luring the family into a package of loans and promises
that destroyed both farm and savings. "I was so brainwashed at that time that I
pushed Bob and his former partner to borrow . . . and expand . . . initially on a
small scale, then slowly increased their reliance on borrowed funds . . . It was
like a 'dope dealer'—take a little now and increase the reliance until it's too
late," Mike Peterson admitted in a memo and in a deposition to the court as he
became a witness for the Stanghellinis.

Yet as Dick Murphy filed a complaint in the Sutter County Superior Court in
Yuba City for "fraud and deceit . . . conspiracy, negligence, intentional inflic-
tion of emotional distress . . . ," the women were still reluctant. "Even to the
last, when I talked them into filing suit, they still had this feeling that the bank
was their friend," said Bob. It was only after the bank's lawyer had accused the
women, in court, of tax evasion—a felony!—that Elide was finally able to
gather enough indignation to rail at her beloved bank: "I didn't think they were
that kind of son of a bitch. We stick with them even when Angelo died, and
that's what we get." But Bob joked nervously to Dick Murphy, as the trial
ground on through its seventh week, "My worst fear in this lawsuit is still that
the lawyer for the bank will say, 'I'm sorry,' he'll hug my mother, and the case
will be over."

Above all, the sisters were struggling to preserve a long illusion, one
fashioned from the days when Amadeo Giannini had known every farmer and
acre he bankrolled and had sat at an open desk where even the poorest man
could come and talk, where service, more than money, had been A.P.'s motive.
His words of commitment to serving the needs of the "little fellow" were
carved in stone in the bank's headquarters building in San Francisco. There
had been compassion. Giannini had been the first to make loans to farmers; he
had saved his old friend Fava and all the bean farmers of the Sacramento Delta,
when the bean market died after World War I, advancing emergency money

and a line of credit to keep the farmers afloat. The branch managers—in Knights Landing or nearby Rio Vista or Woodland—had been men respected and involved in the community. They had known their customers; they had been A.P.'s long arm on banking's front line. But as the court case unfolded, the women had been forced to face what the bank had become. There had been a loss of "that human touch," mourned Giannini's daughter, Claire Giannini Hoffman, now eighty-four, her father's surrogate on the board of directors after her father's death.

Sam Armacost, still president when the lawsuit began, deeply resented the image being painted of his branch bankers as callous Shylocks drinking tea in the Stanghellinis' kitchen while they held a sword over the farm. "Ridiculous!" It was the very softness of some of the branch lenders that had helped bring the bank "to the brink of mortal disaster."

The jury would decide. Playing out in a makeshift courtroom in Yuba City—the Northern California town named by Rand McNally's road map makers as the nation's least desirable destination—*Stanghellini Ranch, Inc.* v. *Bank of America National Trust and Savings Association* would test a farmer's relationship to his bank and a bank's legitimate conduct. A victory for the Stanghellinis would almost certainly send waves far beyond Yuba City, escalating the story from the *Yuba City Appeal Democrat* to the *Wall Street Journal;* it would trigger a wave of similar lawsuits that could bring an already stumbling banking giant to its knees. A victory would resonate as a sign of hope through an agricultural industry as troubled as at any time since the Great Depression and speed the demise of the image of banker as community leader and farmer's friend that had been the essence of A.P.'s banking style.

But these implications did not reach into the farmhouse at Knights Landing. There two sisters distracted themselves from the call that would come soon from Yuba City by watching the TV set with the photograph of their parents on top. They were numbed by the options: If they lost, everything was gone. If they won, they would have to accept that the Bank of America had betrayed them. At 1:20 P.M. the telephone rang. The housekeeper took it and gave the phone to Elide. It was Bob's boy, turning fourteen next day, a sweet boy in spite of the pet python he kept in his bedroom. "Grandma, Dad says to tell you we won fifty million dollars."

III

ON OCTOBER 19, 1987, the stock market dived 508 points. Black Monday. The first truly global market crash. Loss of confidence in the American market had rolled in waves across oceans and continents, satellite-bounced electrons transmitting the news instantaneously, ahead of the sun, as panic swept the stock exchanges of New York, San Francisco, Hong Kong, Tokyo, London.

Two days after the crash, on October 21, on the twentieth floor of B of A's headquarters, Frank Newman, Clausen's chief financial officer, faced thirty journalists to announce a scrap of good news: Operating earnings had inched up in the third quarter. One of the new Wells Fargo team who Clausen had found running the bank on his return, slight, red-haired with neat brush mustache, Newman stated, "I am particularly happy to report that third quarter earnings are written solidly in black ink . . . a milestone in our recovery effort." The gain was small, but it was not the smoke-and-mirrors one-time earnings of asset sales. The bank had at last crept across the line from red to black ink. Brazil's moratorium, and Citicorp's hit, had demonstrated the bank's ability to absorb "a couple of really extraordinary external shocks."

But "these results have to be viewed as the first part of the journey," Newman admitted, for in spite of this promising quarter, the loss for the year would be staggering: $955 million. Nearly $1 billion because of Brazil. Negative perceptions ran at full tide. Corporate declines spawned a cynicism with a momentum all its own. And "Brazil" was not over. In two weeks, at their meeting in Washington, a powerful troika of regulators was almost certain to declare that nation "value-impaired" and force B of A to write off some of its loans to that nation, a hit that, unlike voluntary reserves, would deplete the bank's capital. A terrible blow. At a question from a *Journal* reporter about what might happen on Brazil, Newman lost his smile. "I will not comment on politics."

As the confident decade had begun, BankAmerica's stock had traded at $32. As Newman spoke, BAC, its symbol on the stock exchange, was coming across the ticker at $7^5/_8$.

PART
ONE

Chapter
One

THE BELLOWING GIANT A. P. Giannini had died quietly in his bed on June 3, 1949.

Of all the tributes, none would have been more relished by the "Giant of the West" than the thunder of the Sacramento's waters pouring over the crest of the Shasta Dam at its dedication in mid-June 1950. A.P.'s spirit—and his bank's money—were there on the crest as the floodgates were raised on the crown jewel of the Central Valley irrigation project and the largest hydroelectric plant in California. For, through loans to industrialist Henry Kaiser, the bank had helped fund the world's second-largest concrete structure. From a crest higher than the Washington Monument, *three* times higher than Niagara Falls, to use the hyperbole rampant at the time, fanned a sloping spillway that covered the area of six football fields (including bleachers), containing enough concrete to build a three-foot-wide sidewalk around the girth of the globe at the equator.

As the waters leaped from impoundment behind the dam and raced down the spillway, a roar as deep and reverberating as a thousand bass drums joined the rousing flourishes of sound rising from the festive crowd at the crest. The cymbals and bassoons of the United States Marine Corps Band backed the glittering voice of San Francisco–born Metropolitan Opera soprano Florence Quartararo as she sang "The Star-Spangled Banner."

In the nearby town of Redding, a snow-capped make-believe Mount Shasta loomed over a pioneer-costumed cast of hundreds as a smoke-belching locomotive chugged across the outdoor stage in Redding's "Shasta Cavalcade," the historical pageant staged to celebrate California's entry into the Union. For during the five years that surrounded A.P.'s death, all California became a stage as the state honored the hundredth anniversaries of virtually all its significant founding events. A staggering compression of history, 1946 to 1950 celebrated the discovery and the rush for gold, statehood, the Constitutional Convention in Monterey, the Bear Flag Revolt, the reconquest of Southern California, the first newspaper, first American-type school, first steamer, and on and on.

The empire that Giannini, as much as any frontiersman, settler, or argonaut, had helped build had enveloped his death with pomp and ceremony he himself would never have permitted for his own funeral.

It was a moment, mandated by the state, to pause and reflect. A breather from California's headlong embrace of progress—of the postwar consumerism, suburban fecundity, and industrial growth that had catapulted California to the status of a nation-state. It was a celebration of the conquering of the frontier by men like A. P. Giannini who had not only matched but moved and remade its mountains, rivers, and resources, who had built its dams and bridges, blasted out its roads and railways, and transformed its swamps and deserts into food factories. The centennials became a display of hubris by a new sun-kissed culture lured to continent's edge in a migration more massive than the barbarian migrations that swept Europe at the collapse of the Roman Empire; California's population had grown 10,000 percent in that hundred years!

It was that moment before *Silent Spring* when no ethical hurdles stood in the way of growth, and expansionists were still seen as master builders, not plunderers. "It's progress. You can't stand in the way of progress," A.P. had told his daughter, Claire, embodying the mood, as his own gracious home and gardens, Seven Oaks, were encroached on by highways and apartment buildings in the path of rampaging proto-Silicon Valley. Striding to the bluffs above the great, sandy beach on San Francisco's Pacific flank, he had bellowed approvingly, "Claire, this'll all be inhabited when you're older."

A.P.'s ONLY SURVIVING CHILDREN, Claire and Mario, had been at his side as the stubborn pulse stilled at 6:55 A.M. The ferocious energy that had always been recharged by challenge—by the Great Earthquake, panics and bank runs, by depression, power wars, and the combined forces of Wall Street and Washington—had finally been drained by a series of bodily assaults that congested his huge chest and overwhelmed his heart. Although the *San Francisco Chronicle* apparently deemed his death less sensational than the local linseed oil refinery explosion that dominated the front page, journalist Pierre Salinger suspended a young reporter's cynicism toward big business to pay tribute to "the once-poor San Jose farm boy with vision and foresight who wrote one of the great chapters in the history of California and the Nation." The state's, the city's, and the nation's political and financial leaders responded to the news with an outpouring of praise and converged on San Francisco and San Mateo, south of the city, for the two funeral services staged to accommodate all the mourners.

By his wishes, A.P.'s funeral was as plain and simple as that of an earlier Italian banker, Cosimo de'Medici, whose bank had blazed the path for modern banking. The man who had financed the wars of kings and the trade of Europe and learned the risks of foreign debt five hundred years before American bankers, Cosimo had been buried, by his orders, as an ordinary citizen of Florence. Giannini's mass was said in San Francisco over a casket of silver gray metal adorned only with an embossed cross. There may have been scant pomp and ceremony, but there were A.P.'s people in their worn shoes, shiny funeral suits, and battered fedoras—the little fellows he had invited into a banking system that, since earliest recorded banking, had been for the rich and privileged. The casket was carried into the church by the ten men who had been with A.P. and the bank the longest, honoring tenure and loyalty.

The bank's 520 branches in California stayed open throughout the ceremony; not a transaction was missed, no customer left unserved. In the Wilshire Boulevard branch in Los Angeles, a twenty-six-year-old midwesterner who had joined the bank just a month earlier, Tom Clausen, had been given the afternoon off to attend the rosary on the eve of the funeral of the founder he had never met.

The news of A.P.'s death had been whispered to the bank's cashier, Russell G. Smith, in the midst of negotiations in New York for a loan of $15 million to help a Jewish appeal solve the problem of $300 million subscribed, but uncollected, funds for Israel. When he'd called San Francisco right after the meeting, Mario had told him, "If A.P. were living, he'd tell you to finish your job," and Smith had stayed on in New York. But his mind and emotions were full of A.P. Favored with a position of power, he liked to joke, because "I was a high school dropout and had a graceful Spencerian hand, like A.P.," Smith had been in the trenches with Giannini through the Great Crash, through the repeal of Prohibition, when the bank had helped the grape and wine industries cling to life. They had fought together in the legendary Transamerica proxy fight, when A.P. stormed back from Europe to save from liquidation by alien New York masters the holding company he had created as a vehicle for national expansion.

A.P. had never bothered to tell Smith formally that he was the bank's first international banker. Even in the mid-forties A.P.'s baby was still an entrepreneurial bank, with promotions and assignments made ad hoc in response to galloping growth and the need of the moment. A messenger boy like Smith could rise to senior executive status in a bank that had grown from 75 to 525 branches since he had joined the Bank of Italy in 1923 and was still expanding. Smith first suspected his own new status in London when A.P. would say, "Russ, here, looks after my international stuff." And in New York A.P. had marched Smith into the office of the chairman of National City Bank (Citibank), on whose board A.P. sat, and said, "This is Russ Smith. He's going to look after our international affairs. He doesn't know a damn thing about it, and I want your fellows to help him."

He and A.P. had flown in the steel seats of military aircraft into a Europe still smoking and in ruins. In Rome A.P. had dragged him into an audience with the pope that would make the Gianninis, like the Medici, bankers to the Vatican. Smith chuckled, still hearing the commanding voice that shrank not a decibel in the presence of Pope Pius XII: "Your Holiness, this is Russ Smith. He's not Italian and he's not a Catholic, but I brought him over here so he could tell you what he thinks about Italy. Now, go on, Russ, tell him, *tell* him." That audience led to another, and to a very large papal account.

With A.P.'s blessing, Smith had opened up Japan after the war but had warned against going into China on his first trip in 1946. On a private visit for the Republican Party in 1949 he had watched Madame Chiang Kai-shek run Nationalist China's war against Mao Zedong from her luncheon table, while the generalissimo sat serene, a luncheon that ended abruptly when Madame Chiang stood and said, "Gentlemen, I'm awfully sorry, but there's a battle going on up north and the generalissimo should be there." Smith had just returned from China before A.P.'s death and, sensing the curtain of communism coming down, had again warned against going into Shanghai even though New York's National City Bank was making a handsome profit there trading in silver. He would refrain from saying, "I told you so," when the Bank of America was forced to bail out of its Shanghai branch with a loss of half a million dollars after the Communists took over.

Railway trains rumbled through so many memories of A.P. When they traveled to bankers' conventions with their wives during Prohibition, there was Clorinda Giannini washing telltale signs of devil booze from their glasses after they'd had a scotch in their compartments before dinner. There was a barber on the Overland Limited who was probably telling every man he shaved that A.P. had offered to make him a loan. "He never shaved himself—remember, this was before the safety razor—and he'd give the barber a tip and say, 'If you're ever in San Francisco and need any money, why, come on in and see us. We'll take care of you.' " Smith marveled that A.P. always took his golf clubs on those trips, but never played golf. Time spent on the golf course was morally suspect. " 'You mean, he's got a handicap of *four*?' he'd say, 'That's *disgraceful!*' "

The extraordinary presence of A. P. Giannini would never be duplicated. But Smith had no worry about the bank at A.P.'s death. His son, Mario, was there. "Mario had been giving excellent leadership since he became president in 1936." Mario's experience in the bank filled three pages in the personnel files; he knew the bank's operations more intimately than any employee. A brilliant student of law at the University of California's Hastings Law School, he was a man for times more complex, less frontiering than when A.P. had built the bank. "A.P. was decisive, the salesman for his visions; Mario was more analytical," says Smith. "If you went to A.P. with a piece of paper in your hand and said, 'A.P., I think you'd like to read this letter,' he'd say, 'Tell me about it.' If you went to Mario . . . you couldn't get away without letting him read it. He'd take it home and give it back to you the next day with marginal notes on it." Supporting Mario was a tight-knit Giannini-trained executive group that, Smith believed, would never fall prey to "petty rivalries" after A.P.'s death. They were living models and transmitters of A.P.'s way—the original BankAmericans.

Walking slowly with a cane as the hemophilia that had plagued him from birth became more debilitating, A.P.'s son had entered St. Mary's Cathedral for his father's funeral service through a side entrance and sat with his sister, Claire, in the front pew; the stairs at the church's front entrance were now mountains he could not conquer.

Engulfed by grief, Claire wanted only to be left alone. Yet she had to endure two funerals, one in San Mateo, where the church had overflowed, and this one at St. Mary's. She hated funerals. They too often became social events, she felt, where people came to see and be seen and expected you to feed and entertain them. For the four years since her mother's death in 1945, she and her husband, Biff, had lived with her father at Seven Oaks, the large but unpretentious family home her father had deeded to her. It, and good champagne, were the only things he indulged her in. She had resented his values at times. "He didn't care about money and prestige." From 1945, when he "retired," he received a salary of a dollar a year. As A.P.'s will was read, it was astounding to learn that he had left an estate of less than half a million dollars—a paltry fortune even by the greater value it would have in today's dollars. As he pledged half a million dollars to found the Giannini Foundation when, in the early forties, he felt himself "in danger of becoming a millionaire," Claire "didn't like him giving away all his money; Mother and I could have used some." He had often cautioned his daughter, "Money controls you; you don't control it." Over time, she says, "I learned his humility."

IT WAS MARIO who took command at A.P.'s death. Claire was honored to be given her father's place on the board of directors. Smart, forthright, and intuitive, she had gained incomparable insight into Giannini banking on her many trips with her father. "But I don't think my father would have liked me as an officer in the bank." At family dinners described by niece Anne as "board meetings," with A.P. and Mario arguing with each other down a twenty-foot table, "I never entered the conversation. Nor did my mother," says Claire. "I had no activity in the bank until he died. And then my job was to perpetuate his policy."

Under Mario, there was no pause, no panic, no disarray. Mario had run the bank as president since 1936 and at last came into his own. Insiders and his family knew that Harry Truman had offered him the post of secretary of defense, knew he had driven banking innovation and entry into the international field as aggressively as his father. It was Mario who had initiated the program to save the wine industry and conceived the idea of the holding company that became Transamerica. Yet he had been the invisible man. "He gave all the credit to my grandfather, and it just drove my mother crazy that he wasn't getting any recognition for the things he did," says Mario's elder daughter, now Anne McWilliams. "He'd be annoyed and tell my mother not to interfere." Mario's family were thrilled to see him finally honored with Italy's highest civilian medal and named by *Forbes* magazine as one of the United States' top fifty businessmen. A loving biographer says that A.P. tried to force Mario to take a more public role during the latter years and that Mario had refused. Russ Smith, who was at the elbows of both men during the last years, confirms that "Mario kept himself in the background. Anything that was done, A.P. was given the credit for.

"I think," says Smith, "A.P. had a driving desire to show the old established institutions that he could develop a growing bank," a striving that may have had its origins in ethnic sensitivities. Although he joined the Bohemian, Giannini had been turned down by the establishment's stronghold, the Pacific Union Club on San Francisco's Nob Hill, "and he hated that club ever after," Smith reports. "Italians have always been frowned upon," Claire explains. "We were wops and dagos. My father grew up in the worst of it."

Mario revealed no visible resentment of his supporting role. He had quietly increased his work load during the last years of his father's life, leading his father's long fight with the Federal Reserve Board. In 1932, when A.P. encouraged the Bank of America board to vote for someone other than Mario for president, Mario's wife, Mercedes Giannini, complained, "He's taking Mario's *job.*" But Russ Smith believes that in relieving Mario of some of his load, A.P. was also conspiring to lengthen his son's life. "A.P. just loved Mario," says Eugene E. Trefethen, Jr., who, as president of Kaiser Industries, became a close friend of both Gianninis. Mario was working himself to death.

Yet the bank Mario inherited could not have been more robust. Knowing his territory better than any banker before or since, A.P. had seen the direction California was going and forged a remarkable collaboration with its destiny. It is easy to say that with the state's inexorable growth through the forties and fifties, he could not go wrong. But A.P.'s capacity to bring his bank, thriving, through the depression reveals his success to be based on far more than riding with the good times. Never trapped by the herd thinking that still characterizes most bankers, he was able to identify lending opportunities before trends were clear, well ahead of the pack, and bet the bank on them. He managed his risks by bringing his own hands-on scrutiny to the evaluation and judgment process. He had begun banking in hard times, just before the San Francisco earthquake of 1906 and the bank panic of 1909, and never let banking become too easy. But as the best of times began to roll at mid-century, there seemed little need to search back for the roots of the success Mario had inherited.

Postwar migration had made the West, as a region, the most dynamic of the nation. Within that region California was the prize, and the Bank of America was its banker. "The first thing you did when you came to California was you got a hundred dollars, went down there, and opened an account at the Bank of America. You established yourself as a legitimate citizen," says Santa Monica–based banking consultant Salvatore Serrantino, who first wondered at the phenomenon on a visit from Connecticut in 1954. "Its image was the personification of a bank for everyone. You were dealing with the largest bank in the world." Sixty percent of California's savings sat in its deposit accounts. In 1945 the bank had tasted, for the first time, the heady status of "world's largest bank" as its deposits passed $5 billion. If the size of individual deposits—five million of them by the end of 1949—was a measure, it was still truly the bank for the "little fellow," for the average savings account was $891. There were 525 branches statewide and 7 foreign branches. B of A now employed 14,600 people, up from only 3,500 at the end of the war four years earlier. Nearly 1,000 of those BankAmericans had been with the bank for a quarter of a century.

The branch system A.P. had forged gave both the bank and California a strength and resilience New York's great banks, the so-called money center banks, did not have. With branches scattered throughout the state B of A could mobilize the resources of many branches to concentrate emergency funds in a drought-hit ag region, for example, or extra millions for construction and home mortgages in a booming suburban city. Branch banking was the source of the stability that is "one of the great things about California," says former California Superintendent of Banks Carl J. Schmitt. "In the case of a bank run, the branch banking system has generally been able to move cash from one community to another community in order to stave off, in essence, the loss of confidence."

While the rest of the nation demobilized, California's wartime boom had never ended. Its climate, space, labor force, and activity in the "ultra-new fields" of aerospace and electronics were seductive lures to the defense industry. Fed by military contracts, California blossomed a whole new peacetime industrial base. As the state's population passed ten million and the national income reached the highest level in history by 1948, the momentum to produce and consume was relentless.

The bank funded the infrastructure needed to house, feed, school, and move a state whose GNP, by 1952, would rank it as the seventh-largest nation in the world. Its loans built the freeways, subdivisions, schools, water and electrical systems, dams and irrigation, the heavy and light industry. In 1951 it passed National City Bank as the nation's largest buyer of municipal bonds, the enabling millions for the new communities that were filling the old agricultural valleys and arid hills. It continued to be the largest lender to the farms that made California the fruit and vegetable basket of the nation, with captive markets in California specialties like wine grapes, avocados, artichokes.

With California's food and infrastructure in place, Bank of America proceeded to bankroll the culture whose products and images would become one of America's most potent exports: fashion, trucking, the movies.

It backed the garment trade that gave the world the backless bathing suit, dirndl skirts, and slacks. It backed the big rigs of a trucking industry that moved into second position behind agriculture and made convoys of red and white lights glittering from the freeways at night a classic California sight. As Los Angeles registered more cars and trucks than any foreign nation in the world, Bank of America moved past even General Motors Acceptance Corporation as the state's number one provider of automobile loans.

A.P. was one of the first to take his checkbook to the movies. In 1919 his brother, Dr. Attilio Giannini, had lent $250,000 to First National Distributors, which used as collateral the cans of film holding Charlie Chaplin's *The Kid*. It proved a better investment than government bonds. An industry requiring a shrewd feel for people and the marketplace, movies were the perfect showcase for A.P.'s hands-on banking. He was the first to finance Walt Disney, a relationship that began at the Biltmore Hotel when A.P. and his team came to see if sketches of a small animated creature called Mickey Mouse warranted a loan. As Disney presented his sketches, Mario shook his head as it was reported to Claire, who was in another room. Dr. Giannini, the sophisticated New York banker, scoffed, "No, this is a crazy thing to do!" A.P. took a look, eyeballed Disney, and said, "We're going to do it." He backed Disney's first feature film, *Snow White and the Seven Dwarfs*. The philosophy reflected in Disney's films—"a stubborn, uncritical optimism that things are getting better and better"—matched A.P.'s well. By the early 1950s Bank of America had become Hollywood's banker. It had financed five hundred feature movies.

YET AS A.P., banker to the California dream, was buried, tensions underlay the state's golden glow, nudging the bank toward an ideological rigidity it had never had under the entrepreneuring A.P., whose politics could switch pragmatically from Republican to Roosevelt's New Deal if it served his purpose. Mario became the embodiment of those tensions. He found himself field marshal in a fight against forces perceived as threatening not just the peace that had been won but, indeed, the American way. The cold war had replaced the hot war. As the centennial pageants played out in 1950, the Russians exploded their first atom bomb. In the same year armed conflict began in Korea. In 1956 Russia's Sputnik launched the space race. The Red menace had replaced the Nazis, and whipped by the federal government and Senator Joseph McCarthy, the world's biggest bank became an instrument for defense of the free-enterprise, capitalist, democratic system. A potent symbol.

The bank's, and thus Mario's, mission became, as *Biography of a Bank*, B of A's official history, states, "a titanic struggle to save the world from economic chaos, and thus from Communism." Mario was thrust to the heart of the mobilizing of American aid and capital to shore up allies against communism when he was appointed by Truman to the Foreign Trade Financing Commission.

Mario's identification with the bank's mission was so strong that, having been appointed to A.P.'s seat as a University of California regent two weeks after his father's death, he leaped into the raging loyalty oath fight, which had caused twenty-seven professors to resign. "Regent Lawrence Mario Giannini, son and successor of the founder of the Bank of America, said that if the board rescinded the oath, 'flags would fly in the Kremlin' in celebration, and he himself would feel compelled to 'organize twentieth-century vigilantes' against the subsequent wave of Communism in California," Professor Walton Bean records in his book *California, An Interpretive History*. Mario, alone among the regents, voted for requiring the oath, and resigned from the Board of Regents in a case that became a landmark in issues of academic freedom. The Bank of America became an icon of conservatism. The essence of A.P.'s legacy—risk, innovation, and flexibility—was being cut adrift.

The Gianninis had long had a sense of combat with the financial world east of the Rockies and a conviction that Wall Street and Washington were allied against them. The new sense of menace from without intensified the ongoing fight at home with the Federal Reserve Board, which Mario had shouldered fully at his father's death. Mario testified at hearings in Washington and San Francisco, fighting the Fed's "perfidious . . . adroit and devious . . . attempt to prove that the Bank is controlled by Transamerica," the pioneering holding company A.P. and Mario had created in 1929 to protect Bank of America stock from the speculative excesses that preceded the Great Crash and as the vehicle to achieve A.P.'s dream of creating a nationwide branch banking system. In 1930 A.P. and Mario had fought, and won, banking's most famous proxy fight, a battle for shareholder votes, to save Transamerica from takeover and dismantling by New York bankers who had gained control. He would not let the Feds win now. The ordeal of testifying was so draining to even a healthy man that his lead counsel collapsed and was hospitalized after a round of testimony.

Under the pressures, Mario was declining. "It was just excruciating pain," says Mario's daughter Anne of the days before development of the clotting agents that now control the hemophilia of her sister Virginia's son. "Whenever he had to have a blood transfusion, it was a *whole* blood transfusion, so his veins were distended, and he had terribly painful times. Two or three times a year he would have a very bad bout and might be in the hospital a month each time or laid up at home." To conserve energy, Mario ran the bank from the office in his apartment on Green Street during the last years, though he still went to the bank as often as he could.

His family knew his plans. He would leave the bank when he was sixty—in 1954, the bank's fiftieth birthday—and become involved actively again with Transamerica. San Francisco–based, too, Transamerica was Bank of America's mother ship; from his chair as B of A's president, he cheered its diversifying, over the years, into a variety of businesses that foreshadowed the financial services conglomerate of the 1980s. "He just wanted to make it a very profitable company; he knew it could be. He was going to have two people in place in Bank of America so that he could graciously move out and turn the reins over to the new president and chairman," says Anne.

MARIO DIED ON August 19, 1952. "He had just driven down to Palm Springs with a family friend when the last crisis occurred," says Anne McWilliams. "He was flown up to San Francisco on a chartered plane and went into the hospital in early March. He never left. The last three weeks or so, there was nothing they could do for him. He just lay there. Terrible!"

Mario's, too, was "a funeral just like anybody else's," Russ Smith observed. Yet Mario's power was apparent. The mighty filed into the church. Henry Kaiser. The presidents of the National City Bank in New York and of R. H. Macy. James Roosevelt, the late president's son. The governor, mayors, and judges. Eulogies poured in by phone and wire from the secretary of the treasury; from Isaias Hellman, president of Wells Fargo, his father's old banking rival; from the heads of the great New York banks, National City and Chase. At nine fifty-five, as the hearse pulled up before St. Brigid's Church, there was a minute's silence in the bank's 536 branches worldwide.

There was now no Giannini to run the bank. Claire was on the board, championing the branches, but she could only advise, not manage. She could argue passionately for the "human touch," but she had only one vote. Claire had learned her father's lessons on thrift and service well and began to impose them with a disciple's zeal after her father's death. She became the keeper of A.P.'s flame.

THERE WAS NO Giannini. But rituals were being put in place to perpetuate Giannini's way. In May 1950 Claire had unveiled a bust of her father at the San Francisco headquarters, and Carl F. Wente, called back from early retirement to be the new president, broadcast a Giannini tribute to all branches, launching Founder's Day, an annual ceremony that would gather the Giannini family, longtime employees, and senior officers together to honor A.P. At Mario's death there were thirteen hundred quarter-century employees still at the bank, a loyal cadre of BankAmericans who had been trained directly by A.P. and Mario.

As president Wente represented continuity. A member of the well-known Livermore grape-growing family that still makes Wente wines, he had been one of A.P.'s most trusted lieutenants. A "hard-nosed agricultural banker," acquired when A.P. bought the Wente family's bank in Livermore, he would

surely keep the spirit of the branches alive as well. Wente had been manager of
the Bank of Italy branch in Modesto when Russ Smith joined the bank in 1923.

But it would not be easy to sustain the spirit and intent of the Gianninis. "A.P.
knew he couldn't expand anymore in California. He saw interstate banking as
the next step, and international," observes Russ Smith, a man so close to both
men that he had become a direct expression of their goals. He had just opened
Bank of America (International) in New York as a means of competing with the
eastern banks for their well-established foreign business. BAI took advantage of
the new Edge Act of 1919, which permitted U.S. banks to handle international
banking business in the United States. But it would take Giannini determination
to make serious inroads on Citibank and Chase, which, by 1950, were the only
really active American banks internationally. B of A had only its London and
Italian branches. Smith feared a parochial outlook was taking hold of the
eleventh floor at 1 Powell Street, the new bank headquarters. The legendary
BankAmerican Fred A. Ferroggiaro handled Henry Kaiser's multibillion-dollar
loan portfolio but he had never, to Smith's knowledge, been outside California.
And as months passed, Smith saw "no vigorous attempt by Bank of America to
develop the business that Citibank and Chase had abroad. The thinking simply
wasn't there that it was important."

"WENTE'S VISION WENT about as far as the end of a grapevine," was the
blunt way Alvin C. Rice put it, with the irreverence of youth. Emboldened by
his shiny new Phi Beta Kappa key and a degree from Stanford, a young officer
trainee who joined the bank two years before Tom Clausen, Al Rice dared
question the management philosophy that, with Mario's death, became Holy
Writ. Rice was part of the junior advisory committee, begun in 1944, a group
of ten selected each year by senior management for accelerated training. They
were invited to speak up. Rice did. He had only seen A. P. Giannini, but Mario
had come and spoken to his group several times; he had met and talked with
Mario about the bank's management style. After the prescribed swing through
the branches to learn bank operations from the trenches, Rice had dared find
more than "a little unusual" Mario's belief "that you could hire grammar
school graduates at clerical positions, keep them in very low positions for five
or ten years, pay them very little . . . and through some magical transformation
that was never quite clear to me those people . . . would flip over into grand
managers capable of managing a large and diverse institution."

There was nothing wrong with the leadership coming from within the
institution; he believed in that himself. A.P. had identified some superb talent
from the ranks. Wente was "very much like the Gianninis, a manager of the old

27

school"—and a good one for his day. But it was a system, Rice feared, that rewarded loyalty over the drive and innovation that had been A.P.'s hallmarks. As its banking market stretched beyond the Rockies to the world, B of A would need A.P.'s nimble responsiveness to opportunity and change more than ever before.

AS THE LEGEND BUILT, A.P. was increasingly only half remembered. His sayings were collected up into a book of aphorisms, frozen in time. Founder's Day was marked by a minute's silence and a red rose laid at A.P.'s portrait. The most celebrated Giannini story—his response to the Great Fire and Earthquake of 1906—was enshrined in banking, San Francisco, and California history. His bank had been tiny, only two years old. But as the city burned, A.P. salvaged $80,000 cash, mostly gold, from his banking office before the flames destroyed the building and hid it that night in the fireplace of his home in San Mateo. The next day, he raced to the docks to set up a makeshift bank. Erecting a rough plank as his counter, on the Washington Street wharf, he stuck up a homemade sign, BANK OF ITALY, and started making loans to the burned-out Italian families of North Beach. While other bankers met and talked, he was handing out money, infusing confidence into shattered immigrants, telling them to "go home and get that house fixed." This event inspired one of his most famous aphorisms: "Aim to put yourself in a position to do something the other fellow can't do—particularly in an emergency. . . . The glad hand is all right in the sunshine but it's the helping hand on a dark day that folks remember to the end of time."

But in the glorifying of that event, only his zeal for service to the disenfranchised "little fellow" was celebrated. A. P.'s stirring act is never celebrated for its importance as an entrepreneurial tour de force, a classic example of the resilience and innovation that were basic components of his banking style. His riposte to the Great Earthquake was a visionary and hardheaded act, for he won a city, and half a century, away from the competition. Without that dimension of A.P., the bank remembered only half the man.

AS THE CENTENNIAL CYMBALS clanged and the Bank of America began to carve A.P.'s memory in stone, an eleven-year-old from Woodland, just a few miles south of the Stanghellini farm in the Sutter Basin, was starting his first entrepreneurial enterprise, collecting and selling walnuts, and investing his earnings in the stock market. Too young to place his own buy and sell orders, Charles Schwab, son of a Yolo County district attorney, had to have his dad do it. "Nineteen-fifty was a good year," he said, grinning, as he moved on into the chicken-raising business, honing the business skills that would weave him into the bank's history thirty years later. Already hustling summer jobs that taught him the "human touch," he was spontaneously following a training program that would bring him far closer to A.P.'s populist spirit than the grand training tour being followed by the heirs to the biggest bank in the world.

Chapter Two

"THIS IS THE BEST PLACE to be in the *world*," thought Al Rice in 1952 as he rolled down the top of his brown Ford convertible, turned the radio up, and headed north to Highway 40. He'd kissed Joan and their sleeping baby good-bye, and now he could leave headquarters behind for a week and be a frontline banker. Flashing the smile that would become a familiar and compelling beacon on the international bankers' route on three continents, Rice smiled to himself as he pulled out of his quiet Palo Alto suburb on a Sunday night and drove off to his battlefield. Loan supervisor to the branches: it didn't sound like a job to inflame adventurers. But he believed he was working at the very heart of the machine that drove the Bank of America. The branches.

He lived for that one week a month when his "great little old brown Ford" became the chariot of the commanding general in charge of loan performance of all thirty-five branches between Sacramento and the Oregon border. His boss, Everett Iversen, supervised the cities and big towns in the territory— Sacramento, Redding. But Yreka, Knights Landing, and Susanville were, cumulatively, important profit centers. They were where Al Rice, son of a small-time Southern California ranch manager, had the power to recommend the hiring and firing of the minor banking lords who ran the imposing marble outposts of empire which dominated every downtown. "My assignment: Make them continually more profitable, increase the penetration against the competition, and *don't* make any bad loans."

He was one of thirty loan supervisors. Among them they had the Bank of America's 538 California branches covered. He might be employed by a bureaucratic giant, but out here he was an entrepreneur, pitting the performance of his thirty-five branches against the others. Yet he was seeing precious little talent. "There was practically nobody in it that offered any competition as far as the path to the top."

It was years before the eye of an ambitious young man would focus on international lending as the fast track to promotion; there were only three loan supervisors covering the bank's whole overseas operation at that time. The rural and suburban branches were where deposits, the stuff of life for the bank, poured in, where you cast your net into the apparently bottomless pool of Californians' earnings—unprecedented wealth that would reach $25 billion that year, one-tenth of the nation's income. As he drove north, more than five million depositors slept well with their savings secure in the friendly arms of Bank of America. Growing at an average rate of $1 million each banking day, the deposit base swelled that year to nearly $7.5 billion.

Those deposits meant $7.5 billion to lend to the farmers, workers, and teachers who were buying houses, refrigerators, TVs, and, above all, cars. Big, gas-guzzling Fords, Chryslers, Chevies, satisfying the pent-up hunger for wheels. As Al Rice raced up Highway 40, he joined what was becoming the world's first automobile culture, a culture of speed, change, excitement, and opportunity that had revived the American Dream after depression and war. People were streaming west in such numbers that planners tried to give them some comprehensible reality: California was gaining enough newcomers to create a new city of seventy-five hundred every seven days, or a city as large as Philadelphia or Los Angeles since the postwar boom began. Six out of every ten were customers. Even children were initiated into Bank of America at school, where bankers came each month to collect their pennies and enter them into the treasured blue passbooks.

Rice's last vehicle had been a twin-engined Beechcraft F-2; his territory had been the jungle rainforests of Brazil. That had not been his goal when he signed up for the air force at eighteen. He had been tapped for the South Pacific, where heroism lay. "But just before my reconnaissance wing was sent to the South Pacific, I was detached from the squadron and sent to South America to map the interior of Brazil." Cruising at twenty thousand feet, he scanned thousands of square miles of densely carpeted tropical rainforest. "The country had barely been explored. There were no maps." With the depth perception of 3-D cameras, "we found eleven-thousand-foot mountains that nobody ever knew about." His photographs confirmed what some remote hill people had told him: that there were vast iron and manganese deposits, the mineral trove ultimately extracted for the furnaces of Bethlehem Steel and U.S. Steel.

He had glimpsed the resources that would be golden collateral in the minds of bankers as they made billions in bank loans thirty years later. And he had awakened the impulse to adventure that would not easily be satisfied in a staid bank.

The potential in Brazil still lay so buried when A. P. Giannini did his grand tour of South America with his granddaughters four years later that he closed the door on the bank's entry there for the time being. A.P. came home convinced that rather than the many millions it was asking from banks and the Marshall Plan, Latin America "needs more stability, greater literacy, more teamwork, less confusion, and a middle class." B of A's map of South America would remain empty for many years as a result of A.P.'s trip.

After the war Rice put himself through Stanford on part-time work and $50-a-month veteran's pay, as tuition soared to $143 a quarter. Drawn to the stylish and attractive, he spied his future wife, Joan, at a Phi Beta Kappa reception. Starting graduate school, "I was really going to Stanford and looking for a job at the same time. I thought of the bank as a prestigious organization, one that was very low-paying but where, if you worked long enough, you might finally get up to a position of decision making." In 1947, he had become a Bank-American.

Only at the top could he make the kind of money he had in mind. "Money is what motivates me, more than power, because that's the way you keep score." He had been raised in Whittier—Richard Nixon's hometown—"on what in California you call a ranch, but in Texas would be called a postage stamp." His father grew mostly citrus, and his cash income fell, during the depression, to $500 a year. "My mother used to take surplus eggs and butter down to the grocery store and exchange them for flour and the groceries we needed. We lived well . . . but I obviously knew that we had much less than most people around us. My ambition was mainly reflected in trying to live a better life-style."

Rice had none of the traditional agrarian style and outlook that had shaped, and still shaped, Bank of America's culture when he joined it. With a confidence that verged on brashness, and having completed his training program, Rice would arrive in Yreka for his week's tour of his branches and check into his motel as if it were Gstaad at the height of the season. This was such a *good* system of controlling the quality and performance of the bank's loans, Al believed. With direct contact with your branches, "you learned swiftly who the good or the bad performers were. There were no layers between you and the president of the bank—only two people, and your reports were sure to get at least to the head of the loan supervision department." He marveled at how "very, very profit-oriented" the branches were, with their "day-to-day measuring of performance. Each manager had his operating profit and balance sheet land, daily, on his desk. That balance sheet was an accurate reflection of what was happening, when interest on each loan accrued." Bank managers *knew* if their loans were bad. Rice saw no reason why the same system could not be expanded to a bank of a thousand branches. Thirty good men could still do the job.

What a training ground the branches were! Rice, like all Bank of America officers in training, had been run through every assignment in a branch. Bookkeeping. Commercial and savings teller. The operations and note departments. Personal loans. And, finally, the experience that is, for the young banker, like a medical student's first cadaver: collecting on delinquent installment loans.

In Marysville, in the heart of the Sacramento Valley, he had learned how to make agricultural loans, an "all-important" part of the training of a young BankAmerican. Because a farmer's credit risk couldn't be scientifically quantified, you had to bring Giannini's face-to-face judgment to bear. "You learned that the same farmers were late every year in their planting, had trouble every year getting their harvest done, had to buy feed every year," Rice says.

Watching Marysville's superb manager, Hartley Weichert—inherited by B of A when it had bought another bank—Rice was suddenly struck by a risk the bank faced. "A.P. had built the huge branch system by *acquiring* banks. He rarely started from scratch, *de novo*." He had *bought,* not trained, his best people.

"When Giannini bought his banks," Rice mused, "he bought some very good people." They were the founders. Entrepreneurs like A.P. Men of enormous prestige in the community. Respected. Sound. They made good loan judgments because they knew their customers. They were legends, models, to the young bankers. Christiansen in Redding. Herman Perry in his hometown of Whittier. The Alexander family in St. Helena, where Paul, the founder's son, was still manager as Rice did his rounds. "There was Vandenberg in Sacramento, son of the founder. He gave B of A a *great* reputation there. Giannini kept those people interested and was great pals with them."

But what would happen when these people retired? "I never heard of another Vandenberg coming along in the bank. And no serious effort was being made to think about who's going to manage this after the Vandenbergs retired." Yes, there was the M.B.A. training program the bank had just begun. "But that appeared to be the first time the bank had gone outside the lower levels, and outside the bank, to find people capable of managing an institution that was becoming huge." For forty years B of A had been rewarding loyalty, promoting low-level people from within, relying on alchemy to transform tellers with sixth-grade educations into grand managers. With the low pay and little reward for an aggressive spirit, "this is not going to be a place that will attract the great entrepreneurs of the Western world," Rice feared.

Rice had been rebuffed by the bank's chief of personnel when he revealed his ambitious style. "If the bank wants real estate loans, I'll show these people how to make real estate loans," he had declared to the Richmond branch secretary, Gloria Carnes, as he had looked around at his first branch training assignment for opportunities to make his mark. "We did real estate loans like you cannot believe. And I got a salary increase of twenty-five dollars, raising my salary from three hundred fifty to three hundred seventy-five dollars a month!" Bristling, he packaged documentation of his triumphs, made up a short and concise speech, and delivered both to the bank's personnel director in San Francisco, Frank Risso, a classic example of the bank's promotion policies. For Risso had been A.P.'s chauffeur. He had worked his way up. "Lurking behind his desk as I delivered my speech, he looked up and said, *'Young man, you can easily be replaced.'* "

Despite the rebuff, Rice was convinced that with this system, there could be very few Renaissance bankers out there blocking his route to the top.

But he saw that he would have to leave the branches. "If they find anybody with any talent out in the branches, they transfer them to headquarters." As a loan supervisor Rice had been reversing the pattern. "If I found somebody bright in headquarters, I'd transfer him to the *branches* . . . because the only way you make any money in the banking business is the time you're talking to customers. You don't make money with these big headquarters staffs talking to each other." He felt even more urgent about this as he felt himself being pulled into the corporate banking orbit.

In 1954 S. Clark Beise, a former bank examiner A.P. had lured from Washington, succeeded Wente as president. Rice could now see the first signs of what would become a cultural and political schism within the bank, as Beise stepped up the M.B.A. hiring program. After training in the branches, this new breed was being fed into the fast track. That track was, increasingly, corporate banking—lending to companies.

It was a subtle thing, as most great transitions are. The branches were still treasured as the heart and soul of the bank. They continued, well after Giannini's death, to be the most direct expression of his commitment to serving

Californians. The bank went where the people were. Leaping at even temporary opportunities to open a teller's window or loan officer's desk, the bank
carried the spirit of A.P.'s famous plank on the docks to military bases, new
shopping malls, state fairs. It opened a turn-of-the-century branch at Disney-
land in 1955 with gaslights and rolltop desks. As Orange County exploded
with growth, "We knew we ought to be where the Bank of America is," says
banking consultant Sal Serrantino, then working for a competitor. "We'd watch
where they filed new applications for branches." When he noted B of A had
filed for an intersection in the newly planned city of Irvine that was not even on
the map yet—"there was nothing but orange groves within two miles!"—
Serrantino felt the awe one might feel for an intelligence coup that changes the
winds of war. "They were positioned for what was going to be happening three
years down the line."

The loans made in the branches surpassed in numbers and dollars the
commercial loans made by the corporate department at headquarters. The
branches were, above all, the source of funds for lending; on the bank's fiftieth
anniversary in 1954, lyrical tribute to their importance was paid in the annual
report, which celebrated a deposit base of over $8.2 billion and well over 5.5
million individual accounts. The bank paid them 2 percent interest for leaving
their money, the legal limit—and lent it out at 8 and 9 percent. In that 6 or 7
percent spread between the two lay MotherBank's profits, the golden envelope
known as net interest margin.

The bank prided itself on the balanced mix between checking and savings
accounts, which allowed it to make long-, intermediate-, and short-term loans,
giving more breadth and depth to the bank's service and earning power. The
dynamic in-and-out flow of money through checking accounts, or "demand
deposits" in banker's language, allowed the bank to make short-term loans,
while the stable "savings reservoir" permitted it to make longer-term loans—
home loans to the "little fellow" building his tract house.

The branches, too, had been the proving ground of the great loan officers
who were the model of every trainee. Lending the money out had always had
more prestige than gathering it in at a teller's window. That relative status was
reinforced by banker's language and the layout of the balance sheet. On the
balance sheet, loans were the bank's "assets." Deposits—the assets of the
depositor—were the bank's "liabilities." From the bank's point of view, they
were simply "funding" for their loans, money borrowed from their depositors,
at a price. With interest rates a bank could pay frozen by regulation, the
gathering of deposits was considered an essentially technical task. Loans
made at negotiable interest rates required persuasion, analytical ability, and
judgment.

For the young recruits who would be the bank's senior officers thirty years later, it was a lender's paradise. As the nightmare of the eighties unfolded, as real estate, ag, energy, and third world loans went belly up, bankers would remember these as the golden years of real estate lending. In 1947, 70 percent of the bank's real estate loans were in home loans, most of them insured by the government's National Housing Act or GI Bill of Rights and secured by single-family houses. "Many real estate loans are paid off well in advance of their maturity dates. . . . Our average real estate loan is fully repaid in from 5 to 6 years," the bank could proudly claim. The average loan in a branch then was under $7,000.

But when you lent to Kaiser Steel or Lockheed, you lent hundreds of millions. A farm boy like Rice could feel himself allied with the hallowed European tradition of financing the large commercial enterprises that made and traded the goods and services of the civilized world. Modern banking had begun as a servant of trade and commerce in the ports and trade fairs of Europe, not as a glorified piggy bank for the penny ante individual who was A.P.'s basic customer. The most prestigious New York bank, the House of Morgan, was still wreathed in the venerable aura of "merchant bank," a bank rich enough to go beyond loans to invest its own capital in ventures. New York bankers, Rice knew, sniffed at Bank of America as "that dago warehouse in the West." So there were image as well as profit motives for the pull toward corporate banking. But in a practical sense the need was there. California's explosive postwar industrial and corporate growth had spawned hundreds of companies needing credit lines for production, expansion, export. Bank of America had the money to lend.

Rice left branch loan supervision in 1956 to become assistant head of Corporate Finance, which handled the large corporate customers. He had joined the lending track, the route to advancement. Rice scanned the competition at the meetings of the elite advisory group the most promising had been invited to join. These twice-a-month gatherings augmented their accelerated training and gave them personal contact with the bank's senior management. It was here that Rice, years earlier, had heard and talked with Mario Giannini and that he had first felt doubts about the Giannini management philosophy. Here Rice met the men who would climb the ladder with him. Mostly war veterans, ambitious, and in a hurry, they would gallop parallel for the next several decades. Among them was one who would be crowned king.

THERE WAS Joseph J. Pinola, recruited in 1950, "the skinny Italian who would transmute into Cesar Romero," as a former colleague describes the metamorphosis of the man who would, as the powerful chief of Los Angeles–based First Interstate Bancorp, challenge a weakened MotherBank with a takeover bid in 1986. "Money and I got along well together. I was ambitious. Always," Pinola says. Raised in the Pennsylvania coalfields, he'd honed his drive and toughness in the invasions of the Philippines and Okinawa, and, later, playing college football. Driving a taxi all night to feed his wife and two babies while he rushed through a small sister school of Bucknell University (whose degree he pragmatically co-opted because "I knew it would get me a job a hell of a lot better than a degree from *Wilkes-Barre*"), he regrets that "the GIs like me didn't get an education. I had to get the hell out as fast as I could and go to work." After graduation he was called back by the Korean War to California, where he spent a year on minesweepers out of San Diego. He returned to California with his family, "very hungry and very poor, answered an ad in the newspaper, and started to work for the Bank of America on a training program."

Bored and impatient with even the accelerated training program he had forced the bank to give him, he resigned twice in the first two years. Then, noting that "the competition was going into the loan side, I saw a chance to move faster and be a brighter light in the operations side." It was a high-risk choice, for the tedious, unsung bank operations side was a career dead end. Running the teller line and the bookkeepers and seeing that the books balanced at night, an operations officer never touched the glamour sides of banking—lending, or the integration of new technology. In the little Lawndale branch in Southern California, Pinola launched an aggressive strategy to move himself into number two in the pecking order behind the branch manager, a position always held by a loan man, but one he believed could be attained "if you were sufficiently powerful." His fierce, bright light was seen, and Pinola was quickly plucked from the branches and sent to headquarters with the rest of the "M.B.A. types."

Like Rice's, Pinola's fires of ambition had been stoked by a basic truth he had discovered in the branches: "Bankers, as a fraternity, weren't very smart . . . The old-style branch manager with his stiff shirt and vested suit—the kind who's a pillar in the community, tough-minded and has his collateral, like in the moving pictures—he really doesn't have to be very smart."

MOTHERBANK HAD WRAPPED Alden Winship Clausen up in the arms of family and earned his total loyalty so early in his career that any fire for change he might have had was reduced to a stubborn, smoldering glow. His ambition would burn like a peat fire through the years, gradually eroding the high ground of competitors. The bank had welcomed him into its sacred rites within days of his arrival in May 1949. A.P. died the next month, and Clausen traveled to a downtown Los Angeles church to attend the sad and solemn rosary. He shared a minute's silence and the emotion of old employees at Mario's death two years later. The bank had come to his wedding on Saturday night, February 11, ten months after he joined the bank. Although he had graduated in law and had a job with a law firm waiting for him in the Midwest, he had followed Peggy, a teacher, to California from Minnesota to convince her to marry him. Still not convinced, he says, "that she wanted to marry *me*" when he arrived, he had finally won her. But he had no family in California. When he arrived at the church for the wedding, delayed for hours trying to balance the books, the bank filled his side of the church. He would never forget it.

Clausen had arrived two years after Rice, a member of the same new accelerated training program for university graduates. While Rice toured his territory in his Ford convertible, Clausen's first assignment had been the narrow, nit-picking task of counting cash in a bank vault. Their careers would tend to be characterized by the differences in those early jobs. Both moved on the same upward track, but Rice would fly off on lateral tracks while Clausen moved steadily ahead. Each June 6 Clausen honored the ceremonials of Founder's Day with the staunchness of a wartime Brit standing for the king. "It's the love of the institution that is translated to the founder, whose name is not forgotten," he says of the devotion that began in the vaults of the Rosedale branch. "My whole life has been given to the bank. I am a product of the bank."

IN THE LATE FORTIES it was not just the Bank of America that was hiring M.B.A.'s. All the large banks were trying to hire the talent that had scorned banking since 1929. "When the crash came in the thirties, no banker would admit where he worked. Nobody wanted to work for a bank from 1933 to 1939," explains Citibank's Walter Wriston. "Then the war started. So there was nobody coming into the business from 1933 to 1946." Bank of America and National City hired from the same university-trained pool. But the way they hired reveals some of the differences in attitude that would mark the two institutions. While Al Rice had badgered Frank Risso to raise his pay to $375 a month, National City in New York hired Wriston, the lanky, beautifully educated son of the president of Brown University as a junior inspector in the comptroller's division at roughly the same low pay scale: $3,000 a year, his advanced degree from the Fletcher School of Diplomacy at Tufts University earning him a $200 bonus. But it had recognized in its veteran recruits "a bunch of characters, guys who'd flown P-38s, and been in the water forty-eight hours," says Wriston. "They weren't purchasing the concepts that were around." Instead of suppressing that latent spirit, National City shaped it into "institutionalized entrepreneurship." Says Wriston: "Our personnel system was very simple: Hire every smart man and woman you can find and don't ask the color of their passport or their skin or where the hell they went to college," Wriston says, laughing. Trying to shed its immigrant image, Bank of America was noting the haircuts and polished shoes of its officer candidates.

A rangy six feet three, Wriston was no more born to bank than any of the other recruits. He fell into it when his mother died right after the war and, searching around for work in New York, where he had come to be with his wife, his father suggested, "National City's the best bank." He walked in off the street and applied for a job. National City lacked the prestige of Chase or Morgan. But he throve in its meritocratic culture, which, Wriston believes, was embodied in and created by this hiring policy.

DOWN THE STREET from Wriston, G. Robert Truex, Jr., was entering the banking stream. Banking was calmer than the "titanic engagements" he'd fought in Europe with Patton's Third Army, but the dashing Truex had, in 1949, joined the venerable old New York bank Irving Trust Company, founded in 1812. That bank would find itself target, in 1987, of the first hostile takeover battle in U.S. banking. In its traditional environment, Truex would evolve into the very image of the elegant fiduciary, the suave archetype of the savvy eastern banker. But he settled into his training seduced by the notion of someday being a banker in the exotic Pacific Rim. As head of Irving Trust's national corporate lending, his territory extended to Hawaii. "I made up my mind that the future of the country was out here," in the Pacific. That conviction would bring him west seventeen years later, to Bank of America.

AS RICE FINISHED his four-year stint with the branches, Tom Clausen was already following the corporate lending path. In 1955 Clausen had been promoted to the bank's National Division in Southern California as vice-president working with the electronics companies. This was the leading edge of lending, as the fast-growing aerospace and electronics industries ate up the orange groves of Long Beach and Orange County. Clear skies and spacious desert testing grounds won for Southern California the bulk of the defense contracts that fueled the aerospace industry. Like the rest of the bank's Young Turks, Clausen was turning his back on the branches.

AND YET IT WAS the branches that were A.P.'s singular gift to the history of American banking. Commonplace in England and Canada, branch banking in the United States had languished, after a modest start, for a century. A.P. revived it in California. His bank's movable feast of funds, for whatever city, town, or farmer needed them at a given hour or season, had largely financed the California "miracle." Since the opening of the Bank of Italy's first out-of-town branch in San Jose on January 1, 1909, branch banking had given California's economy extraordinary resilience in its volatile evolution from a booming gold rush territory. By mid-century the cumulative deposits of half of California's population had created a pool of resources vastly larger than any single "unit" bank could possibly accumulate. It had invited competitors who had enlarged that pool—Wells Fargo, Security Pacific, Crocker, banks that had also grown out of California's pioneering days.

A concept created with a giant's eye, those deposit funds, moved around at will, gained the same scale of power as the massive California water projects, and had the same transforming impact on economy and environment—for better or worse. J. P. Morgan might have scoffed over his cigars and old port at A.P.'s plebeian idea of "strengthening the economy with the protected savings of workers, small tradesmen and small farmers" and joined the wall of resistance to branch banking erected by Washington, Wall Street, and most of the states in the Union—a wall not effectively breached until the mid-1980s, when regulations began to fall before free-market forces. Interstate branch banking—the base of truly national banks—would finally become a reality in the early 1990s. But it was A.P.'s populist banking, his mighty branch system based on the dollars of the common man, that created the first distinctly American style of banking. A.P. and Mario both died fighting for it.

Statewide branch banking had never been forbidden in California, as it was in New York and many other states; National City Bank was restricted to branching only in New York City. But by California's Bank Act of 1909, no new branches could be opened or acquired without the approval of the state's superintendent of banks. The negative permission embedded in the Bank Act triggered decades of struggle to *get* that approval from Sacramento. Small independent banks, feeling their rural fiefdoms threatened by the Giannini juggernaut, put unceasing pressure on the state to contain A.P.'s branches. The federal McFadden Act of 1927 "has tended to say that nationally chartered banks can do only what state banks can do," says a former Federal Reserve board governor. In New York, it permitted a national bank to add branches only in the city where it was headquartered, as well as prohibiting interstate banking. A law created to stop the Gianninis, it was another obstacle to be overcome. As their ambitions brought them into conflict with Wall Street and its perceived allies in Washington, the Gianninis developed a sense of "them" and "us"—a "Fortress BankAmerica" mentality intensified by California's isolation beyond the Rockies and by the East's haughty attitude toward the brash young state.

Thriving on challenge, A.P. took out a national charter for his Bank of Italy in 1928, a tradeoff that put him under the long arm of the Federal Reserve Board in Washington but gained him some flexibility in growth. In the same year he formed the Bank of America of California, an assemblage of California banks that, through creative interpretation of the McFadden Act, A.P. had been permitted to buy, with their branches, and merge into the Bank of Italy.

Also, in 1928, he moved toward the larger dream, a transcontinental bank with Giannini branches stretching from sea to shining sea. For that, he needed a prestigious launching pad in New York, one blessed by J. P. Morgan, who still dominated Wall Street and the eastern banking establishment. Giannini had entered New York in a modest way just after World War I, gaining two small banks styled, after his California model, to serve "particularly the foreign elements—Italians, Greeks, Poles, Swiss, Slavonians, Spanish, etc." The banks were run by his brother, Attilio. A.P. ordered "that the managing officers, from the President down, were put out in front and in the open where they would come in contact with and greet the people as they would . . . in the bank [in California]. . . . That is one thing that is lacking in most of the New York banking institutions."

The four thousand miles between New York and California had been un-served by nationwide branch banking since 1836—nearly a century!—when President Andrew Jackson refused to recharter Nicholas Biddle's Bank of the United States, after Biddle had, says B of A's authorized *Biography of a Bank*, "corruptly abused his monopoly." The powerful regulatory agencies—the Federal Reserve Board, the Comptroller of the Currency, the Securities and Exchange Commission (SEC)—held the restraining ropes on A.P.'s imperial goals, each claiming jurisdiction at various levels. But A.P.'s modus operandi was always to proceed with the dream and let the feds try to stop him if they could. "He could never accommodate himself to those regulations," says an old associate, attorney Angelo J. Scampini, of his shouting fights with A.P. over regulatory limits. "He overstepped his power, oh, yes! Most of the time he got away with it. But you're comparing a pygmy to a *giant*. A giant doesn't give a damn what the regulations say. He pushes everything aside."

The crusading tone of Bank of Italy's 1928 annual report foreshadowed A.P.'s planned nationwide push: "We are convinced that the key to our success is to be found . . . in the economic, social and political soundness of branch banking itself. . . . It is difficult to comprehend why, under our existing laws and practices, branches of American banks . . . are permitted to be established and operated in foreign countries, but denied the right of establishment in other American states."

As shareholders were hearing this message in California, A.P. had been on a train to New York to take the first steps: the acquisition of a bank which could establish the beachhead for a national bank, one within the sphere of influence of old J. P. Morgan. His brother had found one at 44 Wall Street, the Bank of America, a small but distinguished old New York bank, founded in 1812, with "Morgan men" on its senior staff. Swallowing his righteous pride, doing what had to be done, A.P. bought Bank of America. Attilio fumed to A.P. from New York by wire that "ingratiating methods will never do with these fellows. For many years they have been impossible and must be told where to head in. . . . The gang downtown never cared for our kind and never will. It is true we need them now, but is not necessary to have them ride over us." But only as A.P. accepted a "Morgan man" as head of his Bank of America did he receive word "that his acquiring control of the Bank of America would . . . have the blessing of J. P. Morgan & Company." With Bank of America sitting just down the street from "the corner" where the House of Morgan sat at Wall and Broad, Giannini had his eastern anchor for the "nationwide banking organization" that had become his goal.

And he had Transamerica Corporation, the key. It was Mario's idea, the company known today by its soaring white pyramid in the San Francisco skyline, now a major Fortune 500 financial services and insurance company with no surviving formal links to the Bank of America. Mario had conceived it, in 1928, as a device for protecting the stock of Bankitaly (the holding company that owned Bank of Italy) from the wild speculation that had been assaulting it in the climate of excess and anxiety that preceded the 1929 market crash. Transamerica would be a holding company, a mother bank, into which all Bankitaly stock and all Giannini assets would be put, out of easy reach of gamblers. Transamerica would trade on the stock exchanges. Bank of Italy shareholders happily exchanged their shares for Transamerica stock, and on January 1, 1929, Bank of Italy stock vanished from the stock exchanges.

On September 3, 1930, A.P. merged Bank of Italy and the Bank of America of California into a national bank, the Bank of America National Trust and Savings Association (NT & SA), the name that endures today. That consolidation made A.P.'s bank the third-largest bank in the United States—only Na-

tional City Bank and Chase National in New York commanded more assets—
and moved him a step closer to his goal.

As A. P. Giannini sailed off to Europe with his wife and Claire in the fall of
1930 to visit the Italian branch bank he had acquired in 1919, the master
structure had been completed. Transamerica had under its umbrella the consolidated California holdings and the Bank of America in New York.

Transamerica would also be a vehicle for expansion nationwide, a holding
company for the network of banks A.P. planned to acquire. Bank of America in
New York had expanded its presence on Wall Street by acquiring, in the spring
of 1929, a fine old investment banking house called Blair & Company. With
Blair, it also acquired its management, New Yorker Elisha Walker and a suave
Frenchman, Jean Monnet, who later became France's minister of finance and
one of the architects of the European Economic Community. As A.P., turning
sixty on May 6, 1930, pulled back from active operating control of his empire
to let his "boys" get used to running things without him, Mario became
president of Transamerica, while New York–based Walker and Monnet became chairman and vice-chairman. Fundamental differences in philosophy
and style had been intensified by the deepening recession, as Transamerica's
stock suffered from soured loans and ebbing deposits and profits. As the
Giannini/Walker schism widened, Walker proposed a restructuring as violent
as any of the 1980s.

By the summer of 1931 A.P.'s banking empire was about to be dismantled by
Walker and Monnet. "The Walker gang had never had much respect for Bank
of Italy officers," Russ Smith knew. "We were 'underpaid with shiny trou-
sers.' " Mario had already resigned from Transamerica, in disputes with
Walker over how best to run and protect the institution in the deepening
economic gloom of '29, '30. But to liquidate while A.P. was in Europe, sick—
to dump the banks, companies, stock, and assets at the knocked-down values
Walker had established—was, to A.P.'s loyal people, tantamount to dismantling the Vatican—a horrifying and venal conspiracy.

The financial press seemed to accept it as a fait accompli. *Time* wrote its
elegy as Mario left Transamerica and A.P. resigned his directorship: "Master
of the temple for one year now has been Chairman Elisha Walker, a quiet,
diplomatic, keen-eyed New Yorker. . . . The great shouts of big, jovial Amadeo Peter Giannini have faded further and further into the distance, are gradually becoming echoes." A *New York Times* headline declared GIANNINIS
LOSE RULE OF HUGE BANK CHAIN, and the *American Banker* cheered that
as "a meteor in the banking firmament disintegrates . . . financially minded
observers abroad as well as at home will be likely to breathe easier. . . .
Giannini overshot the mark. The shortening of his shadow in the banking

world will be good for banking in a future that should look askance at too large financial egg-baskets."

The battle was joined. "Father was very ill, he got this nerve disease— terrible—while we were in Europe," says Claire, in Rome with her parents when the cables started arriving from Mario. She was at the heart of the unfolding drama, as A.P. unleashed a torrent of cables in return. "I was his copy girl. . . . He didn't trust anybody, so I used to take all his dictation. He didn't know I didn't know shorthand, and I learned to write so fast that today I can't write slowly. We sent telegrams that were three or four pages long." As her father's rage and determination built, Claire frantically scribbled A.P.'s cable to Mario: REMEMBER IT'S RIGHT OR PRINCIPLE WE ARE BATTLING FOR . . . AND THERE'S NO COMPROMISING . . . REGARDLESS CONSE-QUENCES. NO, SIR, NEVER, MY BOY. DAD.

"He was too sick to leave. He shouldn't have." But A.P. was coming home to fight. Traveling under the name of S. A. Williams, he sailed from Rome to Montreal with his wife and daughter. Claire and her mother traveled back to California by train, while A.P. sped to Vancouver for a secret meeting with Mario on September 4, 1931. A.P. surfaced next for a war meeting at the Tahoe Tavern near Lake Tahoe, where prosperous San Franciscans spent their summers. Although he still had a deathly pallor, his step was quickening by the minute.

On October 1, 1931, Walker sold the Bank of America to National City Bank.

Scamp Scampini got the call to arms from A.P. himself. He had left his job at the bank's trust department and was starting his own law practice when he read in the newspaper that A.P. was launching a proxy fight to regain control of Transamerica from the Walker group. "I wrote Mr. A.P. a letter telling him that it was about time somebody rose up in arms and sent those Wall Street boys home." Next afternoon A.P. called, and Scamp went hustling over to the eighth floor of 300 Montgomery Street, a small office A.P. had kept to run his wife's estate and other affairs after retiring from the bank.

Several of "the boys" were gathered as A.P. swung around to face the young lawyer. "Scamp, don't tell me you don't have any time to put on this. You've just been made chairman of the stockholders' committee. I want you to accept." Scamp found himself head of the Associated Transamerica Stock-holders, with precious few stockholders whose votes they could count on. A.P. had never permitted a concentration of shares in anyone's hands, not even his own. But in the past A.P. had held voting control of the bank; he had been guaranteed winning any proxy vote by standing proxies for fifteen million shares that had been signed by stockholders friendly to him. But Walker had discovered A.P.'s game. "And he was too damn smart for A.P.," says Scamp. "He had those proxies returned to the stockholders. The proxies had disappeared. The stock on which A.P. had relied to retain control was gone."

If they were to win the proxy fight and control Transamerica and all its holdings, they must have a majority of Transamerica's shares voted for Giannini's slate of directors by February 15, 1932, when the stockholders' meeting would be held in Wilmington, Delaware. They had fewer than five months to win the largest proxy war ever waged in corporate America. There were two hundred thousand shareholders to woo by letter, meetings, court appearances, and the press. The country was in a liquidating mood not unlike the restructuring frenzy of the mid to late 1980s. The *Los Angeles Times* and a number of the other city papers in the state were supporting Transamerica management, the Walker camp. A.P.'s "boys" had been working at it for more than two months and had received only a pathetic trickle of proxies. They must get the Hearst newspapers behind A.P. if they were to win back control of the board.

"So A.P. got on the phone," says Scamp, "and called William Randolph Hearst directly, calls him Bill, and he finally turned around to all of us and said, 'We're meeting Randolph Hearst at three o'clock Wednesday afternoon.' " They would meet at San Simeon, the overblown estate Hearst had built on the crest of a hill back from the Big Sur coast north of Santa Barbara. Thirty-year-old Scamp began to feel that he was moving into a Hollywood movie as he, A.P., and the committee took a train south to San Luis Obispo and were whisked by waiting limousine along the winding coastal road to San Simeon, where Hearst met them and insisted on a tour of his life's delight. Finally Hearst, wearing the old gold railway watch and chain given to him by his father, got down to business.

"What's your strategy?" Hearst demanded of Scamp, who was on orders to speak for the group as A.P. sat back and listened. Scamp outlined his plan to send A.P. on a statewide barnstorming tour to bring the problem directly to the shareholders at a series of big meetings. Out of a cloud of smoke from his Cuban cigar, Hearst said, "Well, I've been mulling it over in my head while Scampini here's been talking, and the more I think about it, the more I like it. Why don't we get started and see how it turns out?" He would not put money in directly. Nor would he put the Hearst papers behind it, yet. But it was all the encouragement A.P. needed to launch the blitz of shareholder meetings.

Scamp had done precious little courtroom work or public speaking. But as the meetings began, he transformed himself into an eloquent orator, rousing crowds with his impassioned pleas to cast their votes for Giannini. For Scamp, it was absolutely thrilling. "That first meeting at the Pacific Auditorium in San Francisco. We had *twelve thousand shareholders,* and they couldn't run fast enough down the aisle—they stampeded over each other—to sign their proxies." The Giannini supporters had tapped the underground stream of loyalty that characterized B of A shareholders even into the 1980s. They took the show to San Jose, San Luis Obispo, San Diego, Bakersfield, with the triumphant finale in Stockton, the heart of the bank's agricultural support. Hearst had been following reports of the road show and called Scamp up to congratulate him. That Sunday morning Scamp opened the *Examiner,* and there it was: Hearst's endorsement. Now the proxies poured in.

A.P. and his troops set off for Wilmington in a specially hired five-car train full of the proxies they had received. When they arrived at the elegant Du Pont Hotel, they found that Walker had taken the entire sixth floor for his entourage, and Giannini spies reported the Walker forces were busily counting and arranging their proxies alphabetically to present to the shareholders' meeting next morning. Scamp and the Giannini group feared their rooms had been bugged, but by now "we figured we had nothing to lose. We had counted and re-counted. We *knew* we had more than a majority. We had enough to elect the board."

At 11:00 P.M. Walker's attorney, the senior partner at the prestigious New York law firm Cravath, Swaine & Moore—the "fine-looking" Mr. Cravath himself—knocked on the Giannini suite to do some back room negotiating with A.P.'s attorney, "which, as the only lawyer present, happened to be me," Scamp recounts. Gathering their aides, Cravath and Scamp huddled in a private room. "Mr. Scampini, before I start congratulating any of you gentlemen, we've been counting all our proxies, we know exactly how many we have, and—"

Scamp, the California upstart facing the consummate New York corporate lawyer, summoned every inch of his orator's bearing and cut in. "Mr. Cravath, you don't know a damn thing about how many you have. Because whatever you have, you can figure that more than half of them have been revoked. We have the last ones signed, *voiding you!*" It had been A.P.'s most effective device; as employees had called in, wanting to vote for A.P. but worried that their jobs might be in jeopardy if Walker's management was monitoring employees' votes and found them out, A.P. had told them, "Go ahead and vote for Walker at work. Then vote for us later. It's the *last* vote that counts."

"I don't think it's necessary for us to re-count them," Cravath responded. "I've been authorized to say that we concede the meeting to you." Next morning, when the meeting was called to order, there was only one party responding with a proxy count—the Associated Transamerica Shareholders. Giannini had won. In San Francisco Mario fired all the officers who had been disloyal to A.P.

The great Transamerica proxy fight became a celebrated part of the nation's banking lore. It was the bank's Battle of Britain.

Giannini had won the battle but not the war. Continuing efforts by the federal regulators to unbundle Bank of America from Transamerica were royally denounced as "persecution" by Mario in the annual reports of the last few years of his life. The grueling process of hearings and filings clearly sped his death at the age of fifty-seven in 1952. When the SEC finally withdrew from a decade-long struggle to sever the connection, the Federal Reserve Board picked up the banner, with Fed chief Marriner Eccles making it an obsessive personal cause. Thwarting the Giannini empire became so preoccupying that Eccles, Mario's great friend turned bitter enemy, would not retire from the board until he saw it beaten. Mario was dying when word of defeat was received from Washington, and he was not told the news. Although orders that Transamerica must divest itself of all remaining Bank of America holdings were reversed briefly after Mario's death, the systematic separation of the two continued until 1958, when the last links were cut.

That divestment in 1958 of a chain of twenty-seven banks in the seven western states, the last remnant of Mario's creation—now renamed First Interstate Bancorp—would be run two decades later by the same Joe Pinola who had traveled the fast track with Rice and Clausen.

Chapter
Three

"BREATHE FROM HERE, breathe from here," Claire Hoffman would tell herself as she took her seat at the boardroom table, trying to make her voice lower and heavier as her speech teacher was training her to do. "When I got on the board, there were about twenty-five members then. I was the only woman . . . I had this high, shrieky child's voice and I felt so conspicuous." Fighting for her father's principles, she had been in combat with the directors and management since she joined the board. His creed became hers: "Serving the needs of others is the only legitimate business in the world." That meant maintaining the "human touch" for both customers and employees. She identified branch managers who "exemplified the spirit" and became their voice at the board level.

Her sense of mission intensified as she found herself increasingly alone. "Within eleven years I lost the people who were closest to me. My father and mother, my brothers Virgil and Mario, my uncle, Attilio." Then, in 1956, "I lost my husband, Biff." Living alone at Seven Oaks, the young woman who had loved dancing and tennis and horseback riding matured into the personification of MotherBank. By the 1960s she had become heavier and more bosomy and had the same challenging, chin-up stature of her father. Wreathed by dark hair pulled back into a knot, her face had almost precisely the same facial structure as A.P.'s, the same square jaw, and the same overlapping eyelids under thick brows that gave their eyes a look of squinting scrutiny.

A.P., however, had always kept one eye ranging over the future. "Claire wanted to keep everything the way it was when her father and Mario were alive," says a fellow director. "If either of them were alive today, that's the last thing they'd want; they were both people who changed with the times."

WENTE WAS NOT CHANGING fast enough for Robert Di Giorgio, the rookie director on the B of A board. As Rice, Clausen, and Pinola tried to break from the pack of rising young corporate bankers, Di Giorgio was about to employ the board's ultimate power: to remove the chief executive officer from command of the Bank of America. It was the kind of chutzpah A.P. would have understood.

In choosing Carl Wente as president at Mario's death in 1952, the board, in crisis at the deaths of both Gianninis, had retrenched and wrapped itself in the familiar. "The old-timers had wanted some continuity with the past," Di Giorgio knew. But they had chosen a caretaker. He liked Carl Wente. "But if Carl said it once, he said it ten times a month: 'There's nobody's going to do anything to rock the boat while I'm running the bank.' " There was no written rule that you had to retire at sixty-five. But it was strict Giannini policy. As Wente's sixty-fifth birthday approached in 1954, there was no talk of his retirement. In fact, in the aggressive young Di Giorgio's view, "the board never said anything, never did anything. It just listened and nodded approval."

On the surface, the bank was still growing—still the biggest bank in the world. In this, its fiftieth anniversary year, total resources rose above the $9 billion mark, and the board had begun to talk with great excitement about reaching $10 billion, a level no bank had ever reached before. But beyond the landmark numbers, Di Giorgio saw slippage in *relative* growth, compared with the state's dynamic gains—and worse, the subsiding of Giannini's innovative drive. "The bank had been *gaining* penetration; now it was losing it. . . . It was no longer a growth bank; it was becoming a *standstill bank*!" Wente had to go.

Wente was "a big, unruffled man who never seemed to have a worry in the world. But Carl was not a man of as great breadth as Mario," Di Giorgio feared. He was not even the successor Mario had planned. Mario had been training two men for president and chairman to succeed him: S. Clark Beise, the national bank examiner who had so impressed A.P. that he had lured him to the bank in 1936, and Jesse W. Tapp, a former government agriculturalist hired by Mario to head the bank's effort to save the wine and grape industry in the late thirties. Beise would be president; Tapp, his chairman. During the last months of Mario's life, Beise had been effectively running the bank as chairman of the Managing Committee, a senior management group formed by A.P. in 1944 to act as a shock absorber if Mario were to be incapacitated; Wente had been its first chairman.

Di Giorgio was just turning thirty-one as he determined to force the birthday issue. "I was the newest and youngest member of the board, the youngest director the bank had ever had. I was amazed that Mario sought me out. He knew me because I had the relationship with the bank, but I was a minor officer and the youngest member of the family." But he was a Di Giorgio and brought a special clout. "We were the largest fruit grower in the state—the largest grape grower, pear grower, plum grower—and the largest packer and shipper of fruit for other growers." Di Giorgio was the bank's most important agricultural customer.

Ranged around Di Giorgio at the boardroom table the day he planned to act were captains of industry and commerce. The CEOs or board chairmen of Macy's, Lehman Brothers, United Vintners, Sears, Roebuck, Broadway-Hale Stores. "It wasn't easy to do. Alfred J. Gock—another Giannini protégé, who had been chairman of the board since A.P. retired from the post in 1945 and would be turning sixty-five shortly—was presiding, and Wente was sitting next to him. Beise was there. But it had to be done," Di Giorgio says of the last board meeting before Wente's birthday, the meeting when Wente's retirement should be announced. Di Giorgio had checked the agenda. It wasn't there. The two men "were going to bullet through because they didn't think anybody'd have the courage to get up and do anything about it." The issue could still be brought up as new business, of course. Di Giorgio had done no lobbying but had found a fellow director who had agreed to second his motion, if he made it. The meeting droned on. Not a word of retirement. "At the end, when Gock said, 'Any new business?' I said, 'There sure is.'"

If, as a San Francisco banker has said, "Being a director is like being a pilot of an aircraft—it's years of boredom and seconds of terror," Di Giorgio's "seconds of terror" had come swiftly.

A husky man with a fleshy Italianate face you might expect to see topping the marble bust of a Roman general, Di Giorgio spoke in a confident rush: "The bank has a long tradition that not just the president but everybody in the bank should retire at sixty-five. A.P. believed in it. Mario believed in it. A.P. respected the rule himself, he felt it was an essential thing for the bank, and I see no reason to change his precepts." Wente and Gock listened politely, as their power was assaulted. "I think we should follow them, and since no one has made any motion about who is to succeed Mr. Wente—and he's not indicated that he has any intention of retiring—I suggest that we refer the matter to the personnel committee and ask them to come to us with a recommendation for his successor." He had evoked the thing that could not be denied—A.P.'s principles. He paused, waiting for questions. Nothing. Not a word. Di Giorgio nodded to his ally to leap in with his "second," he called for "a vote, please," and the motion was passed unanimously. Even Claire Hoffman, abrasive to anyone who did not live by her father's principles, did not object. Di Giorgio had launched the Beise era.

A.P. HAD SERVED the "little fellow," but it was that special relationship Giannini had had with his corporate customers Di Giorgio hoped would be preserved, too, in Beise's era. The bonds between Bank of America and corporate customers like Di Giorgio were like family. Doing business with relish and informality, they had been aggressive collaborators in the growth of the nation-state of California.

Di Giorgio had been part of B of A's so-called "Great Wine and Grape Save" just before World War II. Created to rescue an industry about to collapse from the double blows of Prohibition and depression, the event offered a rare view for Di Giorgio of the combined force of A.P.'s grand-scale concepts and Mario's skill at complex strategies to manipulate agricultural economics. The program involved 250 wineries, and 10,000 growers, and was a program, like many of A.P.'s, that invited hostile attack as price-fixing—as a monstrous cartel manipulating supply and demand to the advantage of the large growers, wineries, and the Bank of America.

With a large percentage of the bank's loan portfolio at risk in agricultural loans, the Gianninis took the calculated risk of infusing millions more into their own massive subsidy program, banking on eventual recovery of the industry. "The concept was to take wine off the market and to take the surplus grapes off the market in the form of wine or brandy," says Di Giorgio. And to keep it off the market "until it began to have maturity."

When World War II erupted, the strategy paid off. For the inventories of brandy became pure gold as the grain needed to make gin and whiskey was diverted to the food supply. "Wine became in short supply because they were taking grapes off the market to make alcohol. The bank, the growers, and the wineries made a lot of money. When the war was over, the industry and the growers were healthy," says Di Giorgio. And Bank of America came out of the war "owning" agricultural banking in California.

Sound judgment underlay the dozens of profitable loan deals B of A had done with Henry Kaiser. Eugene Trefethen speaks from sixty years of contact with Kaiser and Bank of America, many of those as Kaiser's president and key financial negotiator with the bank. Now retired and proprietor of one of Napa Valley's most elegant wineries—and a valley neighbor of Bob Di Giorgio—Trefethen recalls the kind of relationship that characterized corporate banking through the decades that flanked mid-century. "The Bank of America never lost a cent on Kaiser. Number one, they had to have confidence in you, know you were honest and had a good track record. That was A.P.'s foundation for both the big and little customers. He had to know you; he wanted Mario and all his people to know you. Number two, they made sure the feasibility studies had been done properly—the estimates of costs on the construction projects. But once they had faith, they really bet on you."

A.P. had introduced Henry Kaiser to President Roosevelt in the 1930s, a prelude to major dam contracts. B of A was the primary private lender for the big wartime shipbuilding contracts that made Kaiser's Victory ships a household name. Mario initiated new banking contacts for Kaiser as the industrialist's empire demanded credit lines beyond the bank's $43 million limits. For Kaiser Aluminum, the Bank of America and Kaiser jointly pioneered the first big syndicated loans, sharing the risk with the New York banks.

Bank of America's board of directors reflected these familial relationships. Di Giorgio and Kaiser were joined by other customers. Foremost Dairies. United Vintner. Fruehauf Company. Levi Strauss. Union Sugar. Miller & Lux, the pioneer farming giant. Arden Farms. As California became an industrial state through the war and postwar decades, it became a game of musical chairs as the same small club of men danced not only onto the B of A board but onto each other's boards. Bob Di Giorgio became part of a California corporate network of such Byzantine interlinkages and self-perpetuating power that it still dominates the Bank of America board today. Over the years Di Giorgio shared the B of A board with the presidents and chairmen of Pacific Telephone and Broadway-Hale Stores. He was, in turn, invited to join their boards—as well as the boards of Los Angeles–based Union Oil and Newhall Land and Farming. Di Giorgio invited Bank of America's retired presidents Rudy Peterson and even Carl Wente to the Di Giorgio board. Even as Bank of America expanded its corporate lending to the national level, it remained a dominantly California board.

The B of A board has become a lightning rod for criticism since the bank's decline. Although capable men like Di Giorgio moved through the B of A board, the dynamics unique to *this* board—combined with the dynamics unique to *bank* boards—conspired to dilute even the strong voices and make them lead players in the most significant banking decline of the century. If its responsibility was to monitor, advise, and even replace management on behalf of the shareholders who elect it, then the B of A board failed. But why? "I think the weakest link of American capitalism is the board of directors of the commercial bank, partly because of its interrelationships with the bank as borrower," suggests a critic, Anthony M. Frank, president of the nation's seventh-largest savings and loan, San Francisco–based Nationwide Savings, before becoming U.S. postmaster general in 1988. "Their borrowing relationships are terribly important to the corporations involved. So you certainly don't want to offend the management."

As in most American corporate boards, B of A's management chairs the board. There, as ombudsman for the shareholders who own the company, management, in fact, monitors itself. In 1955, the year after Di Giorgio made his move against Wente, thirteen of forty-one members on the board were current or retired Bank of America officers. Both Gock and Wente remained on the board, without a vote, but still influential. "Bank boards tend to be pretty populous compared to other corporate boards," says Frank, a tendency that diffuses decisiveness and creates more opportunity for the installation of retired bank officers who continue to wield great influence although out of touch with the daily feel of events.

The board's instrument of control over management was its structure of committees. When Di Giorgio joined, however, the important ones were dominated by management. "The real running of the bank," he quickly saw, "was done by two committees—the board's Executive Committee and the Executive Personnel and Compensation Committee, which set all wages, stock options, and bonuses and determined the most senior executive appointments." Di Giorgio was appointed to that committee and served as chairman for twenty years, putting him at the center of the selection process.

He was also put on the Executive Committee three years after arrival and discovered that he was the only "outsider"—that almost all were retired bank officers; by tradition, the retired president was always chairman of the Executive Committee. "That isn't good. It's the hand of the past running the bank now," he quickly learned, "and I worked like the dickens to get that changed—and did. Eventually it became a preponderance of outside directors."

To Di Giorgio, "The Auditing and Examining Committee was the other key committee. It concerned itself with the financial health of the bank. One of its principal roles was the responsibility for making sure the bank has adequate reserves for possible loan losses. I don't think this bank's auditing committee was any more lax than others," Di Giorgio reflects, as history's—and government regulators'—measure of the board increasingly focused on the explosive issue of the adequacy of reserves in the 1980s. But he could not always see how rigorous it was, for he was not on it. He was gone by the early eighties, when the roof fell in.

Even in the fifties, when Di Giorgio first brought his forthright voice to the board, the Bank of America, like all banks, functioned in a tight regulatory cocoon that made it more difficult for a bank board to shape policy than in other kinds of corporations. But Tony Frank, who was close to several B of A board members during its later troubles, believes that the bank's very "aura of enormous success" may also have discouraged directors' assertive use of their own good judgments.

For MotherBank was looking fine through the Beise years. "Clark Beise was shy and retiring," says Di Giorgio, "but he was a banker's banker. He knew the banking business from A to Z, he ran the bank by delegating, made very good appointments, had the respect of everybody—and Clark got growth going again." The bank's helping hand to the world after World War II had gained it stature, and Beise was nudging the bank gently toward a more competitive international posture. Great power and community respect still resided in the branch managers, the bank's front line, even though the best talent was draining to corporate banking. To cheers and the popping of champagne by the board, the bank had reached $10 billion in total resources in 1957.

In 1956 introduction of a revolutionary electronic check-handling system, MICR, driven by Beise and developed by B of A's A. R. Zipf and the Stanford Research Institute, put B of A at the leading edge of the technology revolution within American banking. In 1959 ERMA made its official debut as the world's first fully automated checking account system. That same year the BankAmericard was introduced, bringing this forward-looking new kind of credit to two million California families in its first year. Beise's neat silver-haired bearing bespoke prudence and seemed to embody MotherBank's having emerged, like California, from raucous adolescence into confident maturity.

Chapter Four

THE CALIFORNIA GOLDEN BOY, Charles Schwab, had not been raised with that hard edge of depression memory that whipped veterans, like Pinola and Rice, of both depression and war. But he had the same drive for success. Son of a district attorney, he was already active in the stock market and an excellent golfer at fourteen, when his father moved the family from the Sacramento Valley to Santa Barbara. By that age, too, he was showing entrepreneurial hustle in a small chicken operation, which he discovered at Stanford—to his delight—was a "fully integrated operation" in business school terminology. A strong scholar-athlete, Schwab had a solid work ethic that had been reinforced by a traditional education at a parochial high school. He had been student body president and had the sun-bleached all-American good looks and athlete's body you saw on California's surfing beaches. Maturing at the tail end of the passive fifties he delighted in voting for the student who ran, and won, the race for Stanford student body president on the "apathy ticket"—a droll comment, he thought, on this campus full of superachievers. In the lockstep pattern of the day, he had married an attractive Stanford girl, Susan, after getting his B.A. and had one baby. Soon he would have a suburban tract house.

There would be nothing lockstep about his career. Buoyed by an unquenchable optimism that let him believe anything was possible, he had the stuff of the big-time entrepreneur.

As Chuck Schwab left Stanford, another good golfer from Southern California, a handsome dark-haired young man named Sam Armacost, entered the business school on a leave of absence from the Bank of America. Both were men of extraordinary confidence nurtured in well-educated upper-middle-class families. But Armacost was following a conventional path, already moving along an accelerated career track within the giant institution. Steeped in a cultured academic background—his father was president of the University of Redlands, east of Los Angeles, and his mother had been just short of her doctorate at Columbia when she married—Armacost was the more articulate and polished of the two.

Armacost, like Schwab, had met his bride in college, as an undergraduate at American Baptist–founded Denison University in Granville, Ohio, which his family traditionally attended. Bored with being a swimming teacher while he waited for Mary Jane to graduate, he joined the bank and found his calling. While Susan Schwab developed the steely nerves of the wives of test pilots or entrepreneurs, Mary Jane Armacost learned the political and support skills of a corporate wife. The two men were already exhibiting the very different impulses that would promise conflict more than two decades later—Armacost the patrician, Schwab the populist.

Schwab had tried banking one summer, hated its bureaucratic constraints, and went to work for a financial rebel named Laverne Foster in Menlo Park, near Stanford. There, in the same dynamic "start-up" environment in which Silicon Valley was forming from the fruit orchards of Santa Clara Valley, Schwab entered the ragged outer fringes of "diversified financial services." Within a few miles of the A. P. Giannini branch of the Bank of America and of Claire Hoffman's home, Seven Oaks, he joined the scattered band that would wage guerilla warfare on the traditional bastions of investment and commercial banking power.

Banking's powers and freedoms were strictly bound by regulations that buffered it from harm but restrained it from joining the American game of open competition. This regulatory blanket had been cast by a frightened Congress hoping to prevent a repeat of the 1930s. Commercial banks, savings and loans, investment banks, and other financial services such as insurance and consumer credit, operated within boundaries defined by the Glass-Steagall Act of 1933, which prevented one from invading the business territory of the other. Banks could no longer do investment banking—the underwriting and selling of securities—as they had before the '29 crash. Savings and loan associations as well as commercial banks could take deposits and make loans, but only a commercial bank could hold *demand deposits* (checking accounts), an enormously profitable franchise for the banks, for customers were paid no interest on them. They were free money for the banks. And the interest they did pay customers for their savings deposits—3.5 percent in 1962—was kept under a ceiling set by Regulation Q. Charges of "cartel" raged over commercial banks, with their protected sources of cheap money. By the early sixties customers were getting restless for a higher return.

There were few places other than a bank where people could put their money to work. There was the stock market, of course. But the public was hungry for more.

As Schwab entered the stream, there was plenty of money around, particularly in California, where the annual income reached $60 billion in 1961, leading the nation. Schwab picked up the vibrations of the "go-go funds" that were popping up through loopholes in the regulations in New York, Texas, California. Mutual funds. Hedge funds. Limited investment partnerships. The first of the "products" that let customers invest their money outside the banking system or stock market. Bright young traders in Wall Street were charting stocks on graph paper, sweating nights and weekends to develop a better stock analysis technique and start their own little fund. The hottest "go-go" stars like Jimmy Ling in Texas were becoming cult figures to aggressive young men like Schwab struggling to find their niche.

"I was the guy with the slide rule," says Schwab, as he helped Laverne Foster create, register, and market anything he could devise that could legally attract investors to the products of Foster Investment Services. Then Schwab met Desmond Mitchell, an Australian who had made a modest fortune in Canada, and John Morse; in December 1962 the three formed Mitchell, Morse & Schwab. Mitchell was the moneybags. Schwab and Morse were the "worker bees" doing the painstaking analysis of market cycles that made Schwab thankful for the mathematics the nuns had drilled into him.

But Mitchell ran the show. He moved the tiny staff to San Rafael, north of the Golden Gate Bridge, and installed the company in a small linoleum-floored second-floor walk-up office on downtown B Street. They started funds and a market newsletter, *Investment Indicators*—"great products but few customers," says Schwab with the irrepressible good humor that would serve him well. He saw setbacks not as failures but as "learning opportunities"—hallmark of the entrepreneur. With direct response advertising Schwab learned the power of marketing and of measuring your results. "We were, and are," he says, "among the most measured marketers in the country." But the impatient Schwab was tired of working for Mitchell. Schwab was desperate to build the business. In this fragile phase of the infant operation, growth was the only route to survival. He bought a controlling interest from Mitchell, built his staff to a large handful, and began to hire young Wall Street investment bankers eager to join the revolution.

Schwab barbecued weekends in the backyard of his Eichler tract house in Marin County's Lucas Valley, a valley of rolling hills and cattle farms turning to suburban housing, and put every penny he could into marketing his ever-changing bag of products. With his earnings consumed by ads in *Forbes* and the *Wall Street Journal*, he was always short of capital, too busy inventing new products and struggling to keep the regulators at bay to pay much attention to the operations side—the "back office," where transactions were handled and recorded. His operations became a disaster, as Schwab's magic at marketing began to test the capacity of his primitive back office.

By 1967—as the flower children rejected capitalism and took over San Francisco's Haight Ashbury—Schwab had established a tenuous but strengthening beachhead. He had started a no-load mutual fund, the genesis of the discount investment concept, and built it to assets of $20 million. He had gained ten employees on B Street and twenty thousand customers and was marketing all over the United States. Customers were earning 20 to 25 percent in his mutual funds and racy little Laurel limited partnerships, more flexible than mutual funds—all riskier, but vastly more profitable than Bank of America's passbook savings accounts. Schwab was riding the rising tide of defection from commercial banks.

BANK OF AMERICA could flick off a Charles Schwab like a mildly bothersome fly on the hide of an elephant. Its bottomless pools of deposits, fodder for the loans that were the bank's principal product, just grew and grew. If Schwab's funds siphoned off scraps of the bank's deposits, losses were overcompensated for by new customers who kept walking in the door.

But in New York banks could not afford to be so sanguine. Working on slimmer margins in a world very different from California, they had to hustle. "The demand deposits in the city of New York hadn't grown for ten years," says Citibank's Walter Wriston. "You wouldn't have to be too smart to know that the banks were out of business. The Bank of America had this enormous consumer base, and it was sort of sweeping through life because they had a ceiling on what they could pay for deposits." New York banks had never had business laid at their feet as had California banks.

California had always permitted statewide branch banking. But New York City banks, the prestigious money center banks—Chase Manhattan and Morgan Guaranty, Citibank, Manufacturers Hanover, Chemical, and Bankers

Trust—were limited to the five boroughs. Five of the banks held 75 percent of all deposits in New York State, and competition to hold that share of the deposit dollars was fierce. As new deposits in New York shriveled and banks faced a funding crisis—where to get money for their loans—Wriston addressed the problem with the conviction that "Laws and regulations are not sacred; they are there to be changed." Wriston had had some training from the master. He had observed A.P.—to whom regulation tweaking was the stuff of life—at close range during Wriston's first two years at Citibank. Transamerica, A.P.'s holding company, was "the largest owner of Citibank, and that put A.P. on our board. He was a director, and I once reported to A.P. on a special project when I was in the Audit Department. He was a genius. He had a vision."

Citibank did not have the rich capital base and corporate connections Morgan had as its legacy from J. P. Morgan's long dominance of New York finance nor Chase's network of elegant global bankers—"the closest thing America has ever had to the Swiss banker," as former University of Southern California banking professor, consultant Dr. Robert Metzger, describes the men who had made Chase, under David Rockefeller, the dominant U.S. bank overseas. Citibank had its history: Its parent bank had been founded in 1812; it had been in London since 1902. The product of the 1955 merger of National City with a blue-ribbon wholesale bank, First National Bank, Citi was gauche and parochial compared with Chase and Morgan. But it had the ambition and resourcefulness of the underdog in a harsh banking climate. And it had Walter Wriston.

Searching for new funds to lend, Citibank, in 1959, had started buying money from the Eurodollar market. The Eurodollar is simply an American dollar owned outside the United States—a repository of dollars first accumulated in the wake of World War II by iron curtain countries that feared confiscation of dollars left in the United States. By the mid-fifties, they were being deposited in banks in London, which quickly became the center of the Eurodollar market. What gave Eurodollars their mystique beyond their very large volume—a pool of $800 billion by the late 1970s—was the almost complete absence of regulations governing their dizzying international movements as they flew, in the form of entries on accounting sheets, from bank to bank, country to country. They became a means for bright young bankers to display lending virtuosity; Bank of America's Tom Clausen pulled off a $236 million Eurodollar financing package in 1960, raising his visibility dramatically in the San Francisco headquarters.

With Eurodollars, Citibank no longer had to wait for customers' deposits but could simply buy what it needed to fund its loans in the market. Eurodollars were exotic and profitable. But they were not the complete solution to the growing funding crunch. With an innovativeness born from having his back to the wall, Wriston kept searching for some new domestic source of funds to feed the insatiable maw of Citibank's corporate lenders. Yet his career path was sending him overseas.

In 1960, one year after George S. Moore became Citibank's president, Wriston rose to a position of considerable power as chief of the Overseas Division, an expression of Moore's bold decision to commit the bank's money and its best men to catching and surpassing his haughty New York competitors in the overseas market. The goal had emerged from a process of corporate soul-searching Bank of America felt no need to begin until the 1980s. From intense brainstorming sessions "to define the vision of where the bank should be going," as Moore recalls it, the declared mission emerged that "We would not be merely a bank. . . . We would seek to perform every useful financial service, anywhere in the world." Citibank would "be everywhere and do everything."

To "be everywhere," Wriston began his drive to build the bank's international business. He would not do just trade finance for corporations, as in the past, but would move directly into consumer retail banking within his target countries; Citibank would compete directly with the host countries' domestic banks. In seven years Citibank established 85 foreign branches. It had swept ahead of all other American banks. By 1967 it had 148 direct foreign branches in forty-two countries and 93 bank subsidiaries or affiliates in twenty-one countries.

To "be everything," Citibank would go beyond traditional banking and create new ways of making money, new services, new "products." Driven by the imperative of finding new sources of money for funding loans, necessity was still the mother of invention. In 1961 Wriston drove a major wedge into Regulation Q—and changed the way banking was done. By introducing a *negotiable* certificate of deposit (CD), he created a new medium for short-term investment and tapped the great pool of temporary excess funds held by corporations, funds the companies moved quickly in and out of the marketplace at the best interest rates they could find, mostly in Treasury securities. Corporations had avoided locking these funds into commercial banks' non-interest-bearing demand deposits. Wriston created—with the blessing of a Federal Reserve that saw its banking constituency threatened—a "secondary market" for Citibank CDs: interest-bearing deposit certificates that could be sold in the market, just like stock. Corporations bought them from the bank at competitive market rates.

Wriston's CDs had given birth to market funding for banks and given Citibank freedom from dependency on the savings and checking account deposits of the private customer, still B of A's basic source. CDs were a triumph; by 1965 the bank held $1.3 billion in CDs. "It saved New York City banks for ten more years," claims Wriston, with inventor's pride, "and it probably changed the world [of banking] as much as anything."

"But market funding would come at a price," Citibank's biographers admit. Forcing banks to the "cost-conscious management, imaginative product development, and aggressive marketing" other businesses had always had to address, it demanded smarter bankers. Before, with deposit rates fixed, the only variable was the interest rate banks charged for loans. The spread between the two where their profit lay—their margin—could be easily calculated. Now, paying fluctuating market rates to lure the CD money in, bankers had to pay attention to both ends of the lending cycle. They had to juggle interest rates and maturity dates of both CDs and loans to make sure they matched in a way that guaranteed the bank a profitable margin. If you didn't balance them properly, you had a *mismatch*—that is, you might be paying more for funds than you were getting from your loans. "You could play the mismatch both ways and *profit* by it, too," Wriston reminds. But the most common negative mismatch was to be stuck with long, low-fixed-rate loans while the cost of money at the borrowing end soared. Under the threat of a costly mismatch "asset and liability management" was also born then.

Wriston could not relax. As the CD took hold, Citibank's most important source of profits, its corporate market, began to trickle away, eroding the kind of privileged corporate lending relationships A.P. had had for so long with Henry Kaiser, the kind of banking in which, says Wriston, "Loyalty had substituted for innovation." No longer in the Big Apple. The industrial plants of the eastern seaboard were moving south and west. Corporations were increasingly going to Wall Street to raise equity through investment banks and turning to the Eurodollar market, where they could dip into the great pools and borrow more cheaply than from a bank.

And then, in the mid-sixties, bankers shuddered as corporations began borrowing from each other, bypassing the bank. The information revolution was placing in the hands of corporate financial officers the data that had been the priestly knowledge of the banker. Computers gave them access to what New York Federal Reserve chief E. Gerald Corrigan calls the "credit-judgment decision information" banks had controlled. Now a corporation in need of short-term funds was calling a corporation with excess cash and buying its money directly, at a cheaper rate of interest than Citibank could offer in its CDs. The "IOU" issued by the borrowing corporation was called "commercial paper."

By the mid-sixties, Citibankers were speaking an eastern language of *market funding* and *asset and liability management* BankAmericans had no need to learn. And *mismatch* had become a code word—a word analysts and the press would not pick up for another fifteen years. But in the humming calculators of auditors, examiners, and bank cashiers, *mismatch* would become a measure of a bank's ability to adapt to change. Throughout the country another new word was being added to the vocabulary: *disintermediation*—the natural migration of money toward the place where it can earn the highest rate of return. It was an ancient concept, as old as the idea of interest. Commercial banks became its victims, as restless consumers withdrew money from their banks and searched for better returns. "Disintermediation was triggered by the Gray Panthers," says California banking consultant Sal Serrantino. Older folks on fixed income were being discriminated against, they complained. Not fair, they said, that while they were limited to 3.5 percent interest on their savings accounts, large corporations could get 5 and 6 percent on CDs. They were attacking the cheap money on which Bank of America had based its spectacular success.

Congress listened to this large and increasingly vocal constituency. And in 1966 the Federal Reserve Board allowed noninsured financial institutions— large brokerage houses and insurance companies, but not banks—to pay a higher rate for a new type of investment product called "money market accounts." The pioneer appears to be Merrill Lynch's cash management account. By the early seventies, money flowed from bank deposits into money market accounts; Merrill Lynch's Ready Assets Trust, begun in 1975, leaped in one year alone from $8 billion to $40 billion. Total assets in money market funds had reached $45 billion, a number that grew to *$207 billion* by 1982. The revolution Wriston was leading from within would now, increasingly, be driven from without by the market's compulsion to circumvent rules that no longer served the nation's and banks' needs.

Citibank responded to the double jeopardy of erosion of both deposits and corporate loans. With the CD market becoming saturated, Wriston found a loophole in the Holding Company Act of 1956 that would permit a holding company that owned only *one* bank to operate free of many regulatory restraints. *It could issue commercial paper.* In 1968 Citibank formed a holding company, Citicorp, which became the parent of Citibank, and rushed to raise money by issuing its own commercial paper. "Commercial paper gave New York banks another few years of life," Wriston says. Banks had found a new tool to pry open the regulatory prison they felt unfairly restrained them.

In 1967 Wriston became president of Citibank and "became both a creator and a benefactor" of the change that assailed his industry, says Dr. Robert Metzger, a financial services expert for international consultants Kepner-

Tregoe, Inc. As a result of the brainstorming in 1960, Citibank had moved aggressively to "do everything" and "be everywhere." In 1969 Wriston sat down for another brainstorming session. He added the goal that the bank should *"serve everyone."*

He assigned a young banker who had joined Citibank in 1966, John Reed, to figure out how to do that within a year. With a degree in industrial management and metallurgy and an M.S. from the Sloan School of Management at the Massachusetts Institute of Technology, Reed began with scrutiny of the bank's back office—of the operational side of banking lending officers disdained. Under the direction of William I. Spencer, who would later become president of the bank, he analyzed every step of the banking process as if it were part of a manufacturing assembly line, looking for inefficiencies. The bank must aggressively implant computer technology, he determined. He circumnavigated the globe and "could give the ratios of every bank in the world off the top of his head," says a colleague. When Reed came back with his answers, Wriston bet the bank on them, and Reed's star began to soar. South American–raised but trained as a banker in the crucible of New York, he shaped his message to Wriston from an environment in which profit depended on fighting for every penny, every point. He saw early that banks that poured their resources into making the dreary operational side of banking efficient and state-of-the-art would inherit the earth in the competitive, deregulated, globalizing, computerized world that was tumbling toward the financial industry, a world of unfathomable volume and velocity. "This isn't a bank; it's a factory," Reed declared to shocked employees in New York in 1970. That year, Spencer became president, Reed became head of the Operating Group, and Citibank was on its way to realizing the computer's potential as B of A had held the promise of doing in the mid-fifties.

They operated in the same nation, under the same federal regulations. But Citibank and Bank of America were beginning to go in opposite directions. Since pioneering the automation of basic banking operation in the mid-fifties, Bank of America had not made the moves that suggested it saw the same future Reed and Wriston saw. If one was right, the other must be wrong.

THE PRESSURES OF THE SIXTIES were being felt all along the eastern seaboard, not just in New York. "In California they don't know how tenuous it is just keeping the money in the house," said Thomas A. Cooper as money market funds siphoned off the deposits of Girard Bank, the mid-size regional bank in Pittsburgh Cooper had joined in 1962. A former Methodist minister, he had quit the ministry without a job or prospects, had driven trucks and painted houses to feed his wife and the first two of his six children. He had run the finances of several churches, adding practical business experience to his academic credentials, and had turned, finally, to banking. At Girard the scale was smaller, but Cooper struggled with the same conundrums as Wriston in New York. The declining East. Social and economic crises in the old urban centers. More competition for the shrinking deposit base. As profit margins shrank, a spirit of belt tightening and disciplined reform took hold in the East. Cooper became an evangelist for that spirit.

By mid-decade Cooper was experimenting with the use of technology to bring better customer service, as well as lower costs, to the teller's window. Where Reed was a back office man, Cooper focused on another of the seminal issues of the banking revolution: the bank's relationship with its customers. How could you put computers to work without sacrificing the "human touch" that had been the hallmark of the American—and certainly of A. P. Giannini's—style of banking? Cooper appeared to be doing some antipeople things, replacing personal interface with one of IBM's earliest automated teller systems. He was closing branches. "But we made the customer's name the basis for the whole relationship. To call up an account on the computer, you punched in a *name,* not a number."

Tom Cooper had left the church but found his calling. Working night and day with messianic commitment, scarcely seeing his family during these years, he had made implementation of the revolution he knew must come to banking his "thing." In a geographic region where banks had to trim and cut, be lean and mean, he was becoming a skilled corporate surgeon, skills that would make him a candidate for president of Girard Bank and, years later, of Bank of America.

Chapter Five

BURSTING CONFIDENTLY from the pages of B of A's 1961 annual report are full-color pictures of gas-guzzling, tail-finned convertibles and block-long station wagons filling the parking lots of shopping malls. A well-fed young family of five, flashing perfect teeth and happy smiles, waves out from a showy white convertible driving across the Golden Gate Bridge as if to say, "Thank you, Bank of America, for lending us the money to buy our car, washer, fridge, house, toaster, and TV on Timeplan." These were families of inflation who believed, as did the bank, that everything would keep going up forever. The bank, in fact, thrived on inflation, with its dynamic spending and borrowing; soaring incomes and home values only made the bank's loans more secure. The real value of people's savings shrank, of course, but that did not show up in the bank's balance sheet. "The bank seemed capable of anything," says banking consultant Metzger. Its strength was not an illusion. Fine-tuned to thrive in the regulated world that had been its habitat for forty years, "the bank was a stellar performer by every meaningful measure right through the sixties."

California was on the cusp of passing New York to become the most populous state, and B of A's deposits were growing at the rate of $1.5 million a day. In 1957 the board had celebrated reaching $10 billion of total resources—

capital, loans, securities, due interest, "brick and mortar," real estate; by 1961 resources had grown to over $12 billion. The economy was beginning what would prove to be an eight-year boom. In addition to its dominance as personal banker to Californians, B of A was bankrolling the birth of two sophisticated industries that held great promise for the state and for the bank. First was the semiconductor and computer technology being pioneered in Silicon Valley, where high tech's "tilt-up" bunkers were growing up around Stanford University, its brain bank. With smart young bankers like Tom Clausen heading up electronics lending in Northern California, the bank was placing loans with exciting growth companies like Memorex. North of San Francisco, B of A was also banking the boutique winery explosion that would give California and the nation the cosmopolitan image it had lacked.

As Rudolph A. Peterson succeeded Beise in 1963, one of the most capable of the Giannini protégés took the helm. A Swedish immigrant raised in rural California, Peterson had joined the bank in 1936 and had followed a circuitous career path. He had left the bank after ten years, then returned to Transamerica in 1952. In 1955 he left again to join Bank of Hawaii, where he quickly became its executive officer. It was assumed by some at Bank of America that Beise had encouraged him to go to gain experience in running his own bank. In 1961 he had been hired back from Hawaii and installed as heir apparent to Beise. He knew agriculture, B of A's bedrock. For six years as president of Bank of Hawaii, he had been getting the feel for a large branch system. But he saw that the future also lay abroad and quickly announced his plans for aggressive international expansion. Trade was growing fast, and Citibank's thrust abroad was leaving Bank of America far behind. Peterson would transform an oversized regional bank into a global force.

Peterson was more dynamic than either president since A.P.'s death. With a strong, muscular jaw and dark hair that turned a sleek silver over time, he had a commanding presence. "He's a room filler," says admiring colleague Bob Truex. "He's probably five foot eleven, but you're convinced, until you're standing next to him, that he's six foot three." Beyond charisma, says Truex, "Rudy was a listener . . . capable of accepting creativity and innovation." A man of great style and confidence, he did not seem threatened by having strong people around him. And he was backed by a team that held promise for the bank's future.

RESTLESS WITH BANKING and always attracted to the excitement and complexity of big corporate projects, Al Rice had left the fast track and quit the bank late in the Beise era. The lure of money and of the chance to orchestrate the finances of a heavy engineering construction company had been irresistible. Like the prodigal son, he had returned to the bank in 1964. He'd loved the complexity and adventure of helping achieve a massive project, the Seymour Falls dam in a remote region of British Columbia. He had loved the high pay. But lunching with his old boss in loan supervision, Iver Iversen, who was now head of the San Francisco Loan Committee, Iversen asked, "Why don't you come back to the bank?"

Iversen called Beise and said, "I think we can get him back for eighteen thousand dollars a year."

"I think it would be a good bargain," said Beise.

When Rice pressed for a higher salary, he was told, "We can't pay you that. It's more than Clausen gets paid." Clausen, promoted a year earlier to head of Corporate Finance, soon to be merged into the National Division, was leading the lending to Silicon Valley. He had moved ahead of Rice, but Rice was not in awe. "Then pay the poor bastard more," he said, laughing. They did.

Before Rice returned, Beise, still chairing the Executive Committee on the board, had a talk with him. "Will you promise me you'll never use the bank as a stepping-stone for your own ambitions again, Al?" Beise gently demanded.

"I promised. I gave my promise to Beise that I would never leave the Bank of America again. I committed forever," says Rice. "Hell, I loved the bank. I told Joan, 'I'm tired of fighting all these battles. I'm just going to go along with things this time.' "

Beise had tempted him back with the invitation to be part of a dramatic expansion of the bank's corporate lending. He had the idea of expanding beyond the boundaries of California and of making an aggressive assault on the corporate business now dominated by the New York banks. They would also take the large corporate accounts out of the branches and have them run by the new division—a blow to the branches. Beise took that initiative in 1963, just as he retired, but it was Rudy Peterson who implemented the strategy. He assigned Rice to create the new National Division. Lloyd Sugaski headed the Southern California arm of the new division. Joe Pinola was his chief loan officer.

In the north one of Clausen's first hires was Sam Armacost. Returning to the bank after finishing at Stanford in 1964, he met Clausen for the first time as he interviewed for the job. "Tom Clausen had just come up from Southern California to run Corporate Finance. His recruiting pitch was: 'You don't need to go to New York to do corporate finance. It's a highly specialized lending function that we've organized here, and it's just going to be a small cadre of people.' It was B of A's first large push into wholesale lending, dealing only with the major corporations. We all knew the fast track was corporate," says

Armacost. He and Mary Jane got married and, posted to Clausen's unit in San Francisco, continued to live near Stanford. His first impression of Clausen had been "very favorable." As he worked with Clausen, he found him "a very powerful, perceptive guy. Extraordinarily demanding, though I don't think unreasonably so. I think he demanded good work; you did it over and over, if necessary, until you got it right."

Even in his first years there were clues that Armacost was on a faster track than most. Reporting to Al Rice, he was given access to the biggest of all corporate accounts, Kaiser. He was the first BankAmerican chosen to spend a year as an intern in Washington on the Presidential Interchange Executive Program, an honor awarded to only one from the bank each year, an envied opportunity to see government at work and learn how to work the Hill.

Rice. Pinola. Armacost. The best and the brightest were galloping to Camelot. Several of the men who would be the bank's leaders in the 1980s also joined Clausen's corporate band. Robert W. Frick was among the first of the M.B.A.'s. Frick, an engineer and M.B.A. from Washington University in his native St. Louis, had been hired just ahead of Armacost. Mont McMillen was also recruited.

MONT MCMILLEN'S stomach knotted with tension and his chest pounded as he approached the imposing doors of the executive-floor conference room in Los Angeles. So far doors had opened easily for him. He was second-generation Bank of America; his father had retired as president of the spun-off Transamerica bank chain, Western Bancorp, and Mont E. McMillen, Jr., had grown up with warm family feelings about the bank. He had been chosen as one of the first of the Golden 100s, an elite group designated as rising stars. He was about to pay his dues. Within a few months of joining the bank in 1966, he faced his first significant rite of passage as an officer trainee and member of the BankAmerican family—his first loan review by the Southern California Loan Committee.

Bank of America was, above all, a lending culture. To be known as a good loan man was the highest accolade, the highest ambition. A good loan was defined as one that got paid back. You'd never learn without making some bad loans. But not too many. Bank of America placed highest priority on learning how to do it well. Armed with neat files, McMillen approached the great and terrifying ceremonial event.

Raised in Los Angeles, summering in Laguna Beach, McMillen had acquired considerable polish from Stanford and from being around successful bankers, his father's business friends. There was no danger that the tall, dark, and well-groomed young officer trainee would have offended the personnel man who hired him, a man "who hated butch haircuts and bow ties." Also Birkenstocks. A different breed from the hippies who were dropping out of the mainstream and moving to the Haight Ashbury, McMillen was already thirty and had matured just ahead of the counterculture. The choice to join the bank was becoming a consciously conservative one, requiring trainees to cross ideological barricades to enter. More than other banks, Bank of America had become a symbol of American capitalism and economic imperialism in the early years of the cold war, an image reinforced by B of A's large-scale lending to the defense and aerospace industries concentrated in California after World War II.

McMillen had worked for an Arizona real estate developer and had been a salesman for Bethlehem Steel in Pennsylvania. There he had seen symptoms of America's loss of industrial competitiveness and had been alarmed as the company proudly showed off the polished old brass of its World War I-vintage factories.

He had not liked the Pennsylvania climate much. He missed the beaches of Southern California. B of A offered it all: the life-style McMillen wanted, as well as association with a world-class operation with a reputation for quality so high that it was becoming known as the University of America, a prime training ground for the banking profession. The loan review process, defender of credit quality, was at the very heart of that legend. The chairman of the committee sat at one end of a very long table, his back to the fireplace; McMillen sat at the other end, with five or six of the bank's most senior credit officers along the sides. A. P. Giannini's portrait frowned down from the wall.

For nights he had been reviewing every calculation and judgment that went into his analysis of the requested loan. It might be a $10,000 loan for a small paint manufacturer in the San Fernando Valley. But he would have to defend it as if this were his doctoral orals—or a $10 billion loan. It contained a thorough history of the borrowing company and painstaking pages of numbers run by hand—before calculators. Nearly twenty pages, single-spaced. You could be sent from the room in disgrace for even a typo. You submitted your report first, for preliminary review, to several members of the committee. They'd clean up most of the errors. If it was a new officer making his first presentation, his boss would sit beside him for moral support. The stress was terrible. Many threw up before it.

Among the group ranged around the table, facing McMillen, was Joe Pinola, head of corporate lending in Southern California. And K. D. Martin, an accountant whose obsession with nit-picking scrutiny of balance sheets and tenacious pursuit of error would make him the bank's controller by the mid-seventies. Those traits would cause his sword to cross Al Rice's in bank-jarring events in the late 1970s. To McMillen, Martin was a young banker's savior. Screening reports before presentation, "he was an absolute perfectionist. If you could get it through Ken Martin, you were almost surely going to make it through the committee. He was there to keep you from being roasted."

The loan review was one of the bank's prime teaching tools, a way of transmitting credit policies and practices evolved over sixty years. It was an invaluable opportunity for a junior officer to vet his own unpracticed judgments against those of men who had earned their spurs. "They never told us, but they were teaching us how serious it was." They impressed on McMillen that banking, as they knew it, was largely a matter of credit quality. But it was far more than a loan review. The sessions were also transmitting the bank's values, imprinting its culture. Pinola and Martin were like tribal shamans conducting an initiation rite, teaching the behavior required to keep the tribe strong. With powerful ritual, MotherBank was burning her ways into malleable young brains, shaping the BankAmerican.

But loan reviews did not teach that traditional California loan making was shrinking in importance as market forces forged a new kind of banking, that this event would become a museum curiosity as profits increasingly came from other sources, and that loans made by the simple parameters of the past would become the problem, not the answer. Evaluating a home mortgage or credit line to a rice farmer was quite a different game from negotiating a billion-dollar consortium financing package to a multinational's copper project in Bougainville or, a few years later, from evaluating the creditworthiness of Nigeria as loans to sovereign states began. Lending to Silicon Valley required a new, more sophisticated kind of analysis.

It was the impact of the corporate thrust on the bank's credit control system that some see now as a critical stress point in the bank's decline. At the time size was still the measure of success. "Volume was a proxy for profits," says Stephen T. McLin, a strategic planner at the bank ten years later. "With regulated interest rates, you knew your spreads, and it was easy to estimate your profits just by knowing the size of your loans. Loan officers would report their profits by calling in and reporting the size of their portfolio to the cashier's office in San Francisco. The numbers all came together in Baumhefner's head."

Clarence Baumhefner dominated the sixties and seventies as the bank's cashier, its senior financial officer—"one of the most powerful men in the bank," says Iver Iversen, a senior credit officer through the Baumhefner years. "No one ever called him Clarence, *ever.*" Baum's extraordinary command of figures permitted him, the legend goes, to give an accurate report of the bank's worldwide cash position in an hour or two—something that took later cashiers several days to do, with the aid of computers. "I don't think his mind was a substitute for computers," jokes Iversen. But Baum brought his own formidable bearing to a natural seat of power to carry the cashier's power to new heights. As chairman of the Money Policy Committee he set the bank's interest and loan rates. In touch with London every day, he stayed on top of global exchange rates and money markets. Responsible for the overall integrity of the bank's financial condition, he influenced decisions on capital, loan loss reserves, the balance between assets and liabilities, and, of vital importance, the new market funding. Controlling the place where mismatch would develop, he "kept the funding function directly under his control," says Armacost, who would succeed to cashier four years after Baum's retirement in 1977.

The man Joe Pinola considered "probably the finest CFO in the West" won, for BankAmerica, special dispensation to maintain lower capital ratios than other banks. "With our reliable funding sources, we don't need *any* capital," Baumhefner boomed to federal regulators, a colleague reports. He was of heroic stature, with piercing blue eyes set in a ruddy face, strong clefted chin, and a dramatic shock of white hair in later years, and the blaze of his presence shriveled many. Even Clausen, an associate felt, "had a hard time finding out what was going on" in Baumhefner's office—or head. But some feared that Baumhefner's dominating style, his powerful memory and command of numbers allowed "a woefully weak financial group, guys all out of the old school" to grow up around him. The bank had almost no trained accountants.

Would Baum's head be enough in the days ahead? With its captive market, the bank had not felt real urgency to track earnings and profit systematically. Information on where the bank stood at any given moment was still "seat of the pants." Even a decade later it was the loan—the asset—side that was the last to provide its numbers for the annual report, "as if they'd been caught surprised to have to get it together," says one of the public relations staff who waited impatiently.

The laxity in the system lay beyond a captive market and Baum's remarkable memory. It seemed related to the idea of the bank as a family, which assigns jobs, ad hoc, as the need arises and makes stringent checks and balances seem unnecessary—inappropriate even. Russ Smith had become cashier in that informal way in 1931, after the Transamerica proxy fight when Mario had fired defectors and the loyal Smith had survived the purge. With Baumhefner there, the mighty machine seemed to be working. Overseas activity was still small enough that it had not, so far, challenged the bank—really, an overgrown California community bank—beyond its ability to cope. But with the expansion to national corporate lending, the system would be tested.

* * *

THE FIRST SIGHTINGS of problems came from outsiders' fresh eyes. "Nobody knew if they were making money," says Bob Truex, the former Irving Trust banker who joined B of A the same year as Mont McMillen, in 1966. "I was surprised at how relaxed they were about lending. They thought that being the biggest put a magic shawl around their shoulders. It was a flaming administrative nightmare." Tom Cooper later said of the system that still survived when he arrived twenty years later: "If they made a profit, they didn't know *why* or what it had cost to make a dollar—there was no cost accounting."

Truex observed a lack of communication, too, that persisted years later, when he was hiring for Rainier Bancorporation Jim Kearney, who had been a chief credit officer in Europe. Truex had called Lloyd Sugaski, senior credit officer of World Banking while Kearney had been posted in London, to ask him about Kearney. "Lloyd said, 'I hardly knew him at all and had practically nothing to do with him.' " Truex had been shocked. "Here was the senior credit officer of World Banking saying that he didn't even know the credit head of one of the four divisions! There was nothing wrong with Sugaski or Kearney—the *system* that there was no contact was wrong."

The B of A job had been broached when Truex had dropped in on his old friend Rudy Peterson in San Francisco en route to his camp, the Druids, at the Bohemian Grove, a camp with "big shooters" like David Rockefeller and Wally Haas. At Irving he had headed up national wholesale lending, B of A's new focus. But it was his dream of the Pacific Rim that had finally pulled Truex from seventeen years at the New York bank. He was attracted by B of A's arc of offices, branches, and investments strung from Japan to Australia. Building on the branches opened up by Russ Smith after the war, B of A was in Thailand, Malaysia, Hong Kong, the Philippines. Truex brought with him a suavity and poise, a cosmopolitan bearing and cut to his suit that marked him as a banker who had been playing the game with Chase, Morgan, and Citi. Square-jawed and handsome, the consummate charmer, he loved the atmosphere of exclusive men's clubs and his weekends with campmates at Druids and, later, Stowaway at "the Grove." Impeccable in both appearance and credentials, he entered as a $38,000 executive vice-president in the Los Angeles headquarters. He was taking a substantial drop in pay to join a bank that was "a totally different kind of animal from the Morgan Guarantys and Irving Trusts. But I wanted to raise my children in the West and to be involved with a bank that had a major commitment to the Pacific Basin. Peterson was an inspiring leader, but . . . international banking had not been inspirationally led. Rudy had only been there a short time himself, but he *knew* that, and he brought me in and said, 'Go down there and fix it.' "

Above all, Truex had been attracted to Peterson. He admired a man "born in Sweden into a poor, agrarian family, raised by a childless uncle and aunt in

Turlock," who had evolved into "a streetsmart, decisive man, handsome, distinguished, urbane, who earned every honor that Sweden bestows. One of the strongest personalities I have ever encountered. Beise is an intelligent, decent man and a good banker, but of a custodial mentality. It was Peterson who put the bank on the map, domestically and internationally."

Truex shared responsibility with Clausen for international banking in California within the National Division, as did Al Rice. But Clausen was the boss. Clausen had also been promoted to senior credit officer, as well as chairman of the General Finance Committee. "All authority flowed from San Francisco," Truex observed. And, increasingly, from Tom Clausen. Peterson's tenure would be up four years later, in 1970. Truex thought he might get the chairmanship when power changed hands. Peterson and chairman Louis B. Lundborg had told him as much. He clearly had the experience and style for a bank breaking out from its parochial bounds. But Bob Truex did not find an easy welcome in MotherBank. "The reputation was of chewing up and spitting out outsiders who came in midstream," says Truex. "If you started there, you were safe for a lifetime, but if you tried to penetrate that dragon, they got you." As he tripped over "a lot of feet in the aisle," he was discovering a characteristic that would become a dangerous pathology in the decade ahead: the spontaneous reaction of the organism to reject aliens that threatened its self-contained sense of place and purpose. B of A's was "a bankwide culture I can give you in a word—arrogant," says Truex.

Truex and Clausen symbolized the culture conflict in their personal styles. "The trouble is, Truex is a thoroughbred, and this bank is full of quarter horses," Clausen told a colleague, with considerable insight. "He didn't apparently mean that one was superior to the other; they just had different gaits," the colleague comments. Those different gaits were revealed in the way in which each ran his half of the state in the new regional branch structure created "to get the decision making closer to the market," Clausen in Northern California, Truex in the south. "Clausen set his up in the San Francisco headquarters building and had it do its job by remote control; I had mine out there on the ground, in Orange County, where the business was, where the branches were," Truex recalls. The tension between the two men was also, Truex believes, "a reflection of insecurities" felt by Northern California toward Southern California; headquarters would "cook something up and be so afraid that Los Angeles would come in with a better idea that they'd go all the way with it until it was too late to change, *then* they'd tell people in Southern California. . . . Even the *chairman*, Louis Lundborg—a *wonderful* man and the senior officer in the south—had no line authority."

Yet the dour and earnest Clausen couldn't have been warmer at first. He astounded Truex by pouring out his innermost feelings at one of their first meetings. The unexpected burst of intimacy came at a reception at the Bohemian Club. "He told me that he had never stayed in good hotels, never eaten in good restaurants, that he didn't really know how to behave, was having to learn all this stuff, and that it was very difficult for him." Truex listened "in utter amazement" to hear this from the man who appeared to be just inches away from becoming the chief executive of the world's largest bank. "He'd already been annointed. Why he delivered himself of this to me I don't know. But as sure as I'm sitting here I'm sure that he regretted that, and regretted me, from that day forward. He never opened up that much again." Clausen had betrayed to Truex social insecurities that may help explain the overweening drive for size, performance, and global stature that would characterize the Clausen years. Sightings of this private side of Clausen would be reported during the Clausen era only by underlings, never by peers. It revealed itself as a need, in Clausen, never to be embarrassed before those he saw as powerful and influential in the bankers' hierarchy. Truex had been Clausen's junior. But Truex would quickly gain strength and stature. Di Giorgio identified Truex early as "a prince."

The bank used Harvard's Advanced Management Program (AMP) as a finishing school for the designated stars. Those watching for clues to Peterson's choice of heir noted that the session Clausen had attended was the program's twenty-fifth anniversary, a session stacked with prestigious corporate leaders. Peterson was watching Clausen. Clausen had moved up on a very narrow track, the lending track. He was an obsessive detail man, an administrator. But he had "no funding exposure. No international exposure. No exposure to anything but the credit side of the bank. He had a very, very thin background," an associate thought, for a man apparently being groomed for the top. Perhaps Harvard would provide some of the breadth, confidence, and polish he needed.

IN 1969 AL RICE approved a loan to a friend, Joe Duffel, for an apartment development in the seaside town of Sausalito just north of San Francisco. Negotiated by George Quist, president of the bank's small business investment corporation and later a founder of the successful venture capitalists and investment bankers Hambrecht & Quist, it was "a very liberal loan," says Rice. Quist brought it to Rice for approval. "I knew Joe was getting a tremendous buy on it, so, in exchange for making the liberal loan, the bank took part of the equity in the project through SBEC, the bank's venture capital subsidiary. If it all worked out successfully, we'd make more money that way." It did.

Rice had always loved money. In 1970, Duffel offered Rice and several other well-known Bay Area businessmen participation in a real estate syndicate in Daly City, just south of San Francisco. Rice invested $30,000 and, a year later, was repaid with a profit of over $60,000. He was delighted at the success of the deal and a few years later joined Duffel in a partnership in building four condominium units at Lake Tahoe, where Rice's growing family loved to ski.

The Duffel deal would change Rice's destiny within the bank.

IN HIS LAST YEAR as head of BankAmerica, 1969, Peterson gave the bank a new dress and image for the seventies. After sixty-five years of being housed in neoclassical marble, the world headquarters of the Bank of America now flaunted a glossy modern facade. A fifty-three-story skyscraper of flame-finished black-red carnelian granite seized the skyline of San Francisco's financial area, the tallest building west of the Rockies. Any architectural merit was overwhelmed by the building's insensitivity to its setting. Seen as a black slab from across the Golden Gate Bridge, it rose like an alien megalith from the pastel city in defiance of the human scale San Francisco had stubbornly protected. Into the plaza at the foot of the tower was installed a five-ton liver-shaped lump of shiny black stone, a sculpture quickly nicknamed the Banker's Heart.

And a new logo was unveiled. San Francisco's world-rank graphic designer Walter Landor had struggled with the board and with the bank's senior staff to translate the bank's sense of itself—and how it would like to be perceived—into a symbol that would be broadcast to the world on every branch sign, credit card, and memo pad. The project was taken very seriously, for a new logo was an opportunity for the bank to redefine itself. After months of presentations of hundreds of different designs, plainspoken Samuel B. Stewart, the bank's chief counsel, finally told Landor, "I don't care what it looks like, as long as it's got a *B* and an *A*." Using only those stylized letters, the logo finally chosen had a monumental quality. Even in miniature, one could imagine it chipped from stone, thirty feet high. But studies had shown that the bank needed to counter the image of giant with something that suggested the human touch. "The letters were designed to look like a monogram, a personal stamp," says Landor. Where the two letters interlink, a graceful, abstract bird form emerged. Landor thought of it as a dove, although it later evolved into the BankAmerican Eagle. Some corridor wags, with what came to seem prescience, joked that the bird was flying backward.

But in 1969 the BankAmericard held its position as the world's largest credit card. That year, also, BankAmerica Corporation, the holding company, was formed. Following Wriston's creation of Citicorp the previous year, it was a quantum leap toward the diversified kind of banking Citibank had pioneered. BankAmerica immediately issued its own commercial paper, expanding its market funding. And within months it had acquired its first nonbank subsidiary, Decimus Corporation, a computer leasing start-up company that would let the bank gather fees for selling data-processing services. Fifteen years later a corporate chart would show BankAmerica Corporation at the top of a family tree with thirty-six-plus subsidiaries.

In addition, 1969 was a year of offshore successes for B of A. The bank pulled off a stunning coup in the Great Alaska Oil Rush, triggered by ARCO'S major oil strike at Prudhoe Bay. Beating out the New York money center banks to assist Alaska in the investment of funds from the biggest oil lease sale in U.S. history, the deal involved a dramatic eleventh-hour airlift of documents from Anchorage to the nation's money centers. Internationally the bank opened thirteen foreign branches that year and was syndicate organizer for a $350 million multination Eurodollar financing package for Rio Tinto-Zinc Corporation's open-pit copper mine on the South Pacific island of Bougainville. A deal that gave exposure to both Clausen and Armacost, Bougainville involved complex currency transfers, a consortium of foreign banks, and global commodity markets. BankAmericans were entering a heady new world.

These grand-scaled multinational financing packages were the "cutting edge," Peterson claimed, of a new stage in international banking. Until recently little more than trade financing for corporate customers' activities abroad, the financing of huge projects that involved the resource development of emerging nations was evolving to within one step of direct lending to developing nations.

But inside the sleek new headquarters beat the heart of a country bank. "B of A operated as a multinational bank with a community bank's funding," says former Comptroller of the Currency John G. Heimann, identifying a lag in sophistication at home base. The sense of purpose that had been clear as long as MotherBank's identity was defined by California's boundaries was wavering as the bank responded to the lure of the glamour and profits that lay beyond the Golden State. In the bank's closed system, the culture was not evolving at a pace with its worldly activities. "No bank can survive when it loses its sense of purpose," warns banking consultant Serrantino. By 1969 Bank of America had "foraged far from its traditional pastures," *Business Week* observed.

CLAIRE HOFFMAN was disappointed in Peterson, especially his efforts to try to kill the school savings program, and now believed that Beise had been the last of the presidents to follow her father's principles. The board, though, was reluctant to let Peterson go. But he was turning sixty-five and must retire at the end of 1969. As Di Giorgio, chairman of the board's Executive Personnel and Compensation Committee, began to have informal discussions with Peterson about his heir, he was shocked when Peterson suggested bringing in Robert Anderson, a former secretary of the treasury, a financial man of stature equal, at the time, to Walter Wriston's—even though he would plead guilty to tax evasion and illegal banking operations in 1987. "It would be terrible for morale to bring somebody in from outside. You're supposed to be bringing people along inside the bank. That's your job," Di Giorgio told Peterson. Among his colleagues, Tom Clausen had appeared to be the heir. At a board meeting several months before his retirement, Peterson presented his list of candidates: cashier Clarence Baumhefner, chief counsel Sam Stewart, and Tom Clausen. Baumhefner was within two years of retirement and would be a caretaker president. Stewart, hearty and, at times, profane, was not generally deemed polished enough. "I'd be happy with any of them, but my choice is Clausen," Peterson told the board.

A. W. Clausen appeared as president-elect for the first time in the 1969 annual report. Flanked by Chairman Louis Lundborg and the suave Peterson, Clausen, with glasses, slick-brushed hair, and tightly clenched fists, looked earnest and older than his years.

With Clausen, the bank would be cutting its ties with the ag-based, Giannini-trained tradition of leadership. He was only forty-six. To Di Giorgio, the prospect of any president's holding power for nineteen years—as Clausen could—was horrifying. He would accept him only if he agreed to a ten-year limit on the job. An influential member of San Francisco's corporate establishment, Walter A. Haas, Jr., of Levi Strauss, feared Clausen's rough edges and surly style. "The job to some extent is that of a roving ambassador, and you have to have the kind of personality that is effective," he was quoted as saying. "I was concerned that Tom, to my knowledge, had very little international experience." Clausen had insecurities, Peterson admitted, but had come back from Harvard with new poise and assurance. Everyone agreed that Clausen's familiarity with every number on the balance sheet was nothing short of miraculous. "And he had a good credit record," Di Giorgio believed. "He was a good loan man."

To be known as "a good loan man" was still the highest accolade. In 1970 the Clausen years began.

PART TWO

Chapter Six

"THE FÜHRER!" Claire christened him as Clausen came to power in January 1970. "I can't care about people," he had said, defensively, when Claire had challenged him on a branch issue. Yet, as never before, it was the time for a humanist at the helm.

In February 1970 the Isla Vista branch near the campus of UC Santa Barbara was torched, symptom of the charged environment through which Tom Clausen would walk. A national sensation, the event presented a frightening TV montage of charred Bank of America signs and mobs of rioting students, their rage and disaffection unleashed by drugs and the armed presence of the National Guard. Young Californians, whose parents had proudly handed their pennies over to the bank's school savings program, hated the B of A as banker to the Vietnam War and symbol of American capitalism. Rudy Peterson made a plea for peace with the students: "We can afford to lose a branch; we cannot afford to lose a generation." Nine months later the Irvine branch burned.

Clausen responded to the bank's first serious public relations challenge since the 1930s proxy fight by ordering a vigorous reevaluation of its social policy. Through the Giannini Foundation, the bank had been a generous supporter of civic institutions and schools. This required more. In speeches, in directives to department heads and branch managers, in the annual report, the bank raised social responsiveness to highest priority. It dedicated itself to hiring and lending to minorities and to providing credit for environmental improvement projects. The annual report was printed on recycled paper. And Chairman Louis Lundborg, in a much-quoted speech, "Lessons of Isla Vista," told the Seattle Rotary Club, "We can divide into armed camps and shoot it out; or we can try to find common ground so that we can grow together again."

Mont McMillen, Clausen's executive assistant at the time, saw a tenacious commitment on Clausen's part to an effort organized by David Rockefeller to bring politically radical youth into regular dialogue with corporate leaders. "He would not miss one of those meetings," says McMillen, of the unheralded program. In San Francisco a special Social Policy Committee was created, reporting directly to the president.

Yet the campaign of response was largely the product of the Corporate Communications division; in a bank grown to forty thousand employees, compassion had become a bureaucratic function. And the slot of executive vice-president for Social Policy became a useful political tool—a "Siberia" where the out-of-favor could be shelved. Few were ever overtly fired at Bank of America.

When Bob Truex was appointed the first executive vice-president of Social Policy in 1972—with Clausen proclaiming that Truex would "put the bank where my mouth is"—Truex knew he had been sent to Siberia. In the shelving of Truex, Clausen revealed what would become a pattern: that men with the promise of strength equal to his own—and human skills surpassing his own—would not stay long at his elbow.

Truex left the bank a year later. The early intimacy had turned to resentment as Truex—sophisticated, yet congenial, and highly favored by powerful board members like Bob Di Giorgio—became one of the top two or three contenders for the chairman's seat. "Truex had come in right at the top and thought he'd be president of the bank one day," Iver Iversen suspected. Truex was prominent as the senior corporate loan officer for Southern California. A western bank heavy with farm boys, B of A had profited from Truex's urbanity and from his Big Apple banking experience. "I was good at making loans, if I do say so myself," says Truex, laughing.

The chairmanship vaguely promised to Truex—and prematurely announced by the financial press—went to Chauncey Medberry, Clausen's choice. Truex's champions Lundborg and Peterson were no longer in control. Medberry was everyone's favorite Renaissance man, admired and loved. But he was not considered a forceful leader. "He tends to kiss hands at cocktail parties and has the greatest grace. But from the time he became chairman until he retired, he dedicated himself to never making a decision," Al Rice says with a chuckle.

"All I want is to be given a job with some responsibility and be treated like a human being," Truex said, groaning, as he moved from Los Angeles to a hotel in San Francisco. Within the year both Medberry and J. A. Carrera, head of branches, took him aside, told him, "Tom knows you're a good man, but he doesn't know what to do with you," and advised him to take any other good offer he might have. Both men had Clausen's ear; he knew he had been warned from the top. He accepted the job as president of Washington's second-largest bank, Rainier, in Seattle—a regional bank with a surprisingly well-developed Asian business. At last, Truex would be banking the Pacific Rim.

THE FAILURE TO KEEP Truex was not an isolated event. More would leave. Clausen was inspiring in very few the affection and loyalty Beise and Peterson had engendered. More often he inspired fear. "He was just not nice to people," Bob Di Giorgio said later. That was the public view. Yet he could be kindness itself. It was his young executive assistants who got the closest view of a complex and ambiguous personality.

"Rather than endure terrible, terrible castigation from Tom, nobody wanted to allow their mistakes to become public before they had a chance to correct them and possibly hide them forever," says Bruce A. Koppe, Clausen's executive assistant following Mont McMillen's time in the role. "No matter how good the report, or how thorough the preparation, he simply kept asking questions in more and more detail until you either had to say you didn't know, or he caught you in some contradiction or mistake. And then he'd put you down. It almost had to reach one of those conclusions. His management style was one of showing you how superior he was to you by the extreme detail of his knowledge."

Clausen's fabled obsession with rules, numbers, and details seemed driven by fear of being caught unprepared and embarrassed. After presentation of a competent report in which earnings had been given to two decimal points, an impatient Clausen snapped out the number to three decimal points. At that point, even the conciliatory Chauncey Medberry got up and left and was heard to mutter an uncharacteristically biting comment: "What an unimportant damn thing to destroy somebody for when, good Lord, the numbers are all available."

"I think Tom would love to be the world's most generous, warmhearted human being, but he doesn't have any idea how to go about it," says Koppe, who, as his assistant, occasionally saw the soft side. "Morning was not a good time. He made no bones about it. But if I'd walk into his office about six-fifteen, an hour after everybody had left, I was liable to get a princely reception. There were good odds that Tom would sit there and talk to me about things that I was embarrassed to hear, about people, about his inner feelings, about sensitivities to things that were going on. It could be an absolutely super time." But Koppe had become thin-skinned. "I couldn't do anything right. It was painful. For a few weeks most of my business with Tom was by attaching notes to things. He kept saying, 'My door's always open.' And it was. But a bee's nest is open, too. One night at about six-thirty I was beavering away at my desk when this voice comes from the inner sanctum, calling me in. He was seated there at his desk. He put his head in his hands, almost hung his head, and said, 'Why don't you come in and see me anymore?' For the next two weeks I've never had a better relationship with any boss in my whole life."

Clausen could surprise with spontaneous compassion. His assistant Mont McMillen had quaked at receiving a phone call from Clausen while on leave in Los Angeles to visit his sick father. Expecting a frightful dressing-down for some error he had made, McMillen had ventured, "What is it, Tom?" The response was: "I just called to see how your father was." One Christmas, Clausen warmed the heart of a mid-level employee at a tree-lighting ceremony on Giannini Plaza by asking about his wife and child by name. "He had great recall and sensitivity for the personal affairs of employees," Koppe confirms. Clausen tells the press to this day, "I'm the nicest guy I know."

Yet the larger pattern of behavior suggests a man who found the "human touch" hard. Clausen worked studiously to prepare for meetings with lower-echelon staff, examining their backgrounds and records to find the pressure points where they might be motivated; he showed real concern for giving off the right message, "and he did it for the bank," says Koppe, applauding the effort. But it did not come naturally, as it had for Bob Truex. "I'm a student of those kinds of things. I like the full body language of communication," Clausen would say years later, describing how he places himself behind an "intimidating" desk if he has a heavy message to deliver or on a comfortable sofa if his goal is to "make someone feel good." He claims, "I've never lacked confidence in my own style."

Evidence abounds, however, in the accumulated vignettes of close associates, that Clausen's blustering confidence may be partly a pose. A single incident with the Federal Reserve Board reveals the pattern: A member of the Fed's rotating Advisory Council, Clausen had received a questionnaire from the Fed chairman. In Clausen's absence, Koppe had responded as best he could, explaining Clausen's unavailability, and sent the questionnaire back. The Fed had set up a telephone conference to discuss it, Clausen had participated, then exploded at Koppe for usurping his prerogative. "Tom's insecurity with a group of people of the caliber he thought the Federal Reserve Board constituted would simply not allow his taking a backseat, even in that minor way.

"That inferiority complex. I think it's his downfall," Koppe speculated. "Short of being led to the gallows, I don't think, in those days, you could have forced Tom Clausen to do what John Reed was doing, risking losses now for the long-range good of his bank."

ALTHOUGH FIERCELY AMBITIOUS, Wriston's boyish protégé John Reed did not have his ego invested in his image. His background clearly bred more worldliness and confidence than Clausen's midwestern upbringing in a town of eighteen hundred. Son of an Armour executive, Reed had lived in Brazil and Argentina as a child and could negotiate in fluent Spanish and some Portuguese. With an undergraduate joint degree in American literature from Washington and Jefferson College and his sciences and management from M.I.T., he read five books at a time and had been photographed relaxing in a lab coat doing gene splicing. Like Wriston, Reed considered the status quo less than sacred. A cool and pragmatic corporate scientist with few personal friends within the bank, he saw banking as a competitive industry; super marketers like General Foods and Philip Morris were his models. He joined the board of Philip Morris so that he could study its marketing techniques.

The investment Citicorp was making in the visions that had emerged from the sweathouse of the late sixties—to be everything, to go everywhere, to build efficient computerized operations for the deregulated days ahead—was enormous. It would take years, not quarters, to achieve. It would lose pots of money, and for several years Wriston himself would not receive the annual incentive compensation. Citibank would suffer from comparison with B of A by the influential Keefe, Bruyette & Woods, Inc. *Bankreview* as late as 1980, a full decade after its plunge into the daring strategy. "Citi's expensive venture is highly uncertain as it pertains to future profitability," Keefe, Bruyette would tell the financial world, while "BAM should appeal to investors because of its high quality and undervalued status." But Wriston did not panic. "Everybody was angry, unhappy, and the mortgage payments were high. We made a lot of mistakes. But we built a hell of a business."

AS BANKS BURNED, Clausen had other fires to put out. Memorex, financed with such pride, had gone sour. Clausen had led the team that made B of A the principal founding shareholder and lender to the high tech Silicon Valley

company. By the early seventies Memorex was coming apart. As head of the
venture capital unit, Al Rice had been criticized for selling some of the unit's
Memorex stock at $134, as it climbed to $172. "Then, suddenly, all didn't
seem too well . . . and when we went down and took a look at it, it turned out to
be a financial disaster," Rice recalls. "Memorex had a negative net worth of
eighty million dollars—and they *owed* four hundred fifty million dollars."
Jealous of its relationship, B of A had remained its only bank. "We had
enormous investments in it. . . . We had a hundred million dollars in loans, at
risk."

The bank burning in Isla Vista had been a shock to the bank's image. Now
customers were reading in the press that the impregnable B of A—California's
Rock of Gibraltar—might take what Rice believed would be "at that time the
largest loan loss that anybody had ever taken." Inside Memorex, Harvey
Gillis, who would join B of A as a senior financial officer in time for the
decline of the eighties, had wondered why B of A had not moved in sooner to
protect its risk. He'd watched the hostility between the two Memorex founders
paralyze the company. He had seen the decision to diversify from its successful
disk drives to go head-to-head with IBM on small computers go forward until
it brought Memorex to the edge of bankruptcy.

Clausen assigned Rice, one of his favorites, to work out the loans. Known as a
troubleshooter, Rice was, by that time, the bank's chief credit officer as well as
head of the venture capital unit. "For a year I was de facto head of Memorex,"
he says. Running the workout from San Francisco through 1972 and into '73,
Rice dispatched a workout team led by Bob Frick, one of the handsome young
straight arrows following the same corporate fast track as Mont McMillen and
Sam Armacost. "I tried to hold off the creditors and keep them from pushing
Memorex into bankruptcy," says Rice. He leaped up on chairs to calm panicked
creditors, blitzed corporate America for a merger partner, initiated an aggressive restructuring. "If it had gone into bankruptcy, the bank would have lost a
hundred million dollars," Rice claims.

As the loans were repaid, "the B of A got a hundred percent of their dollars
back, plus interest, plus just a little bit more," says Rice. As its Memorex stock
was converted to preferred stock, the bank made more profit. When Burroughs
Corporation bought Memorex, the Memorex executives met in Palo Alto and
presented Rice, their "knight on a white horse," with a big white Stetson. "It
was one of the greatest saves in the history of mankind," Rice loves to claim.

Patrick L. McClung, a mid-level management executive from Decimus who
had worked with him through the crisis, had seen Rice cool, polished, and
forceful in marathon meetings with the heads of IBM and Control Data and
with Ross Perot, the Texas financier. He had identified Rice as a "fantastic

leader." The obvious one, of all the BankAmericans he'd seen, to be Clausen's successor.

The Memorex crisis was a shock. Rice worried that "something in the system was fouled. Memorex shouldn't have happened." But it was explained away as an aberration, an isolated event. The board, employees, and the public were happy to accept reassurances from management. Banking was, after all, a game of risk assessment, and some losses were expected. And ultimately, Memorex was not a loss. But it should have sent up a red flare, an alert that there was, within the biggest bank in the world, a potentially dangerous mismatch between the bank's supreme confidence and its capabilities in a fast-changing banking climate.

It was the problem glimpsed by outsiders like Bob Truex in the mid-sixties, a credit control system that had never really been put to the test as long as it functioned within the simpler world of farm and home loans. But bankers now must grasp, and the system must accommodate, an exquisitely complex new world. "As a business, banking has been so simple," Rice knew from his forays into manufacturing. "No inventory or purchasing problems, no union problems, no cost standards to comply with. All you had to do was be smart enough to take in some deposits and put the money out at a margin." Not anymore.

IN MEMOREX the bank's checks and balances had failed less than fifty miles from headquarters. How would they hold up as Clausen made the boldest move of his entire tenure as president? While Rice was hollering from chairs at Memorex, Clausen was making massive structural changes within the bank. He was decentralizing and dividing up the world.

In a bank where the reins of power and decision had been held in Clausen's authoritarian hands and where ultimate credit authority had been held by the daunting General Loan Committee, he was dispersing credit and lending authority, as well as armies of personnel, to the front lines. To many, that act, begun in 1973, is seen as the beginning of the inexorable chain of events that led to the devastating loan losses of the 1980s, the blows from which the bank may never fully recover the size and stature Clausen inherited in 1970. "It's what broke down the bank's great credit controls," Chauncey Medberry, Clausen's chairman, told a colleague. "When he decentralized, he fixed something that wasn't broke."

In California Clausen regionalized the retail bank. He abandoned the system of loan supervision Al Rice had so admired, a system in which a platoon of well-trained supervisors carried the awesome rigor of the Loan Committee reviews out to the branches. Led by a "core of real experienced loan old-timers," as Iver Iversen knew them, these guardians of loan quality had been a direct line of contact between the branches and headquarters. In decentralizing Clausen created regions and gave them high lending authority. Instead of reporting to headquarters with loans that were over their limits, the branches reported to their region. "Growing your loans was rewarded," says one of the old-timers, "That's dangerous ground." Shielded from headquarters by their new autonomy and buffered from San Francisco's scrutiny by the regional layer that now blanketed the branch system, the lending lords of these new baronies became cavalier with their lending limits. At times they pooled their lending limits, two people combining modest $50,000 and $25,000 limits to make $75,000 and $100,000 loans. "One and one equaled *three*!" Promoted to chief credit officer in 1973, just as decentralizing was implemented, Iversen "was concerned that we'd get too involved in volume and maybe forget a little about quality." But as power poured out to the California regions, Iversen's warnings fell on deaf ears.

IN 1974 CLAUSEN decentralized the world. He put the bank's international operations into a new structure called World Banking Division, divided the world into four parts, and dispersed thousands of shiny-shoed BankAmericans to bases abroad and to New York and Chicago. "It was the most dramatic thing Tom ever did," in Joe Pinola's view, as chairman Chauncey Medberry was appointed head of the new global structure. As the bank's presence and lending power swelled overseas, the gradual expansion of foreign business under Beise and Peterson exploded. This foreign thrust was true to the ambitions Clausen had always had. "I've been a transnational thinker for decades. I got it in my roots. My Norwegian family. My service in the navy. In 1947 I wrote my father from the Azores and said, 'If you're saving the newspaper business for me to come back to, I love you, but it's not for me. I want to be on the global scene.' "

Posted in London in the early 1970s, Sam Armacost saw the strength of Clausen's concept: "Putting people out in the field close to customers developed business much more effectively." It was a way of reviving shrinking corporate lending, which had reached "a kind of saturation." Through the fifties and sixties B of A had been building an indigenous presence overseas; only Citibank surpassed its network. Now, with this bold dispersal of its best talent to the outposts, the bank could target "foreign-domiciled major corporations with the officer serving the account in the same general geographic locale. Yet we could marshal all the resources of a major global bank," says Armacost.

But there was more to Clausen's thrust abroad than playing out his long dream or exploiting the global network. An irresistible opportunity was shining before him, the most glittering bonanza in the history of banking—Arab oil dollars. Petrodollars. Bankers of the 1980s would reap them as the third world debt crisis. But at the time they turned every bank and banker who touched them to gold.

Petrodollars were triggered by the oil embargo in the Mideast in 1973. As Arabs who controlled the world's oil supply shrank the volume of oil they sold to the world, the law of supply and demand sent the price of oil soaring. In a single year, 1973, the price *quadrupled*. As oil-poor nations from Japan to Zambia scrambled for dollars to fuel their needs, desert-bound sheikhdoms, some of them scarcely emerged from nomadic life, watched the world shower them with unimaginable riches; billions of dollars poured in like gushers. More dollars than the countries could put to use for their own social and development programs. As petrodollars flooded the coffers of the oil producers—Saudi Arabia, Iran, Venezuela, Mexico, Libya—American banks had a unique advantage. For oil traded in U.S. dollars.

If banks could attract them as deposits, petrodollars could be put profitably to work as loans. Just as a recession and the accompanying "liquidity crunch" of 1973 and '74 were shrinking the corporate loan business, there were—in Africa, Latin America, Southeast Asia—dozens of industrializing countries that desperately needed infusions of capital to buy oil and to maintain their momentum of growth. A vast new lending market lay open to exploitation: "sovereign risk"—lending to nations, to governments and their state corporations. It served America's strategic interests, for it kept the developing nations as markets for U.S. products and as friends of democracy. It was a chance for bankers—despised moneylenders several centuries earlier—to become financial diplomats speeding a mighty global process in which "the center of industrial dynamism has moved from North America, Western Europe, and Japan to rapidly developing countries in Latin America, Asia, and Africa," as UCLA political scientist Jeffry Frieden describes it—a process that bred new trading partners and political alliances.

With countries hungry for the money, the interest spreads were seductive; banks could lend for at least a point over Libor, the going Euromarket rate—higher than rates they could get at home. As Walter Wriston, one of the era's more eloquent apologists, says, "If the banks had not recycled, the world would have stopped." Whatever the motives—and in this environment greed could be cloaked with an aura of high purpose—petrodollars made the world's commercial banks the conduit for the greatest transfer of money in the history of capital and currency. For a few, euphoric years in the latter part of the twentieth century, bankers would be host to a world-altering phenomenon that would become a metaphor for the naive and parochial thinking that would dethrone the United States from world dominance by the 1990s. At the time, it seemed banking's Golden Age.

BANKAMERICANS PACKED THEIR bags to join the adventure. Clausen's first two World Banking appointments were promising. He was sending the stars of the fast track. Al Rice and Joe Pinola inherited half the world.

Joe Pinola headed North America and Mexico, and "I can tell you that I did not like it," he says of commuting between his headquarters in Los Angeles and New York. "As hungry and ambitious as I was, I liked visibility. Seeing the president when he came down once a year was not going to make me happy. . . . If I wanted to go to New York, I'd go to work for Chase or Citi or Morgan," he grumbled. He saw the merit in Clausen's decentralization—that "putting very good people there and having a shot at leading the hundred-million-dollar credit lines to big corporate customers was a strong reason for . . . taking the bank to the customer." He had a dynamic, oil-rich nation, Mexico, at his doorstep, a candidate for both deposits and loans. But he basically opposed Clausen's concept. "I felt that if the customer wanted another New York bank, it would add Irving to its list, not B of A; it wanted B of A because it wanted the things you could deliver in California. . . . But Tom got behind it, and when Tom got behind something, don't argue, do it. Being a good soldier, I did the best I could to put it together." He expanded the Edge Act international operations in New York, Miami, and Houston, and flew Armacost back from London to establish the new regional office in Chicago. It wasn't all bad. The bank's name still invested its officers with magical power. His division had glamour.

As his power grew, a new Pinola emerged. The "skinny Italian kid" from an Appalachia coal town had gained style and presence. Although some found his self-confidence "egomaniacal," Pinola had the deep commanding voice and motivational skills of a leader. He lacked the multilingual charm and graces of a Chauncey Medberry, but his well-cut suits were now filled out by a barrel chest, and as his hair went prematurely white, the straight-talking Pinola began to look rather like the stars whose movies his division financed. He was backed by Doris, the high school sweetheart who had evolved into a tall, impeccably groomed lady he proudly called "the perfect corporate wife." He had followed Clausen into aerospace and high tech lending in Southern California earlier, a high track move. He was still on track. Now, with North America and Mexico as his territory, Pinola had moved to within striking distance of his goal—the top.

*   *   *

AL RICE WAS ebullient. He was off to London. He was leaving one of the bank's most powerful jobs, that of chief credit officer. But sitting in San Francisco, he had been restless as "I'd read in the newspapers that the price of oil was going up. . . . It didn't take a genius to figure out that there were going to be a lot of dollars floating around." As he packed up Joan and the three children in January 1974, "the dollar totals had just started to be tremendous, and B of A had just started to be one of the principal international banks." As the race for petrodollar deposits began, Al Rice was moving "right to the heart of it." He knew he was going to love decentralization when, as he left, Chairman Chauncey Medberry, "my boss at the time, said, 'Al, if you never call me, I guarantee you, I will never call you.' It was a perfect relationship!"

He ran his empire of one thousand people in London and several thousand in bases scattered from Frankfurt to Kuwait to Kenya from "one of the great offices that ever was created! It was magnificent—semicircular with big windows that looked right out at St. Paul's dome." "Every noon, almost without exception," he lunched in the bank's dining room with current or potential customers. With his cook and butler, he and Joan entertained bankers and businessmen at home. "Nobody pounded the table and said you have to overtake Citicorp," Rice claims, "but you were trying to improve your position in the markets and always trying to get their customers away from them."

He commanded "footings"—total assets—of $17 billion, with half of that in loans, the size of a good-size bank in themselves. But they were not being productively managed. "The reason I went to Europe is because they couldn't balance the books. It was a disaster. The Italian bank had never even been looked at in detail." Constance M. van Vlierden, who had been head of all international operations and a man Rice admired as "articulate, urbane, visionary . . . but not a detailed operating man," was being replaced in San Francisco by Medberry. As chief of international van Vlierden had, in turn, followed Roland Pierotti, by then retired. At Managing Committee meetings in the late sixties, Rice had relished the unequal combat as Pierotti, "this internationalist—this intellectual and gourmet who loved opera, knew history and the arts, and spoke three languages—parried with the provincial Carl Wente." Pierotti had carried Peterson's international ambitions abroad. "He was very intuitive about finding a good deal for the bank. He did a great job of building a network around the world. You need a flamboyant person to get it started." But Pierotti had scattered branches across Europe with wanton abandon, in Rice's view. "They positioned us for great opportunities, but I would have opened five branches where he had about *sixty!* There were buildings and offices the bank didn't even know it had." Pierotti and van Vlierden "were an expression of the bank culture. They didn't pay attention to measuring profits and costs."

Rice demanded of his managers as he took over: "How do we measure our success? How do we monitor performance? Where's our competitive advantage?" He targeted foreign exchange trading, moving into the vacuum created by the Herstatt crisis. Bankhaus I. D. Herstatt, a fast-driving German bank, had been abruptly closed by the German regulators after severe foreign exchange losses in June 1974. Hitting New York in the morning just as banks were settling their foreign exchange accounts, Herstatt had interrupted the international payments mechanism, giving U.S. banks their first frightening taste of the damage that could be done by events abroad. As "everybody got fearful and dropped out of the market," Rice saw his opportunity. Within twelve months B of A's London trading desk was making "about a million dollars a month. We became the largest forward foreign exchange trader in the world." Rice replaced inept managers with a ruthlessness that was alien to MotherBank. He fought with Clausen by phone over raising the pay of the country manager in Germany, a battle over $500 that revealed to Rice that despite decentralization, "Tom wanted to have such tight control that he didn't even let you approve salary levels." With every confrontational "win," the division's power—and Rice's reputation as a stubborn maverick—grew. Rice's division hustled handsome fees for writing letters of credit for importers and exporters—from wheat and corn to Coca-Cola and Caterpillar tractors. It made loans to Greek shipping owners, "loans made in 1974, '75, '76, on a very cherry-picking kind of basis as to our clientele . . . a very good niche strategy" that only later was "prostituted by the drive for profits and . . . very severe recession, and went 'down market' as more marginal shipping companies became a larger part of the portfolio," says Rice's chief credit officer, Richard Puz, of the lending arena that later became a nightmare. At least until he left London in 1979, Armacost claims, "B of A was a conservative belt-and-braces lender in shipping—it lent against cash flows of charters, took hulls as security. It was *not,* in those days, a lender against just mortgage value."

"We were trying to put the B of A on the map. We would work so hard during the week that every couple of months I would say to my country managers, 'Gang, we is going to have a meeting in southern Spain,' " says Rice. They would get in the Learjet, with old pilot Rice sharing the controls in the cockpit, and fly to Marbella "to talk about how we were going to make B of A the most successful bank in Europe." They would come home convinced that "We is going to conquer the *world*!" says Rice, laughing. Clausen "never pushed inordinately to build the portfolios," Rice claims, "but with those enormous petrodollar deposits . . . obviously, we had to use the deposits for something." Loan portfolios still held the glamour, excitement, the prestige. Lending was still the bank's core business.

The true pulse of the petrodollar flow, and its seduction, could be felt only beyond the English Channel. Traveling 50 percent of the time, Rice streaked in the Learjet to Malawi and Abu Dhabi. He donned a burnoose like Lawrence of Arabia for a feast in the luxurious desert tent of billionaire Kuwaiti financier Khalid al-Marzook and fought back "an inferiority complex" among the Goyas and hilltop grandeur of the Spanish banking family the Botins. He visited the homes of the Lamberts in Brussels, the Rothschilds in Paris. "The name, Bank of America, was a great door opener. I think half the time in the smaller countries the finance ministers thought you were the Federal Reserve Bank," he says, chuckling. "There was no finance minister who would ever say, 'I don't want to see you.' "

Rice was the personification of the international lending boom. In the late sixties he had pioneered the early "sovereign risks," staying in "motels tackier than anything in Daly City" in Saudi Arabia's capital, Riyadh. Now, staying in luxurious Hiltons, he shared the petrodollar glory days, when American bankers were seizing from Britain the haughty preeminence it had held in the international banking community through its colonial era and the current Euromarket—that moment before Japanese banks rode their massive pools of capital to top rank when boys from Whittier, California, could feel themselves swell, inside their pinstripes, to something close to statesmen. To trace Rice's movements is to glimpse the seeds of the third world debt crisis and to understand that the awesome buildup of debt was in great part a product of provincial naiveté, bankers' herd mentality, and the blindness of greed.

As American bankers bashed on with frontier enthusiasm, where was Britain, with its centuries of colonial contact with the third world? Why did it not provide a rational model for assessing country risk? Instead, the former colonial powers moved cautiously into the new game. "They were financing mainly trade flows, drawing on experience dating back to the days when the Royal Navy would make an appearance and keep the lid on," says an observer of the international banking scene.

Not all of the world was welcoming. Lebanon—the Paris of the region when Rice had first come in the early sixties—was swiftly deteriorating. B of A's Mideast headquarters in Beirut had survived a terrorist attack in which the local police, foolhardy heroes, had freed hostages by charging down the stairway into a blazing shooting match. The day before Rice had last visited the Beirut office, two bullets had gone through third-floor windows, barely missing Yves Lamarche, his Mideast manager. Rice ordered the staff evacuated and closed up Beirut.

But the addictive recycling of petrodollars overrode concern for political volatility. As deposits flowed in, Rice flew to Africa to lend them out. His missions to Zambia were typical: to win for B of A the role of lead bank in a $40 million financing of a copper mine and milling facility being put together by a syndicate of multinational banks. Subsisting on cornmeal, dependent on copper exports, Zambia was being drained of capital by the soaring oil prices, was starved for money, and was already borrowing heavily from the World Bank and the IMF. After cordial meetings with the president, D. Kenneth Kaunda, and his finance minister, Rice knew he had scored when he was flown in the president's plane for a day of viewing the great game herds at Lake Victoria.

"We thought we were doing great," says Rice of the judgments that went into making larger and larger loans to nations many Americans had never heard of. "In Zambia, Ken Kaunda had been in charge since independence, a benevolent despot trying to do the best he could." Things weren't perfect. "He was working through a primitive society, with corruption." But what better collateral than a nation's resources—Zambia's copper? In Egypt, Zambia, Nigeria, South Africa, Malawi, Morocco, Sudan, "usually you'd put the money out for a specific purpose: build a copper plant in Zambia or an earth fill dam in Nigeria, or help them develop ag land," Rice recalls. It was an extension, really, of the resource development projects the banks had financed so profitably for multinational corporations. "You'd work with the minister of finance. And before you lent, you talked to the U.S. government representatives in the country. You had feasibility studies by the Bechtels and Morrison-Knudsens. You checked on political stability. I'd sometimes personally meet with the U.S. ambassador."

In San Francisco Iver Iversen, a tough and conscientious credit chief since assuming Rice's job in 1973, says, in hindsight, "I can't absolve myself of responsibility . . . but I can't think of what I would have done that I didn't do. We analyzed countries the same way we did a company. We drew on the country ratings made by the bank's own economists. They rated them A to F; Mexico and Brazil *were rated A* at that time." Mexico had discovered rich oil reserves; Brazil was in the midst of an industrializing "miracle," moving from the manufacture of shoes and shirts to "a world-scale export offensive . . . in automobiles and trucks, engineering services and, as soon as possible, electronics," its planning minister proudly boasted. "We loaned to Mexico and Brazil. We even made loans to iron curtain countries—Poland, Russia, Yugoslavia. We thought Russia would never renege; it had *resources*." The bankers basked in smug righteousness, and raked in the interest.

But there were warning signs, if bankers had cared to see. Nations had been bad debtors in the past. Latin America's defaults in the 1920s and '30s had cut that region off from credit for four decades. Loans to Cuba and Ghana had soured in the sixties. Currently, in 1975, Indonesia was having difficulty. Even America itself had been a slow-paying debtor in the late eighteenth century. But bankers had developed short memories. "Country risk" analyses were being constructed largely on hope. From newly independent African nations to blossoming Latin republics, "everybody was hopeful that these grand plans would be more successful than they undoubtedly were," Rice recalls. "We naively accepted what our economists told us," Iversen now says. "We were too naive," Rice agrees. "We never dreamed that central governments would be such ineffective managers. Or imagined that the foreign exchange that those central governments got their hands on from the projects the loans built would not be used to repay the debt but would be used for social programs to serve their political purposes." They never dreamed that billions of borrowed dollars would exit the countries as "capital flight" harbored in banks abroad, lost as working capital at home. "We had a limit we were going to lend to a country," Pinola admits, in hindsight, "but those limits were anything but rigid. It was the euphoria of the times."

"While I was there, Zambia was servicing her debts. The loans were not troubled," says Rice. But the components for disaster were already there: her dependence on just one export, copper, for foreign exchange dollars to pay her debts made Zambia's economy intolerant of another oil shock or a global recession. By the mid-seventies Zambia was a prototype for a global pattern of vulnerability that would grow as B of A's $40 million loan to Zambia joined the sea of debt that would swell, by 1989, to $1.2 trillion—$600 billion of that to commercial banks.

In the euphoria they all had overlooked one fundamental fact, a fatal blind spot in the lending, claims Professor Albert Fishlow at UC Berkeley, "Neither party to the transaction (banks or borrowing countries) fully understood the *inherent temporary character* of the access to credit. . . . Profits were initially large, particularly for the lead banks, and . . . very little thought, and less concern were given to the importance of the continuous stream of lending." In other words, petrodollars—created by the artificial manipulation of oil prices—would eventually dry up. They had not been generated by rising industrial productivity and exports in the borrowing countries. Yet, adds Fishlow, "the capital inflows became a regular, and increasingly necessary, input. . . . Borrowing today was necessary to pay the interest on yesterday's loans . . . and it was attractive to take on still more ambitious, slow-maturing investment opportunities." "This just isn't *true*," Al Rice retorts, "we were making self-liquidating project loans that were generating hard currencies. We didn't think more petrodollars were needed to pay them back." But by 1975 dozens of nations had been hooked on what became a vicious cycle of debt—

Argentina, Thailand, Peru, the Philippines, Algeria, Turkey. The debt of the oil-poor countries alone had grown from $10 billion to $15 billion, and would grow to $50 billion by the end of the decade.

There was another vital question: How could banks collect from a nation? "If a domestic debtor defaults, creditors have legal recourse; but if a foreign debtor defaults, the creditors may have no court they trust to turn to. . . . Creditors can hardly foreclose on foreign territory," UCLA's Professor Jeffry Frieden points out. For all the jaunty talk of "country risk," its two aspects, political and economic, were given short shrift as the banks plunged on.

As the third world debt crisis gestated quietly, Rice's division was stunningly successful. "Profits increased hugely," says Dick Puz, Rice's credit chief; by 1976 Rice's Europe/Middle East/Africa (EMEA) produced 35 percent of World Banking's total earnings for the year, while Latin America was still insignificant. Rice, Puz observed, was bringing "direction, purpose, style, motivation," to the bank's European operation and "a cohesive marketing structure to what had been a fractured, country-by-country approach." "Al Rice had a *great* deal of authority," Iversen observed.

JOE PINOLA'S AUTHORITY was being challenged. Running North America and Mexico, Pinola rankled at his country manager Jose "Pepe" Carral's end running of his Los Angeles headquarters. Carral's operation in Mexico City was an example of the powerful empires that quickly developed within the World Banking Division. Living in a palatial hacienda, Carral and his wife were socially well connected, knew everyone, were invaluable resources for the bank in beating the other U.S. banks in the Mexican market. Carral was supposed to go to Pinola's team in L.A. for loan approval. But if L.A. said no, he would go to Clausen or Iversen directly. "I approved several of Pepe's loans," Iversen confirms. Pinola resented it, but Carral had boundless leverage because of the big Mexican deposits he was able to attract to the bank, deposits the Mexican government deplored as capital flight, a vote of lack of confidence by its own citizens that drained the country of needed capital. Bankers chose not to speak of the fact that much of the money fleeing Mexico to the U.S. was the same money just lent to Mexico by the banks.

Pinola was also worried about the quality of some of the Mexican loans being generated by Carral. He confronted Clausen about them at a meeting in Los Angeles. It is one of the earliest clues to concern within the bank about the petrodollar loans. In an angry exchange Pinola was verbally "manhandled," he says. Bob Truex had observed years earlier that Clausen never liked Pinola "because Pinola spoke up to him. He didn't like me, probably, for the same reason. He is utterly intolerant of dissidents." Rice had promoted Pinola over Clausen's strong objections.

Two years later, in 1976, Pinola was gone. He had been offered the presidency of United California Bank, the flagship 350-branch retail bank of Western Bancorp, UCB's parent bank. "Leaving was enormously hard. I had a division when I left that was larger than the bank I went to." He denies that it was his conflict with Clausen that caused him to leave a successful sixteen-year career with the bank. "I left the bank because this opportunity came," he says, but adds, "The next officer to be either chairman or president was, clearly, Al Rice."

Western Bancorp held a special attraction to any B of A man. It was the surviving multistate banking chain that Giannini's Transamerica Corporation had owned and been forced to spin off in 1958 by Federal Reserve order. Pinola was swiftly promoted to head the entire system with its twenty-seven banks and more than seven hundred branches; he now commanded the chain of banks A.P. had planned as the core of his nationwide interstate network. Running California's fourth-largest bank—and backed by a strong team he had lured from B of A—Pinola had become a major competitor in the home market. More important, his branches in nine western states had been permitted to continue to exist after the spin-off from Transamerica, despite the ban on interstate branch banking. He was positioned with an enviable lead if interstate banking should come. And surely, with building market pressure, it would come in the 1980s.

BOB DI GIORGIO, too, worried about the growing size of the loan portfolios to developing nations. He had seen what unreliable debtors they could be in the 1920s and '30s, when his family's Di Giorgio Fruit Company had stopped doing business with Mexico, Venezuela, the Caribbean, and Africa. He feared the bank was being driven by "growth for growth's sake, getting all excited about any new country, any new continent." Clausen, he felt, loved the hobnobbing with finance ministers and central bankers, at the expense of the bank's core, the California branch system. Visalia. Dinuba. Knights Landing. Di Giorgio spoke up at board meetings, questioned the Auditing and Examining Committee. "But there's only so much complaining you can do without evidence—when all you're going on is feelings."

In 1975 Clausen declared that he was going to pull the bank back from its long posture of growth, shrink his loan portfolio, and refocus on "quality." He appeared a courageous statesman, sacrificing growth for prudence, recognizing that profitability must keep pace. His plan was to shrink assets by 25 percent in 1975. Major stories in *Forbes* and *Business Week* cheered his move.

But Di Giorgio believed Clausen was reacting to pressure from the Fed. The Federal Reserve was becoming increasingly concerned about B of A's overseas growth; growth in the bank's capital was not keeping pace. The Fed had "slapped the bank's hand" in the summer of 1974, when it rejected the bank's bid to buy a foreign insurance company, and bank examiners had ordered Clausen either to raise more capital or to shrink his loan portfolios to keep the ratios acceptable. Clausen soon softened his "slow growth" stance at home and abroad. "Beise and Peterson had expanded the loan portfolios gradually," says Iversen. Clausen had already grown the bank's total assets from less than $30 billion when he took over in 1970 to $66 billion in 1975—more than doubling in his first five years. He would have nearly quadrupled them by 1980. His earnings were keeping pace very nicely with growth. How could he be criticized?

IT WAS NOT loan quality worrying Al Rice in London at mid-decade. There had been no major defaults. It was costs that concerned him. And lack of computer systems. Rice had run into a serious flaw in Clausen's decentralization. Clausen had leapfrogged from a domestic bank into the sophisticated petrodollar market without an equal effort to upgrade operations, computers, and systems of credit and profit control. When he was posted to London, Armacost would fret over the "four to six weeks it could take to get a response on a loan back from San Francisco." Clausen had not invested in technology, as Reed had at Citicorp. "Baloney," Clausen blusters. "In technology, we were at the cutting edge in the mid-seventies. We were the *most* efficient bank in expense/revenue ratios—fifty-nine percent in 1979. There are a lot of uninformed people. Look at the record!" His is a lonely voice. In skipping the overhaul of the bank's operational systems and technology before taking on the world, Clausen made, many feel, the most serious strategic mistake of his career. His four elite armies were stretched beyond their support systems.

Rice made a head-on assault on costs and controls, says Puz, who particularly admired his tackling the weaknesses in computer, auditing, and information systems in EMEA. There had been a "terrible mismatch of computer hardware to processing problems." The London office could not get accurate information on the fundamentals: its earnings; profit; cash position. It found itself in thrall to one of MotherBank's more formidable creations—the Bank of America Systems Group. The model for the industry in the 1950s under Al Zipf, computer systems technology had lost its edge and vision and become "a swollen organism with a life of its own." Housed in a huge white block of a building south of

Market Street, it had a staff of five hundred, roomfuls of near-obsolete IBM mainframe computers haphazardly adapted to do jobs they were not designed to do—a Babel of software programs unable to talk to each other.

Rice had pledged not to rock the boat. But with confidence verging on arrogance and impatience for poor performance and bureaucracy, he invited conflict with headquarters in San Francisco, where different mind-sets reigned. He raised the hackles of the controller, Ken Martin, the man whose scrutiny in the loan reviews was still an awesome memory for those who had endured it. Distressed at the "absolutely incompetent" job Martin's team of auditors from San Francisco had done, Rice sent them home and hired his own, telling Martin by phone, "Mr. Martin, don't ever send those people over here again." He set Puz to creating an independent reporting system in London. For the first time the division knew where it stood and could measure results. It had created the beginnings of a computerized system of information and controls adapted to international banking needs. Armacost, and then McMillen, Rice's successors in London, would develop it further. In time, known as IBS, the system would be adopted by the entire World Banking Division. But to gain a beachhead, Rice had insulted some powerful people in San Francisco.

As head of the board's senior personnel committee, Di Giorgio made a point, on his travels, to get to know the people whose names would be coming before him for promotion to the top spots. He knew Rice was a Clausen favorite and visited him in London. "I just didn't think the depth was there, the grasp of Europe," says Di Giorgio, who had favored Pinola and Truex and had been distressed when they left. Despite Di Giorgio's reservations, Rice's achievements were a powerful argument for promotion. In triumph, Rice returned to San Francisco in 1976 to one of the three most powerful jobs in Bank of America—head of the World Banking Division. It had not been announced that he was the heir apparent. "You didn't need to," says Rice. "There was nobody even in second place."

From the hush-carpeted elegance of the fortieth floor of the headquarters tower, Rice would reign over the last two years of foreign lending's glory days—"the last time a bright young banker could uncynically claim to believe that the system was working, or that it was a strategically and morally sound enterprise for moving the world's money from the haves to the have-nots," as a young banker of the period, S. C. Gwynne, has described it.

IN NEW YORK Citibank had left the herd again. As always, its back was against the wall.

The collapse of Herstatt in 1974 had reverberated through the Eurodollar market, damaging New York banks more than B of A because of their greater dependence on it for their funding. While Clausen was deploying his A team, establishing powerful principalities in the four corners of the world, New York's big banks were receiving more shocks. They had taken heavy losses from the collapse of a real estate investment bubble, REIT, from which B of A—and, in New York, Citibank—had prudently stood aloof. The interest they had to pay in the market for their money was rising close to the interest they could charge for loans, wiping out their margin. Then New York City had gone into financial crisis when it defaulted on its bonds in 1975. Led by Wriston, the banks had gathered in collective agony to help the city restructure. The recession of the mid-seventies had slowed their mainstay, corporate lending, while California and B of A "rode the back of a consumer-led boom that knew no boundaries. We never felt that discipline," says Sam Armacost. "Now those guys in New York really got their act together." It was a turning point in the long rivalry between the two banks.

Citibank mounted a new offensive. Fenton R. "Pete" Talbott, the handsome midwesterner who had helped implement John Reed's rebuilding of operations in the late 1960s and who, as one of Robert S. McNamara's "bean counters" at Ford, was one of the new breed of corporate technocrats, now learned that that had been only the first step of a larger strategy. For Reed had been assigned to do another study of where the world was going and decided that profits in the decades ahead lay in the pockets of the prosperous American consumer. While Citibank's hard-driving army of global bankers was pushing loans in London and Hong Kong in the early 1970s, making up to 75 percent of the bank's earnings, Wriston's "killer M.B.A.'s" were coming home, supplanted abroad by foreign nationals trained in Citibank's aggressive style of banking.

Citibank had changed direction 180 degrees. Reed had identified the most fundamental change coming to banking: the shift to services and fees, a revolution that would transform the traditional loan-making banker into a marketing man. It would create agony for bankers whose identity lay in the old image. Wriston backed the decision and committed the bank to a multibillion-dollar investment in a long-range program to expand Citibank's franchise into the American heartland. Citibank could not branch bank there, but it could provide "diversified financial services" through the nonbanks it had begun to acquire through its holding company, Citicorp: insurance and consumer credit companies; savings and loans. Entering the credit card field, Citibank had taken on the mighty BankAmericard, world's largest. "He told me it would take seven years before we'd be there," says Wriston of Reed's new consumer strategy, as he girded for screams from shareholders and analysts.

Wriston was spreading Citibank perilously thin. The bank was still pushing third world loans, while building the consumer business. It was building bigger foreign portfolios and more risk than any of the other banks. But Citibank faced it with controls and operations in place. And it drove its people hard.

IN 1974 AND '75, Don Griffith, a young loan-making Citibanker posted in Mexico, was "suddenly seeing the international staff go from five hundred to three hundred, to thirty" as they went home to become domestic bankers. But he would not be part of the next stage of the grand strategy. As Citibank's front line shifted, he quit to return to his roots in California. It had been grueling to live up to Wriston's goals of 15 percent growth each year, Griffith found. There was fierce competition with his peers within the bank. And fierce pressure to perform. "My orders were to *double* my loan portfolio in six months." Griffith had had tea with Wriston when he was hired and saw him as a giant. He'd miss the class, the quality of Citibank.

He joined B of A when his job with a small family business did not work out. Pasadena-raised with a UC Berkeley master's degree in political science, Griffith had "realized in the Peace Corps that international banking was colonialism, where mediocre people live fabulous lives," and he felt you "paid a price away from headquarters. You lose the fast track; you have no roots. You become dependent on the bank, and they buy you with the lure of lots of perks." In Los Angeles he was posted to Pinola's North American Division of World Banking, where he would apply his Citibank hustle to placing energy loans in the West and Mexico. That connection would lead him, later, to Pinola's executive floor at Western Bancorp, where he joined the team of BankAmerica expatriates who would lead an assault against MotherBank in 1986.

"What do you think of Walter Wriston's strategy, Mr. Clausen . . . pulling all his people back to the U.S.?" Griffith asked Clausen when, at a large bank lunch, all others avoided sitting beside Clausen, and Griffith found himself in the feared seat.

"Wriston doesn't know what he's doing," Clausen snapped.

Chapter Seven

IT WAS AN UNBELIEVABLE MESS of a back office William Pearson discovered as he poked around in the basement of Chuck Schwab's little discount brokerage on Montgomery Street. Here, amid mounds of paper tickets and stock certificates, this man was operating in the Stone Age! *This* was the leading edge of diversified financial services? Schwab himself was down in the basement, opening mail. "I answered phones with the secretary and trader, licked envelopes after the market closed, and *then* did strategic planning," Schwab admits.

Visiting from Dallas in the summer of 1975, Pearson had walked in off the street, applied for a job, and found himself sharing the birth pangs of Charles Schwab & Co. and of a new industry. Pearson had been a back office man in go-go funds in Dallas. As a junior functionary he had been part of the pioneering that had brought technology to the brokerage business and had worked for the fabled Jimmy Ling until Ling crashed when the market collapsed in 1971.

Schwab, too, had crashed in Texas. When Pearson met him, he had just pulled himself up from the collapse of the promising enterprise he had run from his upstairs shop in San Rafael. His mutual funds had been going beautifully in 1967, '68 . . . '69. Then the regulators had challenged him on the legality of marketing his funds in Texas. He was not properly registered there, they claimed. He had been forced by the Fed and the SEC not only to suspend sales, killing income, but to rescind—to repay!—the original investment of every Texas investor. "As my fund was losing this Texas shoot-out between 1971 and 1972, I hit bottom in my own personal bear market," he says. He was wiped out. His debts were more than $100,000. "Largely because of the incredible strain I had been under, my marriage got into trouble. Soon I found myself divorced." He borrowed from his uncle Bill, in Sacramento, and from Crocker Bank and began the long crawl back. He brokered a few deals, scratched to begin repaying the bank, and looked for a new vehicle.

In late 1973, he had lunch with a Santa Barbara high school chum, Hugo Quackenbush, at the time an institutional portfolio manager in San Francisco. Quackenbush planted the seed. He was seeing the explosive growth of institutional business, the buying and selling of massive blocks of stock for pension funds and insurance companies, "create awesome profits for New York Stock Exchange brokers because of fixed commission rates. But the movement toward fully competitive rates is irreversible," Quackenbush told Schwab. "Chuck, there's room for a new kind of business," one that slashed commissions and targeted a new customer—the investor who, relative to the institutional leviathans, was the little guy. Not A.P.'s little guy, but the sophisticated, active, experienced individual investor who could make his own decisions. Schwab changed his corporate name from First Commander to Charles Schwab & Co. and galloped into the action.

Like horses gathering skittishly at the starting gate, the old-line brokers and the mavericks like Schwab jockeyed through a trial year of deregulated commissions permitted off the Big Board in the regional and third markets.

The test came on May Day. May 1, 1975. The day regulated brokerage commissions vanished. "A truly devastating May Day for the traditional, button-down clique of high-priced brokers," says a satisfied Schwab. His new company, Charles Schwab & Co., had participated in the trial year, but no one knew what would happen on May Day. All the retail brokerages had waited to see what Merrill Lynch would do. Schwab bet they would raise commissions. On May 1 Merrill Lynch raised its commissions 10 percent. Schwab slashed his and charged into "a niche large enough to drive a freight train through," says Quackenbush. Discount brokerage was off and running. A year later Quackenbush joined Schwab as his close adviser—his sounding board and spokesman—and has never left.

Pearson had turned up just a month after May Day. Schwab's capital was at borderline levels. With the "little fellow," the private investor, as his earliest customer, and his commission rates so low, he needed hundreds of thousands—millions—of transactions to get the earnings he wanted. His uncle Bill helped again, buying thirty percent of Schwab's corporation on the condition that the first branch be opened in Sacramento, an outpost for a financial entrepreneur. A small storefront office near the capitol building, "it had desks hammered together out of hollow-core doors," Pearson remembers. But people started walking in and placing stock orders; the office was a success. Offering a limited menu of services at first—just stocks and options, with a Brownie Hawkeye camera as a come-on for new accounts—Schwab soon felt ready to open branches in Los Angeles and the western states; he opened forty in the first five years. In 1977, he committed to a daily ad in a choice location on the inside back page of the *Wall Street Journal*. But success held a catch-22. He had to maintain a certain level of regulatory capital. The SEC required it; he needed it as a safety net. Eighty percent of his customers paid up, all cash, within five days. The rest put up margin for only part—typically, half—of the value of the stock he bought and sold for them. The rest he borrowed against his own capital, then lent to his customers at a reasonable interest rate to cover their stock purchases; it gave him interest income. Customers had to pay up, of course, when their accounts settled. But if the market turned down suddenly, and his customers were caught without the cash to cover the stocks he'd bought on their behalf, he could be caught without an adequate reserve of capital. The more margin debt balances he got, the more capital the SEC required him to have. And the more complex the bookkeeping in the back office became.

Pearson went to work, started a nationwide search for a computer system that could handle Schwab's ambitious goals, and played the office heavy, balancing Schwab's softness with people. Although Schwab lived with risk, "conflict was not his thing."

Schwab had learned his marketing lessons well in the walk-up office in San Rafael. Through rigorous measuring of the results of his advertising, he discovered that, next to his products, his most powerful marketing tool was his own smiling face. His business would be based on state-of-the-art computerized systems; most orders would be placed by phone or computer. But as an industry that had been personal became cold and transactional, Schwab's picture smiling out from the *Journal* each morning established a face-to-face relationship with his customers. With a face as open and trustworthy as the boy next door, glasses giving a bankerly look, his own face, Schwab believed, "showed people that the boss is real, he's committed, he's putting *himself* behind the product. He's not a flake."

But harassment never ceased. Schwab would be in a perpetual state of war with the establishment. At first it ignored him, assuming he'd go away. But as he grew, commercial banks eyed his company with increasing lust as they tried to catch the wave by buying up the new discount brokers through their holding companies. The big brokerage houses hated him; charging higher commissions, they fought to protect their turf. They brought the enormous influence of Wall Street to bear on the regulators in Washington. "The major firms employed the rankest discrimination against us," says Schwab. They fought his getting office space. "In Seattle, Phoenix, and Chicago . . . they would threaten to break their leases if we were allowed a puny thousand square feet way up on the twentieth or thirtieth floor." Schwab had to get "down in the trenches and fight" for a seat on a stock exchange, one of his highest priorities. Finding discounters distasteful, the brokerage house he had used to place stock orders threw him out.

The greatest threat came the day the SEC ordered Schwab to fly to Los Angeles with his books. There, while Schwab fumed, examiners scrutinized accounts, looking for problems. "We were in total control by then," says Pearson, "but they could have confiscated those records if they didn't believe us. We were that close to not being a firm anymore." The impatient entrepreneur "hated those meetings with regulators," Pearson saw. "They represented restraint, control."

Schwab, the entrepreneur, was teaching himself to be a manager, learning how to build an organization, drawing on the theories of consultants, among them one he had heard speak in May 1979 at a meeting of the Young Presidents Organization (YPO) in Rio, Dr. Ichak Adizes. A "therapist" to corporations, the dynamic Yugoslavian-born Israeli had the presence of a tent-filling evangelist. Having lectured to the YPO all over the world for more than a decade, Adizes spoke with characteristic modesty of his popularity, "I'm the guru. Period." Excited by his ideas, Schwab bought his tapes and his book.

Driven by the energy of an idea whose time has come, Schwab was bursting with growth at 120 Montgomery. "We were knocking down walls," said Quackenbush, laughing. "You could tell where we'd expanded by the color of the carpet." And Pearson had found a computer system. Gearing up for its launch, they built, on a neighboring roof, the water tower that provided the vital coolant for the data system—without it, the system would be destroyed. Given twenty-four hours to remove the tower by the angry building owner, Schwab posted a guard armed with a shotgun with orders to "point that gun out the window and say 'Stop' " if anyone dared try to dismantle the tower.

On Friday the thirteenth, 1979, Schwab was there in blue jeans with the rest of his crew as they went on-line with the new BETA computer system, a state-of-the-art system that automatically updated every transaction "instantly, right on the screen, for the first time ever in the business," Pearson proudly explains. BETA, a brand name Schwab is no longer free to use, would make him the first in the infant industry to have an automatic electronic sweep of cash and customer accounts in money market funds, to have instant execution of transactions, twenty-four-hour service. But the moment was incredibly tense. As Schwab pressed the button, he was cutting the cord, breaking his tie with a paper environment, committing every bit and byte of data to a system from Milwaukee that was untested by Schwab's velocity and volumes. If it failed, the business would be wounded. If it worked, it would enable him to grow as he must to catch up to his endless capital problem. It would put him ahead of any of the competitors crowding into the discount brokerage field, and make him rich and famous. "There was fear of the unknown and apprehension as we made the transition from making out paper tickets to sitting at the computer," says a veteran of that day, "but we just sat down and did it." As BETA responded and pulsed with life in the back office, they drank champagne, and Schwab gave Pearson a gold Rolex engraved on the back with his thanks "for loyalty and incredible ability." Though small, Schwab had been the biggest since day one; a fierce competitor, he now had the tool to help him stay there.

. Now he could expand his customer base. And his products. "One-stop shopping" in mutual funds. Schwab One, his asset management account, which was in direct competition to banks and S & Ls. Insured money market accounts that would, at last, end his regulatory capital problem. CDs. A financial advisory service.

As SCHWAB MOVED to technology's leading edge, Anne Giannini Mc-Williams, A.P.'s granddaughter, was reading the *San Francisco Chronicle* while having breakfast with her husband, James, an investment consultant, when she saw the ad. Crocker Bank was advertising its new automatic teller machines. ATMs. *Crocker!* She was shocked, suddenly frightened for her father's bank. "Jim, what's happening? Crocker's got *hundreds* of them. Why haven't we got them yet?" Anne had spotted one of the first visible clues to MotherBank's near bankruptcy in the thing that had set her grandfather's bank apart—innovation.

By the mid-seventies it was generally recognized that automating the process of money handling was a way of cutting operating costs. But automated teller machines (ATMs) were the subject of thundering ideological arguments. It was the symbolic struggle between traditional people-based banking and Information Age banking that embraced the computer and reduced the human interface. It was the conundrum Tom Cooper had faced at Girard Bank in Pittsburgh in the early 1960s. The banking industry had come down in two camps, each led by one of the biggest money center banks in New York. Citibank had made its stand *for* automated banking, installing four hundred Automated Banking Centers by 1977, the first to popularize banking by machine. Chemical Bank, with its three hundred New York branches, had rejected ATMs and was committing its resources to personalized service and the human touch. Bankers watched to see who would win.

In California Crocker took Citibank's path. As Anne McWilliams banged her paper on the breakfast table in dismay, Crocker had installed nearly three hundred machines in the San Jose area south of San Francisco. To her knowledge, B of A had none. And what were Wells Fargo and Security Pacific doing? Like the New York banks, Wells and Security were aggressively compensating for their lack of B of A's boundless deposit funds. Always fighting to get some of B of A's market share, Wells was pouring resources into its California retail bank, its basic business. A creative Wells marketer, Richard M. Rosenberg, was winning customers with his consumer innovations: scenic checks; conveniently packaged checking accounts. Security Pacific was pursuing nonbank financial services, adding "products" to its arsenal. Each was finding a niche and could no longer be ignored. B of A was losing market share in California.

For Anne's aunt, Claire, the battle over automation was critical to the survival of the Giannini spirit in the branches. She hated computers. They were dehumanizing, the antithesis of what B of A's branch banking was all about. She was deaf to the argument that properly used, machines could do the drudge work, freeing the staff to give customers even more personalized service. Computers were enemies of the "human touch," as, she believed, was Tom Clausen. Her fears had been confirmed when the editors of *Time/Life* gave her a lunch in New York and warned her that the bank must guard its unique human touch. Alarmed that "cold-blooded editors" should see the dangers, she stiffened in her resolve to fight the technocrats.

In London, Al Rice had watched Citibank and sensed he had seen the future. "Among the big banks, they are much farther along than anybody in computerization. Wriston saw the future accurately, and is spending a lot of money getting there," said a frustrated Rice. "I wish B of A had put computers into all the branches instead of centralizing them all into one big, insensitive center."

But in California, Claire Hoffman had an ally in Joe Carrera, head of the branch system. A profane, lusty, charismatic Portuguese who had risen, in the Giannini tradition, from high school dropout to head of B of A's crown jewel, the California bank, he symbolized the difference in style between "A.P.'s boys" in the branches and the M.B.A.'s in corporate/international.

Carrera was a forceful champion of his branches to the board and Executive Committee at a time when their prestige within the bank was flagging. Seeing a threat to his people, Carrera came down against ATMs. Dick Puz, back from the wars he and Rice had fought for technology in Europe and now chief credit officer at World Banking headquarters, was stunned to hear Carrera tell a large gathering of executives in San Francisco, "We've done surveys, and our customers don't want to deal with machines. They want to deal with people. We're not going with ATMs." Clausen trusted Carrera. Confided in him—he was one of the very few he did confide in. Since 1972 the bank had run a small five-machine pilot project in Irvine. As Crocker installed its three hundred machines, B of A was planning a thirty-machine trial in Northern California. "But it was a clearly articulated policy that the bank would not install ATMs, because for the California banks with massive statewide branch systems the cost would be just enormous," says bank analyst Donald K. Crowley, a research analyst within B of A at the time.

The issue was far broader than the role of people in banking's future. ATMs were a further step toward electronic funds transfer, the revolution in money handling that would make possible the global financial marketplace that was a key component of the new banking paradigm. The "globalization" of financial communications was leading to a world where money physically never moved, yet could be bought, sold, and shifted through infinite worldwide transactions in a day by one trader sitting at a computer terminal. A taste of the dangers inherent in the fantastic speed, volumes, and complexity that were coming had first surfaced in Herstatt, when foreign exchange problems in a German bank threw a wrench into the interbank payments system. The catastrophic potential would be brought home with shocking force on October 19, 1987, when the world's stock markets crashed as one. There were risks that could not yet be predicted or regulated. But it was already clear to the thinkers within the financial and economic community that as power shifted to those who controlled the satellites, lasers, and electronic clearinghouses of the payments network, those banks or corporations that held that power would gain control of a dominant share of the banking business of the future. Seeing the power of controlling the electronic information flow, Citibanker Walter Wriston predicted, "Tomorrow's competitors are Reuters and IBM and the telephone company."

With the naive clarity of the newcomer, a junior officer, James Cerruti, thought he saw the nature of the problem within B of A. "I saw that the glamour was on the credit side . . . that the bank's vulnerability was the separation of operations and credit as career paths," Cerruti says. "If you got stuck in operations, where computers and payments were, it was a career deadend. Yet it was vital. But operations started getting its M.B.A.'s and strategic plans ten years too late."

Clausen finally addressed the issue. A junior strategic planner, Stephen T. McLin, had dared tell Clausen in 1977 that "EFT, electronic funds transfer is the way the world is going." In 1978 Clausen ordered that a new computer czar be found to bring the bank up to speed. As big budgets were promised, visions of creating a global computerized financial services network danced like sugarplums. Leading the search was John Mickel, who managed Decimus, the computer leasing subsidiary. Mickel himself got the job. "He had been an IBM salesman. He'd turned the bank into an IBM showroom. But he didn't have the experience or talent to lead this massive undertaking," says Al Rice, who had discovered the inadequacies of the information systems in Europe. "He was chosen because he was loyal, he was family," a Decimus colleague of Mickel's believes. "Typically, they did it on the cheap; they could get Mickel for fifty-five thousand dollars. Why go outside?" adds another colleague, who worried, as he saw grand computer schemes building in Mickel's department, that "computer guys have no concept of cost."

AL RICE WAS arguably the second most powerful man in the bank when he returned from Europe in 1977 as head of the World Banking Division and vice-chairman of the bank. With his natural élan enhanced by the exposure of his three years at the heart of the petrodollar scene, he also sat on the Managing Committee, the inner circle that effectively ran the bank. He was presumed to be Bank of America's next leader.

Sam Armacost, sent to London to replace Rice, says, "I saw Rice as the next president, and maybe a place for myself nine or ten years down the line." Like Mont McMillen, Armacost had been on a track so fast that he rarely stayed in one post long enough to see the results of his efforts or to spend Christmas in San Francisco. Defending his series of assignments as "one of the greatest positives," Armacost claims that "it intensified learning. You only stay fast-track if you continue to perform. Your results follow you." In London Armacost had picked up Rice's battle for a sophisticated computer system. In Washington for the annual IMF/World Bank meetings, "I cornered Chauncey and extracted a promise that we could get the computers we needed for BAI [BankAmerica International]." The loan approval system was still so slow that Armacost frequently risked losing a customer waiting for response from San Francisco. "With Al back at headquarters, I'd call him direct. . . . He'd always give me a quick answer." For the aggressive, circumvention had become the way of getting things done.

Rice returned determined to bring costs under control. He ordered a rigorous investigation of all the departments that impacted on the World Banking Division: operations; personnel; computer systems; auditing. "That meant going inside and challenging the Controllers' department, Ken Martin's," says Puz. Of all people in the bank to cross, thought Steve McLin, watching tensions build. Yet McLin suspected that Martin was "not out to 'get' Rice, he was protecting the virginity of the bank. He would examine every nickel and dime. Ken Martins are watchdogs, like the IRS. Not bad people to have around a company." McLin had learned in his earliest days as a banker at First Chicago Corporation working for then-chairman Robert Abboud "not to change the system by confrontation, or to ally yourself with any one faction or person, or you'll go down if your mentor goes down." As a young strategist making acquisitions for the holding company he had an intimate view of bank politics but had carefully kept himself "unaligned, a little Switzerland." Rice, he observed, enjoyed "tweaking the system. He loves the thrill of getting things done by going *around* the system." He wished Rice would play ball with Martin. Work *within* the system.

Within a year Rice had torn World Banking's computers free of the bank's Systems Group and set up his own. He had created a set of rational operating systems and substantially reduced costs. But Puz, McLin, and others feared he had made dangerous enemies.

AL RICE WAS at his Lake Tahoe ski house with his family in February 1978, when he got a call from a man from the main branch in San Francisco, where he kept his checking account. "Al, I think you better be alert to the fact that there have been some audits here of your records and your checking accounts going back forever." Rice was amazed, and touched. He hardly knew the caller. "But the guy went to all the trouble to find me clear up at the lake on a weekend. He must think it's serious." Rice did not. "I don't care if they go back to day one. What have I ever done?" he thought, and dismissed it.

That spring Clausen asked Rice and Mont McMillen to fly to Brazil with the legendary financier and shipping magnate Daniel K. Ludwig to evaluate an agricultural scheme Ludwig had developed in the Amazonian rainforest. Ludwig was wooing the bank for financing, and Clausen wanted an evaluation. It would be interesting to see the country again. "But I didn't expect to have a life experience!" says Rice. Hundreds of square miles of jungle had been cleared and planted with Gmelina trees—a bizarre tree of Southeast Asian origin, transported by the British to Africa, which, in that equatorial climate, grew like some mad scientist's dream into tall forests almost overnight. The wood, Ludwig dreamed, would be used to build Brazil, to export to the world—and to make Ludwig even richer than he was. A project on the scale of A. P. Giannini's.

Rice could see that the project was not being well managed and could feel the old attraction for the grand-scale corporate adventure he'd suppressed since returning to the bank in 1964. But he would honor his promise to Beise never to leave the bank again. He flew back to San Francisco. Looking back, he says, "If I'd had any idea of what would happen, I'd have stayed."

In August Clausen called him to his office. He handed Rice a memorandum and said, as Rice recalls his words, "Al, this is very bad news. You've been self-dealing"—*the* taboo in a profession based on unimpeachable integrity and public trust. He confronted Rice with the two Joe Duffel deals—the Sausalito loan and the real estate syndicate Rice had participated in. Duffel, the astounded Rice heard Clausen telling him, had paid Rice off for the liberal loan terms he gave him by including him in the profitable syndicate. Rice, he said, had made money by doing favors for a customer, an unconscionable breach of banking ethics.

Rice stood, stunned, as the charges went on. There was the matter of the country club membership. Rice had moved his membership from the Claremont Country Club to the San Francisco Golf Club, "a vastly more prestigious club," Rice had thought. The bank had paid for his membership in Claremont. An audit had turned up the fact that he had taken the $2,300 sales proceeds of the Claremont membership and put them in his own bank account as he wrote his own $6,000 check for the San Francisco membership, a procedure which had been approved for others. But Clausen was an uncompromising stickler for rules and propriety; if he had been presented with even the slightest appearance of an ethical lapse, Clausen would have to fire him.

"Tom, you have to be fooling," Rice said in disbelief as his mind raced for some clue. He remembered the call at Tahoe. So it had been going on since then. Twenty-eight years of his personal banking transactions, combed for damning evidence by the gnomes of the auditing staff in the controller's office. The office that had the power to open the books on anything, the bank's Big Brother. Rice's head had apparently been handed to Clausen on a platter. He intuitively suspected that "the people who really wanted me out of the bank were the Controller's department." He would soon be told by a friend that Martin had ordered the investigation and had put two full-time auditors on his trail for a year, "trying to find something I had done wrong." If that were true, had Martin's hand been directed by someone higher? Rice got on fine with Clausen. "We were very compatible." They had traveled extensively together in the Far East—Singapore, Japan, Hong Kong. Clausen might be abusive to some, "but it never happened to me." Clausen even asked Rice for advice and seemed to listen. He suspected that this confrontation was agony for Clausen. "But I have a way of being very direct and positive. . . . Did he feel I had everybody under control? . . . I have no idea whether Tom felt insecure."

Rice ran through Clausen's charges in his mind. He replayed his past actions with Joan at home. Scanning his maverick career, he saw that "I didn't always play the game by all the rules, I suppose." But if he was to be punished for investing with Duffel, then other officers, including Clausen, should be punished for some of their personal investments, Rice thought. Of course, no bank officer dared invest in, or profit from, a project the bank was involved in; being given a car for financing a car dealer was the classic no-no. "But if there was a prohibition against investing with anyone who had an account with B of A, how could you make an investment? You couldn't buy a security from Merrill Lynch." There were few corporations that did not have a relationship with Bank of America. And if Duffel had brought him in as a favor for the liberal loan, he had offered the same favor to all his partners in the deal, some very distinguished San Franciscans among them. The only thing Rice felt sure of was that "my bad positioning started during my three years in Europe," where he had ordered the auditors home and won the angry facedown with Clausen over a pay scale. If that's where it began, "I certainly lost the war," he said, shrugging.

"For several weeks, I went about my business, and tried to put it aside. The controller's staff started saying they had to talk to me about this. Suddenly I was getting harassed. I could see this was going to be a terrible fight," says Rice. He called several of the board members who had seemed friendly over the years, hoping for offers of support. Ruben F. Mettler. Baumhefner. He found a wall of silence. No one would speak about the issue. "Al, we're not even going to talk about your terrible conflict of interest," he was told.

He called Wally Haas. "Wally, you and I have been—"

"I'm not going to talk about it," Haas snapped back.

"Everybody deserted me. . . . Tom Clausen is a very good politician, and he had everybody eating out of his hand. Nobody was going to . . . " Rice finally forced himself to say, "I don't want to be in a place where nobody wants me," and gave Clausen his resignation.

For Rice, the pain would not be prolonged, as Bob Truex's had been, by a period of shelf life in Social Policy. He cleaned out his desk and left. He and Clausen had worked out a press release that would couch his leaving in positive terms. Rice approved it. Ambiguity and innuendo could damage the bank's stock, as well as Rice. He was leaving just two years short of full retirement pay of $150,000 a year. He would now receive $1,500 a month. Making lots of money had been one of his goals. But more than the money, it mattered to Rice that he leave with dignity; he had a brilliant career behind him and a professional life ahead. The announcement was to appear that Thursday. But he searched the paper, and it was not there. It had not been released as agreed upon. Instead, a brief statement was released Friday night for the Saturday papers, stating ambiguously that Rice had resigned "to follow his personal interests," leaving all the tantalizing questions unanswered. "I will never know if Tom did it with malice aforethought." It was the only comment the bank ever made. Clausen had ordered official silence, Rice was told; Corporate Communications was never to refer to Rice again.

The mystery cast over such a sensational corporate event drove the press wild; Rice's telephone rang off the wall the moment the news hit the wire. In a stroke a scandal—L'affaire Rice, as the press dubbed it—had been born.

At the bank, throughout the banking industry, the hundreds who knew Rice searched their memories for any clues to what had happened. A senior credit officer reflected, "I brought him another Duffel loan that had gone belly-up, and we were going to have to declare a default. Al never lifted a finger to try to intervene for his friend." Rice was colorful and freewheeling. He'd had some wild ideas. A critic called him "slick." He was a "freewheeling personality," Pinola had always thought, and wondered if, with his ebullient confidence and the knowledge that he was the heir to the throne, he just hadn't been careful enough to protect himself. Hadn't watched his flanks on the executive floor. "But Clausen didn't want him gone. He'd just promoted him," said one of the inner circle.

Mont McMillen tended to agree that "Al Rice was done in by Ken Martin all by himself, without Clausen's help." But he saw it not as the conniving retribution of a man who had felt the sting of Rice's forthright style, but as the act of a man whose soul and identity lay in impeccable standards of loan quality and business deportment. "Ken's self-esteem lay in maintaining this standard." He had been a symbol, to young bankers, of the best of the bank—a man who "was like a father" to junior loan officers like McMillen as he screened their loan reports before presentation to the terrifying Loan Committee. "But he may have felt threatened by Rice," McMillen reflects, "Al was a guy who operated outside the system. Ken Martin was a guy, like Clausen, who was born in the vault. The bank was his whole life. He was a humorless, chunky guy with graying, wavy hair, who did not dress like Al Rice. He couldn't move as easily as Al. I think he was terribly distressed to see Al Rice, with his wheeling-dealing, about to come out on top."

Rice's behavior had been "possibly unethical" was the guess of a senior colleague, expressing the view of the fastidious hard-liners from the credit side. Iver Iversen, an unimpeachable voice for the decency and integrity that had characterized the best of the BankAmerican, ruminated sadly, "He was a good loan officer. But he was not a great respecter of authority."

"My God, what happened, Al?" asked a shocked Gene Trefethen, who'd worked with Rice for a decade on Kaiser's financing. "We had done dozens of deals together. I mean, I *knew* Al Rice, and I'd never seen even a hint of anything unethical. He gave better service and just worked like fury for his customers."

"I don't know, Gene," Rice responded, mustering the broad smile that effectively masked pain. "One day I was in, next day I was out."

"Once the internal auditors smelled blood, they wanted the whole heart," said an anguished Steve McLin.

Clausen called Armacost in London and told him the news. Like everyone else, Armacost was stunned. From afar he'd heard rumors of the Ken Martin conflict. He guessed that "a lot of Al's problems had to do with his battles over the systems stuff"—the battles Armacost was continuing to fight in London. He wrote Rice a note and told him, "Al, I always thought you'd be our next president." He had thought Clausen should have given Rice the presidency and made himself chairman.

Rice moved into a small office across the street from the bank and started picking up the pieces. But the horror had only begun. The next headlines declared that there would be a grand jury investigation of the Rice affair. Alarmed that a major scandal might be lurking in B of A, the Comptroller of the Currency had urged the attorney general to order the investigation. "A grand jury has no holds barred. They can do anything they want, and you have no retribution," Rice feared. As the FBI investigated within the bank, Rice hired attorneys and accountants to satisfy the jury's demands for tax records and accounts. For six months the press followed the story. His children were ridiculed at school. He tried to explain to his young son and two daughters what was happening, but when the grand jury claimed his son's savings passbook, his son Ted said, "Daddy, I don't think you're a crook." "It didn't undermine my feelings for him," says Ted. But for Rice, "it had become intolerable, absolutely impossible." The distance that had been growing between him and Joan was becoming greater with the stress; he wasn't sure if the long marriage would survive.

Then, suddenly, it was over. The grand jury had scoured his past and found no wrongdoing, it announced as it disbanded. One of its members confided to this author that the jury had felt cynically exploited—that its work had been terminated before its investigation was complete, before the grand jury had explored, to its satisfaction, Rice's guilt or innocence. The veiled suggestion was that whatever, or whoever, had triggered the investigation had achieved the goal: Rice had been destroyed, and the investigation could be halted. Rice had been vindicated. "But the papers reported it on page thirty-eight," he says with a bittersweet laugh.

"I believe the organization essentially nailed Al Rice," says a close associate. "I don't know what he did, but I suspect it was no more or less than a lot of others. I think the powers that be wanted him out." Had Rice—like Pinola, Truex, and others—been simply too strong and independent for the culture to digest and been spit out, like the rest? The system had never assimilated ambitious mavericks. Clausen was strong, but he was a creature of the bank, its obedient servant. Consciously he may have been unhappy at what his sense of propriety had forced him to do; he was close to Rice. But perhaps, intuitively, he had acted as an instrument of the culture's will.

With the investigation halted, the full facts would never be revealed. Corporate history would record Al Rice's word against the bank's silence. And a cloud would always hang over him.

"IT'S A TRAGEDY," said Pat McClung, who had been on the Memorex workout with Rice. "He's the only one who could have led the bank." According to Dick Puz, who had been at Rice's elbow through the events of the last few months, "The real tragedy for the company is that Clausen did not take advice well. He only listened to three people: George Skogland, head of Personnel; Joe Carrera, head of the branches; and Al Rice. Of the three, Al was head and shoulders the best businessman. Not just in putting deals together, but in making a buck. He was the only one of the three with a sense of the larger world. Now Clausen's only going to get part of the picture. It's like a wheel out of balance." Puz feared there would be no one there to bare the problems.

"Clausen was forever saying, 'Don't be afraid to tell me,' " an executive floor colleague says, but in reality, "he shoots the messenger."

There was concern that the young stars who had survived were those cut from Clausen's preferred mold—tall, dark, and polished, as if in compensation for his own lack of native grace. Consummately polite and presentable, they had been kept moving too fast. Armacost and Mont McMillen were prime examples. "Mont had a good reputation as a corporate lending officer," says a peer at the time, "and then he was pushed from one job to the next—eighteen months here, eighteen months there. Which is hardly long enough to find the men's room, for God's sake, much less know whether you have accomplished anything."

* * *

CLAUSEN TOLD ARMACOST in a Paris hotel room that he was being tapped for a powerful promotion. "I'm bringing you back as chief financial officer," Clausen told him. As cashier. Armacost was unprepared. He'd thought he'd be brought back as head of World Banking, like Rice. What he really wanted was the retail bank. "I'd pretty well covered all the bases. Had exposure to almost every phase of the bank. Clausen had made sure of that. That's what all the moving around was about." Clausen had never had any funding exposure— "Baum" had held it tight—or a major credit crisis. "Tom realized those frailties. He wanted senior managers to have the exposure he didn't have. That's why he specifically wanted me to come back to take over the financial job. I hadn't done that."

As Clausen and Armacost met for "three long agonizing hours," Armacost lobbied hard for retail. "We had a battle royal over that." It was "that powerful, incredible resource"—the consumer base Wriston was spending a fortune to capture, Armacost argued. "As I looked at the bank, the place where it was in the greatest risk and disrepair was the retail side." It needed to pay attention to technology, to become efficient as deregulation thrust protected industries into the competitive jungle. Costs were too high. Its potential as a distribution point for selling the new financial products had been ignored. Rice had wanted the California bank, too. "I'd say, 'Let me run that damn thing,' but nobody would ever let me because they knew I'd make changes and heads would roll," says Rice. "Finally, Tom said, 'Sam, you're not hearing me,' " says Armacost. " 'You *are* coming back as chief financial officer.' "

CASHIER. The chair that had been held by members of the power circle— Russ Smith, Baumhefner.

For all his resistance, it was the best place in the bank to find out what was going on. The cashier held the power to probe into every aspect of the bank's financial condition. It was the place to identify and prevent disasters. The cashier had nothing to do with the structure or approval of loans. But he saw their impact on the balance sheet. Bringing the eyes of a competitive internationalist, Armacost could see that there were several serious problems he would be inheriting, that all was not as healthy as the numbers seemed to the analysts who led the cheers for the biggest bank in the world.

The problems lay deep in the system, invisible to most in the bank. The two most distressing were disguised by cryptic code words: *Wellenkamp* and *mismatch*. Not the catchy stuff of business-page headlines at the time, they were, nonetheless, vital symptoms of problems to come.

Wellenkamp was a curse the bank had brought on itself. Costing the bank dearly in lost earnings—ultimately a loss of several hundred million dollars, to the bank—it was "just a terrible drain," says Armacost. *Wellenkamp* was the binding landmark case that had tested the issue of whether a bank could continue to raise the rate on a mortgage, as it always had, when the mortgage changed hands. The bank had lost. Armacost returned to San Francisco to find the bank had made "the fateful, the stupid—absolutely stupid!—decision to persist," carrying its appeal to the Supreme Court and losing there. The bank had lost its opportunity—essential in these inflationary times—to adjust mortgage rates upward when someone sold his or her mortgage. The bank was locked in on the "earnings" end, as the rates it had to pay on the funding end skyrocketed. Had the bank let the issue die away, it might have been business as usual. "I think the Legal Department stuck its neck out, and the business guys accepted their judgment without understanding the implications." Clausen seemed to have missed them, too. When Clausen had given Tony Frank, head of Nationwide Savings, a ride in the bank's jet shortly after the ruling in 1978, Frank had raised the issue of *Wellenkamp,* "a macho I'll-fight-you-in-the-streets-and-in-the-alleys deal," in Frank's view. Clausen's response was "one of the great moments in my life," says Frank, chuckling at the memory. Clausen was a man he knew well from business and the Bohemian, a man who had recently invited Frank and the top management of Nationwide, "not a giant at the time," in for lunch and "pushed on us to transfer our overnight collections account to B of A. I was deeply impressed that he viewed himself as the bank's top marketing officer, and he *did* get our account. We were flying along, and I said, 'Well, Tom, that *Wellenkamp* decision that your guys headed into, it's costing you about a million dollars a week.' And he said, 'What's *Wellenkamp?*' He'd never heard of it! I didn't know whether to throw him out of his own airplane."

Mismatch was a stepchild of the market funding born in the early sixties—of asset and liability management where you had to watch the interest rates and maturity dates at both ends of the funding and lending cycle. An analyst defines it simply: "*Mismatch* is the imbalance between assets where interest rates don't change and liabilities where they do." There had been no risk in mismatch as long as the rates paid for short-term deposits were lower than the yields from thirty-year fixed-rate mortgages—as they always had been while deposits were regulated.

"But those of us who'd been abroad knew, when mismatch really started to bite, that we were in about the worst place you could be," says Armacost. In Europe, playing the mismatch had been a daily part of funding one's portfolio by playing interest rates up and down; you could make money as well as lose it. In the Euromarket, how profitably you played the mismatch was a measure of your sophistication, your nimbleness in a fast-moving market, your feel for trends and changes. But with flexible market rates on the funding end, and traditional fixed-rate loans at the other, "this greater volatility increases both the risks and possible rewards of 'mismatching,' " cautioned a report by the Group of Thirty, the influential international economics think tank, on the risks of international lending. As Armacost discovered B of A's growing mismatch, he knew that "The consequences of *Wellenkamp* you see in the mismatch. The bank was booking billions of dollars of real estate loans on the backs of low-interest Regulation Q savings. All of a sudden, all of those loans on your books at four, five, six, seven, eight percent, which would have been turning over every three to six years, based on the transiency of the California marketplace, were locked in by *Wellenkamp*. But they had to be funded, as it turned out, in 1980, '82, at increasing rates of loss as interest rates approached twenty percent."

B of A's losses from the mismatch had climbed to nearly $7 billion as Armacost returned. That $7 billion was the negative net difference between the two interest rates. On the balance sheet it appeared as a reduction in interest rate earnings. But the analysts on the street hadn't picked it up yet. They were so conditioned to B of A's positive trend that "they often don't pay attention to an erosion in the quality of things," Don Crowley observed. The duty of monitoring mismatch lay in the Money and Loan Policy arm of the Cashier's Department, Leland S. Prussia's department until Armacost replaced him, and Baumhefner's before Prussia. The problem lay, Armacost felt, in the practice of Transfer Pricing, a system of buying money at rates arbitrarily set behind the doors of Money Policy that had isolated branches from the real world. Armacost's chair, the cashier's, controlled "an internal pricing system which gave the branches artificial lending rates from which they would construct a profit and loss, but they had no control over funding. They weren't getting the real experience of live or die in the marketplace. They were charging seven or eight percent for their loans. That's great. But the problem was that the cashier was out in the market paying eleven, twelve percent! The money all came through the cashier's pipe." The "comfort of Transfer Pricing" left the bank ill-prepared for the high volatility of change. That, he felt, was the deep-rooted structural problem.

Armacost laid the immediate blame on Lee Prussia. "Lee had been putting some sophistication into the cashier's office, but the exposure in fixed-rate mortgages had been taken on Lee's very strong assumption that we were going into a major recession and interest rates would go down. He was three or four years off track." During the late 1970s the creeping inflation cushioned the bank. While interest rates the bank paid were artificially low, the interest rates it received on its loans were rising. As a result margin spreads remained fairly stable. But if Paul Volcker at the Fed tightened money to curb inflation, as he was being urged to do, and the bank had to pay rising interest rates of perhaps 12 percent or 15 percent, those fixed-rate mortgages would wound the bank badly. No one knew that in October 1979, within months of Armacost's return, Volcker would do just that, turning mismatch from a minor drain to a balance sheet nightmare. "By the early eighties, we were funding those mortgages at twelve, fourteen . . . sixteen percent, and earning seven or eight percent from our customers," says Armacost, shaking his head at the memory. "Tom Clausen and Prussia rolled the dice that interest rates would go down, and lost. It was catastrophic," says an executive floor colleague at the time. "Tom told me it was the biggest error he ever made."

Armacost had started correcting the mismatch as soon as he'd become cashier, easing the portfolios from low-fixed-rate loans to floating rates that reflected the market. But the size of the mismatch revealed to him that at the highest money policy level as well as at the line level in the branches, the bank simply didn't understand the basics of asset and liability management that had been a daily, fundamental fact of life in Europe and New York for more than a decade. It was the most alarming kind of symptom. It was the mismatch of the bank with its age.

The banking industry was clearly in revolution. Pent-up deregulatory forces were about to become a flood tide. Jimmy Carter was in power, and there was no way of knowing, in 1978, whether there would be a Democratic or Republican president in 1980. But deregulation had become irresistible under either party, already affecting many industries—airlines, communications, trucking, railways. Wall Street had deregulated commissions in 1975. In banking, competitive market forces had been whipping deregulation along, as Congress dragged its feet. President Carter had ordered a report on interstate banking. And in the works was the Deregulation Act of 1980, the first sweeping piece of legislation to liberate banking powers restrained since the 1930s. It would, at last, remove the limits on the interest rate banks could pay for deposits. By the mid-eighties Regulation Q would, at last, be dead. And American commercial banking would no longer be the best and easiest game in town. For Armacost, the mismatch was a strident declaration that "the old earning power of the bank was just not there. You could no longer generate enough interest earnings in the car, ag, and real estate loans that had been the bedrock of our earning power." The pincers of history were closing on "the spread"—the net interest margin that was a bank's profit. It would shrink and narrow, leaving any bank that depended on it vulnerable, for banks lacked the bursts of profit that manufacturing industries could achieve with a successful new product.

*   *   *

WHEN WOULD CLAUSEN leave? Bob Di Giorgio worried, feeling that the time had come. "The bank is losing too many good people," he fretted. Rice was gone. "I wouldn't have voted for him as president." But admittedly, he was strong and experienced. Di Giorgio had liked Pinola. "Joe wasn't in the top rung yet, but he was *the* star of the second tier." His potential was being revealed at Western Bancorp; he had become a formidable competitor.

And Bob Truex. A real loss. "A leader. An incredible banker. He could definitely have been president or chairman." He was doing beautifully at Rainier, up in Seattle.

Clausen had never dared be openly hostile to Di Giorgio. Di Giorgio held the power to dethrone him. "But I'd question him on something, and his neck would go red and his hair would bristle," says Di Giorgio. "He wasn't a villain. He'd just been there too long." Clausen did not look willing to relinquish power, so Di Giorgio started putting pressure on him. He had a series of private talks with Clausen, told him that it was time to go and that he should take any good offer that appeared. "If he didn't, he'd be forced out, I told him." Di Giorgio had done it before.

In the months of behind-the-scenes lobbying through late summer and early fall 1980, Di Giorgio's allies, he claims, were two influential Southern California board members, Philip M. Hawley, head of Carter Hawley Hale, and Donn B. Tatum, CEO of Walt Disney Productions. Many believe that Clausen had always intended to leave after ten years. He was getting prestigious offers and had just declined an invitation to head the Federal Reserve Board; Paul Volcker, six foot seven inch president of the New York Fed, had taken the job instead. "It's nonsense that he was forced out," says a senior executive. In either case, the invitation to head the World Bank offered a dignified resolution for them all.

To make an orderly transition, Clausen's successor would be named at the same time that his departure for the World Bank was announced. As Armacost assimilated the surprise of Clausen's leaving, he assumed he had a good shot at the presidency. But he found himself the front runner. Suddenly Clausen made it a horse race between Armacost and Prussia. "Every day there were new rumors: 'It's Lee. It's Sam,'" says Katherine Neville, a computer systems manager in Travelers Cheques. "I don't know why he did that," says a senior executive. "It just caused a lot of trouble and gave Lee expectations that would leave him a little bitter. But he was never in contention. The board would never have had him." Some board sources surmise that Clausen's choice of a successor was very clear even as he worked to create the impression of a competition. Perhaps he had been trying to create the illusion that a depth of talent surrounded him. But the strong contenders had been driven out. As Armacost would learn, top management "was really pretty thin."

"There had been three candidates," Di Giorgio reveals, "Medberry, Lee Prussia, and Armacost." Armacost was only forty-two. But Medberry would have been a caretaker—already sixty-three. "He didn't have the outgoing personality to be head of the bank," says a longtime colleague. Cashier Lee Prussia was not perceived as a banker, or as a manager. "He was an economist, cerebral," says Armacost. "Sam seemed like a dynamic leader. We'd got to know him well at board meetings. He was full of energy and vision, very dynamic," says Di Giorgio. A colleague in London cheered Armacost as a man who had brought "focus, refinement, execution" to the European operation. In the outposts Armacost had been able to gain luster, far enough away from San Francisco not to be consumed by the culture. The throne would be his.

A board member rushed the news to the public relations staff to prepare for release and asked, "How do we handle this? We're about to leap a generation."

When the announcement was made, Gene Trefethen was not at all surprised. He remembered visiting Clausen early in the seventies on some Kaiser business, and Clausen had called in a very personable young man and introduced him. It was Sam Armacost. After Armacost left, he'd said, "That young man is going to be head of the bank someday." Di Giorgio's retirement from the board had finally come. At the board meeting before his sixty-fifth birthday, in November 1980, he was toasted with champagne and thanked for thirty-one years of service, as the new president, Sam Armacost, was voted into power.

THERE WAS A SIX-MONTH transitional period before Clausen left at the end of May. During this interregnum the Argentina debacle occurred. Argentina was one of those monumental errors in judgment B of A was capable of at times. The Banco Internacional S.A., a substantial Argentinian bank with sixty branches, had gone bankrupt, and the central bank had tried to retrieve something by selling it off. Rumors were out that the peso would be devalued soon, and few banks were interested in taking the risk of bidding for a bank whose $142 million of capital and assets could be worthless tomorrow. Only a small handful of bids sat on the desk of the central bank as the envelopes were opened. But *caramba*! Bank of America had bid $150 million. It was not to be believed. The next closest bid was $32 million.

Word of B of A's bid flashed through the banking community in Buenos Aires. A week later the peso was devalued 10 percent. "The Argentine peso had been twenty-five hundred to the dollar. When the peso finished its collapse, it was three hundred fifty thousand to the dollar. The one hundred fifty million dollars was worth nothing," says David L. Rothstein, then chief of Bankers Trust's Latin American operations. "The American bankers in Latin

America were just laughing up their sleeves. It became a very well-known giggle in the international financial markets."

The fiasco had been inspired by a stubborn determination to dominate foreign retail markets—founded perhaps on the long rivalry with Citibank, on the success of B of A's Italian retail bank, and on the belief that B of A's success in California could be exported anywhere. "It saw itself as a Citibank clone," says Rothstein, now manager of First Interstate's International Private Banking and European operations, "but Citibank had been in Brazil and Paris since before World War One . . . and the manager of the San Jose Main is not necessarily competent to function in a retail system in Argentina or Europe, where he doesn't have the language, the culture, or the connections, as Chase and Citibank did." Like the losses on the mismatch, it was a symptom of minds that had failed to tool up for change.

The acquisition was credited as the strategy of William H. Bolin, the slight, gravel-voiced longtime BankAmerican with the dapper mustache who had been made head of Latin American when Clausen divided the world into four parts in 1974. While Armacost waited to take over, Bolin was rewarded by being given the ultimate plum in World Banking. He would replace Prussia as head of the division, as Prussia, who had filled the vacuum left by Al Rice in 1978, moved up to be Armacost's chairman and cashier. Armacost would inherit Bolin as one of the senior management team, a man later called by a colleague "the key destructive force in the bank being in Latin America."

"But Prussia had a great appetite for the Argentina bank, too," says Mont McMillen, who had sat in his pajamas in the middle of the night in London participating by conference call in the special meeting of World Banking's Executive Council, at which B of A's bid for the bank was decided. Talking into a crackling connection, unable to hear a word from San Francisco, McMillen made his statement, "My people have looked at it, and we think it's worth about twenty million." Then he hung up, got on a single phone line, and had the rest of the discussion relayed to him by the recording secretary. Interrupting McMillen's urgent queries about what was going on, she had finally said in an incredulous voice, "Be quiet. *They're up to one hundred twenty-five million!*" McMillen hung up, went to bed, and learned next morning of the final bid number. In Panama two weeks later with Bolin and Prussia, with the bid submitted to Buenos Aires, McMillen, fishing for the rationale, said, "Lee, that's a lot of money to pay. It must be very important." Echoing Bolin's bullishness, Prussia said, "I think maybe we're not bidding enough."

As the bids were opened Steve McLin saw his chance. At his desk in Corporate Planning, he had sat reading about the Argentinian bid in the *Wall Street Journal*. As word of the deal spread through San Francisco headquarters, McLin had fumed. Beyond overpaying, the bank had clearly not asked "the broader strategic question as to why we wanted to buy a retail bank in Argentina." No one had consulted strategic planning. Hoping the final decision had not yet been made, he went to Armacost and asked to get involved, but Armacost had told him he could not. That would be the decision of the World Banking Executive Council. He talked to one of the men in Latin America and "asked them if they had signed the definitive agreement on this. They hadn't. I said, 'Maybe you better recheck your arithmetic. Maybe you guys missed a decimal point; maybe it should have been *fifteen* million dollars.' " But McLin could not force the issue; he was not head of Corporate Planning. Peter Nelson was.

He watched, in horror, as Bolin proceeded with the most embarrassing and expensive blunder McLin had yet seen. It would not even give B of A a commanding banking presence in the country; Banco Internacional was the sixteenth-largest bank in Argentina. "The thing that was funny," says McLin, "was that the Council had authorized a bid of up to two hundred million dollars." The $100 million-plus excess over the next highest bid was not overpayment, the argument went; it was "goodwill." Goodwill was a credible balance sheet entry—the price of winning friends. It would cost, McLin guessed, $20 million a year in interest payments to service. The shareholders would be paying for years. And as the new head of World Banking, Bolin had the power to buy more Argentinas.

Stunned, as many were, that Bolin had been promoted rather than fired, McLin asked Armacost, "My God, Sam, what makes these kinds of decisions happen?" Even though he was the bank's designated president, Armacost would not, or could not, override World Banking's Executive Council. McLin recalls Armacost saying, "Look, I'm not going to rock the boat at all until after the annual meeting—till Tom is really out of here. But I'm not happy with this." Clausen still ruled and "was big on the chain of command," McLin knew. "Sam and I . . . [were] sort of outside . . . the process." World Banking voted yes on Argentina. The board voted its approval. The deal was signed.

But as Armacost prepared to take his seat as president, Latin America was looking golden. Lending fever again gripped the World Banking Division. Another leap in oil prices in 1979 had led to the wildest binge of petrodollar recycling yet. "The level of lending to the developing countries only began getting very high in late '79, '80, '81, after the second oil shock," confirms Anthony M. Solomon, then head of the New York Fed. Latin America became the star borrower; by 1978 Mexico and Brazil alone consumed half of the entire lending to the third world. As S. C. Gwynne says in *Selling Money*, "Never before had the herd instinct of the international commercial banks been as pronounced as it was in Latin America in the late 1970s."

B of A was no more or less prudent than the thousand-odd international banks joining the party. In fact, Latin American loans were still a small part of its $50 billion World Banking portfolio in 1979. But events unfolding within the bank tended to intensify the lending mood. Lloyd Sugaski, an Ohioan whose fifties hairstyle and manner belied his U of Pennsylvania M.B.A. and smacked of the old-guard BankAmerican, had replaced Iversen as chief credit officer in 1976, over Iversen's strong opposition. "I lobbied for Ken Martin to have my job," says Iversen, "but Tom Clausen was solid for Sugaski." Ultimate credit authority moved into the hands of a man, Iversen feared, "who would be very liberal." A man, some feared, who couldn't say no. Prussia, too, had contributed to the buildup, Armacost believed. "The '79 to '80 time frame when he was in the World Banking chair was when a lot of the big increases in sovereign debt exposures were taken. Lee had no direct lending experience. He'd never run a major line division. You can say, 'Wait a minute, he had experienced line guys under him abroad.' But they were driving their own business." Argentina sat there bleeding, a reminder to Armacost that "the baronies out there were run pretty independently at that stage of the game," a product, he believed, "of the major decentralization through the seventies with outdated control and monitoring structures. There was no real close scrutiny."

Sovereign risks were being taken just as the bank lost its most basic credit controls. Iversen winced as Sugaski disbanded the General Loan Committee, that bastion of credit quality. Killed were the committee's legendary loan reviews that had, Iversen joked, "put a generation of young bankers on tranquilizers before they appeared." Lewis Coleman, with Wells Fargo at the time, claims, "Most banks dumped their loan committees in the late seventies. They just couldn't get through fifteen to twenty loans with all the time zones in a day. But most substituted by creating a credit organization in the field." Armacost says, "Citibank was the epitome because they had a dual signature system around the globe which put individual accountability right at the heart of the decision-making system. There was career risk in their decisions. Our people had become inured to the real risks of the big loans because the decisions were made far away by somebody on a committee. We tried to close the link down by merging some of the credit and lending functions in the senior officers in the field, like Citi or Wells . . . with a delegation of larger and larger responsibility to the field." But when Coleman arrived at B of A to run World Banking credit in 1986, "They still kept credit and lending functions strictly separate. They never came together in the field as they did at Citibank or Wells."

On the mainland, trumpets of alarm had begun to sound by the late 1970s.

"It would be totally misleading to say that there was a whole squad of people wandering around with an understanding of the problems of the LDCs," says then Comptroller of the Currency John Heimann, "but it was readily apparent that the spreads the banks were making on sovereign loans did not match the inherent potential risks. . . . Numbers of bankers were attempting to emulate Walter Wriston without his intellect or grasp." In Washington a trio of powerful regulatory bodies—the Federal Reserve, the FDIC, and the Comptroller—had, in 1979, formed a committee called ICERC that "classified" borrowing countries as to their creditworthiness; its "value-impaired" rating quickly became the dread of any country with troubled debt, for it made it a pariah in the world's financial markets.

In airports and bank offices around the world, economists from headquarters and country managers began playing out a hostile drama. As one of those economists recalls it, a manager would demand, "What the hell are you doing? You lowered the rating on my country last week. After three years of work, I finally get a three-hundred-million-dollar loan syndicate, and what do you clowns do?" The economist would say, "Yeah, that's exactly the reason we lowered the rating. They really need the money. They're in bad shape." B of A, like other banks, assigned teams of credit men to the field. "But their loyalty was to the country manager. He signed their paycheck," says the economist. And the country managers had too often succumbed to "a phenomenon that is well known in the State Department where an ambassador who has been in a country for three or four years begins to reflect the views of the country rather than the view of the U.S. government." As field and headquarters economists met, the conflicts "left much blood on the floor."

Stirrings of concern were there. Within governments. Within the banks. But it was hard for bankers to take the issue of country risk seriously when the loans were performing so well. Interest was being paid. And Clausen played from what appeared a very strong hand. In defense of Clausen's continued bold lending through the late seventies, Armacost observes, "The bank was booking double-digit earnings while everybody else was scraping along." Armacost was cashier, a post of overview and power. "I think, as staff, we could probably have constrained it more," he reflects, "but there weren't enough red flags flying, warning of future troubles. Petrodollar recycling was under way. The whole world was moving that way. B of A wasn't out there pushing sovereign credit alone. It was the major trend line in the world."

DEEP IN THE BALANCE SHEET, an unimaginable event had occurred. For the first time in Clausen's tenure the rate of earnings had not increased. Clausen, perceived as the world's most successful banker, would go out under a cloud. He had asked Armacost to clean up the numbers. And before Clausen handed over the scepter on April 1, Armacost gave him a very special going-away gift. He devised ways of showing the earnings for 1980—Clausen's last year—as higher than they were. "I knew the market would call it aggressive," says Armacost. He had found several clever devices—marking long-held assets up to market value, for one. Retiring CEOs are given the privilege of tailoring their legacies a bit. It was all perfectly legal—obvious even.

In his last annual report, in the president's letter, Clausen was able to boast: "We extended to 18 consecutive years our record of full-year earnings gains, a rare achievement for a corporation with the size and scope of Bank-America. . . . We are the first bank ever to earn over $600 million." He did admit the damage being done by mismatch and confessed that "the rate of earnings increase was the lowest since '72." But he turned decline into triumph by declaring that it had been "achieved in one of the most turbulent economic environments we have ever faced." That turbulence would pale before the economic events ahead. But next year it would be Armacost's problem.

THE ANNUAL MEETING in April 1981 was a personal triumph for Clausen. Shareholders gave him a standing ovation. What a bank he had delivered to his shareholders! Dividends had been consistently high. Earnings had set a new record each year. Dun & Bradstreet had just named it the best-managed corporation in the United States. As profits surpassed Citibank's, *Business Week* praised "a record that has never been equalled in the history of banking."

After the meeting Clausen called out an invitation from his limousine for Claire Hoffman to ride over with him to lunch. She gave Clausen a fierce stare and snapped, "I wouldn't ride with him." As she stepped into her own car, a young bank officer heard her parting volley: "I'm glad to be rid of the Führer."

PART
THREE

Chapter Eight

THE WORLD, ACCORDING TO CALIFORNIA, only went up. But as Armacost took the throne, the state was being pulled, with the world, into a recessionary decline. With a grand manipulation of forces on a scale and scope surpassing even A.P.'s most audacious schemes, America's own central bank was demonstrating its power to play God. Banking as Armacost had known it would not survive.

THE GOLDEN AGE of Banking had been given its deathblow in 1979, as Paul Volcker unfurled his six-feet-seven-inch frame before a hall full of bankers attending the American Bankers Association (ABA) convention in New Orleans and declared war on inflation. It was an act that would, within the next two years, "lock the wheels of the world," as Walter Wriston has described the event. In a stroke Volcker ended the era dominated, since the 1930s, in theory and often in practice, by Keynesian economics. He proclaimed as new savior a pragmatic form of monetarism, a competing theory which had won for University of Chicago economist Milton Friedman the Nobel Prize. Manipulation of money supply, rather than interest rates, would be his tool.

Using the banks as his instrument of policy, the Federal Reserve chief turned off the mighty Fed spigot on the nation's money supply, triggering events that would spread recession worldwide, bring the fragile economies of the third world to economic crisis, and give banks a ruthless testing of their preparedness for the new age. His act would transform banking into an act of survival and leave the Bank of America revealed for all the systemic weaknesses disguised for so long by inflation and California's good times.

Volcker launched the historic experiment on Saturday, October 6, at a meeting at the Fed of its all-powerful Open Market Committee—an event that has been dubbed the "Saturday Night Special." Wall Street was thrust into confusion as the news broke that Monday. For no one, not Volcker, the governors, or the Open Market Committee—where it had been hotly debated before an aye vote—knew what would happen. Tightening the money supply could lead "to slow, flat, or even negative growth. To recession," feared the vice-chairman of that committee, New York Fed chief Anthony Solomon. But democracy itself was at stake, he believed. "We had already gotten to double-digit inflation. If we had not tightened monetary policy, we would have become a banana republic."

Since the Vietnam War, inflation—destroyer of hard-earned value, in the American view—had grown steadily. Spending, and the magic of money creation, had outdistanced real productivity. Climbing wages were pricing American products out of the world market. And America, like its citizens, was borrowing recklessly, building the debts and deficits that would haunt the eighties. By the late seventies, like a tenacious virus that no longer responds to known treatment, inflation could not be contained. It was creating the illusion of riches as the market value of that classic measure of the American Dream the single-family home soared exponentially. But the value and stature of the dollar were being eroded, hurting savers and investors. The dollar—the economic gunboat that had defended U.S. preeminence around the globe since World War II—risked becoming disarmed.

Banks flourished in times of inflation, to a point. But inflation, this time, had brought the country to a state of near panic and the markets to wild instability that was no longer healthy for banks. While middle-class families smugly paid low-fixed-rate mortgages on homes that had quadrupled in value, the value of capital shrank, and risk grew that people would pull their money from the economy and sink it into "safe" savings: jewelry; gold; art; land. Would stop using the banks. Memories haunted of the inflationary excesses that had preceded the crash of 1929, forerunner of the hated regulations that the banks were now trying to shed. This was the fiftieth anniversary of the crash. Volcker was being pushed and pulled by Congress, Fed governors, bankers, and Wall Street, with increasing numbers arguing for control of the money supply—the amount of U.S. money allowed to circulate in the economy. Until now, controlling interest rates, which slowed or speeded borrowing and spending, had been the principal way the Fed had tried to keep inflationary forces contained. International Monetary Fund (IMF) meetings in late September hammered home the need to halt America's inflation and the accompanying decline of the dollar's value, which was undermining international exchange rates. Yet strengthening the dollar would hurt American exports, make U.S. products too expensive to buy. Volcker was torn by his double mandate: to maintain the global equilibrium and to protect the strength of the U.S. banking system. As inflation hit 12 percent, monetarism won the day.

As the new policy was announced, the Fed's troops acted to implement it. The trader at the Open Market desk at the New York Federal Reserve moved into the market, selling Treasury bills and bonds, sucking liquidity from the system. Banks were central to the control of the money supply. The Federal Reserve raised the rate banks pay to borrow at the "Fed window" a full point to 12 percent, slowing the outflow. In theory. Over the coming months, as the higher Fed rates drove already high interest rates dramatically higher, the cost of borrowing money did increase. But lending, borrowing, and spending didn't slow. A perverse psychology had taken hold. Volcker had warned the bankers in New Orleans, "This is hardly the time to search out exotic new lending areas or to finance speculative or purely financial activities that have little to do with the performance of the American economy." But with a new oil crisis, the '79 "oil shock," spilling a new infusion of petrodollars into the system, banks went into a frenzy of lending through '80 and '81—at home and abroad. During Armacost's first year, Bank of America increased its foreign loans by over 17 percent, loans that would earn the bank irresistibly high interest rates as oil-buying countries were forced to borrow more to pay for higher-priced oil. Worldwide, commercial bank loans grew to $100 billion, the raw material of the debt crisis a few years later. As with the earlier oil shock in 1973, admits Solomon, "we in the government encouraged the banks to recycle the money."

Getting mixed messages, American consumers did not halt their spending as interest rates rose; feeling the general uncertainty and vacillation, they bought at a more hectic rate, assuming that inflation would regain its hold and prices would be higher tomorrow. Inflationary expectations, economists saw, were ruling the consumer. Those who were beginning to feel the first twinges of retraction—small businessmen, real estate developers—had to borrow more to cover the interest payments on old debts.

Banks were being jerked around chaotically. As they continued to borrow from the "window" even as rates there rose to an unprecedented 12.5 . . . 13

percent, the money supply kept swelling. Inflation still flourished. The Fed tightened, then eased, then—reluctantly implementing controls invoked by President Carter—imposed credit controls across the board in 1980, freezing lending altogether—an "unprecedented action that . . . restricted our lending activities for a major part of the year," a bristling Tom Clausen wrote in his annual report as he attempted to preserve his reputation against Bank of America's first decline in rate of earnings growth in eighteen years. Nothing was unfolding as the governors had anticipated. Within the first year of the monetarist experiment, banks roller-coastered through two dips of recession, were lurched to a standstill by the credit controls, then, when controls were lifted, pitched headlong into another lending binge, in spite of Volcker's New Orleans caution. Inflation seemed immune. The great experiment was quivering at the edge of failure.

Volcker finally decided to turn the screw abruptly tighter and keep it tight until he forced inflation to its knees. He drove the Fed rate to 14 . . . 15 percent. There had to be a threshold at which he could break inflation's back. He was relentless. Interest rates soared to 18 percent . . . 19 percent, to a breathtaking 20 percent, reaching their fifty-year apex in the summer of '81, just after Armacost took the reins. The cost of money was reaching the limits of the society's capacity to borrow. Finally, starved for fuel, the engine of growth began to slow and sputter. Unemployment rose perceptibly; prices inched down. The dollar was strengthening against other currencies. At last, the inflation rate was dropping. By late summer 1981 it had dropped to 7.5 percent. As Volcker kept the money tight, anxiety over what they might have wrought flared among the Fed governors.

"A U.S. recession . . . meant a world recession," Solomon knew. It was America again playing God, some argued. But Volcker kept rigid restraint on the money supply. At home, whole segments of the economy began to feel the impact of deflation. Small businesses. Agriculture. Real estate. Energy. The states where those were concentrated were hurt first. Texas and Oklahoma. The Corn Belt. Even California. Bankruptcies and default on bank debt began to erupt. For the first time since the 1930s, banks, especially savings and loans, were failing. Racked by high-flying excesses and corruption as well as by recession, savings and loans would be a dying industry by the end of the decade, its claims against the federal insurer of "thrifts," the insurance pool of the Federal Savings and Loan Insurance Corporation (FSLIC), so overwhelming that the agency was bankrupt as the Bush presidency began. Commercial banks, though, are often the last in the chain to feel the economic despair of their customers; there is a time lag between recession and default on loans. Banks were still not feeling the recession pervasively in their loan portfolios.

As the American economy faltered, shock waves reverberated beyond the United States. Compounded by the '79 oil shock and a strengthening U.S. dollar, the infant recession migrated abroad. As the United States, the world's biggest market for the exports of developing nations, pulled back, international trade slowed. Oil prices, falling now after soaring with the oil shock, ravaged the earnings of oil-producing countries like Mexico and Venezuela. Those countries borrowed more to cover the shortfalls, as interest rates continued to rise. The Fed's Solomon saw that the elements that could shatter the fragile balances that underlay even the lustiest-looking third world economy had converged: "the higher real interest rates, the lower commodity prices . . . the fall in world trade." For bankers, as well as for the third world, Volcker was creating unspeakable hell. Just as banks were sailing into quickening deregulation, needing flexibility and resilience to compete, the loan portfolios filled with such ease through the 1970s and early 1980s became vulnerable, as whole industries and nations stumbled toward default. Interest payments on foreign debt went overdue. Thirty days, sixty days. Banks watched with alarm, for loans that are ninety days late must be declared "nonaccruing," the point at which banks must set up more loan loss reserves, depleting precious earnings, and declare them on their balance sheets.

The recession then boomeranged back to the United States and swiftly deepened. Starting with the core commodity crops in the Midwest—corn, wheat, soybeans—farmers saw their domestic and export markets shrink dramatically and prices dive as the world's consuming slowed. The cash flow farmers relied on to service their loans vanished; the land—collateral for their loans—collapsed in value. Recession reached out. Tract homes and office buildings sat empty, and construction slowed. Oil rigs stopped drilling. In November 1980 Carter lost the presidential election to Ronald Reagan. Volcker's act had helped bring down the president who had appointed him. Carter's defeat lay as much in the oil shock and in the Iran hostage crisis, which hounded the last months of his presidency. But a recession that was sending unemployment climbing to 10 percent had been insurmountable for Carter.

In October 1981 President Reagan finally declared the nation and the world in full, rolling recession.

Even without Volcker "locking the wheels," banking had been undergoing a paradigm change, as the globalized market, telecommunications, deregulation, and the changing needs of an Information Age society invalidated the past. But the violence and trauma of recession turned an evolutionary process into convulsive revolution from which American banks would emerge diminished in the new power balances that were reshaping the world's economic order. Volcker had won the domestic battle but lost the larger war. By the mid-1980s the United States would have lost, perhaps forever, its global preeminence and its power to orchestrate the world's financial symphony. By that time efforts to control the value of the dollar by "intervention"—a concerted buying or selling of vast volumes of dollars by Germany, Japan, and the United States—would be only fitfully effective as the global market became bigger and more powerful than the choreographed dance of the dollar by the world's great powers. And, of American banks, only Citicorp would still sit on the list of the world's ten biggest banks, soon to be pushed off by Japan's banks, fat with savings. The American financial system would find itself increasingly vulnerable to events triggered by "the mob at the gates," as liberal Harvard economist Robert Reich describes the fear that has lingered in America's primal brain for more than two centuries. Volcker's global shake-down sped the painful discovery that all nations were ensnared in a web of economic interdependency. Any wall could be breached by the punch of a computer key.

Volcker had set in play forces that would inflict catastrophic damage to some industries and give a bonanza, through high interest rates, to the already wealthy. But he had broken the dangerous pattern that had hounded three presidents. He had regained the confidence of the financial world. The rumpled giant had wrestled with the beast inflation and won. Volcker became something of a folk hero. A federal bank examiner driving through Washington was astounded to see on a brick wall in a black neighborhood the sprayed graffiti "Volcker suks." "*Sucks* was spelled wrong, but *Volcker* was spelled right." He laughed, amazed.

ON APRIL 1, 1981, Sam Armacost assumed the chair that only three men had occupied since the death of the Gianninis at mid-century. At forty-two, he was president of the Bank of America. Though it lacked the princely robes of the Renaissance, his position still carried inestimable stature; commercial banks were still, as they had been for six centuries, the principal conduit and repository for the world's wealth. As B of A's president he joined that informal international financial establishment that guards and controls what is termed the "Western banking system." He had access to the inner sanctums of the Treasury and the Fed. Access to prestigious clubs, to the bank's private air force and limousines, to private meetings with third world rulers, and to Paul Volcker's ear. He had a salary of $475,000 a year.

He sat in a deep blue velvet chair in a setting as imperial as a modern sky-scraper permits. His office on the fortieth floor must be approached through deep-carpeted acres of reception area decorated with the spoils of global banking—rare sixteenth-century Japanese screens, ceremonial urns, and ancient bronzes, a fortune in paintings and sculpture. On a pedestal was the austere bronze head of A. P. Giannini. The vast corner office commanded a spectacular view of the bay and, below, of the North Beach neighborhood where the bank began. The patina of old wood and the richness of Oriental carpets surrounded Sam Armacost as he launched his era.

Certainly, he brought the style and polish of a world-class banker to the job. He was a classically smooth and polished product of MotherBank, with a pleasant, even-featured face saved from blandness by a high, intelligent forehead and keen eyes. The only imbalanced note was a slightly bulbous nose that gave him the look of actor Karl Malden's handsome younger brother. With dark hair receding slightly, he was attractive, volubly articulate, and though under six feet tall, he carried himself with a jaunty confidence and country club athleticism that made him seem taller. As if in compensation for his own inadequacies, Clausen had chosen a man who, in physical terms, was all the things Clausen, as he moved into his middle years, was not.

Armacost came from a family steeped in institutional gentility. As his father retired from the presidency of the University of Redlands in Southern California, his brother Michael was rising toward assignment as undersecretary of state, the second-highest-ranking career officer in the State Department. His oldest brother was now president of Eckerd College in Florida, while his sister had returned to graduate theological studies.

Yet Armacost was perceived as having, under the polish, the toughness the times required. Headlined NO TIME FOR A GENTLEMAN, a *Forbes* article published as he took over suggests that Armacost had the toughness his rival, Lee Prussia, lacked. What could not be measured was Armacost's true grit. Profits had been easy in the California boom times and petrodollar era in which Armacost had learned and plied his trade. A banker weaned on inflation's rising values and expansionism, he had never seen a recession. He had always been known as "very bright." But nothing in Armacost's upbringing or experience had taught him the ruthlessness that revolutions require. Would he have the right stuff, as unprecedented challenges came from without, and within?

ARMACOST WAS NOT ALONE. All banks shared the same tumultuous environment. Recession. The first rumblings of third world debt problems, as Poland's and Zaire's loans defaulted as the eighties began. Frustration with the Fed's smothering blanket of regulations. Erratic deregulation. A banking industry divided among itself, as big and little banks lobbied for their disparate self-interests.

He was buffered, at first, by California's unique economy. The defense spending that had buoyed the economy since World War II would continue to grow under Reagan's presidency; California won 40 percent of the nation's defense contracts. The Golden State had the momentum of the world's seventh—and by 1985, the sixth—largest economy; it still led the nation in population growth, income, and GNP and promised to be the portal to the Pacific Rim, where the future lay. The diversity of its farm crops gave it more resilience than one-crop states in the Midwest.

But relatively, California was no longer racing ahead of the nation; it was leveling off. North Dakota was, relatively, growing faster. Recession had reached the state. Its banks, heavy with energy, real estate, and agriculture loans, were particularly vulnerable. B of A's loan portfolios, especially in home and farm loans, were fatter than most. If California's consumer culture spent less, banks would reel. Recession had not begun to reach bottom.

And war had broken out among his peer banks in California. As the barriers to nationwide interstate banking began to break down, they all were trying to strengthen themselves against the assault from New York and abroad that would come by the end of the decade. Wells, Security Pacific, Western Bancorp were nipping at BankAmerica's heels, trying to break the bank's impregnable hold on the nation's richest consumer market, stealing some of the golden market share B of A had always owned.

Joe Pinola was becoming the embodiment of the aggressive challenge in B of A's own backyard. Armacost's old colleague was head of Western Bancorp's region-spanning banking network, with twenty-one banks in eleven states and $22 billion in assets. Still only a third the size of Bank of America, his bank was the nation's ninth-largest holding company, and he was neck and neck with his ambitious western peers, Wells Fargo and Security Pacific. Pinola was becoming a forceful spokesman for change. The strong nose was balanced now by a face that had squared, tanned, and beefed up handsomely. With a deep, authoritative voice, silvery hair that glinted off the spotlight, and the timing of an actor, he had warned a bank directors' meeting in Acapulco in 1979 of an environment in which competition that became "more banklike every day" siphoned off deposits and market share: "Foreign banks already own 10 percent of total U.S. banking assets . . . and Sears Roebuck, with 3,700 offices and a credit base of twenty-three billion, could easily become the first—and largest—nationwide bank."

Pinola was battling within his own bank to achieve a top secret project he believed would dramatically reinforce the competitive advantage he already had in an interstate banking network that stretched from Washington State to Arizona. For three years and three months he had been secretly preparing to unify his entire network of independent banks under one name. Each still operated under its original name. First National Bank of Arizona. American National Bank of Denver. Northwest Pacific National Bank. United California. "We realized we wanted to pull them all together so that we could compete in this new deregulated world," and he had determined, in 1978, to unify the banks as First Interstate Bancorp, a name that revealed Pinola's ambitions. He felt urgency: If he was to gain the high ground regionally, he must make his breakout soon. A just released presidential report endorsed interstate banking, giving momentum to the movement. By the mid-eighties a new breed of banking consortium would be forming up to challenge his unique interstate advantage as the nation's prime geographic zones formed reciprocal banking regions. Powerful territories were being carved out in New England, in the Southeast, in the Far West. Less burdened than the giant multinationals with third world debt, blanketing the market in a block of states, the regions stood as a wall to interlopers. Within the regions a new breed of bank was evolving: the superregional. A multibillion-dollar bank with a huge regional presence. Banks like First Wachovia in Winston-Salem, SunTrust in Atlanta, NCNB Corp in Charlotte, PNC Financial and CoreStates in Pennsylvania, Banc One in Columbus, Ohio, and—before its real estate loan losses in 1989—the Bank of New England in Boston. They were making higher returns on assets, the magic measure of success, than the great money center standard, Morgan Guaranty in New York. Although Pinola preferred to think of himself as a multinational, his renamed bank would be the most visible superregional in the country. To achieve surprise, a code name was used for the three years of planning the changeover. But Pinola was having a difficult time getting the individual banks to accept the concept. No one wanted to give up the independent identity, the prestige and tenure in the community that attached to the old names.

"Finally I put them on a boat. . . . I got them as far away from the bank as I could get them, sat them down, and said, 'We're going to change our names, boys.' " In 1981 the red, orange, and brown signs of First Interstate Bank started going up on 900 branches across the West. Pinola then started franchising the name and network, signing up banks in states contiguous to his western base. He carved his niche: "the two-hundred-fifty-million-dollar to a billion-dollar bank, too small for Bank of America or Citibank." He would have a presence in thirty-two states by the mid-eighties. "Stay flexible. Stay flexible as hell!" he said, as he searched for new opportunities to widen his network nationally.

Pinola's 327 California branches did not seriously threaten Bank of America's dominance in the nation's best market. B of A still held a nearly 35 percent share of California. But cumulatively, the California competition—the Wellses and Security Pacifics as well as the little independent banks that lavished service on their customers—was eating into B of A's historic franchise. Bob Di Giorgio had been alarmed at the decay in the heartland before he retired from the board in 1980. When the bank stopped "holding our share in Dinuba, Visalia, and St. Helena . . . that's when we stopped being the Bank of America."

THE EXTERNAL BATTLEFIELD was challenging enough. The greater battle, for Armacost, lay inside the bank.

Wellenkamp. Argentina. Mismatch. As he had uncovered them in the cashier's chair, they had scarcely scuffed the glittering veneer of the world's biggest bank. A little cosmetic work on the balance sheet had neatly disguised the slight slippage of earnings in Clausen's last year. But Sam Armacost knew, as he took the throne, that a common thread united them all: that they were symptoms of an elusive systemic illness that ran through the bloodstream of the bank, symptoms of something deep in the culture that, under pressure, was working its way to the surface. He would not let his worries show. Unruffled, he would let the word *aberration* flow glibly from his tongue. But he knew that the disease itself must be dealt with if MotherBank was to hold her preeminence through the Armacost era.

The symptoms were still minor as he surveyed the year that was already five months gone when he took over—the first year history would record as his. On the surface, they appeared as much a product of the difficult climate as of any corporate disease. Avoided by accounting tricks in 1980, for the first quarter of 1981—for the first time in memory—a decline in earnings must be declared. Earnings were the bank's lifeblood—the source of capital, profits, dividends, and growth, watched by analysts and investors as clues to strength and health. Earnings were in trouble, partly "because of deregulation and high interest rates." But there was also "the cost equation . . . a very expensive branch structure that was going to kill us."

Credit quality, Bank of America's greatest pride, seemed, fundamentally, to be holding. Yes, there had been increased charge-offs on bad loans, up 28.5 percent from the year before—an increase that was "as would be expected in the economic cycle that we could see," Armacost stated, as he raised the loan loss reserves 33 percent to cover an increase, too, in "nonaccrual" loans that were ninety days overdue in their interest payments. "Modest increases in loan losses" he blamed on "difficult domestic climates . . . and political uncertainty" abroad. Demonstrating his confidence, he joined the international banking community in expanding foreign and domestic lending, the surge begun with the second petrodollar flood in 1979. In 1981, Bank of America co-led one of "the largest syndications ever arranged," a $4 billion financing for Pemex, Mexico's state-owned petroleum agency. *"No red flags were going up that there was anything seriously wrong with our credit quality,"* he reaffirmed.

THE TEAM ARMACOST HAD in place to help him through the eighties was Clausen's team.

The board had been appointed by Clausen. "Mostly over-the-hill retired CEOs," observed a colleague. "They would have approved Howdy Doody if Clausen had recommended him," said one B of A executive of the appreciation the board felt for Clausen, the man who had delivered record after record. He had made the post of director one of the most envied board seats in corporate America. Each was paid $12,000 a year, and $500 a day for meetings, but it was the prestige, more than the pay, that attracted; even Robert S. McNamara, Clausen's predecessor at the World Bank, joined the board in 1982. McNamara's appointment, some felt, was typical of the way in which Clausen insinuated his people onto the board and senior management. Clausen had asked, then—when the World Bank job came up—unasked, McNamara. But he had left Armacost with a moral commitment. As a new CEO, Armacost could have seized the opportunity to name a board member of his own choosing. But he recalls that while technically he was given a free choice because the McNamara seat had been temporarily rescinded, he felt "a sense of obligation to follow through with Tom's appointment." Clausen had also appointed John R. Beckett, sixty-three-year-old board chairman and retiring CEO of Transamerica, during the last months of his era, while Armacost would have been inclined to ask Transamerica's younger James R. Harvey, just assuming Beckett's chair as CEO.

Armacost viewed the Managing Committee, the handful who ran the bank. A team that had evolved from seventy-six years' experience in molding bankers, that had risen above eighty-three thousand fellow BankAmericans as the bank's leaders, they represented the culture's climax growth. All older than Armacost, they were, like Armacost, well groomed and mannerly.

James P. Miscoll, an ebullient personality with a love of banking lore, history, and fey Irish humor, a well-educated man with broad foreign as well as retail experience within the bank, but not perceived as a heavyweight banker. James B. Wiesler, a loyal thirty-three-year bank veteran who had moved up through the California retail bank. Bill Bolin, small, dapper, nearing retirement with little indication of the bankerly skills needed for new wave banking and carrying the stigma of Argentina—the gross overpayment for its bank there. Arthur V. Toupin, who, a colleague says, "worked within the frame" of bank tradition. Lee Prussia, a Stanford-trained economist and a gentleman, an introverted technician at home in the cashier's chair, but who, Armacost saw, "had never been in a position where he had to really make major decisions, be accountable for them, and stand up to scrutiny. . . . Lee is not a manager." As brief head of World Banking Division, he had not gained a great reputation. Lloyd Sugaski, head of all credit quality, a man promoted by the Peter Principle beyond his high competency in analyzing individual old-time loans, some associates felt. Bob Frick, a friend and colleague of Armacost's, "with an engineer's kind of mind that can never make a decision because it has to look at all sides of the problem," he felt. Although he had traveled the fast track in corporate finance, his indecisiveness drove the public relations writers mad. "He'd wait for weeks to approve a press release. He just couldn't make up his mind." John Mickel, a man "so nice you'd love him as a brother-in-law," an associate said of the man Clausen had appointed to bring the bank's computer systems into the eighties, but widely regarded as limited by his background as "just an IBM salesman"; a Nebraskan and mathematics graduate from Northwestern, he had not brought the bank's technology to within shooting distance of Citibank. His power was eroding as Armacost took over.

Good BankAmericans all. But were they equipped to carry forward Armacost's "proactive" program? The word, defined, meant "to intervene positively between past and future events." It became Armacost's mantra. "The bank was a little lacking in depth," Armacost admitted as he scanned his team. Perhaps it was the result of Clausen's "weak lieutenant" theory, as he had described it to Armacost: If you have three strong and one weak man, you choose the weakest of the four as leader so that the other three won't quit. A theory that, some thought, explained Clausen's choice of Bolin as head of World Banking, it stood in opposition to Wriston's policy to "Choose men stronger than you, and be prepared for a lot of humbling."

Why hadn't Armacost tried harder to influence decisions during the eight-month interregnum before he took over from Clausen? When Clausen anointed Sam, he gave him two messages, an associate suggests: " 'Here are the keys to the kingdom. And, by the way, Sam, here's your team.' It was the team the board appointed the day they appointed him. And I reckon . . . he never felt that he had a charter to vaporize them."

Steve McLin speculated, "I think Sam was playing it cool to get the job, and then he was going to figure out what he was going to do when he got it." This was the moment, in hindsight, he could have disowned the past and begun the Armacost years with a tabula rasa, a clean slate. The moment he could have fired and hired his own team. It was the moment he could have declared a massive loan loss reserve, shedding, in a stroke, responsibility for any losses Clausen might have left lurking in the portfolios—a declaration that they would accrue to Clausen's record, not his own.

He would naturally resist raiding his shaky earnings to create the huge reserve that might have freed him of Clausen's legacy. Short-term, at least, he needed to dedicate his earnings to "grow" his assets, to grow out of trouble, as the bank always had. With a big bank's tremendous leveraging power, every dollar of capital frozen into reserves could be $16 or more invested in loans.

But there was something else. He would not, could not fully reject the past.

FROM DAY ONE he struggled with a powerful internal conflict, one that would pull him simultaneously toward the past and the future, a basic conflict that underlay the image of indecisiveness that would come to haunt him. Intellectually he had embraced the banking revolution. But he, too, was a BankAmerican trained since college in the culture. On the surface he took the aggressive posture of the "proactive" man of tomorrow. But inside, he was a conservator of the BankAmerican world.

From his family and his work, all his life, he had known only institutions, whose role in society is, partly, to be a force for continuity through times of change. Institutions had obligations beyond profit. They ground forward with the inexorable momentum of glaciers, and their goal was more often to hold their course and let others lead change. Only a handful of American corporations had also become national institutions—Ford, IBM, the big airlines and networks, Standard Oil, McDonald's. B of A was one of them. Few, other than IBM, had successfully played the role of both institution and leading-edge innovator.

Yet Armacost knew most, though not all, of the bank's weaknesses. As he took the helm, he saw that "above the surface, the ship looked like it was in great shape." Later he mused, "Maybe I should have told them on day one, 'You work for a lousy bank. It's rotten inside.' " But he was concerned about undermining morale and crushing motivation by roughly imposing new leaders and ideas on a culture in which loyalty, not initiative, had been rewarded.

Armacost knew that change must come, that he must nudge eighty thousand people into a new world. The basic banking on which B of A had flourished would no longer work. "The bank had been driven on a growth strategy through the seventies; it was roaring with growth," he said, summing up the "old bank." "Its operating strategy was high asset growth, low return on assets, go for size, highly leverage your capital, and with decent earnings you show your shareholder high rates of returns."

"B of A got in trouble because it played *the size game* instead of market positioning," Armacost would later say. He had seen this game of "biggest bank" played from his London office in the late seventies when "the chief financial officer would call at the end of the last quarter and say, 'I need two billion dollars in five hours' "—an infusion of the short-term, low-yield inter-bank lending that puffed the bank's assets in the annual report but which constituted billions of dollars of "water" in the balance sheet when he took over. He would wring out $18 to $20 million of it, a high risk move for Armacost. For the sharp shrinkage of assets made the bank's already high expenses look even more swollen in relation to its assets. He feared, correctly, that analysts would not see the "perverse expense ratios" for what they were, the by-product of some needed housecleaning, and would attack him for it.

But the size game, which he, too, had played had become a dangerous anachronism. And his talks to the troops would promote a new message, one never before heard in a bank fattened by the cornucopia of California. "It was a message about scarcity of resources and the need to allocate much more effectively than had been done in the seventies, when the world was full of growth and no one really worried about where the next buck was coming from. . . . *We couldn't be all things to all people.*"

By the time he made his first address to the management forum, a monthly meeting of two hundred senior managers, he had determined to distance himself from Clausen's fear-driven style and inaugurate an era of candor. "We need to open up the environment around here. I want an open forum where people feel free to object and dissent with each other in order to get the best ideas put forward. And we need to do that in a disciplined way," he urged. Although he claimed, "I always got on fine with Tom. I was one of the few people who would argue with him," he knew that most had been afraid to bring him problems. Candor would come more easily, he hoped, away from Clausen's favored Managing Committee meetings, very formal, structured affairs with tight agendas. "We started a series of budget review sessions that were really one-on-ones between the chairman and me and the financial officer." In these sessions he was shocked to discover that there was no cohesive idea of the bank's objectives. No vision. A.P. seemed to have been lost. "Making money isn't the reason you're in business," he said, trying to persuade the others. "The reason you're in business is to serve the needs of the marketplace. If you do well, you should get rewarded with profits." He saw "the need to define the strategy for the organization, which had none . . . and to get a much better handle on its strengths and weaknesses."

He formulated his vision: The culture could be—it *would* be—transformed from within. With the help of the Boston Consulting Group, which was already in the bank doing some studies, he would lead a search back to the real A. P. Giannini. To separate legend from fact and find A.P.'s original objectives. Putting the bank on the couch, he would try to probe the corporate memory. He would lead the bank in a corporate quest for MotherBank's true roots and spirit.

This quiet culture search would run as an underground stream as Armacost's "proactive" revolution held the attention of the press, analysts, and shareholders. Like any serious attempt at self-renewal, it required time.

SEARCHING FOR A BREAKOUT OPPORTUNITY to help shape the Armacost revolution, McLin had made his first move a year earlier, in 1980; he had tried to maneuver his way into discussions on bidding for the Argentine bank and been rebuffed. Thirty-three years old, pipe-smoking and balding, the young strategist had been finding very small audiences at the upper levels for his strategic thinking over the past six years. There was no bankwide coordination of planning.

He wanted in on the action. He shared Armacost's proactive vision. Allying himself with Armacost was the only way. The Argentine fiasco was the argument he needed to convince Armacost of the need for bankwide coordination of strategic planning. "This bank has been preserved as if it was in formaldehyde," McLin exclaimed to Armacost. "They've kept A.P.'s room just the way it was when he died. Let's diversify," he argued. "There are going to be lots of new ways to make money. We ought to sell some things which don't fit with our business. . . . We can look at some acquisitions. . . ." With the words *acquisitions* and *diversify*, he had Armacost's ear. He urged Armacost to appoint him head of Corporate Development and Strategic Planning for the entire bank.

If he got the job, if he did get the president's ear, he would be identified as Armacost's man. He risked compromising his carefully guarded neutrality. He would rise or fall with Armacost at a volatile time in the bank's history.

But the opportunity to participate in remaking the Bank of America was irresistible. McLin was Armacost's first appointment after he became president. From April 14, 1981, no acquisition or divestiture would be done without review by McLin's unit.

*   *   *

"IT'S COSTS THAT are killing this bank," McLin and Armacost agreed as the two men began their weekly one-on-one strategy meetings. Their new "best of breed" peer bank comparisons revealed that Bank of America had a 3.6 percent problem—the percentage of its earnings being eaten by expenses. For every billion of assets, it had $36 million expenses. It was impossibly high. A well-managed little savings bank like Golden West in Oakland operated on a 2 percent ratio. With margins getting slimmer, you couldn't stay in business at 3.6 percent.

In spite of his criticism of the size game Armacost needed to expand. To grow his loan portfolio. To find new sources of revenues. He wanted acquisitions that would move the bank into the new financial arenas. McLin cautioned him, "If you've got the profits, the bank can *double* its number of people. . . . You can grow once your costs are down. But they've got to come down." Major surgery must be done on MotherBank. "We have to reduce the size of the bank by about twenty thousand people over the next five years." Perhaps close some branches.

People were the largest cost. "The bank's personnel expenses were over a billion dollars higher than they should have been," says McLin. The branches were the principal source for these overruns. There were fifty-four thousand people in the branches. McLin had learned that "the way you got paid more at B of A was to have more people working for you." Empire building was rewarded.

The cost of operations must be cut, too. "The bank had the advantage of almost twelve hundred branches, then sort of crapped it all away by putting full back offices in all the branches." They were running what Clausen had called a thousand little mom-and-pop stores. "Each one is a little barony, with full services, and computers that only work three hours a day. Each branch had its own proofing machine. They cost about a hundred thousand bucks. The thing runs about two or three hours a day—about seven percent of capacity," said McLin. They must capture economies of scale. They must search relentlessly for "competitive advantage." They must "consolidate the functionality," he said, coining the buzz word.

Now, Armacost and his band moved toward the most sacrosanct area of the Bank of America. The branches. In a big, thick study, the Boston Consulting Group had proposed a major restructuring of the branches—a surgical strike Claire Hoffman would fight as a desecration of her father. It became the core of the strategy driven by Armacost and McLin. They would cluster small branches around a hub, tightening their focus on specific markets. Trying to repair the mismatch between the customers' needs and the existing delivery systems, they would create specialized lending centers. Some small branches would shrink to basic services. Processing operations would be removed to regional centers to capture efficiency and reduce cost. And a burgeoning network of automatic tellers would spread "convenience banking" across the state.

Computer systems must be coordinated, paper handling reduced. The bank was still drowning in a paper environment, as the world moved away from it. The classic example, for McLin, was the ritual, each afternoon, in which the millions of checks written by the customers were hand-stuffed into envelopes. Each day dozens of small aircraft loaded up with bags full of documents and checks and flew to San Francisco, where, in a cavernous Market Street building, "every piece of paper that represented a transaction—the millions, billions of pieces of paper that fly into the bank at night—covered the floor, was captured and crunched by proofing machines, sorters, collators," as a computer systems officer described the sight. It was as outdated as Wells Fargo's stagecoach.

Sophisticated technology was the crying operational need. Especially ATMs—automated teller machines. The bank's token few were an embarrassment. ATMs could be installed without rocking the culture, McLin and Armacost agreed. You could explain to staff that it was being freed from drudge work to give more of its time to personal customer contact. ATMs still cost $40,000 each, an enormous investment. But Armacost committed himself to a massive budget to "leapfrog" to the vanguard of bank technology. The bank would reach three hundred ATMs by the end of 1981, equal to any bank in California.

The strategic eye next shifted to the lending process. Dangerous territory. For branch bankers saw any interference with their fiefdoms as attacks on their very identity as bankers. "For branch managers, identity had been *defined* in terms of lending limits," says Armacost. Here, as everywhere in this maelstrom of change, he felt himself mediator between the purity of McLin's theory and the emotions of threatened line personnel who must "buy in" if change were to happen. Trapped at this point of tension between change and tradition, Armacost would be a target for criticism as troubles deepened.

Surveys showed that the bulk of the loans were made in only a handful of the branches; the "four hundred least productive branches made an average of four a year." Didn't pay their loan officer's salary. McLin's staff pulled samples to see how well mortgages were being serviced; documentation was "terrible." And B of A had lost its competitive advantage in agricultural loans. "The bank was competing with the Production Credit Association. . . . There was no way we could achieve a competitive advantage because (a) the PCA doesn't pay income tax, so their reserve standards are half of yours and (b) they get government subsidized funding. Their cost of funds is fifty basis points less than yours. . . . Therefore, there wasn't anything you could do to be smart enough to beat 'em," McLin and Armacost agreed. The bank would keep only the quality farmers—25 to 30 percent of its portfolio. B of A was the farm bank! They were exploding a shibboleth.

And then another. McLin felt that "the trend to create a thousand Renaissance men or women to run branches was silly," and was, Armacost concluded, "impossible to achieve." The branch staff must become salespeople. "They can fill in the papers for the loan, but they won't have the authority to make it. The most important thing is that the customer perceives that they're still being served," said McLin.

A system of hubs and satellites would transform the branch lending structure. The larger branches would become hubs with ten or twelve branches reporting to them. Loans would be processed in these centers. "The notion was a geographic cluster. The person who headed the cluster would be the president, as it were, of kind of the little local B of A structure . . . with some stability, presence, and muscle . . . trying again to push the power down to the branch structure," Armacost explains. The model was the small independent banks with great personalized service that were stealing B of A's market share in the communities. "They're the real competition," said Armacost, "not the big chain banks. We'd been losing retail market share throughout the seventies, and with each new branch B of A opened it cannibalized its own branch structure." But what was the right number—fifty, seventy-five, one hundred? McLin mused, "We knew eight hundred was too many. Home Savings, which originated about the same volume of real estate loans as B of A, had only twenty-seven real estate loan origination sites in the state." Whatever the final number, it would mean customers would have to go to another center, perhaps a neighboring town or city, to get their mortgages. But surveys clearly showed that "the more important a transaction was, the further people were willing to go for it," McLin reported.

Finally, the last of the big commercial loans would leave the branches. The large corporate accounts had been taken out in the mid-sixties. Now it was proposed to take out the remaining mid-size commercial accounts. It had been proposed in the mid-seventies in a study chaired by Lloyd Sugaski, but never implemented. "Beise and Peterson took the Fortune 500 business out of the branches; what we did was to take out the middle market, call it the Fortune three thousand," McLin says.

"We put in a whole different branch performance evaluation system," says Armacost. "We instituted performance measurement devices which brought the breeze of reality to accountability, holding the managers accountable for revenue generation, cost control, and customer service. Those managers were given five or six objective criteria against which they were measured. . . ." Real profit and loss had always been orchestrated by the cashier's office, which had shielded the branches from the realities of market funding. "Branch managers had enjoyed the illusion that they owned a profit and loss center and played an artificial Transfer Pricing game to look good when, in fact, they had very little real control over true profitability."

In spite of bonuses and incentives "the entrenched status quo felt truly threatened," Armacost saw; there was resistance in the branches. Joe Carrera had been a charismatic leader of the retail bank, but "he had tried to protect the branches from change," says McLin. It was human nature. At the heart, too, was corrosion of the banker's image. People who took pride in being bankers were being forced to become marketing men.

Loan quality was still not seen as the major problem. "Fundamentals are sound," Armacost said often. "At this time our loan portfolios were performing well by the numbers." McLin says: "At the time people thought B of A was good at it. The bank had . . . been praised by the examiners for its credit management. I assumed, since they checked every nickel on expense reports and expense accounts, that they applied the same rigor to the credit process." He still rankled at having an expense account bounce for a $4 breakfast he had bought at the airport after leaving home at 5:00 A.M. "If the same scrutiny was applied to loan review, the portfolios should be *pristine,*" McLin mused. As he and his staff began to examine the portfolios in the branches, it became clear that "some of the credit quality was pretty rancid," says McLin. Isolated aberrations related, mostly, to the general recession, they hoped. But as the process of centralization relentlessly pulled in and examined loans that had been disbursed over 1,200 branches and previously only sampled for quality, Armacost, too, would soon be "horrified at the sorry state of the loans."

ANDREW JOHNSON, JR., watched the assault on the branches from his desk on the "platform" in the St. Helena branch that had "owned" the Napa Valley winery business since the forties. A new wing was being built on the bank, a commercial division with its own entrance and staff of young commercial loan specialists sent out from San Francisco. The largest wineries were already gone from his branch. Now they would be taking all the mid-size wineries as well. Hanns Kornell, Don Chappellet, Schramsberg. Johnson, archetype of the great B of A branch manager—the man who had said no to advancement when Al Rice had asked him, "Andy, where would you like to go? What would you like to do?"—was being replaced by bean counters and computers.

His was a vivid view of the bank losing touch with the "little fellow," a trend Johnson could measure in a few points slippage in Napa Valley market share and would see accelerating in the drop to below 40 percent for the first time just after his retirement, in 1984, and in the plunge to less than 15 percent by the end of 1988.

Johnson's desk was still out in the open, but he could no longer chat with the winery men and keep in touch. By the sheer force of his reputation among his superiors, Johnson was still doing substantial deals. As he prepared to retire in 1983, he had just completed one of his last transactions, a debt restructuring for Warren Winiarski, whose Stag's Leap Wine Cellars has been one of the leaders in Napa's triumphant surge to international stature. He had made his first inventory loan to Winiarski in 1974, permitting him to hold and age the cabernets that would beat Château Mouton-Rothschild in the 1976 bicentennial tasting in Paris that skyrocketed Napa's wines to world rank. Winiarski had left the bank for the Production Credit Association, as had so many other vintners, when he refinanced in 1978 "because of B of A's caution. They were placing the same collateral value on a ten-dollar bottle of wine as on a two-dollar bottle. You'd only get one dollar, instead of *five*, to work with, even after the Paris triumph. And the winery business is very much a financing business. Someone has to supply capital for extended periods."

But in 1981 Winiarski had driven the Silverado Trail north to St. Helena and sat again at Andy Johnson's desk. His partner's shares had come up for sale. He needed a loan to buy his independence. "It wasn't just the numbers; it called for judgment and insight. An evaluation of our winery's potential." The two went painstakingly over the numbers, Johnson analyzing them slowly. Then Johnson stopped looking at the numbers and seemed to muse, silently. "We stared at each other and said nothing for a long time," Winiarski recalls. As he ruminated, Johnson was thinking how often he had gone over his lending limits and said yes before he had approval. "Then, from the pregnant silence, Andy said, 'I see how important it is for what you're going to do, so I'm making the loan.' It was critical to us." Johnson had won Winiarski back for the bank.

From now on Winiarski would go next door to the new wing. Johnson's successor would be a regional manager. A public relations man, not a community banker. "It's a mistake to take the wineries away from the branch," Johnson would continue to believe.

His plan, Armacost claims, had been "to build people like Andy Johnson as the senior bank presence, the figurehead in the new regional structure. An Andy Johnson would not be moved every eighteen months." He would become the prototype for what Armacost envisioned as a new breed of branch banker, a hands-on personal banker who knew the territory and got vineyard dust on his shoes, but a banker kept from the dangerous parochialism of the past by his linkages to the larger region and to the sophisticated information networks, distribution and payments systems, and global resources of an aggressive multinational bank.

Alarmed by the erosion of the bank's powerful Napa Valley franchise, Armacost did not carry through with the dream. He left Johnson on his platform, his power evaporating as his wineries moved next door. "We kept Andy on his platform because he was a unique fixture, a critical part of holding Napa Valley," Armacost says.

MCLIN CALLED Armacost from a phone booth in the federal courthouse in early August of 1981. "What do you think about exploring a discount brokerage?" He had Charles Schwab in mind. It was an uncharacteristically daring move for Bank of America; no other bank had bought a brokerage. To do it would require a major regulatory struggle. The bank would face a formidable lobbying effort by the securities industry, funded by the deep pockets of a Wall Street determined to keep banks out of their territory. But if B of A could pull it off, Schwab would drive a vital wedge for the entire commercial banking industry. A discount brokerage that simply executed stock transactions and did not invade investment banking's underwriting turf might have a chance of getting approval. If B of A could get a Schwab through, it could break the back of Glass-Steagall, the act that, for half a century, had restrained banks from competing in the securities field.

As McLin sat in San Francisco's U.S. courthouse waiting for assignment to jury duty, he began to play with the possibilities. It was aggressive. It seemed perfectly aligned to Armacost's strategy. Might Schwab be open to merger or acquisition?

On September 11 McLin and Peter Moss, a former options trader who was now Schwab's strategic planner, met for lunch at the Banker's Club on the top floor of the BankAmerica tower, the fifty-second floor, with a spectacular view of the entire city and bay.

Schwab looked strong. He was in a self-declared shoot-out to hold the title of biggest discount brokerage in the nation. The numbers were still tiny compared with B of A. He had 370,000-plus customers, 40 percent of them in California. Eight hundred employees. Assets of $151.3 million. But his growth rate was phenomenal. He had been growing at 70 percent a year since he started, was in the middle of an expansion that was adding twenty branches a year, and had just declared that he would double his number of branches by 1985.

After twenty years of peaks and disasters, Charles Schwab was finally rich and famous. His newspaper marketing was phenomenally successful. His was not as familiar a face, perhaps, as Lee Iacocca's, but he was a household face to any reader of the *Wall Street Journal*. At forty-five, he had risen like the phoenix from the wipeout of the early seventies to acquire a luxurious home in a fashionable Peninsula suburb and, soon, a ranch in Montana, a condominium on the Big Island of Hawaii, and a ski house in Park City. Through Young Presidents, his friends were a dynamic group of youngish corporate superstars. He was still a populist in his contacts with old friends and in his identification with his customers—he, like most of them, was a moderate Republican who hated government regulation. He had no corporate jet. But he was chauffeured in his Cadillac Brougham. Married to the daughter of a wealthy oilman from Midland, Texas, he was on the San Francisco Museums board, collected art, and was acquiring a string of prestigious club memberships—San Francisco Golf Club, Olympic, Pacific Union, the Menlo Circus Club, and Castle Pines in Denver. But his net worth, his life's work, and his soul were in the company.

Guarding the gates to growth, like Scylla and Charybdis, were two obstacles: regulations and lack of capital. It was regulations that created his perpetual capital crisis, inhibiting him from the growth he was determined to have. Must have. "We knew in order to remain number one, we *had* to have more money," says Bill Pearson. "We always hated to see Chuck go on vacation because we knew when he came back that he would have a new idea." More need for capital. As they expanded to mutual funds, money market accounts—whatever Schwab's imagination devised—customers poured in, putting further stress on Schwab's ability to maintain the "minimum net capital" required by the SEC. Every month was a moment of truth, as the company filed the requisite FOCUS report with the SEC. Schwab's team grazed ceaselessly for capital to feed the galloping growth.

The solution had seemed to be at hand in the spring of 1980. Schwab was taking his company public. The prospectus for the initial public offering was printed, and Schwab and his staff were talking it up to brokers, preparing the market. At $8 or $9 or $10 a share, they would have excess capital at last. But on the eve of launch the offering crashed, victim of "the computerization of Schwab. . . . That was directly my responsibility," Pearson said. "Because of the computer going down during the conversion, we lost about one million dollars on transactions that we had to pay back to the clients." The two investment brokers scrutinizing Schwab's data before marketing his stock had spotted the loss and thought it would be a negative factor to potential stockholders. They priced the stock at $2.75 to $3 a share. But Schwab's team suspected they had priced it too low because of the old establishment bias against discount brokers, for Schwab had grown to 90,000 customers, and was pressing Merrill Lynch and E. F. Hutton in money market accounts. With an offer from Schwab's friend at YPO, Nationwide Savings' Tony Frank, of an infusion of capital, Schwab had an alternative. The public offering was "kiboshed." Killed.

McLin's call had coincided with this state of urgency. Frank had invested $4 million in Charles Schwab & Co. in January 1981, giving the large savings and loan a 20 percent stake in his company. In September, "Chuck suddenly called and said he was talking to the B of A," says Frank. "His company was not doing that sensationally then. I suppose both Chuck's and my stupid feeling at the time was that if you could get an enormous windfall of capital, take it."

And now, emissaries of the go-go Golden Boy and of the imperial banking bureaucracy were talking. At their lunch at the Banker's Club, Moss didn't try to conceal Schwab's need for capital, and McLin hinted that the bank might just be the source of the "ultimate capital infusion." McLin reported to Armacost after lunch, "It's not only potentially legal but a very good business fit."

Armacost and Schwab lunched together two weeks later in the president's dining room and had an easy time. Both were attractive, affable. Incredibly confident. Good golfers. They shared Stanford's graduate school of business. They were almost the same age. Schwab discreetly avoided talking about his past experience with the Bank of America; it had turned down two requests for loans. They left the lunch feeling bullish about the possibilities.

As Armacost and McLin subsequently toured Schwab's back office just five blocks away from the bank, they entered a paperless environment that made the yellow envelopes in B of A's branches seem artifacts from the Miocene. From the day he had cut the umbilical cord from paper and placed his destiny in the hands of a computer, Schwab had never looked back. Since the BETA system had gone on-line in 1979, Bill Pearson had tinkered with it to bring volume from less than a thousand transactions a day to what would soon be twenty thousand a day. "That's a monster program. Oh, it's big," Pearson explained to the envious bankers. "Similar to making an airline reservation, it automatically updates every bit of transactional information." A broker could execute orders directly on the screen, the first system in the nation to permit that. Yet, even with the burgeoning volume, Schwab's "cancel and rebill rate"—a measure of the accuracy of his execution—was the lowest, thus the best, in the brokerage industry. Schwab had grown from offering simple stock transactions to a menu of mutual funds and money market accounts, and had just introduced Schwab One, which combined high interest checking account, debit card, and discount brokerage all on one account. The kind of account that could help stanch the flow of deposits from banks. McLin and Armacost salivated.

It seemed an impossible partnership: the nimble entrepreneur and the turgid bureaucracy. "I look at an entrepreneur's spirit as a little bird in your hand and it is so easy to squeeze, and it is so important for the top management to be understanding of how essential it is to maintain and keep it alive," Schwab told an auditorium full of businessmen at St. Mary's College across the bay from San Francisco. Now he was contemplating marrying his high tech back office—responsive, advanced—to a monolithic company strapped to an archaic computer system second only to the U.S. government in the sheer size of its daily processing job.

But both companies had compelling reasons to make it happen. For Schwab, it would be a quantum leap in growth through the bank's branches. B of A's imprimatur would give him the credibility that obsessed him. B of A's customers could buy Schwab products through their checking accounts, and B of A could market a host of services through Schwab's national customer network, circumventing the geographic restrictions of the McFadden Act. Schwab self-service kiosks would be set up in B of A branches, giving him that huge flow of customers. Cross-selling possibilities were endless. And the bank had promised a $50 million loan to Schwab whether or not the deal went through.

For B of A, acquisition of Schwab would be the most forward-looking move the bank had made since it pioneered computerized check handling in the 1950s. After years of lagging, B of A would suddenly be on the front lines of the industry's fight for the freedom to compete in the new financial world. With this entrepreneurial unit under its roof, MotherBank could compete with the financial conglomerates Prudential-Bache, Shearson/American Express, Sears Roebuck and Dean Witter, and Merrill Lynch.

With Schwab's branch offices, it also served the territorial side of McLin and Armacost's strategy. Schwab had everything: positioning for interstate banking, entry into investment banking, and product, product, product. Sam Armacost would be scooping John Reed at Citicorp.

With the offer of a board seat and "enhancements" for his senior staff, which would keep the entrepreneurial spirit afire, Schwab was ready to strike a deal. He agreed to sell his company to BankAmerica for $53 million of B of A stock—2.2 million shares. Beyond arguments that it was too much or too little was the fact that the price was three or four times Schwab's book value. On November 20, 1981, Armacost signed a letter of intent to acquire the discount brokerage. In the exchange of stock Schwab would become the largest shareholder of the Bank of America. Nationwide Savings, with a 20 percent holding of Schwab, would, "for an instant in time, be its second-largest shareholder," said Nationwide's Frank. That created a mild conundrum. "To be the second-largest shareholder of your biggest competitor doesn't make much sense!" But Nationwide would own less than 1 percent of B of A stock; there was no conflict of interest.

Schwab might be naive in his trust of people, but he had the protective instincts of a male wolf when it came to his company. As McLin and Schwab had negotiated the deal, it was agreed that the bank would own the right to the name Schwab & Company but *not* to the face and personality. He agreed to a standstill that would restrain him from competing for a mere sixty days if he were to leave Schwab & Co. He would say later, "I could go across the street and, in two months, open up as 'The Charles Project' "—with his face smiling out again from the *Wall Street Journal*.

There was another concession McLin made. The bank could sell the business, but not the name Schwab & Co. It meant, if McLin had been looking for holes to poke in the deal, that the bank had little to sell, for in a marketing-based company like Schwab where the name and face were the competitive advantage, you'd be selling a hollow shell without them. It would tend to cripple any effort to sell the company in the future to anyone but Schwab himself. "But we weren't buying Schwab with the thought that we would ever sell it," says McLin. They were in the euphoric courtship phase, unified against Glass-Steagall, Wall Street, and Sears Roebuck. There was no thought of divorce.

The decision now lay with Volcker at the Federal Reserve Board. Armacost was girding for at least a year of battle in Washington to get a positive decision. He would take Glass-Steagall to the wall—to the U.S. Supreme Court, if necessary.

THE 1981 ANNUAL REPORT would be an opportunity to polish the perception of Armacost's first year. Armacost's vision became the theme of the report: "Extending Our Reach." The theme "expresses our determination to be at the forefront of the rapidly changing financial services industry," Armacost said in the president's letter, revealing a bank "pursuing tactics that will serve us well tomorrow," with the confident hope "that in the transformed financial services industry of the 80s, Bank of America will emerge a leader."

Armacost could not report, as Clausen had been able to in 1980, that the bank had broken its own records. History would record that Armacost began his tenure by serving up the first decline in nineteen years. Although earnings had still been very strong, they had declined, quarter by quarter. Loan losses had increased nearly 30 percent. And there had been corrosion through the year of profits, of return on assets, of loan loss reserve ratios, of rate of capital growth, of "spread"—the measures of health that would be scrutinized. Armacost's "scarcity of resources" was being intensified just when he needed money to bankroll his ambitious vision.

The annual report would offer a list of explanations of the bank's malaise— "Deregulation . . . unprecedentedly high interest rates . . . global instability . . . recession"—while staff and senior executives brainstormed for ways to buffer the news of the first serious downturn since the upward surge began after World War II. Dividends were raised, defusing complaints of share-holders, even though it meant a drain on capital. The restructuring of the branches was presented gently: Only two dozen had been closed, a dozen opened.

The good news was celebrated. Operating profits had grown more slowly than in the past, but had still increased 7.5 percent. Return on assets (ROA) stood at a healthy 0.62 percent. Not the 1 percent that was every bank's dream, but well in the ballpark with its peers. Bank of America still held a 35 percent market share of California's deposits. Although Citicorp had passed Bank-America as "biggest bank holding company in the U.S.," the $88.4 billion that sat in its deposits made Bank of America, still, by that measure, the largest bank in the world.

The report would point to impressive growth in the bank's traditional areas of strength: B of A had headed up the largest syndicated loan ever to Mexico as assets swelled—Armacost was still playing the size game. There was Schwab to announce. The technology surge. ATMs going in at the rate of "one every working day." The bank's astounding success with its first deregulated prod-uct, a money market account that earned an initial 50 percent market share.

But mismatch persisted as a drag on earnings and, increasingly, on image. It made the bank a target of the press, which had discovered mismatch early in Armacost's tenure and was reveling in it like a new toy. Analysts picked it up in their reports. Corporate Communications took a bold step. They would draw fire from other problems by thrusting mismatch up into prominence, make it the scapegoat. It was revealed that the mismatch had its origin in one small profit center called the Money Manager, a unit "isolated from the domestic line divisions," where both liabilities and assets were brought together, and their maturity dates and interest rates matched by computers. The roughly $8 billion mismatch of assets *and an earnings loss for the Money Manager of nearly half a billion dollars for 1981* were centered there. Although a young computer expert close to the unit at the time claims that Money Manager was nothing more than "a reporting tool, a thermometer, that *identified* the mismatch but did not create it," the report explained it as "an internal clearinghouse . . . that buys all deposits and other sources of funds from the branches and other profit centers, at market rates. It then sells to profit centers, at market rates, funds for loans and investments on a matched maturity basis. The profit center spread on any fixed-rate asset is locked in for the life of the asset. The Money Manager, therefore, absorbs any cost of funding long-term assets with short-term liabilities." Although Money Manager was derelict for not triggering action in the cashier's office, mismatch could be treated as an isolated, not a systemic disease.

Focusing on Money Manager as the culprit absolved the two big operating divisions that should have been coordinating mismatch: the California bank and World Banking. Mismatch, the annual report reassured, was being put to rest by "tighter and more rigorous monitoring" and by the "floating rate mortgages and longer-maturity liabilities" Armacost had already initiated as a solution. It was not entirely cynical. "We *were* making progress," a bank officer says. "Quarter to quarter, you could see the mismatch change." If the bank could maintain it—if Armacost could bring it to heel—he would emerge looking like the Paul Volcker of mismatch.

Chapter Nine

IN THE ARCANE UNIVERSE of the bank's computer systems, worlds away from mismatch, Armacost had already become a demigod. "Everybody was just thrilled about Sam. He didn't have capped teeth. He didn't act like a jerk. He wasn't like a back-room politician in a smoke-filled room," Katherine Neville mused as she observed the change of command from computer systems, which had felt like a motherless child under Clausen. B of A's first woman vice-president in Travelers Cheques operations, she knew software, hardware, programming, design. As banks moved into electronically delivered "products," they needed people like Neville to get them on-line. A career technocrat writing a novel on the side, she ran budgets and schedules and drove with a whip, at times, to meet deadlines. She had just been promoted from the retail division to Travelers Cheques, where five million checks and $650 million cash a day were processed. Bank of America was "the sloppiest shop I'd ever seen.

"Sam gave a banquet for us in the Giannini auditorium in the B of A building just a few months after he became president. He'd scheduled it just for Travelers Cheques management because he'd suddenly realized that we were bringing him six hundred and fifty million dollars a day in float that was money in his pockets." In Travelers Cheques float is the delay between the time when the bank is paid cash for a check and the time when the check is cashed and "clears" the bank. This is how banks make interest profits on the sale of travelers cheques.

"Sam comes flying in with no notes, stands up at the podium, in this very small, intimate auditorium, and starts telling us what Travelers Cheques' business has been for the last five, ten years, what we're doing now, and the systems we're developing. We couldn't believe it. He couldn't lie to these people. Not only did he know everything about *us*—our business—but he understood our data processing requirements—enough to impress people with twenty or twenty-five years of data processing experience like me, who are not gullible. Obviously he'd done his homework. And we were one of many, many small areas of the bank that he seemed to understand thoroughly."

B of A had shaken even this veteran. "The management style had formerly been 'cover your ass.' " As people listened to Armacost, "everybody went, 'Oh, wow, we have a leader at last.' We were completely blown away. Ready to go pray at the shrine!" That first image of Sam Armacost was etched on Neville's mind, a benchmark against which to measure the Armacost of the next few years.

Technology had been a second-class citizen, she saw. Operations—computers, the back office, the whole electronic dimension of banking—were the poor relation to the lending side, where the glamour was. She had felt it acutely when she'd had tea with Mont McMillen in London—by the fireplace in the office where both Sam Armacost and Al Rice had sat. What class! "The place was fabulous." The antique desk. There were no Persian carpets in computer operations. She worked in a giant unmarked building at Fifth and Market which housed data processing. The fire department hounded them to move desks and tons of paper from the overspilling aisles. B of A operations were scattered over most of San Francisco, including a warehouse at Fifth and Mission. There were people smelling hamburger fumes above Zim's on Van Ness, some hacking away among the marble columns in the old B of A branch at Powell and Market. The central mainframes for the whole system were kept in the data center at Van Ness and Market. "If the data center had collapsed in an earthquake, the bank would have been out of business overnight."

It wasn't that the bank wasn't putting money into computer systems. "The general attitude was 'Money is no object; it's quality that counts.' " It was the IBM attitude she guessed had migrated over with the technology chief, John Mickel. "However, I had never seen it on a scale like this before." Budgets had increased with Armacost. "Sam had come in and told us, 'We're going to get out of the brick-and-mortar business. We're going to become an electronic bank. We're going to have to deliver to turn this elephant around.' The method was to throw money at it. They were *hiring*, putting ATMs in at a frantic rate. Money was just going, going, going."

But it was being put into the hands of a culture that wasn't getting the job done, Neville feared. When she met with the division vice-presidents to propose three new management tools they might use, she was appalled as they said, "What are Citibank and Crocker and Wells doing? Which one are *they* using?" She confronted her boss. "What comes first—the good project management *tool* or the good project *manager*? Because I don't think these people know how to *use* these tools," she said. "They'd never had to report any kind of measurement against budget and schedules. . . . There was no performance monitoring," she saw, alarmed that this mushy, unsystematic swamp must function as the nerves, arteries, and heartbeat of the whole vast enterprise.

With deregulation coming in, "all of a sudden it was anybody's game." Banks could offer floating rates. New products were where opportunity lay. They should be rolling products off the line as Wall Street's rocket scientists were. "But I'd get status reports that were about where to send Suzy flowers after her hernia operation, and I'd say, 'Yes, but how many modules did we complete coding?' They were throwing millions of dollars into putting in a ten-digit zip code in every system because the post office said, 'We're going ten-digit zip code,' but they didn't know if they were going to it in the next year or five years down the road." When she asked for an inventory check on the delivery of a multimillion Tandem computer system, she discovered there was no inventory list, no experience with doing a physical inventory—and no procurement office for centralized purchasing.

This was the culture, deep, here, in mid-management, that Armacost would have to change. These tens of thousands of people, attracted by the bank's tradition of lifelong security rather than by ambition and challenge, people with a deep, vested interest in the status quo. Good people were pressed between the layers, their ideas imprisoned in the hierarchy. There were a thousand vice-presidents, for Christ's sake! On the line Neville could see and touch it as the men on the fortieth floor could not. It was an enormous civil service, really, cloaked in the tradition of BankAmerican ideology. Functioning like high priests among the old boys was a cadre of senior technocrats, Mickel's men, an elite of "the best and the brightest . . . that was only interested in the sophistication of the design. That's great if you're at IBM developing software in a corner. But when you've got to use the damn software to deliver products that you should have had out on the street *yesterday*! . . . It's *not* Silicon Valley." Neville fumed.

Yet like a miracle, some things worked. Everyone had cheered the day the new statewide item processing (paper capturing) system went on-line "on time and on budget." And the bank's telecommunications network was one of the best, linking up around the world, even with countries like Bangladesh. It was the high-velocity pulses of energy in this network that breathed reality into Walter Wriston's comment: "If it turns out, as I believe it will, that information about money is becoming almost as important as money itself . . . those who can supply that information better, cheaper, quicker, and most accurately will be the winners in tomorrow's world."

B of A was the first non–New York bank to join CHIPS's the New York clearinghouse that, with Fed funds, was the basic daily conduit in the United States for electronic transfers of money. CHIPS's daily payment flows averaged $450 billion. This massive global crisscrossing of funds was done by computers talking to each other, making accounting entries in their data bases. In late '81 CHIPS enhanced its network by a revolutionary upgrading of its electronic processing capacity; it would now close its books at the end of each banking day, rather than the next day. Each bank's books must now balance, that day, with the New York Fed. "On the day of the changeover, BankAmerica smoothly moved $30 billion through the network," the bank proudly announced.

Neville saw B of A's electronic network as the way the bank had to go and cheered Armacost's support of it. But the environment she faced daily made her a frayed nerve end. All she could do was try to bring some cohesion and professionalism to her tiny corner of the system and go home and write. Armacost was still going to have to find a really strong computer guy with the muscle to rip out the deadwood and rebuild systems.

PRODUCTS. They were symbols of the new banking. James Cerruti, a young officer in World Banking, was attracted to strategic planning—and products. He had invented one.

In his immaculate banker's suit, Cerruti was clearly one of the bank's young M.B.A. types. But with his blond-red wavy hair and neat, clipped beard, he had a certain cerebral air that lifted him above the mob. This was a creative maverick, the kind of guy the bank needed, Neville saw, identifying him as a kindred spirit as she met him at a meeting called to discuss his product, one that exploited float in cashiers checks and money orders.

Cerruti's goal was an assignment abroad. He wanted to be an international banker and had taken his master's in international business administration from the Monterey Institute with that goal in mind; he had kept his cottage on Santorini in the hope of a posting to Athens. He already knew that he did not want a career path in the "mature lending culture." It was fees from services and products—not interest from loans—that were the core of future earnings. Marketing was where banking was going.

If the eclipse of the humanist dreams of the sixties can be reduced to a symbolic moment, it may be James Cerruti designing his product. He had discovered the untapped potential of float. If the bank's holding company were permitted to issue official checks like cashiers checks, rather than the California bank, he proposed, it could prolong float time by extending it interstate and, most important, avoid paying reserves to the Fed as the bank must do. A bank must reserve nine to twelve percent of the check's balance, but a holding company was reserves-free. His idea was clever—tricky, even, from the customer's point of view. But as competition pressed bankers to the wall while regulations still thwarted them, exploiting loopholes was where you made your mark. And made the bank money. Citicorp was ten years ahead in float exploitation. The float period could be extended, Cerruti proposed, by clearing checks at a geographically remote center, like North Dakota, which would give the holding company an extra day or two to invest and profit from the use of the money.

His product could also save the bank at least $2 million a year from the reduced reserves requirement, he had calculated. *If* he was able to get the Federal Reserve to change Regulation Y, which controlled what holding companies were permitted to do. It was a knockoff of a credit card product of Citicorp's. But it hadn't done it yet in cashiers checks.

"It's great, let's go with it," Sam Armacost said as Cerruti's product was presented to the Managing Committee. Cerruti had the go-ahead and joined the task force assigned to get it on-line as fast as possible. In a feverish year of work he got Regulation Y changed—a triumph. But that redoubled the sense of urgency. Any competitor could now use the idea. He knew Citicorp would grab the similar product its bank, Citibank, already had and switch it to the holding company. With its head start, BAC could still be first. Fresno was chosen as the float point to which checks would be shipped. Staff was being assembled, and people were beginning to plan selling their houses for the move. Software was being developed, hardware ordered. Cerruti's product was scheduled to go on-line toward the end of 1983. When it did, he would be awarded a $50,000 prize.

Katherine Neville knew that the progress of Cerruti's product through the bank would be a telling measure of Armacost's ability to get the elephant turned around.

AT AMERICAN AIRLINES' headquarters in Dallas, Max D. Hopper scrutinized the Bank of America's 1981 annual report with great care. The bank was clearly addressing technology with vigor. He, Hopper, had been offered the chance to lead that effort. He would not control it all, at first. Jim Wiesler, head of retail, had been wooing Hopper through the spring of '82 and had made him a tempting offer to head up computer systems for B of A's retail operation. It was compelling. Hopper's charter would be to take an organization demanding vastly larger systems than any airline into the next phase—"to broaden into the whole realm of information management—international, everything." He would start with retail. But there were hints that he might ultimately be given the entire bank.

Hopper was attracted to Armacost's vision, his goal to "leapfrog the bank from where it had been to a position of prominence." Although he sensed that Wiesler only "semishared Sam's vision," both men seemed "in sync with the expectation that they would become a nationwide, if not a worldwide, bank, in the retail field, that banking would be deregulated sooner than later, that their systems were not customer-oriented, and that they could not get there without some heavy changes in their systems approach." A massive budget was being projected—$5 billion, to be allocated over five years, from 1985, to Bank-America and all its subsidiaries and divisions.

Deregulation was making it less fun at the airlines. A protected industry dumped more abruptly than the banks into a cutthroat world, airlines were being wrenched by cuts, mergers, and uncertainty, while upstart, no-frills airlines like PeoplExpress stole the business. Hopper had earned recognition for using technology as an aid to becoming competitive in a deregulated environment; he ran American's computerized reservations and ticketing system, SABRE. But in the current mode of belt-tightening, there could well be a cap on new management opportunities.

It was the chaos in the airlines that finally made up his mind: He had been in Tulsa, en route to Dallas, when Braniff abruptly closed down, victim of deregulation. Flights were turned around, canceled. "I flew one of the last flights on Braniff Airlines into Dallas Airport. We had two flight crews on there. . . . They were all in tears, and there was no service." Hopper joined Bank of America.

He had never touched banking. "But from my perspective, banking and airlines systems were extremely similar. An airline has to be largely centralized because the operations are so integrated." So, too, did banks. There was an air of excitement around Armacost. There was no sense of "saving" the bank, no crisis. It was the challenge of moving a great institution into position for the twenty-first century. Leaving his wife in Dallas until he got settled, Hopper arrived in San Francisco in July 1982.

He would soon earn the nicknames among the systems crowd of Max the Ax and Hopper the Chopper. But the general impression of Hopper was of "smiling Max." Of average height and stocky frame, and with a thick thatch of dark hair and a broad and happy face, he looked more the practical computer operations man he was trained to be at the U of Houston than a man of palace politics. He was plainspoken and decisive. But he was also a poised and articulate executive who could sit through hours of meetings with the grace and self-control of a yoga master.

He worked from the confidence of a computer pioneer of the late fifties who "just grew up with it from the ground up. Not many individuals had the chance to get in and learn the guts of the technology as well as the business problems and try to mesh 'em together." He had developed early systems for the oil industry. Working for Ross Perot at EDS, he had introduced computer systems to the complex data environments of hospitals and airlines. Those days with Perot "gave me a bit of an entrepreneurial thrust." He had joined American in 1972 and had brought SABRE on-line. But "in terms of scope and responsibility, it was just a much bigger leap. . . . It was a larger responsibility than I had had at American in terms of people. I had maybe two thousand there; it was more like five or six thousand at B of A." And it would grow.

Word was out "that he was going to come in and growl and chop lots of people. Which we needed," said a hopeful Katherine Neville, her prayers for a strong systems man apparently answered. He was not universally welcomed. Claire Hoffman was not happy. Hopper met her at bank dinners. "She didn't like technology, so she always gave me a hard time. Said it was antipeople. . . . She constantly kind of lectured me, 'You've got to be concerned about people.' " By reaching outside the carnelian tower and the ranks of BankAmericans to hire a corporate management star, Armacost had broken tradition. He had recognized that to leapfrog, he would have to reach outside the bank. He knew he had to build depth. Find people who could "make an immediate positive contribution and raise the level of ability." For Armacost, "hiring Max was a tremendous coup."

Two weeks after Hopper, Bob Beck arrived from IBM as new head of Human Resources—a headhunter for new talent for the top two or three layers of management. Chosen from a culture considered compatible with B of A, Beck was a significant commitment to the cultural revolution. Armacost was about to slice into the upper layers well stacked with true-blue BankAmericans and insert several dozen outsiders. It had never worked. The bank had never digested them. Bob Truex had faced booby traps at every turn and been spit out. Armacost was aware of the bank's traditional rejection of "alien managers." But he was doing the thing that had, historically, revitalized decadent dynasties, in China, India, Persia; he was breeding in dynamic new "barbarian" blood. Beck studied the salary scales at peer banks and moved B of A's up to be competitive, giving Armacost a new tool for attracting talent. Hopper and Beck moved into bank-owned apartments in a fashionable high rise in Pacific Heights, a mile from headquarters, and, bonded as the first members of a new breed of outsiders, sharing dinners and hours of talk.

Declining Wiesler's invitation to take an office on the fortieth floor, Hopper chose the other option, the data center on Market Street. It would remove him from daily contact with the politics around the throne, but it would give him a better platform for his hands-on style. He was immediately thrust into the budget—"a huge budget that had to be put to bed by September or October." The sheer size of the job, and of the bank, now hit home. "You reach a point where no one man or even group of people can run things to the degree that you can a smaller enterprise. You've got to go through a delegation process," he saw; "the bank was so big, with so many products, so many units." As Katherine Neville had learned at a much lower level, performance was almost impossible to measure. "And everybody put forward estimates that they were going to do very well," Hopper recalls with a smile.

Hopper focused, at first, on "efficiency and reducing cost" and on "the *business* use, rather than the technical use," of computers. He imposed "the most rigorous budget sessions any of them had ever gone through," an opportunity for Hopper to ask the questions a mid-level manager like Neville did not have the clout to ask. "What were their goals? How did they determine, and employ, resources? What were the expense levels? I didn't find too many people were concerned with that. In fact, I did not find bankers, as a whole, very good businessmen."

Lifting his head from budgets, he scanned the bank's systems from the top. Looking at the branches, he confirmed McLin's findings that "back room operations in the branches were paper factories." He discovered the same lack of systems coordination, the same anarchy Neville had seen from the narrower perspective of Travelers Cheques. "We counted about seventy data networks. Many branches would have as many as a half a dozen or maybe ten terminal types out there, each connected to a different data network. Not talking to each other. Highly inefficient." As new products came along, computer systems grew up around them and swelled, unmanaged, into monsters. The big smile broadened as he surveyed the opportunities. "For a guy that likes to solve problems, there was a fertile field."

But he would work in a climate of tension. He identified a ferocious two-way turf battle between computer operations—the technocrats who actually created, installed, and ran the systems in two data centers in Los Angeles and San Francisco—and the business units that "owned" the systems. With the all-powerful Managing Committee giving unilateral approval of new systems directly to the vice-president in the business unit, "the operations people didn't even get a chance to review it." John Mickel's computer aces hated being reduced to delivery boys, whipped by deadlines set by the business types. The technocrats continued to function under Mickel's command, even after Hopper's arrival.

Fighting to hold power, Mickel had claimed "architectural control" over the hardware and the hiring of senior computer people. Hopper continued to face his predecessor with equal status on both the Managing Committee and the retail bank's Planning Committee. Mickel had not been decisively removed, just redeployed to marketing, where he was in constant touch with the growth of Hopper's power at the expense of his own. "Conflict was built in, it was inevitable, between Mickel and me," says Hopper.

He began the job of containing the disorder. Of centralizing, systematizing the mess. He ordered computer operations "to create a reasonable set of standards." He forced a 180-degree change in focus to "the customers. *They* were my concern. You don't want to screw up the customers." He centralized the buying of equipment, creating a purchasing group to gain economies of scale and some cohesion. He became so obsessive about controlling procurement that, Katherine Neville noted, "it got to the point where . . . you couldn't buy a pencil without his name on it." Still, she cheered the idea of controls and standards.

Hopper aggressively implemented Armacost's vision. He drove the ATM program hard; the target was fifteen hundred. He introduced "safe keeping" of checks—saving the bank enormous amounts of money in handling and mailing by holding on to the paper check instead of returning it to the customer. Customers were accepting it. He determined to end the archaic "paper factory" he had been shocked to find. And he pruned the jungle growth of projects by selectively canceling some. Neville saw that act creating another problem. "He started cutting back on projects, but not on staff. He didn't fire. You got this floating population of people waiting to be redeployed." He was not firing among the technocrats, where pruning was needed most, in Neville's view. Personnel costs continued to rise, even though they were the prime target of the cost-cutting strategy, a steady drag on Armacost's balance sheet. But Armacost had braced for the investment in technology and good people, knowing they were essential for survival over the long haul. Wriston's strategy. Hopper claims there were steady "cost declines for all operating units for which I had responsibility" for 1982 to 1985, with new people hired only for special or major corporate projects approved by the Managing Committee. His personnel swelled dramatically only, he says, when Mickel's operating centers—credit cards, real estate, and student loans—were shifted to Hopper. "At times," he says, "it rose to ten thousand people."

"Hopper's impulses were right. He just didn't go for the jugular quickly enough," says Neville of the early impact of "Max the Ax." His role in the installation of a controversial Tandem computer system had alarmed her; he had permitted the Tandem system to get installed, over his own, Neville's, and others' objections, explaining, "You've got to delegate and stand behind your vice-presidents when they feel this strongly. You can't have strong managers if you're always second-guessing them." Says Neville: "Baloney. The managers threw themselves on the ground, and Max gave in to them."

Hopper claims that he made major internal budget cuts but that, if he avoided some drastic cuts, it was not lack of toughness, but lack of clear authority. He had been dumped into the bureaucratic morass without clear lines of command. He reported to Jim Wiesler, who kept expanding Hopper's charter. Wiesler had given him the two credit card centers and the real estate loan center in November 1982. In February, "Sam asked me to prepare a paper for the overall consolidation of technology within the bank." He had never been asked a more challenging question: "How do you put a technology in place that solves the bank's strategic directions?" Armacost, it appeared, was finally giving him the world. But it intensified the human tensions. "I had two hats. Jim didn't like me spending my time mucking around with the rest of the bank." Hopper's line of command was becoming a confusing crosshatching of dotted and solid lines.

But hell, it was revolution. You expected power and lines of command to be in flux. "Positive contention" over business issues was natural and healthy; Armacost encouraged it.

Yet at the weekly meetings of the Managing Committee he was glimpsing a disquieting pattern that would build under Armacost, frustrating the talented team of imports Beck would lure: Armacost would hire a high-powered man, giving him a sweeping mandate to get a specific job done, but withholding the clear power and backup support to get it done. Armacost was permitting the same dangerous ambiguity of roles and powers that existed between him and his chairman, Lee Prussia. Before he left, Clausen had created what Armacost touted as "a team," but which, it seemed to some, let Prussia taste just enough presidential power to keep alive his frustration at losing out to Armacost. As cashier he held one of the bank's key power seats. At Managing Committee meetings, Hopper saw, Prussia was showing more concern than most "that things were not going well. But it was more of a Cassandra kind of thing. You didn't know how much of it was sour grapes."

In Prussia's outbursts Hopper was sensing "a lack of unified commitment to

Sam's vision." He had felt it in Wiesler. And others. Hostile factionalism was bubbling up. Explosions were contained by the mannerly code and the tightly structured formality of the meetings. But being revealed to Hopper, the newcomer, were deep-rooted ideological conflicts that could harden into war.

He saw it first, within five months of arrival, when deregulation of interest on checking accounts freed the bank to compete for deposits with its first money market account. Hopper had assumed there would be consensus "that we had to attack with a major thrust" with the kind of product that was at the very core of Armacost's strategy. But pushing for Managing Committee approval of an aggressive new product, the Cash Maximizer, created "almost a major split in the bank." In December Hopper won the fight, and "Cash Maximizer became one of the most profitable things the bank ever did." It would become everybody's pride, as it sucked in $8 billion within six months of its launch in early '82. But he had seen, at the highest levels, that Armacost was permitting resistance to the new world, putting his forward-looking dreams at risk.

The pressures of B of A's internal revolution within an environment of shrinking resources was revealing hostilities that had never before ruffled the inner circle. Hopper felt the hostility himself when he presented the paper on coordination of bankwide systems Armacost had asked him to do. He knew that, not being on the fortieth floor, he missed some of the political nuances. "But I thought Sam had greased a lot of skids. I was surprised that there was quite a bit of negative reaction at that meeting. I stepped on a lot of toes."

But that first year the great ship was under full sail, catching the winds well. An incredibly exciting time, Hopper felt. The Schwab acquisition had received the blessings of the Fed in January 1983. Bolin was going to be replaced in World Banking; a hunt was on for his successor. McLin was sniffing out troubled out-of-state banks for acquisition, taking advantage of a new opportunity: as the recession forced numbers of banks to their knees, the FDIC—to keep them from failing—was closing its eyes to the McFadden Act, which forbade interstate banking, and was allowing commercial banks to cross state lines to buy floundering banks. It was a loophole to territorial expansion, another chink in the wall of regulations. Hopper says, "Sam's view was that we would fill out the West Coast, become a strong operator there, then be able to move geographically."

WITHIN THE BANK Hopper was engaged in the extraordinary "total review of the culture" ordered by Armacost shortly after assuming the presidency. The redefining of the culture was taking visible form in a redesign of the color scheme of the corporate logo. The stylized logo Walter Landor had designed in the early seventies had achieved a high recognition factor, worldwide. That was worth gold. But the colors, white and black, were not compelling; there was concern that they turned the public off, that they did not express the new proactive identity Armacost was trying to spread through the old culture. Landor's designers came back in, conducted series of focus groups and staff meetings. The senior hierarchy of the bank met, in several Managing Committee meetings, to debate the new identity. The bank, Landor's team found, wanted to project an image of itself as "dynamic, aggressive." Landor's people repainted the logo bright red against a strong blue background. "The blue and red were very warm colors. They signaled a more human bank," Hopper said, cheering. Later, wags joked that the new color scheme was appropriate to the red ink that would soon show on the balance sheet. But as new signs went in at every branch, Armacost felt that "everybody felt pretty good about that . . . red was more a sign of aggression, self-confidence, more youthful."

Less visibly, the bank's historians searched through old Giannini materials in the archives "to get the flavor of what Giannini really was as an entrepreneur, as opposed to a patriarch," says Hopper. A.P.'s legacy had been magnified by the old-timers, Armacost felt, but was virtually unknown to younger BankAmericans. "But Sam did not try to glorify A.P. In fact, he tried to push the thrust that he had been very customer-focused, very aggressive in the marketplace." Armacost believed Giannini had been, at times, no doubt, "a tyrant." These revelations risked shattering the myth. Yet given time, this search might lead to resolution of the conflicts of purpose Hopper saw throughout the bank. "I thought it was a very healthy kind of thing. . . . We sat around for hours and debated things like whether A.P. had put service to people first or the bank's interest first." It was a real shock to Hopper that his colleagues didn't understand that banks are about service. "They were not that concerned about the customers, much less the shareholders. At the airline we do a tremendous amount of measurement at airports of how customers are treated, how fast they get their bags, and so on." It took intense debate before consensus was reached that indeed, A.P. had tried to serve the customer interest first. "But I'm not sure, to this day, Lee Prussia ever totally agreed with what we tried to push through." As the culture search deepened, Prussia, the gentlemanly BankAmerican who should have been Armacost's alter ego, his echo, was becoming a contrarian.

It was interminable, the time being taken by senior management in the raging debate over mission and purpose. It could thwart his "action plan," Armacost feared, "but it was critical to alter the culture of the executive suite if there was to be any hope of altering the culture of the whole organization."

For Armacost, the Boston Consulting Group was "wonderful at articulating broad overviews, but it was hard to capture the detail and implement it." He assigned Bob Beck and a senior team to synthesize the results and draft a statement of principles. "We wrote it," Armacost says proudly of the end result, a shiny white booklet published in 1982 called *Visions, Values and Strategies,* which would be pervasively quoted and distributed throughout the bank, worldwide, as the bank's ideological guidepost for the new age. Its tenet, "Leadership through serving people," became the bank's rallying theme. "I really thought it was extremely well done," says Hopper, whose power and visibility expanded with *Visions*'s emphasis on the importance of technology.

Reading it as a middle manager eager for clarity and inspiration, Katherine Neville was unconvinced. She felt it was vague. Gratuitous. Jargony. "It didn't give you a mandate to really go out and *do* anything." But it was, at least, a refreshing antidote to the foot-thick Operations Manual, which decreed that a loan should take 1,702 minutes to make and process. "That really is the mismatch of the culture," Armacost said ruefully to jabs that *Visions* was too vague. "It's the status quo needing to be told specifically what to do, and how and when to do it." Where was initiative? As Bank of America focused ever more intently on its own navel, it became clear that Armacost was going not for a quick, but for a fundamental, fix of MotherBank. A long-term effort that was "entirely appropriate," in Hopper's view.

Through 1982, Hopper recalls, "there was no hint that the bank was in sad trouble. There was almost a euphoric feeling that the bank could just do anything it wanted to."

Chapter Ten

MAX HOPPER'S EUPHORIA had survived two major shocks in the summer of 1982, as the recession that had swept the world's economies finally hit bank portfolios. First, there was the failure of Penn Square Bank. And then, the Mexican debt crisis. Momentum within the bank was so strong he scarcely noticed. But "Penn Square" and "Mexico" would, cumulatively, deliver withering blows to Armacost's vision of the future.

The two historic events hit just as Volcker was about to set in motion the beginnings of recovery that would pull the world back from the edge of depression. Pure monetarism would slink back to the realm of theory. But as the rest of the world began to smile again, banks found themselves in a frustrating position. "Typically bank problems lag behind economic problems because loans don't go bad all at once," explains Lee Cross, speaking for the Office of the Comptroller of the Currency (OCC), whose examiners diagnose sick loans. "You can even have banks getting worse with a recovery going on because they're still reflecting the problems of the recession that preceded it." For banks, the grim days were just beginning.

AS HE CHECKED into the Hilton in downtown Oklahoma City on the eve of the July Fourth weekend, Michael Patriarca used the tricks of a practiced spy to disguise his presence. Sacrificing his government room rate for secrecy, he registered as a private citizen, under his own name. Looking too youthful and academic for the tough job he had to do, Patriarca was, in fact, a senior enforcement officer from the Comptroller of the Currency, a hit man sent to "shoot people" the next day at Penn Square Bank. In his briefcase was the cease and desist order from the Comptroller of the Currency that would shut down banking operations. If word leaked that he was there, it could cause panic, he feared.

How could it have happened? The Comptroller's examiners audited Penn Square twice a year. In their asset quality examinations, they had been sampling loans and scrutinizing suspect areas. Combing SEC filings and the quarterly call reports sent to the Comptroller's Office for clues to where loan losses might come from. They had been monitoring the key measures of stability—capital and liquidity. Reading the board's minutes to see if the board was watching credit quality. Somehow, since the last examination, Penn Square's loan portfolios had become a disaster. The drop in oil prices was hurting loan portfolios throughout the Energy Belt, but Penn Square's management had been "imprudent to the extreme." The portfolios were rife with shoddy loans that would have to be charged off as losses. Examiners were finding "outlandish" personal loans to board members and even to the bank's outside auditors, Peat, Marwick, Mitchell & Co., the same Big Eight accounting firm that had, just months before, given Penn Square a clean bill of health. Several weeks before July 4, examiners had pulled together their preliminary conclusions. Penn Square was smelling like a major scandal. The examiners were going to force the bank to write off so many loans that it would eclipse the bank's capital. Penn Square would be insolvent.

Patriarca had issued a call for the bank's board to meet at 10:00 A.M., when he would make his "surgical strike"; he would deliver his order to the board and fly home to Washington the same day.

In simplest terms, the order was a demand that the board make an immediate infusion of more capital into the bank. If that did not occur over the weekend, Comptroller C. Todd Conover would make the dread declaration of insolvency on Monday. That act would pass the ball to the FDIC, the federal insurers of bank deposits, which must then either liquidate the bank or find new owners. Patriarca wanted to reach and talk to the FDIC men he knew were in the hotel. But they were registered under aliases. As he scanned the dining room next morning at breakfast, the only players he could be sure of were the bankers, there to protect their threatened interests in Penn Square. For Penn Square had packaged and sold off $800 million of its bad energy loans to other banks. "You can tell the Citibank types from the Continental Illinois types," he mused.

"It's Keystone Kops stuff," Patriarca knew. But the secrecy was vital to the "safety and soundness" of the banking system, the only charter of the regulators at the OCC. "Everybody gets up in the morning and salutes to safety and soundness," cracks Patriarca. "Supervising banks is the only activity the place engages in." Confidence was the key. Beyond all the safeguards built in since 1929—capital, reserves, deposit insurance, regular auditing—safety and soundness hung on public confidence. If that failed, bank runs could begin and the American banking system could still come unraveled. It could happen this weekend in Oklahoma, on the grand and glorious Fourth.

Penn Square was a mid-size bank—its assets were only half a billion dollars—but history showed that it took just one shot to start a war. A run on the smallest bank could become contagious and spread to the hundreds of oil patch banks whose energy loan portfolios were deteriorating daily. In the electronic marketplace it could escalate into a global run that, in the worst-case scenario, could close down the international banking system. Patriarca did not believe it would happen. But a run on Penn Square had already begun. It was a sight rarely seen in America since the depression, one which he, at thirty-two, had never seen. Rumors of trouble had leaked before he left Washington. A reporter for the *American Banker* newspaper had broken the story. Local TV and other media in Oklahoma City had picked it up. Stores stopped accepting checks drawn on Penn Square. There were lines outside the bank as customers pulled deposits. Cars lined up at the drive-up window. Holed up in his hotel room, Patriarca watched the chilling event on television.

Although there were some storm troopers among them, examiners were not in the business of closing banks. Hired and trained directly from college, they had the esprit of an elite military corps. They prided themselves on being an independent unit within Treasury. Their job was to catch problems before they became desperate. Pride was badly bruised if any bank scandal made the nightly news. Broadcast around the world by the wire services, Penn Square's crisis was becoming global news.

The OCC must contain the crisis. As Patriarca went through his cease and desist duties in Oklahoma City, the deputy comptroller met in Washington with representatives of the banks that had the most to lose, those that had bought energy loans from Penn Square: Continental Illinois of Chicago, Seafirst of Seattle, and Chase Manhattan of New York. In an eleventh-hour attempt to save the bank, "he told them, in essence, 'This baby's going down the chute. Who *knows* what's going to happen if this thing fails? You guys ought to think about whether you want to, collectively, infuse capital into this institution,' " says Patriarca. "They all said, 'Thanks, but no thanks.' " Over the weekend of the Fourth, the overseers of the nation's banking system—the secretary of the treasury, Comptroller Conover, the FDIC's William M. Isaac, Volcker, and the governors of the Fed—met in urgent debate over the fundamental issue: Should market discipline prevail and the bank be permitted to die of its own greed and ineptitude? Or should the government step in? Free marketeers argued that in an overcrowded banking industry, market forces should be allowed to weed out the weak. But if the government's obligation was to maintain stability, the argument for stepping in went, Penn Square's collapse could give off a dangerous message to the world and undermine confidence in the system.

"The forces of market discipline won out," says Patriarca. Conover, who had joined Reagan's new team as a free-market idealist, acted on his ideology. On Monday he declared Penn Square insolvent and turned it over to the FDIC as receiver.

William Isaac, the FDIC chairman, flew to Oklahoma City the same day. Making it a media event, he held Penn Square up as an example of slipshod banking and stunned the banks with his announcement: Only insured deposits would be repaid by the FDIC. Uninsured deposits—the deposits in excess of $100,000 held largely by institutional investors—would not, as banks had hoped they would be to hold confidence in the system. Many depositors would be hurt; many millions lost. The shareholders would be wiped out, and management fired. "What that said is that the U.S. government is not necessarily going to stand behind its large banks," as virtually every other advanced nation did, as Patriarca saw it. "This may have been a moderate-sized bank, but the implications were significant beyond belief. It made the financial system a much more volatile place," he observed. In the weeks after Penn Square, Patriarca's examiners reported increasing jumpiness among depositors at any hint of bad news about a bank. Japan and London were especially nervous. Examiners were monitoring Continental Illinois, the nation's twelfth-largest bank, and Seafirst—the leading bank in the Pacific Northwest. Two major banks wounded and the world's markets scared by the irresponsible peccadilloes of a little midwestern energy bank.

In samurai Japan the examiners would have committed ceremonial hara-kiri. In the wake of the humiliation of Penn Square, the Comptroller of the Currency dramatically changed the examination process. From now on, examination schedules would be driven "by reality, not the calendar," Patriarca reports. There would be continuous monitoring of the biggest banks. Examiners would have an office in the banks and be there full-time. Suspicious loans would be examined with a microscope. No longer would examiners rely on the honor system, or seat-of-the-pants judgments by loan officers as to the "goodness" or "badness" of their loans. They would pry and probe into loan portfolios and haul the bad loans out. Banking would no longer be played like a gentleman's game.

Bank of America would hate it. Since A.P., it had felt itself in an adversarial role with the examiners, their presence an insult to an institution respected worldwide for its credit quality. But with Penn Square, the game changed. Regulators had been permissive with the big banks, permitting them to operate with less capital than the smaller banks. With the stability of its huge deposit base, B of A had been allowed, and had assumed, more leniency than most. Now there would be more pressure to build capital and loan loss reserves. Straining resources even more as earnings declined, Armacost would face a more rigorous federal auditing environment than banks had ever known.

Patriarca would be the man Armacost must deal with. For he had been promoted, after Penn Square, from enforcement officer to deputy comptroller for twelve multinational banks. He had most of the giants and some large regionals. Citibank, Continental Illinois, Security Pacific, Wells Fargo, Bank of Boston. And Bank of America.

MONT MCMILLEN was in attendance at the birth of the third world debt crisis. Two months earlier he had ruled from London Bank of America's most elegant feudal barony—the Europe/Middle East/Africa Division, most prestigious and profitable of the bank's four international divisions. But McMillen had been snatched home and shifted laterally to head the sprawling North American Division (NAD), whose portfolios were stuffed with the energy, agricultural, and real estate loans that looked increasingly vulnerable as recession deepened through the first half of 1982.

The move had actually been a vote of confidence from Armacost. NAD held all the commercial loans in the United States, plus Mexico. For the first half of '82 NAD's domestic loan losses were running far ahead of foreign losses. NAD was shaping to be the front line, Armacost could see. "We put Mont there because we thought he was strong and decisive enough to handle it," he says. But the move had shocked colleagues who had watched McMillen race the fast track and had expected him to come home and replace Bill Bolin as head of the World Banking Division. McMillen had arrived just in time to see Mexico, a model of hope for Central America and an important profit center for the bank, escalate into an international emergency.

Now, on August 20, McMillen found himself in a large meeting room at the New York Fed, waiting for the arrival of "Chucho" and "Angel," both well known to the bankers. Finance Minister Jesús Silva Herzog and Director of Mexico's Department of Public Credit Ángel Gurria had been wooed and

courted, wined and dined by this crowd. They had been—until yesterday—
superstars of the international syndicated loan circuit as the banks lined up to
pour money into the Mexican "miracle." With oil wealth that poured in from
1977, when PEMEX released word that vast reserves had been found, Mexico
had been able to pay its bills, to borrow as well as spend, and to achieve a
growth rate of 5 to 6 percent a year, apparently catapulting the country from
poverty level to the cusp of industrialized nation status. Its democratic government had credibility in the world's trade and capital markets and an increasing
voice in international affairs.

"The banks were full of petrodollars and were facing a recession in industrial countries—they did not have anyone to loan their money to—and the
developing countries, especially those that had petroleum, became very attractive clients," says Silva, reflecting on the rush of lending that accelerated in the
late seventies, ensnaring them all. "The banks were hot to get in. All the banks
in the U.S. and Europe and Japan stepped forward. They showed no foresight.
They didn't do any credit analysis. It was wild," Gurria agrees. But Mexico
was paying now for an even wilder national spree. "To the oil revenues of just
under fifty billion dollars from 1976 to 1982, we added a debt of almost fifty
billion dollars. We spent a hundred billion dollars in five years," said Silva
regretfully, "but to be nouveau riche is a very difficult situation that almost
nobody can resist, and we were nouveau riche. The country was growing too
rapidly. However, the voices of caution in '80, '81, and '82 were very few, and
those few were not heard."

Telexes had been flying all week giving bankers the skeletal facts. Mexico
was in extremis.

Gurria and Silva carried in their briefcases appalling financial data: Mexico
was almost out of cash to run the country and to pay interest on its foreign
debts. By Monday Mexico would be "illiquid," to use the banker's term. For
Mexico, it was the worst economic crisis since the 1920s. Its foreign debt stood
at $80 billion. By Gurria's calculations, it needed at least $2 billion emergency
money and a $20 billion package of rescheduled and new loans. The two were
flying to Washington to demand help from the world's financial community.
They would say to Paul Volcker, to the secretary of the treasury and the
Comptroller of the Currency, to the IMF, the World Bank, and commercial
banks—to President Reagan, if necessary—that Mexico's crisis was the
world's crisis. Mexico needed time to pay interest. Old loans extended. New
money to keep the country operating and current on its loans. And a long-term
solution that would enable the country to shed the burden of debt without
making its internal growth hostage to the world's commercial banks.

Mexico was not the first country of the petrodollar era to struggle with its foreign debt. Most of the men the two Mexican officials would see in the United States were veterans of debt reschedulings over the past few years. Turkey, Zaire, Peru, Nicaragua, Sudan, Jamaica, Poland had given the banks isolated scares. Troubles were currently erupting in Rumania, Costa Rica, Senegal, Liberia. But there had been nothing of this magnitude.

As Gurria and Silva sped to the airport for the flight by government jet to Washington, their financial condition mirrored Mexico's: The two men were actually penniless. They did not have enough dollars between them to catch a cab from Dulles Airport. American Express had canceled use of Mexican-based credit cards. Searching pockets and petty cash boxes, aides had scraped together $46 American before they boarded. That Silva should be playing the role of hat-in-hand debtor was, he thought, the ultimate irony. "I hate personal debt. I don't like credit cards or owing anybody." How could Mexico have come to this?

Some of the seeds of trouble lay in the last two presidents, Luis Echeverría and José López Portillo, whose term as president would finish in a month. "The squandering and corruption were outrageous; it brought the country down," says then Chairman of the New York Federal Reserve Anthony Solomon, with the benefit of business experience in Mexico twenty-five years earlier. Inflation contributed. The government's lavish spending on infrastructure and industrial development had dumped into the economy "too much money chasing too few goods," familiar prelude to inflation, Joseph Kraft claims in his report of the crisis, *The Mexican Rescue,* published by the Group of Thirty. As the peso lost its value, capital began to flee the country. "By July a hundred million dollars a day was leaving the country," said an alarmed Silva, watching much of it flood into offshore Bank of America accounts. Capital flight meant loss of confidence by Mexicans in their country and bled the nation of the resources it so desperately needed invested at home.

Volcker's recession, hitting Mexico in 1981, had been the coup de grace. The high interest rates that came with it "raised dramatically the cost of servicing their foreign debts," Armacost explains. "Just a few points' rise in the rates added billions to the interest they had to pay the banks. It was billions they'd never borrowed but would have to pay back." With the recession-induced drop in oil and other commodity prices, and sluggish global trade, Mexico's income—its source of dollars to pay its debts—declined. But basically, it was the petrodollar lending coming home to roost; Mexico was the first major country to experience the full rolling fallout.

Trying to compensate for lost income, Mexico had continued to borrow aggressively from the banks, deepening its debt. There had been two stopgap fixes by the Fed. "But six hundred million dollars in April was gone in a week.

A $2.5 billion emergency loan from banks raised by a bank syndicate headed by B of A, vanished in two days," Gurria reported. Mont McMillen had flown to Mexico City in June to preside over the ceremonial signing. Mexico was losing money at the rate of $100 million a day. In the weeks before the meetings with commercial banks, Silva had met with the Treasury and the Fed to arrange for additional emergency financing. But by August 16 the nation would be broke.

It was, officially, Treasury's show. But with the banks at risk, Paul Volcker played a potent intermediary role. He got on the phone and set up a meeting with the chairmen of the central banks of six nations that, with the United States, were to raise $1.5 billion for Mexico. They met in Basel, Switzerland, at the headquarters of the Bank for International Settlements (BIS) on August 18. With Sir Gordon (later Lord) Richardson, chairman of the Bank of England and a sympathetic ally, in the chair, the full BIS membership pledged most of its $750 million share.

The bankers had invited Silva to appoint an "advisory" committee of creditor banks—the banks that were owed the most and had been friendliest to Mexico. By any name, the committee was the traditional shirt-sleeved workout team charged with protecting the banks' interests and collecting on troubled loans. Using secret lists of their whereabouts, Silva reached the CEOs of the 8 key banks and sent telexes to 860 more, urging attendance at a morning meeting in New York, August 20. McMillen flew east to represent Bank-America. Senior representatives from 115 international banks joined him in the large auditorium at the New York Fed.

Solomon chaired the meeting. He had been at the eye of the hurricane as Carter's undersecretary of the treasury during the petrodollar lending rush of the mid-seventies. As Volcker's successor at the New York Fed and vice-chairman of the Federal Reserve Open Money Committee, he had shared in the historic policy change to monetarism in 1979 that had helped drive Mexico to its dilemma.

But even as he introduced the distressed Mexicans to an auditorium full of worried bankers, Solomon stood by the Fed decision in '79 that had set the recessionary chain of events in motion.

After setting the tone, Solomon handed the meeting over to Silva and Gurria. Silva was a man of sharp and subtle intellect, of unflappable poise and wry wit. Sweeping over what McMillen called "the macro stuff," he opened the door to the new order that must ultimately transcend banks' insistence on full repayment. "I am convinced that the responsibility for the debt problem must be shared between debtors and creditors. . . . I don't see the way to resolve this problem unless it is with an adequate dose of debt relief." Rescheduling. New money. But debt relief could mean the banks' forgiving—or writing off!—some of Mexico's debt. A violation of the most basic tenet of banking, a tenet so staunchly held that it would still be the principal stumbling block in 1989.

In contrast to Silva's statesmanly style, Gurria revealed his emotions, turning the crisis into taut theater. He had appeared at one of the high-level meetings in Washington haggard, unshaven, crumpled, spilling his coffee with nervousness. With his black beard, piercing eyes, and heavy brows giving him "a Rasputin look," Gurria riveted the bankers' attention. At the meeting he delivered his wish list: rolling over the old loans; new money to pay the banks' interest.

Gurria kept nervous watch on the bankers. For months the market had been showing resistance to putting new money into Mexico. They would resist this bailout, he sensed. He was hopeful as Citi's Bill Rhodes said, "I believe the banks will be willing to support Mexico in its hour of need." Finally McMillen, one of the most influential men there, rose to speak. The quintessential international BankAmerican, tall, impeccably groomed, and mannerly, Anglo-Saxon handsome, youthful and fit as Armacost, McMillen told Gurria and Silva, "We have so much on the table, we're going to stand by Mexico and help out." Gurria told the press, triumphant, that "all the banks agreed to cooperate with Mexico in finding a solution. . . . It was 'we' will do this, and 'we' will solve the problem."

"It wasn't Ángel's presentation that made me stand up and clap." McMillen shrugged. "We had very few options."

At risk was Bank of America's $2.5 billion Mexican loan portfolios. A fact that would have shocked customers who drew a sense of security from the bank's very size was that B of A's foreign loans surpassed its total capital. Its Mexican loans, alone, equaled 48 percent of its capital. If Mexico, and one or two other Latin American countries, were to default, Bank of America would be as insolvent as Penn Square. Like Bank of America, several of the biggest banks had more than 100 percent of their capital committed to loans in potentially troubled nations. "If just the three biggest Latin debtors default, every major bank in the U.S., except Morgan, fails," said an alarmed Bank of America economist. Compounding the risk, many of the loans were to the private sector, where there was no recourse, no government guarantee, if the loans defaulted. Drawing confidence from Pepe Carral's inside track, Bank of America had plunged in where other banks had shied away. By 1982 nearly half of the bank's Mexican loans were in the private sector. They were high-risk, but they paid high interest. The yields were so high that a senior First Interstate foreign loan man admitted, "We make loans to the country so that we'll have a crack at the private companies." The Fed's Solomon later grumbled, "But the yields were never commensurate to the risk."

McMillen had known a year earlier that all was not perfect in the bank's third world portfolios. He had been directly embroiled in the Polish crisis, "the first big debt experience." At $30 billion, Poland's debt was less than half of Mexico's. But Bank of America was the largest U.S. lender to Poland. "All of us recognized when Poland went that the rest of COMECON [the European Eastern bloc] was right behind." He had seen Clausen cutting back loans to Eastern Europe and trying to exit Africa in 1979 and '80. "But it was not seen in terms of a global crisis. There was no inkling that the rest of the world was going." In fact, dynamic Latin American countries like Brazil had sat at the negotiating table as fellow bank creditors in Poland, a heartening rite of passage into membership in the Western banking system. But McMillen could see, as Mexico shaped to a crisis, that "Poland is where it all started."

Now Mexico was seeking a bailout. A hated idea in Reagan Washington. Tampering with market forces. But the United States could not allow Mexico, unlike Penn Square, to fail. Sharing a thousand-mile border with the United States, Mexico was not only a major trading partner but "the most tempting target for Communist adventurism in the Southern Hemisphere," as an analyst reminded.

The United States committed itself to buying $1 billion of agricultural products and $1 billion of Mexican oil for its strategic oil reserves. Mexico would be paid on Monday in the form of short-term bank loans. It was not a humanitarian gesture. The U.S.'s Office of Management and Budget demanded a fee of $100 million—an oil fee equivalent to *90 percent interest*. Outraged, López Portillo ordered his team home from Washington and all negotiations canceled. It was a dangerous bit of brinkmanship. Mexico could not afford to cut itself off from the world's marketplace—from capital, from trade. Pride would not permit it to be perceived by the club of advanced countries as an irresponsible renegade. Yet this could not be borne. "Those were moments, or hours, in which I felt deep emotions and a great responsibility," says Silva of the climactic deal breaker. "On the following day the history of the world would probably change. . . . Mexico was . . . probably going to declare a global moratorium on all its external payments."

U.S. Ambassador to Mexico John Gavin and the Treasury's point man, Deputy Secretary Tim McNamar, rushed to visit Gurria and Silva at their suite at the Watergate, negotiated a 50 percent cut in the fee, and, by phone, López Portillo agreed. He would be enraged again, later, when examination of the numbers revealed that Mexico had paid the equivalent of over 30 percent interest for the loans. But his country would still be in business on Monday morning.

The long-term fix for the debt coming due in 1983 and 1984 was a larger problem. The IMF was flying a team to Mexico, preamble to the possibility of money and mandatory economic reforms, the "austerity programs" relied on by the commercial banks as a watchdog for their loans, but so hated by the countries that they fueled riots and the overthrow of governments. Most of the money would have to come from the banks.

THE U.S. BANKERS met at Citibank on the afternoon of August 20 to plot the next step. Chairing the informal gathering was Citi's Thomas C. Theobald, who, with McMillen, was still acting cochair of the fledgling bankers' committee. McMillen had appointed as B of A's point man Preston Bennett, an old Mexico hand as well as an experienced credit administrator. But he hadn't arrived in New York yet. Bill Rhodes had been appointed for Citibank. At the Citibank meeting "Rhodes was Theobald's bag carrier." McMillen laughed in hindsight. By the time Bennett arrived to take his chair, Rhodes had been asked by Mexico to take the leadership role.

Rhodes—tireless and "the most pragmatic man I ever met," in Gurria's judgment—was a low-key commercial banker with fluency in Spanish gained from twelve years in Venezuela and the Caribbean, and an unassuming ease in the diplomatic situation. With a style of cultured erudition honed by the study of classical art and architecture and Eastern European history at Brown University, he had cultivated and earned friendly access to everyone—in Washington and in the countries. With dark hair brushed neatly back, slim build, and glasses giving an academic look to an attractive, fine-featured face, he did not look a likely candidate for the Metternich of international debt. Usually in shirtsleeves, he lacked only green eyeshades to look like a back office accountant. But supported by Citicorp's commanding international network, he had the unflappable poise of the British colonial soldier backed by the gunboats of empire—a poise that would survive years of marathon negotiations and the petulance of proud sovereign debtors. As Senior Corporate Officer for Latin America, a vital profit center for Citibank, he sat on Citicorp's Policy Committee with Wriston. He was seen also as a mediator between Volcker and Wriston, a man able to oil the waters between the two towering rivals. He would swiftly be appointed head of the advisory committees for Argentina, Uruguay, and Peru, and in 1983, would be asked by Volcker and Wriston to chair the Brazilian committee.

The very different styles of the two men, Rhodes and Bennett, summed up the differences between the New York money center banks and the big California bank. "Pres was a California product. His shoes weren't quite as shiny as the New York bankers. He didn't have an M.B.A., and he just didn't care about the old school tie. But at the end of the day he'd achieve something of substance," says McMillen, who took pride in the bank's senior role in the committees. "We were respected, consulted," Armacost confirms. But the informal shifting of Bennett to a secondary role paralleled a painful fact of history occurring in 1982: Citibank had won the decades-long race to be the biggest bank in the United States. The crown had passed back and forth for several years. But the "slow-moving tortoise" praised in a *Forbes* article in 1980 as likely to win the longer race had, by '82, been decisively passed in asset size by the "livelier hare."

There had always been workout men—specialists in collecting troubled loans. They were the cleanup brigade; it was the lending officers who were banking's princes. But as the third world debt crisis became the dominant international economic problem, Rhodes and Bennett were the pioneers of a new breed of workout banker; theirs would be the global workout that never ends. Endurance would prove the most valuable trait for a tedious job that would prove as much political as economic. The process would be dressed in an aura of high purpose; the international financial system was being saved. Endless cycles of marathon negotiations would plod to the drums and flourishes of international protocol. Dining, signing, and toasting with presidents and ministers, crisscrossing the Southern Hemisphere with the urgency of a secretary of state, Rhodes would be the first workout man to become an international superstar.

He led bankers who had suddenly been thrust into a new function. Finding creative alternatives to collecting debts in the old-fashioned way was the new challenge. Over the next few years, devising debt and equity swaps, bartering, converting debt to investment in the countries, offering appealing "menus of options" with such devices as "exit bonds" would become as hot an area for the financial "rocket scientist" as creating new money market and float products for the consumer market in the United States. They were more than products; they were potential solutions to the debt crisis.

The first and most pressing need for the banks was to avoid nonaccrual—to avoid having to declare a three-month nonpayment of interest on the loans, a reduction in earnings, and damage to the shareholders. It was clear that the only way interest could be paid was if banks lent Mexico the money to pay it. "The banks were funding countries' financial gaps," says Rhodes, defending the process against attack as a contrived charade. "Not only did the debtor country want to do it that way, in order to retain its credit reputation," adds Solomon, "but also this permitted the banks to continue to show the loan as a good loan." The loan itself wasn't the problem. Loans could be rolled over for twenty, thirty years. It was the interest payments. Over the lifetime of the loan, interest amounted to 85 percent of the country's total obligation, while principal—the $40 or $100 million originally lent in the late seventies—was only 15 percent. If they could keep interest payments coming, it would buy the banks precious time to build up their loan loss reserves and capital to withstand the shocks that were bound to come from other Latin American countries. They could "grow into" the crisis. "The strategy . . . was also aimed at giving the countries time to restructure their economies and grow out of crisis," Rhodes claims. The pattern of banks lending to keep their own interest payments current began.

As they packed their bags for the first rescheduling negotiations, the inchoate beginnings of a new era, bankers resisted seeing the seminal point: "The debt burden is too large for the countries," said Lew Coleman, who would later face the crisis as head of B of A's World Banking but who was then struggling with Wells Fargo's relatively small Mexican exposure. Bankers, he feared, were locked into the sacred idea that, "By God, everybody pays their debts. It's a tenet of banking, even though we've all charged off loans before."

By late September, as the world's financial leaders converged on Toronto for the joint annual meeting of the IMF/World Bank, the sense of unease pervading the banking community had risen to the level of stark panic. "It's surprise that causes panic," said John Heimann, former Comptroller of the Currency, viewing the series of shocks served up in the past few weeks. The deepening recession. Poland. Mexico. And, on the eve of the IMF meetings, President López Portillo, trying to control the flight of capital from Mexico, had nationalized Mexico's banks and ordered exchange controls, sending another jolt of fear through the Toronto gathering.

Armacost flew into Toronto with McMillen, to meetings that had become "an overblown affair where the speeches are just prewritten political statements that achieve nothing," Armacost felt. They had become a great money bazaar. Since the petrodollar lending binge began, the commercial bankers had come not as delegates but to make contacts and do business. Plying their trade over caviar and champagne at private clubs, chic hotels, art galleries, and townhouses, they had learned to scan the ID cards chained around everyone's neck with the acuity of peregrine falcons, to target central bankers and finance ministers from capital-hungry countries, and swoop down adroitly. This year, with fear in the air, the exotics were not the sought-after stars as in past years, when retinues from Zambia, Indonesia, Brazil, and Nepal strutted and preened, picking and choosing among the bankers lusting to be lead bank in huge syndicated loans. With the shock of Mexico, the financial leaders of emerging nations were making the first macho-shattering adjustments to being treated like bad debtors. Protocol would be maintained, of course.

There would be few new loans. But the men from Chase, Morgan, Barclays, and Sumitomo were already shifting to talk of trade financing, currency exchanges, and short-term credit lines. They would soon talk "menus of options"—the smorgasbord of swapping, discounting and investing debt that would emerge from the decade's obsessive search for ways to exit the third world debt arena without having to declare huge losses on their balance sheets.

This year the place was electric. The Mexican crisis dominated everything—the talk and gossip in the halls, the cocktail parties, the private meetings and dinners. Gurria and Silva were the center of attention. They were besieged for interviews by hundreds of journalists, and their elusiveness only fed the fears and rumors.

"Bankers were very worried about collapse," says Robert Carswell, a partner at Citibank's principal outside lawyers Shearman & Sterling and former deputy secretary of the Treasury—a man who had seen banking panic in the Iran hostage, Hunt Silver, and New York City crises—of the Toronto meetings. Walter Wriston described the scene: "We had a hundred and fifty-odd finance ministers, fifty-odd central bankers, a thousand journalists, a thousand commercial bankers, a large supply of whiskey, and a reasonably small city that produced an enormous head of steam driving the engine called 'the end of the world is coming.' "

It was largely Wriston who had led the bankers along the path of third world debt. He had plunged with petrodollars when they first appeared in 1973, and had the most foreign debt: Citibank had $2.8 billion in Latin America, compared with Bank of America's $2.5 billion. "Bankers tend to move in herds," Gurria knew, and more than a thousand bankers had followed the leader. Wriston had held bankers' hands through '73 and '79, the two oil shocks that quadrupled the price of oil, amid predictions that "the lights are going out all over the free world, we all are going to starve to death, freeze to death, and the Arabs will own the world." He had happened to be in the office of the secretary of the treasury when the first shock hit and had reassured the secretary that "Only the market can manage this crisis."

Even as third world lending began to backfire, Wriston was delighted with the bankers' role. He believed that recycling Arab oil dollars had been "the greatest transfer of financial assets in the shortest time frame in the history of the world, with the most minor casualties—really only Herstatt Bank . . . Japan, that imports a hundred percent of its oil—it adjusted. And Brazil. Except for the U.S., the *world* adjusted. . . . Those of us who believed that the market would absorb the shock of skyrocketing oil prices proved correct." With the same optimism in the face of panic in Toronto, he predicted, "No

American bank would fail because of foreign debt. . . . But lots of them will fail on American real estate and oil."

It was Volcker, not Citibank, Wriston reminded, who had brought them to this. How could the banks know, Wriston asked emphatically and often, "that Volcker would lock the wheels of the world and cause the worst depression since the 1930s?" As chairman of President Reagan's economic policy board, he and "our little committee" had been called in at the Mexican crisis to see Reagan, and Wriston had reassured the president, "It's a mess, but it's manageable. There will be all kinds of troubles, but it will not bring down the free world." But "we had a runaway recession, we had a tide moving in public opinion for which there was no counterbalance, which was dangerous. So I decided we needed a counterbalance about the end of the world. . . . We needed to waken the marketplace."

In an essay printed on the *New York Times* op-ed page on September 14, 1982, a week after the Toronto meetings, Wriston made the statement that would prove the most controversial of the third world debt crisis: A country does not go bankrupt. "Over the years, a lot of intellectual capital has been invested in the proposition that massive defaults by developing countries will eventually cause a severe world financial crisis. Those who took that view in 1973–74 have been proved wrong." There were few recorded instances in history, he claimed, of government—including the United States—actually getting out of debt. Debts are rolled over; "in the U.S., it's called the weekly Treasury bill auction. When problems arise, they are problems of liquidity, not insolvency. The country does *not* go bankrupt. Bankruptcy is a procedure developed in Western law to forgive the obligations of a person or a company that owes more than it has. Any country, however badly off, will 'own' more than it 'owes.' " He had planted the idea that the debt crisis was a cash-flow problem that sound programs and time would cure—not the complex economic problem that would be revealed five years later.

"I knew when I wrote it I would be the target of people who didn't understand the problem. But it caused a *fire storm*!" Within a year, as seventeen countries followed Mexico into financial crisis, he was vilified, he says, as "that jerk who said that countries don't go bankrupt"—a dangerous Pied Piper who had lured banks and nations into complacency. "It was wonderful. It diverted attention and gave them a good handle to beat me up." The controversy thrust Wriston into a subcareer of setting the record straight. "What I said was: 'The country has an infrastructure. It has railroads, mines, factories, people, governments; it has enormous resources. The definition of bankruptcy is when your liabilities exceed your assets. By definition, a country is not bankrupt if it has a hundred twenty-five million people, is self-sufficient in iron ore and copper and [has] an export surplus of ten billion dollars.' *That's* what I said. But it's an argument that takes more than one line."

But Wriston's reassurances did not make the Mexican mess go away. Or answer the question, How could so many smart bankers have been taken by surprise in Mexico? De Larosière has said, in hindsight, that even the IMF did not know. It had seen only that Mexico had delayed filing its balance of payments accounts, but did not sense disaster. "The lending went on right through until 1982," says attorney Carswell, defending Treasury's role. "The level of lending to the developing countries only began getting very high in late '79, '80, '81, after the second oil shock," Solomon confirms.

By the late seventies every bank had created its country risk analysis, encouraged—and, finally, forced—by the regulators. Among the regulators, "We had our country risk analysis in place in 1979," says Carswell, who helped draft it, "but clearly it failed." *Risks of International Bank Lending,* a Group of Thirty study coauthored by John Heimann, Comptroller of the Currency in the late seventies, and published just months before the Mexican crisis, had sounded the call, warning, with exquisite understatement: "There have been no major disasters for the international banking system. . . . However, our survey confirms that most bankers believe that risks have increased and will increase more rapidly in the future. . . . Competitive pressures may lead banks to override country risk assessments and engage in imprudent lending." B of A's Chairman Lee Prussia—head of World Banking during the late seventies spurt of lending that swelled commercial bank loans to a $400 billion total by 1981—had been one of the report's ten authors; he *knew* the growing risks. And yet B of A's Latin American loan portfolio continued to grow—70 percent in the three short years from 1979—under both Clausen and Armacost.

Within B of A, voices of concern had been building steadily. Lyle Krapf, a senior credit officer in NAD, had reportedly fought loans to Mexico, actually quit over it—as had Joe Pinola in 1975—but was hired meekly back in another department. In April, five months before the crisis, "Pres" Bennett had run into resistance getting a $2.5 billion syndicate subscribed, sign of shaky confidence among the banks. The bank had had evidence that Mexico was having difficulty repaying capital in 1977, for it led a bailout syndicate for Mexico's biggest steelmaker when the peso dived. "The loans had been getting longer and longer terms," Armacost had noted. Trade financing, usually ninety days, "was stretching out five, six years." Delaying the day of reckoning.

"Bankers knew what was going on," claims Armacost, as a new consciousness pushed up through the panic in Toronto. It was government that did not, he claims, in spite of regulators' efforts to get risk analysis going. "Only Volcker saw the implications and lectured for moderation," he says. The State Department saw banks as "an instrument," says McMillen, still chuckling over his contretemps with a State Department official at the 1981 IMF/World Bank meetings in Washington. "He sidled up to me at a cocktail party in the guarded way they have and suggested that it would be very helpful if the banks were to cooperate in keeping Yugoslavia nonaligned with Russia by issuing new loans. 'There's no goddamned way they're getting any more money from me,' " McMillen had responded.

Like collective grieving in the face of disaster, the IMF/World Bank meetings in Toronto may have been the ceremonial release needed by the community of bankers who shared the shock of Mexico's debt crisis. For the Western banking system survived Toronto. Negotiations for the final phases of the Mexican "save" went on through the fall and into a climactic meeting at the New York Fed on November 16. IMF Managing Director Jacques de Larosière de Champfeu had become the ringmaster. The presidents or chairmen of the thirteen banks on the advisory committee met for the presentation of the plan he had hammered out and had had approved by Volcker and Richardson of the Bank of England. Lew Preston attended for Morgan. Lee Prussia for Armacost. There were bankers from Canada, Japan, Switzerland, West Germany and France. Wriston, there for Citibank, had sent the Citibank plane to the Caribbean to bring Rhodes back from vacation—the last he was to have for years. The bankers were stunned. "When de Larosière said the whole IMF deal was conditional on the banks putting up $5 billion in new money, we were shocked. When he said we had to have the money by December 15, we were appalled," said an officer from a British bank, as Joseph Kraft reports.

A relieved Silva later said of the moment, "It brought out the strength in people. Events made de Larosière rise big and tall—as great events tend to do." But the banks saw de Larosière as a tyrant. With the clock ticking toward the day when they must declare the Mexican loans as nonaccruing, they set feverishly to work, speeding a job that would normally take many months. "Within ten days we had the restructuring done and a twenty-foot-long telex written to send to all the banks," Gurria says exultantly. De Larosière announced that the IMF would pledge its money and play the watchdog role the banks relied on. As overseer and enforcer, the International Monetary Fund had installed itself "at the apex of the creditor pyramid," as Professor Frieden describes the power role the IMF would continue to play throughout the 1980s. But Mexico was "saved."

Mexico had brought the greatest lending boom in history to a crashing halt. It had, as Gurria dramatically stated, "changed the world." To Armacost, Mexico was a "warning bell" that this was not just a short-term, cyclical cash-flow problem. "Mexico was the first shot across the bow that this was a political crisis and would eventually become a taxpayer issue."

Within the year an epidemic of rescheduling had begun, with Brazil, the largest of the Latin American debtors, beginning the process that would lead to its petulant moratorium in 1987. By 1985 *Foreign Affairs'* annual chronology of the world's most significant events would be overwhelmingly dominated by reschedulings of foreign debt.

JUMPY FROM PENN SQUARE, the regulators reacted boldly after Mexico, expanding their control over banks' involvement in foreign debt. Again, they'd failed to stave off crisis. ICERC, the powerful triumvirate of the Fed, Comptroller, and FDIC that, since 1979, had met informally to review the creditworthiness of foreign debtor countries, was formalized in 1983 by an act of Congress. ICERC immediately passed a new rule that would hit Armacost hard. From now on, any seriously troubled country would be examined and "classified" on a one-to-five scale. All banks would be required to put up reserves against loans to any country that had been classified "value-impaired." It was unprecedented. The decision to reserve had always been the prerogative of the banks.

There was another change, one that would strike Armacost's vision a blow. Until now banks took reserves from their earnings against specific losses but still counted them on the balance sheet as a form of *capital*. Now it appeared that, in addition to individual loss, *country risk itself* would have to be reserved. "With B of A's sizable portfolio, the thought is chilling," said Armacost, scowling.

Yet Armacost felt confident about B of A's strength. As Mexico opened the floodgates on the third world debt crisis, foreign write-offs were still a relatively insignificant part of B of A's loan losses in the 1982 annual report. "Net loan losses were $432.7 million," B of A reported, double the 1981 figure. Seventy percent of the bank's losses were still domestic, mostly small and mid-size businesses, even though foreign loan losses had doubled from the previous year. But ICERC's new weapon, combined with the live-in examiners and continuous auditing that were a legacy of Penn Square, meant that deteriorating portfolios and the reserves against them would more quickly be revealed. Armacost wanted it that way. He had been pleading, "Bring me your problems," and had put a hard-nosed new chief, William V. Young, into Latin America. Young had run Eastern Europe through the Polish and Yugoslavian crises and would not be afraid to dump the problems on Armacost's desk. But no one had any idea of the magnitude of the disaster that sat in the foreign loan portfolios filled, mostly, on Clausen's watch.

AS THE WORLD DEBT CRISIS erupted like a young volcano and bubbled up into a dominant world issue, the powerful treasurer of the World Bank under both McNamara and Clausen, Eugene Rotberg, saw with regret that, as the IMF took the lead role, the World Bank "was being looked upon as a minor player." Running the World Bank, aloof from the panic of the commercial banks, Tom Clausen was positioned for statesmanship. Yet a look of fear and blustering confusion still occasionally flashed in his eyes, betraying that even the presidency of the World Bank had not erased Tom Clausen's boyish awe of men of "weight and importance," as a senior Citibanker called the international power pack that was Clausen's peer group. His campmates saw it flash in the firelight at the Hillbillies encampment at the Bohemian Grove, the most prestigious summer camp in the world, during that period after Mexico when third world debt dominated serious talk. Hillbillies, a bark-sheathed hobbit-hole of a compound hidden in a redwood grove, counted George Bush, Bill Buckley, West Germany's Helmut Schmidt, General Dynamics's David Lewis, and Alexander Haig among its guests and members. At a congenial evening gathering by the campfire, Clausen spoke up.

Historian J. S. Holliday listened, amazed. "In the ambience of the forest, he talked with conviction, persuasiveness, eloquence even, of how vitally important it was for the World Bank, on behalf of the Western world, to assist underdeveloped countries to secure economic stability so that *we* wouldn't suffer from disasters that would spread from them to us." Said Holliday, author of a classic book on the California gold rush; "He was appealing to the enlightened self-interest of these men, yes, but he went beyond that to the role of *humanist*. He was concerned that they look out for mankind. He was not being facile, I thought, but revealing his own values. He spoke from the heart."

As Jim Holliday got up to leave a little later, he was seized by the spirit of camaraderie and said to Clausen, in full hearing of the other men, "Tom, listening to you, I see you're an *idealist*!" Clausen turned toward him and, with fire in his eyes, shocked Holliday by snapping angrily, "*I am no such thing!*" Clausen could not allow this group to see him as anything but a hard-nosed pragmatist, Holliday guessed, saddened by the revelation.

The World Bank was not proving the kind of triumph everyone had expected it to be for Clausen as he stepped up from world's most successful commercial banker to the role of global banker-statesman. It had looked like such a promising match of man and challenge. Robert McNamara had been "very much involved in the choice of his successor," says Rotberg. "I think he looked upon Tom as an internationalist. A financial person. A banker. A banker who was totally aware of the LDC debt problem and with a commitment to do some good. All of which were accurate . . . Clausen had good motives, high intelligence."

He had been expected to thrive there. The World Bank was a banker's bank. "The most powerful and the most prestigious financial institution in the world," says Rotberg. A bank that had retained a triple A rating since 1958, a credit record surpassing almost all commercial banks. By most measures, it was bigger than the Bank of America. Having grown from lending a half billion a year, it was lending $7 to $8 billion when Clausen arrived. The bank was "the largest single lender to the developing countries in the world," Rotberg proudly claimed, "the largest *borrower* in the world." Funding itself in the world's capital markets, the bank was an efficient business that made $1.3 billion profit a year. Where the IMF made short-term loans to solve cash flow problems, the World Bank made long-term—ten-, fifteen-to-twenty-year—development loans to build the infrastructure in developing countries, which was the root of growth. The idea of "aid" was anathema. "McNamara insisted on only quality credits—loans to countries who would repay us," Rotberg explains. Unlike the commercial banks, its debtor countries paid principal and interest with clocklike regularity. As Mexico and, next, Brazil rattled the earnings of commercial banks, the bank was able to say with hauteur, "The best borrowers in the world are Mexico and Brazil. They have *impeccable* relationships with the bank." Even when the World Bank was thrown out of Iran for fighting the centralization of industrial and military power under the shah in 1973—and when Iran's assets were frozen by the banks in 1980—Iran missed not a payment on its past loans from the bank. It was a place as obsessed with numbers and balance sheets as was Clausen, a legacy of McNamara, the consummate bean counter.

"But Tom found it difficult to get a hold on the bank, to know which levers to pull to get things done," Rotberg saw. "At the B of A, he knew exactly who to call, what to do. He knew where every skeleton was, every problem. He *built* it. He just didn't have that at the bank. . . . And therefore, he delegated to the brightest people he could find." Delegation of power was not the style of the old take-hold Clausen. But it was the pragmatic Clausen who had always had a shrewd sense of compensating for his own inadequacies by his choice of key people. If he could not take hold at the World Bank, his image in the eyes of the men of "weight and importance"—his place in history—required that he find people who could. Wisely, Rotberg says. "Tom saw that we had a highly professional team in the treasurer's office and in the bank's lending operations ['the most fantastic group of professionals I've ever worked with,' Clausen claims] and respected it. But," Rotberg observed, "that in turn caused Clausen, inexorably, to lose authority."

When he came, "his reputation was for very, very tough, shoot-the-messenger, I-know-more-about-the-business-than-you-do management. He had authority, presence, power, control at B of A," an associate says. "But there was no bullying at the bank. It might have come at Bank of America from a conscious sense of power which he had and deserved at B of A. . . . But he could not exercise that at the World Bank because he didn't have the authority and power over the system.

"It may also have been a question of vision," the associate suggests. Clausen reports that McNamara had started structural adjustments, the broad macro approach to loans, as opposed to the individual projects—the roads and irrigation ditches. Rotberg claims that McNamara had a next step in mind. "He was going to move it in the direction of policy and research . . . into a Nobel Prize level of economists giving advice and research on macro and micro trade policies, looking at a country, working with it to put it into the twentieth century." Clausen continued McNamara's macro approach, the structural adjustments, for a while, then "I went back to the sectoral lending"—to the irrigation ditches. "Clausen came from an environment which looked at every quarter. . . . For anyone earning profits for however many consecutive quarters, there is obviously a lot of attention to short-term decisions and creative accounting, to put it mildly," says Rotberg. "The World Bank never did that. There was a conscious decision never to look at short-term gains. Or short-term profits. We looked only to what might happen in five or ten years from now. Or a decade from now—or beyond the year 2000. . . . Very few men have a vision that seeks to change the world for the better even after they have left it . . . and to take the necessary pain during their tenure. McNamara almost *preferred* present pain for future pleasure."

Might Clausen have moved into the leadership vacuum filled by de Larosière at the beginning of the debt crisis and taken the lead? "De Larosière took the initiative, no one gave it to him," says Rotberg. In Clausen's defense, though, he argues, "He got a bum rap from those who demanded he save the world. It was very difficult for him in the Mexican crisis to take the mandate— to intervene at a strong enough level. . . . After all, the bankers looked to the IMF because they made money available quicker, from governments. Tom did not have that flexibility."

Clausen had played it safe. He did what he knew. He "grew" the World Bank just as he had grown the Bank of America. Total World Bank lending since its founding had been $7 billion when McNamara came. "Under Clausen, following McNamara, it would be lending *double that in a year,*" observed Rotberg as he signed his name to the billions borrowed from institutional investors. B of A's in-house publication, the *BankAmerican,* credits Clausen with "doubling the World Bank's annual profit to $1.2 billion by increasing lending and cutting costs." In the same period he doubled new borrowings in the capital markets. But the World Bank he left was earning increasing anger over the environmental and cultural insensitivity of its projects; its bureaucracy was badly in need of an overhaul.

Not invited to serve a second term, as McNamara had been, Clausen would go out with a whimper, leaving a trail of gossip that he had been less than effective at the World Bank.

Chapter Eleven

IN SANTA MONICA, Dr. Ichak Adizes took a call from his secretary at the Adizes Institute. "Mr. Armacost would like to talk with you this afternoon."

Speaking and gesturing with the exuberant physicality and passionate intensity of Tevye in *Fiddler on the Roof*, Adizes scheduled a call for 4:00 P.M. Fantastic! Wonderful! But not really surprising. If he could be corporate therapist to presidents and princes, why not to the Bank of America? He was an internationally active "organizational therapist . . . not a consultant, but an *in*sultant," he insisted. He was persuasive verging on messianic in teaching the theories that have taken shape in his lively mind as the Adizes Theory. This swarthy, square-jawed man with the stocky build of a wrestler earned his Ph.D. helping his homeland of Yugoslavia debureaucratize as it broke from the Russian central system. He had shared "the best intellectual time of my life" with Robert Hutchins at the Santa Barbara think tank, the Center for the Study of Democratic Institutions. His theories have carried him to diagnoses with clients as disparate as the crew of Australia's America's Cup–winning sailing team, Porsche, and Domino Pizza.

"I've been listening to you till two in the morning, and I think you really have something. I would like to meet with you," said Armacost, who had had an aide deliver Adizes's tapes to him at the San Francisco Airport at eleven the previous night. The two men scanned their mad schedules, discussed meeting in limos at airports, and settled on Adizes's flying to San Francisco for a "tête-à-tête" the next week.

Adizes might be the darling of the Young Presidents Organization, a tenured professor at UCLA, very big in European management circles, but "I'm the best-kept secret in America." It pained him that people did not always act on his insights. "Oh, I could have saved Steve Jobs," he groaned at the power play that forced out the founder of Apple Computer. "It was classic—the founder squeezed out by administrative types. I *told* him, and he didn't listen." Curing a patient as large and prestigious as Bank of America could give Adizes the broad recognition that had eluded him and that his ego and proselytizing spirit craved. He flew to San Francisco in November 1982 to meet Sam Armacost.

He would meet Chuck Schwab first. It was Schwab who had put Adizes and Armacost in contact. Schwab was about to "marry" the Bank of America. The SEC and Justice Department had granted approval, hearings had finished in Washington, and the Federal Reserve was about to give its formal blessing—a triumph for commercial banks over Glass-Steagall. He and Armacost would sign and shake hands for the photographers the moment permission came on January 11. But the entrepreneur and the grand dowager were already cohabiting. In October a pilot program of six Schwab self-service counters had been set up in B of A branches.

As he and the bank merged destinies, Schwab had his first views of the board. He had insisted on board membership, a means of protecting his stake. But this display of the great bank's power impressed him into dutiful respect. He sat with dignified icons like eighty-four-year-old Clark Beise and Rudy Peterson, the bank's voices of the fifties and sixties. There was Ray Dahl, former CEO of Crown Zellerbach, another old San Francisco institution. The chairman of the board's all-important Auditing and Examining Committee was the retired president of the giant California utility, California Edison. Among the active CEOs there were some impressive ones. David Lewis of General Dynamics. Ruben Mettler of TRW. And there were the operating heads of Walt Disney, Kaiser Aluminum, the *Los Angeles Times,* Transamerica, Levi Strauss, the L.A. Dodgers, Standard Oil. The California corporate establishment. There was retailer Phil Hawley, head of Carter Hawley Hale. And the token Hispanic, *La Opinión*'s publisher, Ignacio Lozano. From seats of power in Washington had come Bob McNamara and former Fed Governor Andrew Brimmer. He would soon see it as a dangerously passive board. But at first he was awed.

As the day when he would exchange all the shares of his company for shares of BankAmerica came closer, Schwab's interest in the bank's health heightened. High-profile it might be, but Charles Schwab & Co. would be a very small subsidiary in a $120 billion bank. He could monitor the bank as a board member. He would still be running his company. But his fortunes would rise or fall on the corporate health of the whole bank and the value of the bank's stock. It had reached a high, before a two-for-one split, of $79 in 1968. Now it was trading at $18. He was the bank's largest shareholder. He owned more stock than A.P. had ever owned, a fact that earned him the ire of Claire Hoffman.

Schwab's hopes that she would see glimpses of her father in his entrepreneurial populism foundered in her resentment of Schwab's stock holdings and his enthusiasm for computers. He was an outsider, with no natural ally on the board. His block of stock was too small in the larger context to guarantee that he could shape events. "But I was still very committed, very optimistic," he says.

Schwab cheered Armacost's vision of the bank as a world leader in financial services and his insight that any meaningful change in the bank would require changing the entire culture. The in-house statement of goals, *Visions, Values and Strategies,* had helped define the mission. But what was needed were what Armacost called "operating organizational structures" to transform mission into performance. They must get managers focused "on the business issues, not on personalities, and who's losing authority and independence." Adizes, Schwab felt, would be a good speaker for the B of A seminar coming up at the Silverado resort in the Napa Valley.

"They have a big bureaucracy, and they sure need you," Adizes recalls Schwab telling him when they met at Schwab's office just before his first meeting with Armacost. "They're very slow. They spend a lot of money on marketing, and they don't know what marketing is all *about.*" Adizes liked this fresh-faced master marketer. "There was a lot of respect between the two of us. I respected his growth." Schwab respected Adizes as a consultant and speaker. As an organizational analyst. But Adizes could already see trouble ahead. At that time "all Chuck felt was a little annoyance." Later he would see Schwab's attitude toward B of A as "a classic case of . . . the misunderstanding of a small entrepreneur of the realities of a big bureaucracy."

Adizes had made a mental diagnosis of Schwab as they talked, using the acronym-larded jargon of his methodology to describe what he saw. All organizations, all managers, he taught, had four primary roles: They must be producers, integrators, administrators, and entrepreneurs. P, I, A, E. But no one person could perform all four roles effectively. That essential merging of the four could be achieved only by a team, by choosing people who complemented your strengths and filled the gaps. Schwab was "classically, typically PE: He was big P—very task-oriented, they want to get *done* with, finished. Then he was the entrepreneur, small E—charging, arrogant, and very small A, medium I." But he had applied the Adizes Theory well. Why was Schwab's company successful? Because he had hired good "AIs"—administrative integrators—to complement his own strong "PE." And yet "PEs don't understand the *realities* of an A-based organization . . . they don't have the patience." Oh yes, trouble ahead.

He nailed Armacost instantly as "big I. . . . He's an integrator, he likes consensus, he's sensitive to the political climate . . . has a very global view of what's happening." Adizes recalls Armacost telling him, "What I'm facing here is when I open a discussion, nobody says a word. They're all waiting for the boss to say what he wants. Because Clausen would say, 'Here's what I want.' " The bank had felt itself above consultants, he told Adizes, using them "like manpower, like secretarial help." The attitude had been: "Who can tell *us* what to do?"—a parochial arrogance central to B of A's culture. Armacost invited him to give a two-hour lecture to the Management Forum that would be meeting at the Silverado Country Club in Napa Valley in January. "I want all the people in the room to realize Bank of America has to change—that change is *going* to happen."

Adizes was shattered. "Here I come to be hired as a consultant of change, and all he's going to have is a *lecture*!" Armacost was being cautious. "Big Is cannot disclose their cards easily. They keep it very close to the breast. They want to see what's going on," Adizes ruminated, as he insisted on three hours.

Armacost had made a powerful impression on Adizes. "He's the material of statesmanship. . . . He knows how to maintain distance without being arrogant . . . how to maintain a certain aura—but it's not artificial. And he comes from this incredible family."

THE THIRTY MEN who gathered Saturday morning in their ties and sport coats in a conference room at the Silverado constituted the top tier of management. They had flown in from all over the world for this unprecedented event. With its antebellum architecture, immaculately white against avenues of lofty palms and square miles of perfect green golf course, Silverado is a clone of the world-class corporate resort; sitting in splendid isolation from the Napa Valley vineyards that surround it, it could as easily be in Arizona or North Carolina. Driving past men in golf carts wearing bright Polo shirts and slacks, their woods topped with hand-knit mittens, Adizes was acutely aware, "Here I'm coming. A guy with an accent. Not famous. Not Peter Drucker." He had never worked with bankers before. "But life cycle is independent of the industry." B of A could be a shoe factory.

To Adizes a corporation is a living organism. His methodology is based on understanding its life cycles. It starts out "go-go," goes through adolescence, reaches prime and maturity. As it begins to age, it moves into the aristocratic and then the final, bureaucratic stage before death. "The role of management and leaders is to bring an organization to prime, and to keep it in prime. . . . What causes growing and aging is not size and not chronological age. . . . Prime can be prolonged for hundreds of years. The Catholic church has been two thousand years now!"

Adizes had only three hours to win the job of agent of change to the Bank of America. He was speaking to the right group. For it was in this group that CAPI resided. CAPI was Adizes's key acronym: "The coalesced authority, power, and influence to solve problems. A psychiatrist works with your brain . . . with the ego. With whom do I work? Who has the keys to the consciousness of an organization to change its personality? . . . I work on CAPI. It existed in this roomful of thirty men."

Appearing relaxed but watching keenly, Armacost scanned the faces in the room and thought, "The past is catching up with us." There was some lively interest; Adizes was engaging. But there was some resistance, too, says Armacost. "We had already started to condition our audience to the need for changing more drastically—saying we're going to have to throw away a lot of preconceived notions about how we used to do things—and the market was starting to provide the momentum to reinforce that. But they were paralyzed with thoughts of how to execute the kinds of changes we were starting to articulate—especially in middle management. They were feeling, 'Jeez, we haven't got time to get all these things done and what happens to me in the process?' Many of those feelings had been transformed into really profound, disabling fears about the inability of the corporation to cope with a lot of the challenges. . . . The guys were just panic-stricken."

"You can tell the life stages by how the employees dress, how they address each other, how they deal with conflict," Adizes explained to this power group, exuberantly revealing the concepts that had grown from observing "real life—listening to taxi drivers, by really watching my children. . . . In the aristocratic stage, they wear the IBM look—the darker the better. . . . The drapes are heavy, deep carpets, big table, usually the picture of the founder, life size, looking down upon you, frowning," said Adizes, as they all broke up laughing. He had not known that Giannini's portrait hung on the wall in every branch. In aristocratic, he explained, "Individually, they are scared, but when they get together, they are enchanted with the present and paralyzed to deal with the future." Where was B of A? he asked them. "By and large, the agreement was that the Bank of America was in the aristocratic stage."

Mont McMillen, too busy with Mexico and with getting a handle on NAD to appreciate spending time in what some saw as a group therapy session, grew skeptical as Adizes started talking his arcane language of PIPs, POKs, and CAPI, the acronyms that would become as familiar as "assets" and "margins" to these bankers. "It was a bit hard to assimilate the acronyms. I thought they were unnecessarily jargony—the sizzle that went with the steak. The mystique." But he was finding it a "very interesting lateral way to think."

Adizes's was not the style Max Hopper was used to in Texas. Max Hopper could see "a lot of merit in his concepts. They were not unlike American Airlines—identifying what needs to be done. But he puts a little too much chutzpah on top." And yet, Hopper mused, "This man is a master of group dynamics. He's handling it in a way that's not threatening." He could sense a growing willingness among the bankers to open up.

"Take a piece of paper and write the top five problems that you see the bank has. Nobody will ever see it. I will not correct. Write it for yourself," he directed. Could they? "Clausen was very authoritarian. He didn't allow anything under him to sprout. People were scared shitless from him," says Adizes. Armacost was astounded at what was happening. On three-by-five file cards, the men were writing, writing. Naming their criticisms of the bank—the "PIPs," as Adizes called them, that must be solved. Adizes then demanded, "How many of these can any one person in this room solve alone?" The answer, of course, was none. The response he expected. "How many of these problems will you have three years from now?" Thirty faces fell. He drove on. "You will probably not have only these five, but five more. . . . All right, guys, we want to solve these problems and not to continue to climb in the life cycle. What do we need to do?" The bankers said it: "We need to change."

The next event happened as he knew it would. Tentatively, at first, and then as a chorus, the men suggested, "Why don't we share what we have on all this?" Adizes says: "I had freed them from mutual accusations. Now they were dying to say what it is that together we have to solve." While the men took a ten-minute break, Adizes spread the cards on a table, arranging the problems in a chain of causation.

Armacost was still the observer. But as Adizes arrayed the bits of paper on the table, he felt a rising excitement. Here, to be grasped in one fist, were the bank's problems, named. But beyond that, it was the opening up Armacost found most remarkable. "Most of these men had never been in an environment where they were encouraged, or felt comfortable, saying things about the bank they had long felt. . . . This was a new era of candor and openness and ease with which people were starting to relate to each other. It was the revelation, the watershed." He would remember that moment as the most hopeful of the early years of his era. There seemed hope, in the unprecedented candor Adizes had evoked, that this powerful culture—a culture that had evolved out of A.P.'s memory and flowered, full blown, in the classical BankAmerican—could be fundamentally changed from within. There seemed hope that this elite corps of BankAmericans could transform itself from an aristocratic bureaucracy into a contemporary version of A.P.'s entrepreneurial bank.

Mont McMillen came out of the session thinking, "He did pretty damn well. It was very entertaining and, I thought, interesting. But I didn't come out of the meeting a true believer. A light bulb didn't go on in my head that this guy was going to solve everybody's problems." McMillen had played a part in building the loan portfolios—shipping, LDCs—as had Rice and Armacost before him. He had been sent back to an even more troubled division. In the months since Mexico, NAD's commercial loan portfolios were revealing shocks in real estate, energy, private-sector loans in Mexico. Federal examiners were auditing relentlessly, digging deep in the loan pouches. This very month, January 1983, Bank of America's own economists pronounced California in its deepest recession since the 1930s. Predicting long-term damage to the state, they warned that California's prized double A credit rating by Moody's was threatened. Neither the state nor the bank had any experience of reverses.

Armacost observed later, with a wry smile, that out of the jubilant consensus on hundreds of problems faced by the bank at that first Silverado meeting, "What *wasn't* agreed upon was that the portfolio was in bad shape. There was not a cardinal signal yet; recovery was just starting. The intransigent nature of the portfolios had not yet been revealed by any numbers."

"IN THREE YEARS I can solve all your problems," said Adizes as he negotiated his contract. "It will cost a million bucks a year. If I do not solve forty percent of your problems in the first year, I will pay you back anything you pay me." Compared to the Boston Consulting Group, Adizes was *cheap,* Armacost mused. Adizes was delighted that "Sam was very fair. He said, 'You don't have to return it. We are hiring you. Let's start work.' "

"How do I get them to move off the dime, to commit themselves? By me committing myself," Adizes mused, as he bought $250,000 stock in Bank of America. He would be able to tell his first working session, "I'm the second-largest shareholder in this group. I have more stock than Sam Armacost."

Armacost was still being cautious. He wanted Adizes to start with the North American Division. "No, no, Sam. In an organization so big, if I take NAD, it will never vibrate throughout the organization." He could see that Mont McMillen was in "a no-win situation, with a structure that gave him a lot of responsibility but little authority." He could find solutions only by making broad diagonal cuts through the bank. "In Yugoslavia we say, 'Once you join the circle of dancers, you have to dance.' " He insisted on having at least seven of the bank's thirty divisions as his patients. But Armacost was not going to make it easy for him. He would not deliver the Managing Committee.

Seven divisions were chosen. Armacost had asked Jim Wiesler to try Adizes out in the California retail bank, but Wiesler had begged off. McMillen's NAD was a "more manageable size," he suggested. "If I'd thought about it, I'd have said no," McMillen says. But he was the good soldier. And he was dealing with some fundamental organizational problems in NAD—"the most uncomfortable business experience" of his career. It was a battle between NAD's two overlapping lending arms: its geographic regions and its targeted industries. His commercial bankers were "bickering and backbiting," as both groups competed for contact and control over the customer relationship. "The character of the banking business was changing dramatically. Straightforward loans we used to do were dying away." And a generation of loan officers was fighting fierce turf battles for shrinking pieces of the pie.

"I was willing to put up with the tension and friction. I thought it was a sound division of effort—you got more banking for your buck," McMillen says. The conflicts were the "positive contention" Armacost was encouraging as a healthy symptom of change. "But I *did* think that maybe, with Adizes, we could get it out on the table and talk."

Assigned by Adizes to form a NAD POK—the small group formed to identify and deal with PIPs, the problems—McMillen chose about fifteen senior NAD executives. Its first session was a two-day marathon at the Westwood Marquis, a small hotel near the UCLA campus, in June 1983. The men were sealed off with no telephones. It was the beginning for Mont McMillen of two years of PIPs, POKs, and CAPI.

They came in coats and ties, and so did Adizes, at first. "How are you feeling this morning?" he asked at the beginning of each session, going around the room, inviting the men to say what they felt. It didn't matter what they said: "I've got a hangover"; "I'm feeling good about it today"; "I feel lousy about this whole project." "Rules were very strict. You always went in turn around the circle. Raised your hand. You were fined if you came late," says McMillen. "It ended with 'How did you feel about today?' We played the game." Adizes changed to sports clothes. So, too, did the proper BankAmericans.

They "spent six months discussing 'What is a bank?' . . . and came to the conclusion the banking industry is dead and they better become a financial

California's first family of banking aboard ship in 1923. Mario (left) and Virgil Giannini (right) with their parents, Clorinda and A.P., and sister, Claire. (*Bank of America*)

On May 7, 1941, the day after his seventieth birthday, A.P. (left) lays the cornerstone of Bank of America's new headquarters in San Francisco. Russell Smith, the bank's first international banker, hands A.P. a trowel made of wood from each of California's counties, celebrating the bank's statewide branch system. (*Courtesy Russell G. Smith*)

The "little fellow's bank" fueled California's explosive growth during and after World War II. By the time of A.P.'s death in 1949, it had become the biggest bank in the world. Mario, president from 1936 until his untimely death in 1952, maintained the warmth and personal style of A.P.'s community bank while bringing order to the sprawling giant. (*Bank of America*)

Defender of her father's spirit after his death, Claire Giannini Hoffman attends the unveiling in 1987 of a plaque honoring A.P.'s financing of the Golden Gate Bridge. Saddened by the bank's drift away from A.P.'s "human touch," she resigned from the board in 1986. (*Bank of America*)

The Bank of America was still well matched to its time and territory when former federal bank examiner S. Clark Beise (above right) became president in 1954. Computerized processing and the credit card, introduced during his tenure, made B of A the world leader in bank technology and innovation through the 1950s. (*Bank of America. Photo: Gerald L. French*)

The son of Swedish immigrant farmers, Rudolph Peterson (above left), the bank's most cosmopolitan president, personified B of A's expanding vision of itself through the 1960s. (*Courtesy Andrew Johnson*)

Still the state's dominant "ag" bank, Peterson's B of A underwrote the ambitions of Robert Mondavi (left, with branch manager Andy Johnson) for Napa Valley's wines while boldly extending its reach into corporate and international banking. (*Courtesy Andrew Johnson*)

Watchdog over the bank's financial condition as it grew to a global colossus during the 1960s and 1970s, legendary cashier (chief financial officer) Clarence Baumhefner (left) reputedly kept the bank's financial status in his head. Even his powerful mind, however, was no substitute for systematic controls and sophisticated computers. Their lack would leave B of A catastrophically ill equipped in the era of deregulation. (*BankAmerica Corporation Annual Report. Photo: Leigh Wiener*)

During A. W. "Tom" Clausen's presidency in the 1970s, overseas growth continued. The charismatic Alvin Rice presided from his London office over the petrodollar lending that would later blossom into the third world debt crisis. After returning to San Francisco as Clausen's heir, Rice resigned abruptly under pressure from Clausen in 1979, shocking and mystifying the banking world. (*Photo: Barnet Saidman*)

In happier days, Clausen (left) and Rice, with Yves C. Lamarche (right) in Cairo in the mid-'70s, celebrating a successful trade financing. (*Courtesy Alvin Rice*)

Good BankAmericans all, the power team that ran the most successful bank in the world on the eve of revolution had no giants of A.P.'s stature. Pictured here, the Managing Committee in 1978: seated, from left to right, Arthur Toupin, Leland Prussia, Joe Carrera, Clausen, and Chauncey Medberry; standing, Walter Hoadley, George Skoglund, and Lloyd Sugaski. (*BankAmerica Corporation Annual Report*)

The senior management team that emerged from the crucible of the 1980s smiles, in 1988, at the bank's dramatic recovery. All except Clausen, reinstated as CEO in 1986, are from Bank of America's longtime rival Wells Fargo, training ground for tough managers. Standing behind Clausen, from left to right, are Lewis Coleman, Glenhall Taylor, Richard Rosenberg, and Frank Newman, all candidates for leadership of the bank on Clausen's retirement. In 1990, Rosenberg, leader of B of A's strong recovery in consumer banking, won the crown. (*BankAmerica Corporation Annual Report*)

James Miscoll (above left) and James Wiesler were charged with revitalizing the bank's consumer side and its heart, the vast branch system, which had been neglected in favor of large corporate and international banking. Sole survivor of the old team, Miscoll heads B of A's Southern California operations. (*BankAmerica Corporation Annual Report*)

Archetypes of the global BankAmerican of the bank's Golden Age, Mont McMillen (left) and William Bolin (below) saw their stature within the bank suffer in the eighties as they came to be perceived as symbols of the status quo. (*Left photo: Brian Glenn; below: BankAmerica Corporation Annual Report*)

A towering presence to American bankers as chairman of the Federal Reserve Board, Paul Volcker in 1979 instituted inflation-fighting monetary policies that triggered a worldwide recession and accelerated the most violent shakeout the banking industry had felt since the Great Depression. Volcker, center, is flanked by members of the Fed's Board of Governors, from left to right, Manuel H. Johnson, H. Robert Heller, Edward W. Kelley, Jr., Wayne D. Angell, and Martha R. Seger. Heller was Bank of America's chief international economist before joining the Federal Reserve. (*Federal Reserve Board*)

At times, the members of BankAmerica Corp's board found their seats hot as well as prestigious. In 1953 Robert Di Giorgio (left), as CEO of the agribusiness giant Di Giorgio Corporation, intervened daringly to speed the transition from the presidency of Carl Wente to that of Beise. Below, four directors who influenced the bank's management crisis in 1986. (*Photo: Frank Wing*)

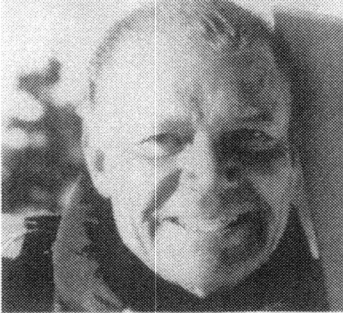

Now retired from the board, Robert McNamara (above left), former U.S. Secretary of Defense and head of the World Bank, warned the bank of the risky condition of its loans and reserves during the climactic decline of the 1980s. John Beckett (above right), then chairman of Transamerica Corporation, was supportive of Clausen's successor, Samuel Armacost, for many years, but he placed the historic phone call that brought Clausen back to the bank's presidency. (*Left photo: Jeffrey Aaronson. Right photo: BankAmerica Corporation Annual Report*)

Chairing the committee charged with hiring and firing senior executives, Philip Hawley (above left), the powerful Southern Californian CEO of the retail chain Carter Hawley Hale, cast the pivotal vote in the ousting of Armacost. As chairman of the board's Executive Committee, Dr. Franklin Murphy (above right), former chairman and CEO of the Times Mirror Company (*L.A. Times*), tried to quell revolt as the bank faced takeover challenges. (*Left photo: Courtesy Philip J. Hawley. Right photo: Courtesy Dr. Franklin D. Murphy*)

Bringing an ambitious vision to the presidency in 1981, Samuel H. Armacost (above) initiated aggressive restructuring to prepare the bank for the deregulated era ahead. Two of his key facilitators were strategic planner Stephen McLin (below left), who drove acquisitions and overhauled the branches, and consultant Dr. Ichak Adizes (below right), whose theories, Armacost hoped, would transform B of A's culture from fear of change and outmoded banking practices to a focus on serving the customer and new banking strategies. But by 1985 devastating loan losses and the growing perception that change was coming too slowly threatened to undercut Armacost's vision and credibility. (*Above: Bank of America. Left photo: Jonathan Reicher. Right photo: Courtesy Dr. Ichak Adizes*)

As a boy in rural California, Charles Schwab honed his entrepreneur's instincts in his own tiny chicken business. (*Courtesy Charles Schwab*)

Armacost (below left) moved Bank of America into the future with the acquisition in 1983 of Charles Schwab & Company, the nation's largest discount brokerage. The smiles that celebrated the marriage turned to tension later as a frustrated Schwab resigned from the board and struggled to break his company free of the bank. (*Photo: Vano Photography*)

"Proaction" was the buzzword as Armacost infused his senior management team with fresh blood from outside B of A. Some saw Tom Cooper (right), hired from Mellon Bank to cut costs, as a threat to Armacost when he was promoted to president of the bank. Cooper outlasted Armacost, only to leave after Clausen's return. (*Courtesy Thomas Cooper*)

Fenton "Pete" Talbott brought Citibank skills to the bank's retail operations, but, thwarted by the lack of a depth of management talent and of clear-cut lines of authority, he returned to New York. (*Bank of America*)

B of A lagged behind its computerized peers when Max Hopper (right) was lured from American Airlines as technology czar. He made strides toward restoring the bank to leadership, but quit over power struggles with Cooper. Talbott's and Hopper's defections slowed Armacost's momentum in turning the bank around.

Urbane New York banker Robert Truex (right), who died in 1988, with President Gerald Ford. Truex was one of several strong and gifted bankers spit out by the bank during Clausen's tenure. Unable to digest the kind of ambitious mavericks being nurtured by Citibank in New York, the bank was depleted at the top just as it was being tested by the banking revolution. (*Photo: Bill Houlton*)

Joseph Pinola left the bank in 1976. Ten years later, as head of First Interstate Bancorp, a vestige of A.P.'s old empire, he mounted a bold takeover bid for B of A. (*Courtesy Sanford I. Weill*)

Also vying for control of the weakened bank was Wall Street financier Sanford Weill, who created the brokerage empire now known as Shearson Lehman Hutton, owned in part by American Express. Rebuffed by B of A's board, Weill launched a new financial services empire. (*Courtesy First Interstate Bancorp*)

A. P. Giannini had been part of their family, yet the Stanghellinis—Elide, her son Bob, and her sister Angelina Fava—filed a $50 million lawsuit against Bank of America for fraud when its loans bankrupted their Sutter Basin farm. (*Photo: Antoinnette LaFarge*)

Even as farmers were defecting to the new, small personalized banks that were seizing market share, B of A's man in Napa Valley, Andy Johnson (here visiting vintner Bill Jaeger at Rutherford Hill winery), struggled to maintain the hands-on banking and human touch that were giving way to computerized transactional banking. (*Courtesy Andrew Johnson*)

After World War II the more competitive conditions on the East Coast produced a different breed of banker. New York's Citibank was forced to be more innovative, efficient, and future-oriented than were California banks. Led by Walter Wriston (right) and his successor, John Reed (left), Citibank passed B of A in 1982 to become "the biggest bank in the U.S." Although "performance" has become the prime measure of success, size is still analogous to power; today no American bank can be found on the list of the world's twenty largest, dominated by Japan. (*Courtesy Citicorp/Citibank*)

Citicorp may be one of the handful of surviving American banking giants by the year 2000, as power and profits shift from the great money center banks to competitors who are less shackled by outdated regulations and by bankers' conventional thinking. Citicorp's world headquarters (right) are in midtown Manhattan. (*Courtesy Citicorp/Citibank*)

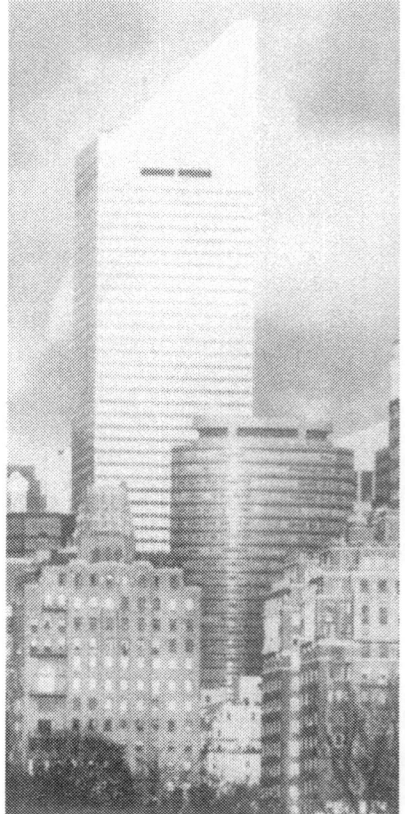

Sidestepping regulatory obstacles to interstate and national banking, Citi moved into B of A territory, the rich California consumer market, by acquiring savings banks. (*Courtesy Citicorp/Citibank*)

The shock that broke the stalemate between intransigent banks and despairing debtor nations was John Reed's announcement in May 1987 that Citicorp would voluntarily take a massive reserve against losses on its foreign loans, a $3 billion blow to its earnings. (*Courtesy Citicorp/Citibank*)

Loans made with eager optimism and signed with chandeliered ceremony, like this signing of a $1 billion loan to Spain in 1976 in which B of A was lead manager, deteriorated into the third world debt crisis that wracked the globe at the close of the 1980s. (*BankAmerica Corporation Annual Report*)

Pioneers of the urgent negotiations that ended the Mexican debt crisis of 1982. Angel Gurria, now Mexico's undersecretary to the Ministry of Finance; B of A's Preston Bennett; then–Mexican finance minister Silva Herzog; and Citicorp's William Rhodes, who became leader for the banks of the debt restructuring marathon that climaxed in the Brady Plan in 1989, sign the historic debt agreement. (*Courtesy Citicorp/Citibank*)

This 1904 frame building in San Francisco's Italian neighborhood, North Beach, was the birthplace of the Bank of America. It was destroyed in the earthquake and fire of 1906. The next day, A.P. reopened his business on the docks and began lending to the ruined and homeless San Franciscans. (*Bank of America*)

Eighty years later, BankAmerica's sleek headquarters is only blocks from its birthplace, but the bank has grown away from A.P.'s founding principles. Although its recovery has been strong, it may never regain the global preeminence it once knew. But B of A can again be the Giant of the West if it recaptures the vision, spirit of service, global outlook, and, perhaps, the passion Giannini brought to his country bank. (*Bank of America*)

services institution. . . . Loans are a very outdated way of financing business. So the banks are trying to buy cheap money and sell it expensive—you cannot make money on that small margin anymore. . . . We had to change it from making money on money to making money on fees," says Adizes, who was learning along with the bankers.

"It was really a very simple concept," says McMillen as he and the NAD POK went through a series of two-day sessions with Adizes. "Identify the problem, put it up on the wall, and be tenacious until you solve the bloody problem. Don't sweep it under the rug or hand it to someone else. *Fix* it." Says Adizes: "It turned out that most of the NAD problems were not at their level, but at the higher level. The corporate level. It was a very centrist organization."

McMillen suspected that "Ichak was manufacturing some of the need to move to higher levels for solutions. Adizes, I think, knew that his hook into the organization was to somehow or other convince the Managing Committee that the problems in NAD needed to be addressed by the corporation. Some were legitimate. But I think it was a tool he used to get to the corporation."

McMillen asked Armacost if he and the Managing Committee would give them a hearing. He agreed, and McMillen's POK flew to San Francisco to present its findings.

Faced with NAD's nasty little stack of problems, all of which must apparently be solved at the highest level, a Corporate POK was created. It contained "the whole power structure of the bank," McMillen observed. With Armacost and Prussia involved, a large conference room on the fifty-first floor became its home. But even this powerful body could not, it seemed, fix NAD's problems alone. "The message was clear. If you're running a profit center with four hundred problems, and three hundred and fifty of them are not solvable inside the organization, you've got to begin to question the organizational structure of the institution," Adizes told them. He was thrilled when the Corp POK said it itself: "We've got to reorganize the bank." At last Adizes had the entire corporate body on his couch.

New POKs were created as Adizes spread his reach in the bank. Max Hopper found himself on three. "Through '84 I was spending fifty percent of my time on the three POKs." McMillen, based in L.A., was "flying up for those dumb meetings every couple of weeks for two days. . . . I, for one, was getting awfully tired of it," McMillen admits. McMillen felt tension on several fronts. He had just been passed over as Bill Bolin's successor as head of the World Banking Division when Bolin retired in the first quarter of '83. "Bill called me and said that it was close, but they felt I wasn't quite ready." The post sat empty, intensifying the politics being played in the Managing Committee, deepening the schisms Hopper had seen. As the Corp POK began to gain momentum, McMillen's NAD POK was abandoned, his problem with battling loan officers left unsolved.

By late summer of '84 "there was great pressure for Sam and Adizes to display some visible success," says Hopper. Adizes was costing $1 million a year. There was the downward earnings trend. "And increasing skepticism in the bank. The POK felt it had to pump something out," says McMillen.

Adizes felt additional pressure. His diagnosis of the bank's life phase had been thrown off track, at first, by a trail of false clues. But they led to an insight as credible as any that has been proposed concerning what went wrong with Bank of America. Inside the aristocratic exterior of MotherBank, Adizes suspected, beat the heart of a go-go organization. The grand dowager had never grown up.

In the aristocratic stage of the life cycle "people call each other by the *last* name." At B of A, says Adizes, "you go into an elevator and people say, 'Hi, Lee, hi, Sam.' That began to give me a clue something was wrong here." The *BankAmerican*, the bank's in-house magazine, used the same informal tone in its stories. It was "Sam" this and "Mont" that. Adizes found Prussia's role "another very interesting anomaly: that the chairman of the board reports to the president. And Lee had functions—financial, economic, legal, with staff reporting to him—but he was chairman of the board. I've never seen that in any other organization—unless you're a go-go, where you appoint someone who is your friend to be chairman. . . . A go-go company is organized around people, not around tasks."

Most disconcerting, the bank "had bureaucratic manifestations, but no bureaucracy. . . . I could not find one bureaucrat in the bank. If you look at the bank from the outside, you believe you see a bureaucracy because nobody is moving. In a bureaucracy, people would rather pee in their pants than make a commotion. You recognize the innovators by the arrows in their back. They dream about how wonderful the world can be. But nobody moves. Bureaucracy is *rules*. It is so many rules, standard operating procedures, and rituals that it freezes the organization." The bank had the paralysis, but without the structure, Adizes believed. "Here what you have is a hodgepodge structure."

"Look at the Managing Committee. It was composed almost exclusively of the retail bank people. This was a retail bank that grew to be an international bank that grew to be a world bank, but management was still people from the retail bank. *It was a go-go structure.* The organizational chart of a go-go company is a piece of paper that looks like a chicken has walked all over it." In the bank "the computers were reporting to the retail bank, but serving the rest of the world. They didn't have cost accounting. They thought they had decentralization, but they had no decentralization that you can measure. No managerial responsibility for profits. They had a lot of data but no information. You cannot have an information base without structure. To whom does it flow? It must flow in a channel; otherwise it spreads around like a swamp. They had a *swamp!*" There were a thousand committees when Armacost came, to make up for the lack of structure; he would remove a hundred standing committees in 1983 alone. "But they became paralyzed. You had to go through many levels to get anything approved."

And the persisting commitment to growth, of course, was go-go. "In a go-go stage, more is better. A go-go company is measured by market share, by sales. That's what Clausen did."

Adizes diagnosed that "the bank went through aging. It lost the flexibility that is the source of vitality and gained the predictability. But it was *premature aging*. They never developed the administrative systems. They never went through prime, when you develop them. They became the largest bank in the world without ever getting to prime of their life cycle." They had entered the adolescent stage and never left. "They are a child in a tuxedo trying to play football," he declared.

But why? How could that happen? Adizes's climactic discovery was that "My God, they're I-oriented." It was there in bank history. "There was tremendous growth with Giannini. Then he went to Europe, and the bank was taken over by the administrative types. A fight occurred. There is always a time when the administrators, the people who want to stabilize it and bring systems, start fighting with the entrepreneur, who wants to keep the freedom. Usually the administrative types kick out the entrepreneur. But Giannini kicked *them* out." How? "Because there is a substitute for 'administrator,' and it is called 'I'—integration. It is people. Social values. Japan doesn't have too much 'A,' but has a lot of 'I.'

"The reason A.P. succeeded was his 'I'—his integration—was very high. Very personable. Very charismatic. . . . Because of the Giannini legacy, the bank could do it. People in Bank of America feel very deeply for the bank. There is a love and affection and dedication I have not seen anywhere. The executive vice-president from the retail bank who talks to me with tears in his eyes about what he thinks about the B of A. *Really*, it's a *family!*

"With the Giannini legacy, and the people doing the best they can for each other, you can overcome problems." Overcome the lack of systems. "It's based more on networking. The Giannini legacy is family-oriented. In a family we don't have rules who's going to wash the dishes; whoever sees dirty dishes goes and cleans them. . . . Giannini appointed his chauffeur to be personnel manager of the bank. He didn't give any importance to personnel. Did you ever see a personnel manager in a family? Personnel you get in a bureaucracy. That's why Sam hired this guy from IBM, Bob Beck, to develop the personnel function. It was hardly existent.

"Deregulation brought the dysfunctionality of their behavior to the surface. But I believe they were paralyzed long before that. *It was the biggest pathology I've ever seen in any company that never went through prime.*"

This revelation turned Adizes's approach around 180 degrees. His challenge, suddenly, was "not to worry about how to cut down bureaucracy, but how to develop bureaucracy—to develop systems, manuals, build accountability." Out of it would come such things as a total overhaul of the credit and financial controls. But Adizes's growing frustration was that if his diagnosis was correct, the serious pathology he had discovered was going to take longer to correct. He had arrived at his "Eureka" revelation during that nervous period of late 1983, early 1984, when Armacost's strong positive momentum rode against a strengthening tide of negative events, a time when the wisest analyst or economist could probably have predicted with equal credibility either glory or disaster for the bank over the coming two or three years. Time was becoming a vital factor. If Adizes had the time, the skill, and the "coalesced authority"—the power—to apply his insight to the bank's structures and systems and correct the chaos, he would be worth his $3 million a hundred times over.

The POKs were getting restless. "We thought we were buying into six to nine months," says McMillen.

Adizes must produce. The Adizes Theory would be put to work first on technology, the forgotten child. The Corp POK would be asked to resolve the issue Max Hopper was eager to be assigned to solve: the anarchy of its computer systems. Armacost knew, as systems people like Katherine Neville did, that "there was very little connectibility between systems. Each guy had his own druthers." World Banking still ran its own computer system, separate and independent from the systems of the retail bank. The issue was: Should they unify the two into one worldwide system?

"They chewed on it far longer than I thought they should have," says McMillen, who was sympathetic to World Banking's independent system. Since Al Rice, the international bankers had fought to free their systems from headquarters and develop a system sensitive to their complex global needs. Just before Armacost had returned to San Francisco as cashier, in 1979, he wrote that World Banking should "pursue automation and systems development." Taking Armacost's seat in London, McMillen had followed up on that by driving the creation of a system that would serve the international network; that cell of activity in London was now working hard to complete what would become known as International Business Systems (IBS).

After months of debate, the Corp POK finally decided that there should be one systems organization for the entire bank. It would be called BASE. BankAmerica Systems Engineering. IBS would be folded into it, an independent system supported by BASE. BASE would follow the concepts laid down by Max Hopper in the report he had delivered to Armacost in January 1983 on how to develop a bankwide system. Says McMillen: "No one said who would head it. But it was assumed it would be Max Hopper." BASE was granted a princely budget of half a billion dollars and given priority scheduling so that it could go on-line, with an international media launch, in October 1984. But word that it was in the works was announced earlier. "BASE was the first surfacing of Adizes," says McMillen.

As he described BASE, Adizes began to sound to some like an empire builder. BASE would be "the largest computer company in the *world* in the service industry. Fifteen thousand people. An incredible budget," said Adizes, though the real numbers were closer to five thousand people. It would be housed in suburban Concord, across the bay from San Francisco in a sprawling new complex that "was like the Pentagon! Nobody could touch us after that."

Other targets were identified, as POKs proliferated through the bank. Adizes's methodology would tackle a total redesign of the bank's credit and financial controls to be rolled out in July '84—before the on-line launch of BASE in October, when Hopper would push the buttons that ended computer anarchy. After that Adizes would take on the global payments system—the dream that had emerged from the early soul-searching about "What is a bank?"

The payments system would use one of the best things the bank had going for it—its worldwide electronic network. Operating through satellites, lasers, telephone lines, and interbank computers, the bank moved more than $1 trillion through the United States alone each day—a quarter of the nation's annual GNP—as well as billions of bits and bytes of information without moving a penny of hard currency or even paper. B of A was inaugurating a fiber optics link that carried money transfer instructions totaling up to $21 billion a day over a beam of light. Its electronic mail route had just been improved to allow push-button transmission of credit memos anywhere in the world. Building on this with the most sophisticated technology, the bank was installing in space over the equator the bank's first earth station, Westar II, which could send the entire text of *War and Peace*—all thirteen hundred pages— from San Francisco to Los Angeles in twenty seconds.

Adizes envisioned a money and information transfer network that would pull all the payments functions together: retail and wholesale payments; credit cards; travelers cheques. Tied into an international clearinghouse, it would operate twenty-four hours a day, seven days a week. "A corporate treasurer could place an order, and we'd execute, anywhere in the world," said Max Hopper. "We are going to leapfrog all the financial institutions and the banks. They're all going to need *us*. . . . The banks—all organizations—would become our clients," declared Adizes. "Once you plug in and connect your computers to their computers, you're in for life; we would become a *utility*! We would make money like a telephone company, charging for the transactions. It is a beautiful vision—taking the largest bank in the world and converting it into a utility system."

That project took the name BAPS—BankAmerica Payments Systems. Having a commanding market share of the world's money payment systems was at the very heart of the successful bank of the future; it was integral to Armacost's goal of keeping the bank a major international player, as the numbers of survivors in that arena dwindled. "The bank of the future would be making money off fees, not interest spreads," Max Hopper reminded, cheering the income-producing future planned for BAPS. "And it would have another fifteen thousand people," said Adizes, exaggerating a number Hopper recalls as in "the eight to ten thousand range."

But first, the bank's monolithic retail side had been targeted for restructuring. It would play off the bold changes already being made by McLin's strategies. Rounds of Corp POK sessions pursued the question: "What is our retail mission?" An intense debate was launched over whether the bank's presence abroad in the future should be both retail and wholesale. Max Hopper noted that Adizes, the detached, was taking positions. Hopper, who argued for wholesale, felt "that Ichak would have supported a retail presence overseas." McMillen observed, "Ichak had begun to do something he said he would never do." He had joined the debate.

"He had always said that he didn't want to know banking—we could be an ice-cream manufacturer—but somewhere early in the Corp POK exercise," says McMillen, "he lost his sense of what his role was. He slipped out of the role of consultant and began promoting his own visions." McMillen speculated that "he just got so bloody wound up in it, and began to feel so intensely that all of a sudden, he couldn't help saying, 'This is the way it should go.' " As he did so, "he began to lose his audience." "The pain was great, and it's easy to bitch about it. But Ichak did *not* lose objectivity—at least not to the degree some of these guys thought," says Armacost, loyally defending Adizes. "Sometimes they misinterpreted as involvement his going to extremes to get a reaction."

In spite of the rising impatience over the time and money Adizes was costing, Armacost was gratified by what he was seeing. *Visions, Values and Strategies,* in which he took such pride, had proven a useful preamble to change. With Adizes, he felt, change was being achieved. He was shaking up dozens of dug-in little empires, achieving a buy-in to change. If B of A were to win the war against decline, it would have to be with this kind of internal transformation. "It was happening," Armacost was convinced. And most important, others were perceiving it. As 1984 began, gains were being seen and celebrated.

On January 3 the *Wall Street Journal*'s influential "Heard on the Street" column reported that "a profit rebound was seen by some analysts who had revised their BAC ratings to a 'buy'." Three weeks later it reported that "the stirring giant . . . seeking a turnaround, seems to gain ground"—in spite of a poor fourth quarter in '83. In-house, Adizes was getting his first recognition. Mont McMillen wrote a major article for *BankAmerican* on Adizes's work in the bank. Adizes grinned. "I was getting, from all over the place, applause, people saying, 'You guys did it.' Because the market was turning. The stock market started recommending the stock to buy."

Armacost cried the good news from the podium of the annual meeting on April 24, 1984. In 1983 "BankAmerica was rated number one in the world in arranging syndicated loans," a position consolidated a month earlier, when the bank drove to the heart of the takeover wars to lead the $14 billion financing that enabled Chevron to acquire Gulf Oil, the deal that snatched Gulf from the hands of corporate raider T. Boone Pickens. But that was the old business, corporate loans. He spoke to the revolution. "We have learned to address markets, and not just street corners." To that end he would have shrunk the brick and mortar of 1,071 branches by 120 by the end of '84—cutting four thousand people from the payroll. The bank had moved from fourth to first place in automated teller machines in California. Becoming "truly creatures of the marketplace," it had seen its money market entry, Cash Maximizer, grab 53 percent of the California bank market—only one of an "armada" of new products. With Schwab, he had "pushed the barriers of what a bank could be." Faced the "pestilence" of nonbanking competitors by applying for permission to open a string of "nonbank banks" across the country. Acquired Seafirst in Seattle when the Penn Square energy loans brought it down, gaining a vital long-term strategic edge for interstate and Pacific Rim banking.

The ebullient Jim Miscoll, one of the "true" BankAmericans and now head of Retail Financial Services, summed up the spirit of "rebirth" that would become his personal theme. Addressing a Senior Management Conference in Anaheim in mid-February '84, he announced, "Watch out, everybody. MotherBank is back!"

But keeping his own counsel, Armacost had seen the red flags go up for MotherBank by the end of 1983. Until the recovery started in '83, "we were not getting any signals out of all the disciplines we had in place. *But when the other banks' earnings started recovering again, our credit losses got worse. That was the first real, real major sign that something was not running right in our portfolio, in particular.*" His private thoughts were: "How deep, how bad is it? How do you contain it?"

The dysfunction Adizes had identified had not crippled the bank during the good times. But as Adizes later said with a shrug of futility, "when the bad loans came through," the intransigent nature of the portfolio that had gone unidentified at Silverado would reveal itself and strike with violent perversity.

PETE TALBOTT had had an alarming view of the deteriorating ag loan portfolios within two weeks of joining the bank in October 1983. After spending six years implementing John Reed's consumer strategy across the United States and two years running Citibank's consumer business in Europe, he had been frustrated when passed by as one of three promised by John Reed to run the entire consumer operation for Citibank. "You'll be promoted next year," Reed had promised him. He knew Reed would honor that. But he was hurt. He was turning forty, and this seemed the time to change, if he was going to. He left Citibank and in mid-'83 called Mont McMillen, still running Europe in London for B of A. The Talbotts and McMillens had become friends. Talbott had heard Armacost was planning to develop a national consumer strategy. After twelve years of frontline consumer banking for Citi, he felt confident telling McMillen, "You need me." Vice-Chairman Jim Wiesler, now head of the renamed Retail Consumer Services, had hired Talbott in October to develop the national strategy. "They wanted one because Citi had one," Talbott says with a smile. He would find himself within six months running the California retail bank as Jim Miscoll was moved to the figurehead role of running Southern California in Los Angeles. A great place for Miscoll, in the consensus of just about everybody.

"At the monthly meetings of regional managers," said Talbott, "Miscoll would conduct the meetings, and portfolios would be presented from each lending sector. Randy Russell presented the ag loans and was very upset to report *that roughly half of the ag loans were not performing.* I became almost feverish hearing this and waited for comments. None came. And Miscoll would say, 'Thank you. Next.' And I'd say, 'Hey, did you hear what I heard? Isn't anybody going to ask some questions?' and I'd be told, 'This is not a problem. We know our farmers. We know the agricultural cycles. Things will pick up.' "

WHILE TALBOTT WORRIED, in the carnelian tower Adizes's Corp POK had revealed, but could not resolve, another problem in McMillen's NAD. It had laid bare the biggest human conflict of the banking revolution: the struggle of the traditional banker to hold on to his identity and self-image as his role was transformed from banker to salesman and as traditional forms of banking shrank and vanished. Common to all banks, Armacost saw it as "the conflict between the old banker/counselor/customer manager and a new breed of transactionally driven capital market specialists." It erupted, specifically, in B of A as "the struggle and conflict between commercial and investment banking. You're starting to hire capital market-type people. They want high salaries. They don't integrate. They want total account access," says Armacost. "They wanted to access our customers directly and sell their products," confirms McMillen, reducing his commercial bankers, the men who had built and nurtured the customer relationships and already fighting among themselves for their slice of the shrinking corporate pie, into little more than door openers. He would go to the wall on that issue. "All we had going for us was the relationship."

The conflict had escalated into hostility between McMillen and John Vella, head of Investment Banking, BankAmerica Capital Markets Group. Watching old-style corporate lending vanish, McMillen's people "were dying to learn about new lines of business so they could sell them to their customers. But the new lines were *not* part of my responsibility," says McMillen. "They were in Vella's. He had a good thing going and didn't want anything to do with commercial bankers."

McMillen wouldn't give an inch. Chairman Lee Prussia sided with Vella, polarizing the issue, weakening McMillen's political position. "Of course, it meant a shrinking of my division," says McMillen. "I was perceived as fighting out of self-interest. But I believed that if we lost that relationship, we had nothing else to sell. I knew when I bucked Prussia and Vella it was curtains for my career, but I owed it to my troops and to myself to fight for what we saw as best." By the accidents of career path and history, McMillen had become defender and archetype of the old system. The classic BankAmerican, standing firm on his principles as the tidal wave engulfed him.

The struggle put at risk the promotion that had looked obvious. Armacost had not yet filled the void in World Banking since Bolin had retired—been invited to retire, many said, as the Latin American loans became an embarrassment. For months the job was empty. In October 1984 Armacost called McMillen and said, "I put a dime on its side, and it could have fallen either way. It fell for Bob." Bob Frick, a longtime fast-track colleague, was the new head of World Banking. McMillen was being moved onto the shelf. It was painful for Armacost. "Mont was great at client relationships. He was marvelous at that side of things. I have great respect for him. I put him in Europe with major responsibilities." And Armacost admitted that as McMillen had gone through the Adizes process, "he certainly did inherit the brunt of some of the NAD tensions." But as two fundamental conflicts continued to run through his division, unresolved, Armacost, with his ear to the ground, picked up rumblings that McMillen was being perceived "as a much greater talker than doer in the minds of the guys he worked directly for. . . . The classic guy with everything needed to succeed in B of A was being stripped by the Adizes process," Armacost suspected, "of the veneer that had allowed some people success in the old culture without being truly measured by their peers." One of McMillen's colleagues on the Corp POK shook his head and said, "His weaknesses showed up in the process. When pushed, he was revealed."

In November 1984 McMillen was moved out of NAD to a World Banking job in San Francisco with the ring of power, but no actual line authority. He would be executive vice-president overseeing a new division called Network Markets. He would also be "senior calling officer for major network accounts." It was the equivalent of Social Policy, to which Bob Truex had been banished. He knew it was his writing on the wall. He would go to pasture, the impeccable BankAmerican in his banker's blues, working the relationship.

"The system is beginning to throw its sacrifices to the lions," said Adizes, who had predicted that the pathology would drive the organism to kill its own as scapegoats.

Adizes, as well as Sam Armacost, now had time running against him. All the ratios, the measures the world watched, were falling sharply. The great bank rated *at the bottom* in performance. Adizes's dreams took time and money, raising costs while the balance sheet deteriorated. Armacost's strength directly affected the success or failure of Adizes's ambitious schedule. "Ichak was the prisoner of two things—whatever Sam wanted and his ego," observed the bank's financial controller, Harvey Gillis, of Adizes's dependence on Armacost. The enormous investment in BASE, BAPS, and the other massive projects made Armacost a target. "I began to tell him, 'Sam, you have to worry about your survival.' He would say, 'We are not going to cut down on our future.' I admired him tremendously for that," says Adizes.

Adizes's admiration for Armacost had grown with the pressure. He had heard that Armacost "had been a fantastic manager in Europe, his desk was clean, he always had time. His people loved him; they would kill themselves for Sam. He was a leader. . . . You can't not love Sam." Adizes speculated that Europe might be the source of some of his strength. "Sam went to Europe, so he was not in the center where he could have been consumed." By the politics. By Clausen. "Most of the good management emerged far away from the central office."

Although the board stood fast behind Armacost, the escalating problems were stressing the Managing Committee. They were also aggravating the tension created by the unusual division of power between his chairman, Lee Prussia, and Armacost. Armacost claims he was making a great effort to work with Prussia as a team, sharing the power and the glory. But in counterpoint to Armacost's view of the future, Prussia had been crying doom and gloom from the time Max Hopper arrived in mid-'82, issuing warnings some felt were more petulant than constructive. In the POK sessions, McMillen saw Prussia "being very aggressive about 'Banking is dead. If we don't change fast, the bank won't survive." Lecturing Armacost by implication. Chuck Schwab observed at board meetings that Prussia spoke up with suggestions for change that seemed to be attacks on Armacost's lack of speed of change. Schwab tended to agree with Prussia. For Schwab himself was becoming an abrasive force. "He was giving Sam a very bad time at the board," Adizes began to hear.

Armacost's poise and the dignified pacing of his revolution demonstrated Adizes's "duck theory of management—above water you act unperturbed, while under the water you are paddling like hell."

And the bank *was* being remade. The restructuring of consumer banking and the creation of Global Consumer Markets would be unveiled in February 1985. IBS, World Banking's computer system, announced in January 1985: "If it were an ocean, it would be the Pacific; if it were a mountain, it would be Everest. . . ." IBS would make BankAmerica's global information system state of the art. It would be fully operational in 1988. BAPS, the payments system, would be unveiled midyear.

"THERE WAS NO SENSE of crisis" at the end of 1983, McMillen says. Red flags had revealed to Armacost that B of A suffered from some systemic illness not shared by other banks, and Armacost overrode his reluctance to undermine BankAmerican morale to warn the entire bank staff, by letter, at the end of 1983: "Among the nation's leading banks, we're currently ranked at or near the bottom of the list of financial measures by which performance is generally judged."

But in the next sentence the salesman's eternal optimism reassured "the women and men of BankAmerica" that "we are turning this situation around. . . . We've always been winners. We're going to continue to be." The bank's true condition had not yet reached the men who ran it. Through the Indian summer of 1984 the bank's management and board basked in its last season of complacency.

Chapter Twelve

NMEC, THE BLOODLESS ACRONYM by which the disaster became known, was the bank's Pearl Harbor. A sneak attack that shocked the bank from its myth of impregnability, it was the beginning of a relentless barrage of hits to balance sheet, morale, and stock price that would leave the great bank crippled, and Sam Armacost's career and visions for MotherBank in disarray. With NMEC, the symptoms that had been presenting themselves for half a decade were finally revealed as a pathology about to overwhelm the organism.

Standing for National Mortgage Equity Corporation, and pronounced "Nee-mek," NMEC began to unravel in the summer of 1983, a full sixteen months before anyone at bank headquarters would hear of it—twenty months before a terse and guarded statement from the bank would give the press its first hint. It was not a story you hurried to release. It appeared to be the biggest fraud in banking history.

That summer David Feldman, a graduate of West Point and a veteran of honorable service in Vietnam, had learned that his appeal against conviction for fraud had been denied by a Chicago court and he would be going to jail. In eight months he would be in Boron, a minimum-security prison in California's desert where white-collar criminals play tennis and order in pizzas. Comforts aside, he would no longer be out there, on the telephone, infusing into his flourishing real estate scam, NMEC, the flow of fresh money on which it all depended. The pyramid scheme he had built with brilliant cunning would almost surely collapse as its pumping engine went behind bars.

The mortgage securities fraud hit Sam Armacost's desk in early October 1984. It came in the guise of a small, even insignificant, loss of about eight million dollars. Harvey Gillis, the bank's newly arrived financial controller, had entered his office just after Armacost had been brought the news. They were meeting to talk about the auditing problem they were arm wrestling through with the regulators, an error on the bank's part that would take a year to correct operationally and reconcile in its books, and that brought more regulatory focus on the bank. Within weeks of joining BankAmerica Gillis had inherited project responsibility for resolving this financial systems blowup. "Here's another surprise we don't need," said Armacost, clearly nettled at the series of "surprises" that had been hitting his desk with disquieting frequency over the past months.

They had only the sketchiest of information so far. It apparently involved the bank's Inglewood branch and regional management in Southern California. The monthly payments to a group of East Coast savings and loans that had invested in mortgage-backed securities had stopped. The S&Ls were demanding action from the bank, which had served as both escrow agent and trustee. The first news was guardedly optimistic. "We appear to have had a bit of a scam in real estate mortgages," Gillis was told as he swiftly checked with the bank's specialists, but old hands reassured him that it was a fairly common scam.

Armacost instantly assigned a task force to find out what was going on. Just six months on the job, Gillis was thrust to the heart of the task force investigation. This would be a core group of about a dozen, meeting in secrecy under intense pressure of time to get the facts and assess the damage before the scandal broke from some other source. B of A would soon be preparing fourth-quarter figures, and had to know what impact NMEC would have.

Gillis had had enough surprises. The "Nigerian surprise" had broken just as he arrived, in June—a failed loan made to Nigeria by BankAmerica's consumer credit subsidiary, FinanceAmerica, to purchase what proved to be outdated and worthless plastic building supplies. The con had been run by a woman who had moved the money to a Swiss bank account, and Finance-America had lost several million dollars. He had been shocked, sitting in on a loan loss committee meeting chaired by Lee Prussia, to find that the people responsible had not been fired. "I had not realized. You just don't fire people at BankAmerica. They didn't want to endanger their status with Nigeria—that was logical. But it was brushed right over."

In addition to Nigeria, the "reconciling surprise," as he called it, had already popped before Gillis arrived, unknown to him. "Although the amounts involved were immense, the potential loss was not large. But nobody *told* me." The job of cleaning it up was proving to be "huge, just *enormous.*" And now there was NMEC, the corporate vehicle Feldman had created for his con game.

The task force faced a meticulously crafted scam. A mortgage broker unwittingly caught up in the scheme explains Feldman's legitimate-sounding deal. "Savings and loans deposit five million dollars or more in an escrow account administered by B of A. That money is used to fund mortgages to individuals. The individuals then repay the mortgages back to NMEC monthly, and NMEC remits the money back out to the investors and collects a healthy servicing fee. We're talking about residential, bread-and-butter mortgages, mostly in California. And, later, Texas apartment houses converted into investor condos." It was a "high-yield, relatively short-term investment, a very attractively packaged deal. It appeared to be risk-free. It seemed almost too good to be true," says one of the men who was suckered in. For its role as "gatekeeper" of the money that moved between investors and NMEC, Bank of America earned the kind of fee income Armacost was urging his people to find. But it was all smoke and mirrors.

An honor graduate from West Point in engineering, Feldman was spruce and articulate, and seemed a serious-minded straight shooter. "His suits were never quite in style, and he wore sideburns, kind of a throwback to the sixties," an insider later reflected. But he didn't look slick. His credentials checked out impeccably. He performed meticulously and kept his promises.

His "risk free" package had been carefully designed to reassure the most cautious investor. His escrow agents and trustees were Bank of America and Wells Fargo. His attorney was the big, prestigious Chicago firm Lord, Bissell, and Brook, major representatives of Lloyds of London in the United States. Lord, Bissell had written the one-hundred-page private placement document that specified quality standards for those mortgages qualified to be included in the pool into which investors—in this case, savings and loans—would pour their money. Those standards—including scrupulous appraisals of the properties' values—were incorporated into the escrow instructions that authorized B of A to release the investors' money to NMEC only if the mortgages NMEC submitted for certification met the predetermined standards. There was yet another layer of security: The mortgages were 100 percent insured by two companies. One of them, a Montana insurer, Glacier General Assurance, had a published Best rating of A+12, in the very highest range of insurance company ratings.

Feldman had worked as a commodities broker for Merrill Lynch's Chicago office, but lived a double life and had been convicted of mail and wire fraud in 1982. Undeterred by the impending indictment, he had constructed the mortgage-pooling scheme as early as 1980. Working with several convicted felons, he had fabricated a convincing story to sell the deal: He was in the mortgage business, was pooling high-rate first and second mortgages and selling them to S&Ls, and had created a structure for doing this that solved a lot of the risk issues. (He had shrewdly chosen S&Ls as his target at a time when they were under tremendous pressure from regulators to expand their earnings to meet increasing capital requirements. The high yields he offered were irresistible.) He had begun selling the mortgage securities to the S&Ls in late '81, and used his early investors as enthusiastic references, an attractive carrot to subsequent investors.

The first thrifts to invest were getting paid regularly and on time. Feldman was proving "a man of his word," says an insider. Through early 1984 he was successful in getting several dozen eastern S&Ls to invest in pools. As much as $200 million flowed through escrow accounts in B of A's Inglewood branch.

At the peak of NMEC's success Feldman went to jail. Believing Feldman's claims of innocence in the Chicago fraud, and thinking the certificate process legitimate, the loyal staff Feldman had left behind, supported by outside interested parties, tried to maintain the monthly payments to the investors while Feldman was gone. Opening NMEC's books, reading the mail, responding to calls, they gradually became suspicious. When investors requested inspection of some of the properties, they discovered that some properties were shabby and abandoned—and some simply didn't exist. They also found that the Montana insurer Glacier had been providing a substantial portion of the payments, giving the investor banks the illusion that homeowners were making their mortgage payments and that the certificates were current. Glacier, it began to appear, was part of the scam.

Like any pyramid scheme, NMEC's required a steady flow of new cash to keep current the monthly certificate payments made to investors. It required Feldman to get new infusions of cash from more and more investors. But he was serving time; the spigot had been turned off. No more certificates were being sold to unsuspecting S&Ls. The cash drought spread to Glacier: NMEC had tried to cover the ceased payments to the thrifts by increasing its claims on its insurer. But by late summer, Glacier had stopped honoring claims, and NMEC was unable to continue making monthly payments. Evidence that the whole scheme was coming unraveled was the worried inquiries NMEC was starting to receive from the investor banks reporting late or even missed payments. The lid was being lifted on a horror story, almost none of it yet known to Bank of America.

Another dimension to the fraud was unfolding. Some of the pool money had not even been invested in mortgages, but had been diverted from the escrow accounts to NMEC's corporate purposes. Evidence suggested that up to $5 million of the escrow monies had been spent buying a troubled S&L. And Feldman had extracted some booty from the pool—incredibly arrogant behavior in a man heading to jail and under constant watch as a convicted felon. Scanning checkbooks, investigators subsequently discovered that Feldman had been siphoning money from the corporation and spending it on such things as home improvements and the massive lawyer's fees related to his appeal efforts. Associates had noticed that he had been doing lavish renovation of both his Palos Verdes and Tahoe homes and had taken to being driven in a limo. The paper trail led to Bank of America, for the NMEC money Feldman had been spending had been diverted from the escrow accounts. It was a shock to the insider: *People at the bank had allowed money to be released out of the escrow account for purposes other than funding mortgages for the investment pool. It was a breakdown of fiduciary responsibility so blatant and severe that it suggested something more sinister than oversight or incompetence. One or more B of A employees must be in on the conspiracy.*

Banks know there will always be some fraud. But even more alarming were the implications for the bank's control and monitoring systems. The explosively growing footings in the Inglewood branch, the burst of escrow activity, should have triggered questions and investigations into the kind of business being taken on, and into its risks. As gatekeeper, B of A had fallen asleep at the switch.

Nor was Wells Fargo blameless. As the original trustee, it had grown dubious of NMEC's credibility and passed the role to Bank of America. But it had not shared its fears, or evidence, with B of A.

In late August, the Inglewood branch staff members handling the NMEC escrows agreed to a meeting at the bank's regional headquarters. It was attended by several of B of A's branch employees and regional executives, Feldman, home on furlough, his accountant, and a few other concerned parties. The meeting had been called in response to an alarming letter from Seamen's Bank for Savings in New York, which was circulated at the meeting. The bank, by this time, had received a call, as well, from Seamen's. Seamen's had invested nearly $20 million into a B of A escrow account. When its payments from NMEC fell behind, Seamen's did its own investigation, and discovered that their money was still in escrow; fortunately it had not been invested on schedule. Sensing something very wrong, Seamen's wrote a strong, accusatory letter that "pointed out irregularities that made the bank look terrible," says a participant at the meeting; they wanted return of their $19.5

million. Sent to senior officers in the bank, the Seamen's letter was now an official bank document, requiring action. Even though it had not yet percolated up to Armacost, it could not be hidden or destroyed.

Claiming innocence of any problems or irregularities, the involved bank staff reported, two weeks after the meeting, that the escrow money was all there and that, in fact, there were excess funds of almost $200,000. Conflicting stories about what money was or was not there raged, as the roof caved in on Feldman's scheme. Subsequently, millions would prove to be missing from the Seamen's escrow. Evidence converging from many sources outside the bank and from the Seamen's letter inside broke over the heads of the involved Bank-Americans. They were temporarily suspended, pending more information, and five were subsequently fired.

Beyond the apparent direct conspiracy of its employees, the bank had indirectly helped perpetuate and deepen what could become a staggering loss to reputation and balance sheet by lending its own prestige to affirm Feldman's personal credibility; it had freely provided references to investors, and Feldman had been claiming he had a large line of credit from B of A to support NMEC's operations.

THE FBI WAS pursuing the criminal investigation. The bank's job was to establish what facts it could and try to calculate its liabilities and obligations. The first job of the task force was to get evaluations on the property—fast, thorough ground appraisals that would give them a good handle on market values. B of A's chief accountant Sarah Collins, a key member of the task force, who impressed Gillis as "a very bright young woman, sharp, quick, analytical," was checking out the insurers, and was going at it with the tenacity of a secret agent. Gillis urged her to "get at the facts," fearing that they were "not as people hoped them to be." A third of the mortgages, she discovered, had been insured by the Texas insurance company Pacific American and two-thirds by Glacier, the Montana company.

With the year-end closing, there was urgent need for the bank to establish the size of the loss. Much depended on what the insurers would pay. There were signs that Pacific American was collapsing. It was apparently going bankrupt and into receivership to the state. Clues were also appearing that Pacific American was controlled by convicted felons who were NMEC insiders. Sarah Collins now pursued Glacier like a sleuth, living on the telephone, extracting information. Gleaning word that the top-rated company was having financial difficulties, she continued to press until she found that Glacier might also be on the brink of bankruptcy. The task force had written off coverage from Texas. But if Glacier went, the bank's only protection from a multimillion-dollar loss was what it could get from the sale of the properties. The task force must get the appraisals it had ordered. By mid-November they had not come. "Look, go do quickie curbside appraisals, *today!*" Gillis demanded. While doing little more than driving by a property could not be relied on for the final figures, it would give the task force at least some grasp of the magnitude of the loss.

As the curbside estimates of the values of the California properties started coming in, they were showing values lower than the values claimed by NMEC. Appraisers could not find some of the properties or addresses. Some buildings were empty, with no evidence of being converted to condos. The first word from Texas was even worse. There were half-finished apartment buildings, abandoned and disheveled, in a market in which all values were diving. As the task force groaned at the results, an apartment building originally appraised at $5 million would drop to $3 . . . then to $1 million. It was clear that the property values had been grossly overstated across the board.

Easier to quantify were the losses to the New York thrifts. They appeared to be in the range of $130 million. "Our lawyers argued that the B of A had to step up and take the loss, not the savings banks. We offered to buy the mortgages back and replace them with good mortgages from our portfolio," says Gillis. The bank's first offer of fifty cents on the dollar was refused by the investors; it paid full price. One hundred and thirty-three million dollars. Those good-faith payments would help contain embarrassment and image damage in the marketplace. It would help keep the scandal quiet while the bank pursued the depth of its loss—now largely contingent on the final appraisals and the ability of Glacier Assurance to cover a massive portion of the money paid to the savings and loans.

By the last weeks of 1984 the original estimate of an $8 million loss was a dream. It had climbed from $10 to $12 to a worst-case scenario of $37 million. Still the reliable ground appraisals had not arrived.

The law required issuing a press release if the loss was "material," Helmut Loring, task force expert on the SEC, told Gillis as they discussed daily, during these weeks, whether a press release had to be issued. If the loss was deemed "material" to the financial status of the company, it must be disclosed. But what was a "material" loss? Loring deemed that $10 million was probably not material. Anything over $30 million certainly would be. Gillis wanted a release.

NMEC was putting great tension on Sam Armacost. He must find out what was going on, assess the loss, and disclose it to Mike Patriarca. The loss might *still* be relatively small. But it would be another goddamned red flag waved before the chief examiner. Patriarca had increased his rigor, his presence, since the banking disaster that had followed Penn Square, the near collapse whose name would send shudders through the big banks through the 1980s: Continental Illinois.

MIKE PATRIARCA HAD BEEN SIMPLY a bearer of stern news to Penn Square. It had not been "his" bank. But the Continental Illinois crisis had been all his—as chief examiner of twelve multinationals—and his examiners'. He had been "bowled over" by Continental.

The OCC had been monitoring Continental Illinois, the nation's ninth-largest holding company, since Penn Square. For Continental had bought "one and a half billion of Penn Square's lousy energy loans"—the loans that had brought Seafirst down in 1983. Continental had a special vulnerability, different from Penn Square—or Bank of America. It had no branches, virtually no checking or savings accounts—no retail deposits that fell under the FDIC insurance umbrella. Of its $40 billion in deposits, the vast majority was uninsured CDs; its depositors were institutional investors, many foreign. The wipeout of the uninsured depositors in Penn Square was still a raw memory in the market, and investors had been jumpy, ready to pull their funds on a rumor, ever since.

These professional investors had brought a new volatility to the banking system. "They rely on a rating agency, Keefe, Bruyette, which grades all the banks, A to E. When Keefe lowers the grade to below a C, the deposits are pulled immediately. It is sudden death," says Patriarca. This volatility had been increased by Penn Square, when the FDIC's Bill Isaac had given his message to the world that the U.S. government would not stand behind its banks or big depositors.

"Continental was in trouble and had been reporting a steadily increasing volume of problem assets for two years," Patriarca says. As Continental's capital was drained off by the bad energy loans, his examiners saw signs of a creeping run on deposits. Market confidence was eroding.

The run started in May 1984 on a false rumor. A Japanese wire service story reported that the U.S. Comptroller of the Currency was discussing with the financial giant Nomura Securities its acquisition of Continental Illinois. "Continental called us and said, 'What the hell are you doing?' " Patriarca recalls. "We issued a press release within hours denying it. But the world was goosey about Continental. The rumors had been going on for months in the trading pits. Once there was sufficient question about Continental's viability in the eyes of those large uninsured depositors, *bang!*—we had a run."

It began in Europe and Japan and quickly struck in the United States. It was like no bank run in history; no lines of depositors gathered outside Continental. It was the world's first global electronic run, with billions sucked from the bank by computers in London, Tokyo, and Hong Kong. The money couldn't all run out in a day. With CDs, depositors could legally pull their money without forfeit of interest when maturity dates came due. It would be a prolonged agony. Patriarca dispatched a top examiner to sit at Continental's trading post in Chicago. He stationed "a funding expert of the first order" at the head trader's desk in Continental's London office. "He was reporting by telephone a couple of times a day. When London closed, he rolled their results to our guy in Chicago, then transmitted to Washington." Computer-scanning the maturities, they calculated the next day's drain, helpless, as the bank raced toward insolvency.

The run still rolled a week later, when Patriarca was rushed to New York for an emergency meeting of all the major banks. Conveniently in New York for a meeting of the Association of Reserve City Bankers, the banking establishment gathered in a branch of Morgan Guaranty Trust Company, with Lewis T. Preston, then chairman of both the bank and holding company J. P. Morgan & Company, Inc., chairing. Armacost and Prussia were there for Bank of America. Only those with money in Continental were directly at risk. But for all the big banks, "it was a meeting of enlightened self-interest." Penn Square had been a half-billion-dollar bank; Continental was one of the "elephants." The untested vulnerabilities created by instantaneous globalized communications and dependence on market funding "were being played out in Technicolor," says Patriarca. "We really didn't know what would happen to the world financial structure. Whether this would be the loose thread that unwound the whole thing. The potential was real."

Patriarca, chairing a parallel meeting next door with the banks' chief lending officers, caught snatches of the heated "wrangling." It sounded like a script from Penn Square. "Some were saying, 'It's in our interest to try to stem the tide and keep Continental on its feet.' Others were saying, 'God damn it, these guys failed, and banks ought to be allowed to fail.' But no one knew what the consequences were if Continental failed. No one wanted to find out." It was decided to provide Continental with a bridge line of credit and interim funding. Patriarca was impressed with Preston's force at the meeting. He was named chair of an ad hoc committee of bankers, and banks volunteered to call all absent members of the Reserve City Bankers to get them signed up to the safety net credit line. A press release was issued on May 16 announcing a shared bailout by the Federal Reserve, the FDIC, and the banks—a $10 billion bailout. The Fed was stepping in as lender of last resort, confirming the growing concerns about U.S. vulnerability to events beyond its borders expressed by Volcker in testimony to the Senate Committee on Banking, Housing, and Urban Affairs just three months earlier:

> The international financial system is not separable from our domestic banking and credit system. . . . We are talking about a threat essentially without parallel in the postwar period.

Patriarca and Joe Selby, Comptroller Todd Conover's deputy, flew to London to try to hold the "confidence factor" abroad at a summit meeting of international banks hosted by the Bank of England. Joining the Fed and the FDIC in a united front, Patriarca declared to the world's nervous bankers that "the government is committed to ensuring that Continental and the U.S. banking system remain intact." An important statement had been made: There was a handful of banks that the U.S. government would not allow to fail. At congressional hearings a few months later, that category was given its abbreviation, TBTF—"too big to fail." Bank of America was one of those banks. Yet they all had seen that even the largest banks could crumble internally to the point of bailout, a fate only a little less terrible than death.

Patriarca's response to Continental had been to form an elite SWAT team of senior examiners who would be assigned, full-time, to the very biggest or most troubled banks. "It didn't make any sense for the biggest banks to have second-team examiners," Patriarca believed. The new team was a flying squad that could be sent wherever in the world the safety and soundness of his dozen multinationals were at risk. Those watching Bank of America "lived in San Francisco but reported to us. We got control of the elite," said Patriarca. By early spring Michael LaRusso, a muscular man who looked more like a union organizer on the docks than a banking expert, would be "on-site a hundred percent of the time."

Another response to Continental was to raise capital requirements for the big banks. Capital was seen, by the regulators, as the best buffer for crises. A shock absorber. The only real source of resilience. Immediately after Continental, the drive to force the banks to build their capital became the major thrust of the Comptroller's Office. At the time B of A's capital as a percentage of assets sat at 4 percent. In June all banks were ordered to raise those capital ratios to 5.5 percent.

But Bank of America was being singled out for special attention, Armacost was disturbed to see. It would be forced to raise its capital *higher* than its peer banks, to 6 percent. "They were petrified of another major bank failure and were on a kick of changing and articulating new capital and credit standards as a proxy for control and new regulation. We were a perfect vehicle. They could use us as a glorious example, and then they wouldn't have to kowtow to any other bank." Armacost fumed. "They were so determined they were never going to let Continental happen again that they started trying to run the bank."

He knew that for the November board meeting, Patriarca planned to fly from Washington and force Armacost, before the board, to sign an agreement that the bank would raise its capital to the new level and more than *triple* its loan loss reserves. It was like being publicly spanked. Humiliated.

AS THE BOARD GATHERED in Los Angeles for the November meeting, NMEC was still a secret, smoldering volcano. Although Armacost had spoken privately to several of the directors about it, the board had been told nothing. The issue at the meeting was capital and loan loss reserves. Mike Patriarca came to read the riot act and force Armacost to sign the pledge.

As the agreement was circulated around the table, each director required to sign off on it, accepting responsibility, Chuck Schwab watched the ritual, appalled. "Sam had to sign this unbelievable, devastating letter of acknowledgment of Patriarca's finding. He had to bring it to the board. It was just awful!" As Patriarca presented his report, the message Schwab was getting was: " 'This is a serious matter, gentlemen. You've got to address these issues.' It was our first warning."

On the surface Armacost maintained his composure. Inside he was enraged over Patriarca's acts. "The bank had been raising its capital for five years," Armacost had argued in a heated meeting with Comptroller Conover before the board meeting. He had been raising both capital and reserves since he was cashier in 1979, he pointed out. This additional pressure on the bank's resources was not needed right now. He needed to grow to bring up declining earnings, not to have to shrink or compromise his aggressive strategy to raise capital and reserves.

But there were a few sources of quick capital that would not compromise the strategy, he told the board. He made a delicate proposal: The headquarters building on California Street was tying up perhaps half a billion in capital. B of A could sell it without changing anything. It would still be the headquarters, still be the Bank of America building and Giannini Plaza. Claire Hoffman was not there to hear the proposal being made. They all knew she never came to the Los Angeles meetings.

Under the spell of Armacost's fast and fluid presentations, the board did not seem to share Schwab's alarm. It was reacting with "hope against hope that this was a temporary problem," Schwab felt. The reserves issue disturbed him most. He sketched a graph—a steeply escalating line of the bank's nonper-forming loans, the reserves line staying static along the base, a widening gap growing between the two. The board, he feared, seemed to be missing the "absolutely critical relationship of loan loss reserves relative to the level of nonperforming loans. How large should their reserves be?" If reserves were too small, losses too high, banks might have to drain their capital. Big reserves were a safety net. When he joined the board, Schwab had not fully understood the role of loan loss reserves. The brokerage business was far more rigorous. "You have to reserve one hundred percent on a troubled loan and write it off *immediately,* that day. Every day you have to close the books." In educating himself, he had discovered one of the keys to banking: "How you manage earnings is by playing with reserves." Harvey Gillis describes it as "an artistic science." A judgment call traditionally left up to the bank. If you wanted earnings to look better, you took less from earnings for reserves. If earnings were strong, you could build reserves boldly, accruing some fat for the lean years when you might want to shift some reserves back into earnings.

Schwab left the meeting aghast. "If they'd got the board to respond then and taken decisive action . . ." he later thought with anguish. More than ever he was convinced he must take aggressive action to activate change in the organization. He had met several months earlier in Washington with Bob McNamara. Washington had been "hotter than hell," but he'd had a "real good exchange with McNamara. Talked about the Schwab business in relationship to the bank . . . I had lots of hats—fast-growing subsidiary, board member, large stockholder. But they, the board, were my overseers, too," says Schwab. "McNamara thought we were underreserved. He said several times, 'You can't lend to third world countries and properly reserve for third world debt. Can't have it both ways.' He was well spoken. Outspoken. Very charming and alert. But he just *talked* about it."

The November meeting had heightened tension between Schwab and Arma-cost when the two met for their regular monthly one-on-one in Armacost's office in December. Schwab's relationship with the bank had been going "ninety-five percent perfect" from a business point of view. Schwab had gained customers and increased his profits. The Schwab minioffices in Bank of America branches had expanded his reach. Always impatient when the bank's lumbering bureaucracy did not seize opportunity, he was frustrated that Arma-cost had not diverted the Trust Department's stock-trading business to Schwab & Co., as he had urged him to do. "Sam, it's costing the bank ten million dollars a year to place these trades with investment brokers when they could give the business to a subsidiary"—a sibling! He was appalled at the trust's performance. "They never make the Dow-Jones index," he scoffed. The business press had been publishing a series of embarrassing stories about rank inefficiency in B of A's trust operations. They had begun to have the smell of scandal.

Schwab had stubbornly held his independence from the bank and ran his operation largely without interference. He and Armacost had been getting along well personally. Proposed by Schwab's close friend banker Donald R. Stephens, CEO of Bank of San Francisco, Armacost had joined Young Presidents. They had played some golf together. But Armacost had heard about Schwab's private visit with McNamara, and at their December meeting Schwab sensed that Armacost was "pissed off." With NMEC and the pressure from the examiners, it was a time when Armacost wanted solidarity on the board, and to him, Schwab's actions smacked of disloyalty. It was, in his view, back-door behavior. As Adizes had predicted, the marriage between the entrepreneur and the bank was turning stormy.

Schwab, starting low-key and gathering steam, as is his style, responded emotionally to Sam's testiness: "I've got everything I have at stake. My company. My stockholdings. Sam, I just want you to be *the best damn president of a bank in the U.S.!*"

WHILE THE RESERVES and capital issues preoccupied the executive floor and board, NMEC was about to explode. The task force could not wait for the final appraisals. It was well into January, and the NMEC loss was clearly "material," even though final numbers were not known. There was still faint hope that Glacier, the larger insurer, would come through with insurance money. The word on Glacier from accountant Sarah Collins was getting worse. It seemed likely that it, too, was involved in the fraud. Glacier's California agent, John Wain, had suddenly died in January; several suspected that he was not dead at all but had dropped out of sight.

By late January it appeared that the bank could not avoid declaring a loss of at least $37 million. "Sam was really upset. We were getting back to a decent recovery. He was a positive sales-oriented man and didn't like receiving bad news," says Gillis. There was urgent debate. Gillis could wait a few weeks, delay release of his fourth-quarter numbers until getting final appraisals to know better where they stood. But more delay risked violation of the SEC's disclosure rules. On January 28 Gillis bit the bullet and issued a press release announcing a $37 million loss involving fraudulent mortgage securities. The release said nothing else. The press went crazy, tracking down the story. Relief that the release had been made vanished as soon as Gillis learned that the loss would far exceed $37 million; it would surpass their worst case number.

The full NMEC property appraisals had started to arrive. "Somebody hadn't done their homework," Gillis said in wry understatement as the task force learned that the properties were worth even less than the curbside appraisals had shown. "It was a full-size scam!" Within two weeks Sarah Collins had rooted out another surprise. She had inside financial information on the Montana insurer, Glacier. She told the team that Glacier was about to declare bankruptcy. It did not have the capacity to cover the two-thirds of the bank's loss it was to have covered. There would be no insurance coverage. The bank's loss could now be as high as $95 million.

A $37 million loss had already been announced. The bank would now have to do the thing banks dread above all others: *restate its estimated loss.* "It would look as if we've been trying to suppress bad news," Gillis said fretfully. "Analysts hate it. It makes them, and shareholders, doubt the integrity of the bank. The bank doesn't know what's going on," said Steve McLin, concerned that bad news would hurt his negotiations for acquisitions and lose the regulators' support. He had the acquisition of Orbanco, a big bank in Oregon, in the works. And applications pending for the creation of thirteen nonbank banks to expand into the financial services area in other states. Part of Armacost's grand strategy to become "the nation's leader in financial services," the negotiations were all the more important since Citicorp had just charged into the California market by buying a failing three-hundred-branch savings and loan and renaming it Citicorp Savings—an impressive toehold. Citi was anchoring its expansion in skyscraping towers in Los Angeles and San Francisco. A negative announcement of this magnitude would hurt B of A's competitive momentum. Gillis had been assured by line officers that McLin's acquisition negotiations would be backed by strong first-quarter gains in 1985. No bad surprises.

The potential $95 million loss would have to be presented to the board at its February meeting. Armacost had not kept the board fully informed. As the board had met in December, the task force had still been intensively information gathering, still guessing that the loss would be small. He had mentioned the problem to the Auditing and Examining Committee but opted not to tell the full board. There had been no regular board meeting in January, and he had not called directors informally. "When there's smoke, he closes the door," Gillis says, concerned that Armacost had not pursued an informational campaign with the board, gently, and in small groups, keeping directors informed and seeking their counsel.

The NMEC mess was finally dumped on the boardroom table in February. Board members had read of the $37 million fraud in the press. Armacost had met with the Auditing and Examining Committee before the board meeting. But most had not had any idea of the possibility of the larger loss. Gillis presented his year-end financial report for 1984 and made reference to the NMEC loss. It was Armacost's job to deliver the $95 million explanation.

In the halls after the meeting as the directors left for lunch, Gillis heard grumblings about not having been told and updated. In his first six months with BankAmerica, he had never before seen the board really "aggravated." He was, in fact, relieved to see the board take an active stance.

By the end of the meeting the board members had come to grips with what must be done. By manipulating numbers, they might still declare a much smaller loss. But with Patriarca breathing down their necks, they dared not open themselves to the charge of imprudence. The bank would take a conservative stance. Grim with the knowledge of the damage it would do to the bank's and his own credibility, Gillis wrote a new press release. On February 8 the *Journal* carried the story: The Bank of America had restated its NMEC loss, adding $58 million to it. The declared loss would now be $95 million. The massive hit would be taken against 1984's fourth-quarter earnings, pulling down the year's earnings 12 percent to $345 million. The only redeeming feature of the debacle was that it would let Armacost start 1985 with a cleaner slate.

But NMEC wouldn't die. George W. Coombe, Jr., the bank's lead counsel, rankled, reportedly, at the idea of the bank's paying $95 million through criminal fraud, the laxity of several employees, and the collapse of its insurers, searched for ways not to pay. He devised a plan to recover the $95 million NMEC loss from the bank's own insurer, Employers Insurance of Wausau, by suing the suspect employees and claiming coverage by the bank's D&O (directors and officers) insurance, written by Wausau. Schwab fought Coombe's plan. He found it incredible. This was supposed to be third-party insurance to protect the bank if somebody else sued it; it was not to try to force your insurer to cover you for your employees' failure! He was sure the insurer would hit back. Coombe pushed it through in what Schwab thought was "a hostile and macho way."

Incensed at the lawsuit the bank had filed against them, the insurers canceled the D&O insurance, just as Schwab had guessed they would. To Schwab the message was clear: "You won't get insurance on this globe." The board was now vulnerable. At a time when multimillion-dollar "lender liability" lawsuits against boards of directors and senior management were proliferating, few insurers would write D&O insurance. Lee Prussia was dispatched to London to try to get coverage from the Lloyds syndicate that specialized in D&O insurance, the Merritt Group. He was reportedly turned down by Merritt's lead underwriter, Robin Jackson, when he explained the mess with the excuse that, in effect, "Our lawyers made us do it." As Jackson described the scene to a banker friend, Jackson gathered up all the haughty British dignity Lloyds still exudes, in spite of scandal and reform, and demanded of Prussia, "What *kind* of institution is run by its *lawyers!*" B of A created an offshore subsidiary to provide coverage to satisfy a frightened board. But it was, in effect, self-insurance, providing minimal coverage of perhaps $40 or $50 million. It would be meaningless if there should be a major claim against it. For the bank's directors and senior executives, NMEC had created a prolonged state of terror.

NMEC HAD BEEN the final loss of innocence for Schwab. As the horrendous fact of a nearly $100 million scam the bank's controls had not detected had settled over the board, he had seen Armacost as he had hoped he would never see him—as a king without clothes. He had wanted Armacost to bring the force and grandeur to the post of CEO the great institution deserved. He felt powerful emotion as the realization swept him: "This man who should be a *giant!* He has feet of clay."

WITHIN THE BANK NMEC had deeply bruised morale. "The mortgage scam. That was pretty shocking," says Katherine Neville of her reaction to NMEC as the full dimensions of the scandal spread through the bank. "We'd been losing money, and other things had happened. But this was the first one that really left a bad taste in everybody's mouth—a one-more-thing-we-didn't-need feeling. How could a few crooked guys at one branch sign for all this stuff without any supervision? Without anybody knowing. Without any checks at all."

Armacost's tone was changing, Neville observed. He sent a letter to senior vice-presidents soon after NMEC in which the idea that he'd been let down crept into his message. The ship, above-water, was still full steam ahead; Armacost assured the *Wall Street Journal* on February 12 that NMEC was an "aberration" that would not hurt "the bank's turnaround or my leadership." But Neville noted that the ebullient man who had captivated the hard-boiled computer pros when he had addressed them in 1981 "started, around the time of the bad mortgages, sending around memos saying, 'I don't want any more surprises, group. Please let me know if there's anything you want to reveal.' He was hurt." His sense of hurt, of personal betrayal, over not being told the bad news before it became a disaster like NMEC, grew in his communications to his people. But he wasn't firing the people who had given him the bad information, a senior PR person observed, shaking his head.

*   *   *

NMEC HAD happened in the retail bank. In the sacrosanct branches, Jim Wiesler's and Jim Miscoll's bailiwick. "Why don't you fire Miscoll and Wiesler? Tell them their people have screwed up, but *they're* accountable," a close senior colleague urged Armacost, as the five employees at Inglewood were finally fired. He hoped the NMEC scandal would force completion of the housecleaning of the last of the old palace guard that had surrounded Armacost when he assumed the presidency in 1981. There had been some changes. Bob Frick had replaced Bolin as head of the World Banking Division. But instead of having their gold braid stripped from their shoulders, Miscoll and Wiesler had been awarded with the newly created title of vice-chairman, lifting them above the other executive vice-presidents with whom they sat on the Managing Committee. "NMEC happened on Wiesler's watch," Armacost admitted. But in the wake of NMEC, Wiesler was elevated from head of the branches to command of Global Consumer Markets, Adizes's proud product. A vast expansion of Wiesler's power, this restructuring of worldwide consumer banking would be announced with fanfare in February. Miscoll had been moved away from retail but would be more visible than ever in the ceremonial role of chief officer in Southern California, where he would reign as the bank's "Mr. L.A." in the sumptuous executive offices on Flower Street.

NMEC HAD HURT the bank in the marketplace. Across the bay in Walnut Creek, the SIFE Trust Fund, a $200 million mutual fund that invests primarily in bank stocks, sold the last of its Bank of America stock on February 8, 1985, the day the *Journal* story reported the $95 million loss. Sam A. Marchese, the partner who buys and sells, picked up the phone and unloaded 57,600 shares, at $19\frac{7}{8}$ a share. BAC had been the very first stock SIFE had bought for its portfolio on December 18, 1962. It had been a blue chip then, selling at $56\frac{1}{8}$. Marchese had been moving BAC gradually out of his portfolio as the price declined. Since NMEC, "you couldn't pick up a paper and not read something negative about the company." The restating of earnings in that morning's *Journal* had been the last straw. "A lot of it is perception. If the Street perceives that there are some fundamental problems, it acts," just as Marchese was doing. SIFE still had a gain of $250,000, but it was eroding hourly. He had walked into his partner's office next door to his own, carrying the paper, and said, "Bob, this is getting to be very painful. I think what we ought to do is sell it—take our lumps, take our gain, get out, and watch what happens." He added: "We were very relieved once the decision was made to sell. A call and it was done."

"NMEC was the watershed. It was the first significant image crisis. It was a huge loss and raised questions about controls. For the first couple of years Sam made decisions which made up in some degree for lower earnings. But with NMEC, things fundamentally were awry," says one of the large Corporate Communications staff trying to contain the damage. "The bank had had no trouble with image. But NMEC was slow bleeding all the way down. We tried to be forthcoming and tell reporters as much as we knew. But the numbers were just so phenomenal. They kept getting kicked up. We lost credibility."

Years later, Mike Patriarca confided to a former BankAmerican, "It was NMEC that told us Bank of America was out of control."

As LITIGATION, NMEC dragged on into the '90s. The bank sued, then settled with, its involved employees. The U.S. criminal case against Feldman et al. would finally go to trial in the federal courthouse in downtown Los Angeles in April 1990. B of A's civil suit under the RICO (racketeering) Act sat, pending the outcome of that trial.

Chapter Thirteen

CLAIRE HOFFMAN READ ABOUT IT in the newspapers. The headquarters building to be sold! No one had had the sensitivity or courage to tell her. Just as no one had listened to her as the bank spiraled into decline. As a nonvoting director emeritus since 1970, "I'd make suggestions. They'd listen but wouldn't do anything about it. . . . I just sat there and expressed my opinion." To no avail. The stock price was a disgrace, and she worried about the loyal shareholders. "A lot of them counted on that money for their retirement, and they're having a tough time making both ends meet." The selling of the world headquarters—the globally recognized symbol of her father's legacy—was the final, intolerable outrage.

She had tried to spur the shareholders to action before the last annual meeting, offering to vote their proxies against management, as she had done with her own vote for the past eleven years. "I told them all, 'You are a bunch of stupids. You think the bank is the same bank you knew. It isn't.' "

Her memory of the man she had enshrined for thirty-six years had been so assaulted by change, so dishonored by a technocratic new breed of Bank-American that Hoffman could bear it no longer. She resolved to use her last remaining weapon. She would resign from the board. A. P. Giannini's daughter would *resign*. The board had never heard her, so now she would take her statement to a larger audience, where it would not be ignored.

That decision was the "greatest emotional pain." She would be relinquishing her father's seat on the board, given to her at his death. She would be severing her last formal links with the bank and further shrinking a life that had been lived on a global canvas since her first trip abroad with her father at the age of six. Now eighty, she'd retired from her many years as an invited guest at World Bank meetings. Living alone at Seven Oaks, she had seen the leafy compound become an embattled island of memories as her father's beloved "progress" overtook the neighborhood. In classic emerald silk shirtwaist, pearls, and the diamond-cluster ring given her by the wife of the longtime head of the Italian bank, she still received an occasional guest and served French champagne herself, in the egalitarian style of the Gianninis. But increasingly, her network of BankAmericans was her life, her family.

In early March she sent a sixteen-paragraph letter of resignation to Sam Armacost. It was a blistering condemnation of a fifteen-year pattern of "corporate self-interest, insincerity and insensitivity . . . of corporate myopia and thoughtlessness." Claire Hoffman had been an aggravation to all CEOs since Beise. "She hated Rudy. She absolutely despised Tom. But I thought I was getting along fine," said Armacost. He had invited her to Founder's Club meetings, got her out for the unveiling of a commemorative stone at the old headquarters at Clay and Montgomery, tried to include her in things. She had been invited to present scrolls honoring longtime customers at the San Mateo branch on Founder's Day in 1984—the kind of event the bank *should* be doing, she felt. But she had become "an increasing embarrassment" to the board, says Armacost. "Claire had all these networks into the younger officers and would ramble, be indiscreet, openly criticize. There were malcontents of the old world who were feeding her all sorts of nonsense. All she heard were the complaints about the changes in the branch system. She never stopped to understand why, on a cost basis, that system would kill us. She would just fire off rockets."

Unwittingly she had blocked the very thing she should have wanted most, Armacost felt: the search for her father's essence. Obsessed with technology as an enemy of the human touch, she never saw that her father would have led the way with computer systems. Nor had she seen that the basic thrust of Armacost's culture search "was not *losing* Giannini, but picking up the *real* Giannini," Max Hopper observed. She was leaving just as the theme she had hammered for nearly forty years was being adopted as the bank's theme for the eighties: *Leadership in serving people.*

When the resignation letter came, "it was the ultimate irony that the thing that caused the great schism was the sale of that building. She had fought Rudy tooth and nail because he built it," said Armacost. "But it's sad. It didn't need to happen." He met with her, tried to persuade her not to resign. The bank's image, currently being battered by NMEC, would be further damaged. "Claire, we're not selling your father's monument. His monument was across the street, where it still is. Your father never knew this building existed. If anything, it's Rudy's monument." It would still be the Bank of America Building. The Giannini Plaza. And the world headquarters. "All we're doing is taking our profit out and changing the ownership." Claire says: "I was begged, too, by other members of the board not to do it, but I just didn't care anymore."

B OF A FOUNDER'S DAUGHTER RESIGNS was the headline on March 9, 1985, in the *Chronicle*. Her statement went out on wire services across the country:

> For the past 15 years or so, I have watched three successive administrations stray further and further from the policies and practices that were such a vital part of my father's leadership: Clear thinking, a willingness to place the human needs of ordinary people above private ambition and a realization that the bank was less a place of work for its thousands of employees than an extended family of fellow workers, each intimately involved with the other in the creation of a corporate trustee of great public purpose.

TO BLITZ FOX, just hired as general manager for the Magoon Estate, owner of Guenoc Winery, in a Northern California wine valley just beyond Napa, the B of A's purpose now was to drive mid-size wineries out of the bank. Out of business.

The bank was now driving the new strategy of exiting from all but the best 25 percent of the farm credits. Fox could understand why the bank would make a strategic decision to leave the mid-size winery market. Farm banks, subsidized by the government and able to charge a point less for loans, were stealing the business. But he could never forgive the way they were doing it. Fox had arrived from Hawaii to find Bank of America using ruthless tactics to collect its loans. Without warning and without good reason, he deduced, the bank was about to declare defaults that threatened to close up Guenoc's new winery and force a fire sale of assets.

To establish the vineyards that were turning this parched rattlesnake country productive, and to build and equip a high tech winery, the Magoon Estate Ltd. had taken on a $6 million debt from B of A—a $5 million long-term loan and a $1 million credit line. Guenoc had never missed paying a cent of due interest. The loans were current. The $20 million winery was pledged as collateral.

Behind that were the $100 million-plus real estate assets of one of Hawaii's wealthiest landowning families, the Magoons. But as Fox had quickly discovered, vineyards and wineries required wealthy owners with bottomless pockets or patient bankers. There was insufficient cash flow to pay back even the interest on loans, much less capital, for six or seven years. It was the fact of the wine business Andy Johnson, a few miles south in Napa, had understood. B of A wanted out. Now.

Fox had met and established relations with the loan officer, Al Gross, who couldn't have been nicer. They were in the midst of negotiations to extend the credit line when Fox received the first blow—a letter of default on the credit line. On its heels came another letter claiming cross-default—that invidious act by which a default on one loan put any and all of Guenoc's loans from the bank in default. Any pledged collateral could be grabbed. Suddenly the young winery—still trapped in a phase of heavy capital investment and little cash flow—must pay back $6 million within the year. Something it could do only by selling off Magoon properties in Hawaii—holdings built up over two centuries—for whatever price it could get.

It seemed a plot calculated with the psychological torture techniques Fox had learned in survival school in the air force: the alternate use of abuse and kindness to break you down. True to the scenario, Gross carried a stick. If Guenoc did not accept his offer, the storm troopers were just outside the door. Fox couldn't believe it. A Special Assets Group (SAG) had been formed to enforce the defaults. Praised in the *BankAmerican* as teams that "aggressively manage existing problem accounts and enhance recovery efforts," those in SAG were empowered to make life-and-death decisions with little experience, he suspected, of the practical realities of agriculture. This heavy-booted group of M.B.A.'s would be tacking up seizure signs on the winery and filing lawsuits within a month. Al Gross, he felt, was a decent, traditional banker. But he was apparently helpless before SAG.

But the Magoons were not about to be booted out of the valley they had reclaimed for grapes. Fox flew to Hawaii, called a special meeting of the board, and with a phone call, the directors switched their loans from B of A to the Bank of Hawaii. Fox called Al Gross at the B of A and told him, "Al, we've taken you out. I'm sure Bank of America will put the money somewhere they think is more profitable." MotherBank had lost a good customer.

BARRY A. STERLING, owner of Iron Horse Vineyards in Sonoma County, west of Napa, and an international attorney with long ties to Bank of America, watched, amazed, as an entourage of bankers' cars drove through his rolling vineyards. It was Lee Prussia, an old friend, conducting what Sterling saw as a remarkable hands-on demonstration both to his young officers and to customers that the bank's great "calling tradition" was still alive and well; the chairman himself had come seeking some commercial business.

Sterling ached for Prussia; he knew from reading the papers the pressure he was under and admired the guts it took to put himself on the line like this before his junior officers. Like all Californians, his wife, Audrey, had a "Bank of America story," a special bond to the bank: B of A had funded her father, a hungry young graduate of the Pacific Dental College, in setting up his first dentistry office in San Francisco. She would always be grateful. But Sterling did his winery banking with Farm Production Credit, which gave better terms to farm-related industries. In the blossoming garden of their exquisite restored Victorian, Sterling served the Bank of America group the same champagne with which Reagan and Gorbachev had toasted peace at the Geneva summit. As at Geneva, champagne softened the awkward issues; talk of doing business drifted off gracefully.

"IT'S A BANK with no heart," said sparkling-wine maker Hanns Kornell, as he pulled his longtime account from B of A's St. Helena branch, where Andy Johnson had held Kornell's hand through the building of his business in the sixties and seventies. Cold-blooded judgments, based solely on the numbers by young bankers who had never seen a champagne riddling rack, in Kornell's opinion, were restricting his ability to function. Armacost had been correct in seeing that it was the little independent banks, not Wells Fargo, that threatened his market share in the branches. Kornell moved his account to Napa Valley Bank, a new, small bank founded by local people who had perceived a need. They welcomed Kornell as Bank of America had welcomed him when Andy Johnson ran the branch.

By the time Andy Johnson retired, the authority to serve Kornell and the other winery customers personally had evaporated. Wineries the bank had nurtured had left; his friend Jay Corley of Monticello Cellars had joined several well-known wine men on the board of the start-up bank, Napa National. They had shrewdly offered Johnson a princely retainer to bring his prestige to Napa National, but he refused to trade on the goodwill he'd earned as a BankAmerican.

Sam Armacost had tried to halt the drain of customers; he had come to St. Helena, staged several dinners for the winery customers and their wives, something not done before or since, says Warren Winiarski of Stag's Leap

Wine Cellars. He had made three visits to the Winiarskis' winery. But Johnson was picking up rumblings of more defections in his chats with the winery
men who dropped by his desk to say good-bye or take him out for a farewell
lunch.

When he arrived at the St. George restaurant for his lunch with Bob Pecota,
he followed the winemaker to their table downstairs. As Johnson innocently
entered one of the banquet rooms, the entire winery fraternity rose from their
chairs and sang "For He's a Jolly Good Fellow" to the man who had put the
bank's money behind them when Napa Valley's triumph seemed more dream
than possibility. At first, Johnson joined the singing: "I had no idea it was for
me." As he grasped it, he was overwhelmed. As tributes rolled, he was made
an honorary member of the Napa Valley Vintners, the second person ever to be
so honored. His heart swelling with gratitude, he managed to thank the men
who had ranked his contribution to Napa's phenomenal surge on a par with that
of its technical father, famed UC Davis oenology professor Dr. Maynard
Amerine, the only other honorary member.

Two days later Bernard Scoda drove up with his truck full of cases of wine
and delivered a gift from the vintners that would permit Johnson to uncork
Napa's best private reserves at the dinner table for the rest of his life.

Some of the vintners still felt a blind, affectionate loyalty to Bank of
America. One of the valley's Young Turks, John Kongsgaard, winemaker for
Newton Vineyards, reminisced: "When I opened my first checking account at
the Napa branch as a high school kid, Casey, the manager, took me into the
back room and said, 'John, if you ever need a little money, there's always some
in this pouch for you.' " Casey and his wife had been killed in a car crash years
ago. Rationally Kongsgaard knew that it was no longer the same bank. But he
would never leave. Gene Trefethen, too, continued to do his vineyard, winery,
and personal banking through St. Helena. He knew B of A from his Kaiser
days. He believed he saw that old tradition of service and quality trying to
assert itself through this time of troubles—troubles caused mostly, he felt, by
uncontrollable economic events that had knocked the pins out from under real
estate and the agricultural industry. Bob Mondavi still remembered his father,
Cesare, introducing him to A.P. in an Italian restaurant in New York, and how
his huge presence had filled the room. Although Mondavi had spread his
banking relationships around, he still had an active corporate account in San
Francisco. Warren Winiarski had to be out of town on the day of the lunch.
"But Andy and I said our private good-bye," he says, recalling the decisive
day Johnson had funded his corporate independence.

In bestowing its greatest honor on Andy Johnson, the vintners of Napa
Valley paid tribute to the best of a dying breed—the great branch managers

who had so shaped the prosperity of their communities. They were saying good-bye to the bank that was.

A NEW BANK was emerging from within. At the cost of the human touch perhaps. But there were increasing signs of movement in the direction B of A must go for survival.

The unveilings of Ichak Adizes's first two products were staged as major media events. On January 28, 1985, Max Hopper's broad smile was beamed by closed-circuit video broadcast to BankAmerica computer centers across the country as BASE—the unification of the bank's hodgepodge of global computer systems into one system—went on-line. Thirty-five hundred employees prepared to move across San Francisco Bay to suburban Concord, where computers scattered in seventeen buildings in San Francisco would be consolidated at the new BASE headquarters in September. Hopper summed up the chaos that had been tamed in a speech to senior management. "We've allowed technology to weave through the organization, to sprout, mature, and undergo transformation, in independent life cycles under a scattered system," he said. BASE, at last, would provide "integrated systems architecture for a total customer relationship." For Armacost, BASE was triumphant vindication of the Adizes methodology. "The whole grain of the bank had been *against* centralizing the computer function and *with* a proliferation of individual empires. With little pain and carping, we had created a . . . structure that kept managers focused on the business issues," not on personalities and protection of their turfs.

With computer systems in place, reorganization of the operating divisions accelerated. A month later Jim Wiesler took center stage and announced the creation of Global Consumer Markets, with Wiesler as its head. It merged the bank's old retail division with other consumer-focused services like credit cards, travelers cheques, real estate, trust business, Schwab's discount brokerage, and electronic banking. "Ninety-nine percent of it was in California," says Armacost, but it also included "some very large and very good retail banks" overseas. The segregation of retail from wholesale banking operations was recognition, finally, that they were different businesses.

Global Consumer Markets was the first stage of a strategy of retreat from the race to be in every country in which Citicorp had a consumer business. The bank was now "looking at the world and saying there may be eight or ten countries where a consumer business for us might be viable," says Armacost. Soon B of A would be making country-by-country decisions to stay or exit as a retail bank.

But as Global Consumer Markets was introduced, Dr. George Parker, senior lecturer at Stanford's Graduate School of Business, tweaked the bank for its time lag, stating to a reporter, "To some extent, B of A is emulating other successful models like Citibank, which went through its reorganization seven or eight years ago."

And why had Wiesler been named to head it? Armacost knew the complaints about Wiesler. There had been NMEC and the growing concern for the consumer loan portfolios, all coming out of retail during Wiesler's watch. By definition, he was part of the problem. Aides were warning Armacost that Wiesler would be a drag on the credibility of his new proactive image. In his favor, Wiesler was given credit for supporting the growth of ATMs from three hundred to fifteen hundred, and he was a definitive link to the branch culture. But there was conflict between the old and new cultures. Some saw Pete Talbott, the retail star from Citicorp who had been promoted to head of a unit within the new group that reported to Wiesler, as the better choice. He carried no burden of baggage from the past. Why wasn't he heading it?

Armacost had his own strategy, driven by his persisting concern with rushing the old culture into change. "With all the changes we were making, I needed to ensure that the retail bank guys thought there was a guy who understood them representing them. Talbott was still largely an unknown or viewed as a Citibanker—not always an endorsement. I had carefully structured Talbott and others down below who I thought could drive the strategy through and get it done, in spite of Wiesler almost." In Global Consumer Markets, Wiesler would be a visible champion for the old retail culture, Armacost continued, "because otherwise we were afraid of losing them. *You're dealing with fifty thousand people who can ruin your business if they want to. You've got to be sure they don't perceive that decisions are being made that show no understanding of their needs or their business.*" He planned, he expected, that Talbott would soon head the retail operations.

But emotionally, he could not decommission the last of the elite platoon that carried the tattered banner of BankAmerican values. That would leave him alone on the beach, the only survivor of a culture still so powerful in the "proactive" man that it was staying his hand at the vital decision points.

Time, a little more time, was what he needed.

TIME IS WHAT Adizes needed, too. The public unveiling of products helped appease growing complaints about the time drain Adizes's strategy sessions— his POKs—were imposing on busy men like Hopper and Talbott at a time when they had increasing pressure for short-term performance. Even Armacost was beginning to fear that "the time it was taking to build group dynamics in the change process was undermining change itself." He sensed hostility becoming focused on Adizes.

But Adizes's messianic enthusiasm continued to drive the grand projects, as he moved forward with the creation of the next product of the Adizes Method, BAPS, the bank's payment system.

"They stood and applauded!" Adizes beamed, describing the response BASE and BAPS received when they were introduced in-house to the bank's annual retail management conference in Los Angeles after the media launch. The presentation was staged with high tech glitz at the Los Angeles Airport Hilton, where dynamic images of a changing bank were flashed on screens positioned to suggest an eagle in flight. The stylized bird in the bank's logo, intended by designer Walter Landor as a dove of peace, had become the symbol of the soaring and aggressive new vision. Eagle pins rewarding special contributions were worn proudly in gray flannel lapels. Armacost presented Jim Miscoll with an eagle statuette, honoring the man who was now "Mr. L.A.," the bank's figurehead chief executive in the Los Angeles headquarters. In his own way, at his own pace, Armacost was changing the guard.

At the conference it was the "New Faces of 1985" that were paraded through three days of speeches, panels, seminars. Talbott—handsome, suave, thick-haired—punched the air with his finger, John Kennedy style, to emphasize that "as a retail banker you will have to be more retailer than banker in the future." Talbott, who had replaced Miscoll in February as head of the California branch system, got star exposure at the conference; his in-action photograph was spread across the front page of the next issue of the in-house magazine, *BankAmerican*. Chuck Schwab spoke out at a "breakout session" on deregulation. IBM recruit Bob Beck, who was bringing to the benign title "Human Resources" the toughness of a headsman, commended managers for graceful handling of "redeployment" during branch consolidation that had cut staff by thousands. Eight thousand BankAmericans were now gone; 132 branches closed in 1984 alone. He was also head-hunting for more new faces.

Armacost spoke of NMEC, the worst of the surprises so far, and exorcised that terrible page of bank history by praising his people for handling it with "integrity and dignity" and reassuring them that "it is an aberration. This failure occurred because people didn't *execute*. We can't, and we won't, tolerate that," he snapped.

With more prescience than he may have known, Corporate Communications chief Ronald E. Rhody, who parried daily with the press as he tried to combine full disclosure with protection of the bank's image in a climate of growing crisis, told the conference, "People's perception of the facts is almost as important as what the facts really are. *Because people act on their perceptions."*

THE PERCEPTION was growing that through the stubborn legacy of the past, Armacost was building a strong new team. In May 1984 Keefe analyst Don Crowley, a former BankAmerican, had commended Armacost for efforts to "upgrade staff." With the addition of Tom Cooper in March 1985, he had his Four Horsemen. Hopper. Talbott. Beck. And Cooper. Outsiders all. The "right stuff" for revolution had not been forged within the old culture, and Bank-Americans must now live, daily, with this visible evidence of its failure.

Cooper came in like an itinerant prophet, full of fire and brimstone, ready to impose salvation through a path of self-denial and human sacrifice. A former Methodist minister trained in the crucible of eastern banking, he had guided Philadelphia's Girard Bank through acquisition by the Mellon Bank and then stayed on with Mellon. Bank of America hired him to shepherd the worldwide payment system BAPS to on-line status and to run it and a staff of ten thousand people. Controlling all transfers of money in the bank, BAPS was more than the bank's payment system. It was the nucleus of Adizes's early dream of making the bank a global utility in electronic transactions, serving other banks and customers throughout the world. But the infant BAPS was losing $100 million a year. It would be Cooper's job to turn that around.

Tuned in to the underground of complaints that Armacost was not cutting people and costs fast enough, Adizes had said to him, "We need to bring in a new guy for BAPS." What Bank of America needed at this stage of its life cycle, said Adizes, "is a doer, a Margaret Thatcher who can *cut!* Cooper is what the climate calls for." There was risk for Armacost in bringing in the person needed for the time. Armacost had been warned by a senior Mellon officer who called to tell him that Cooper was not a team player. And being brought in as Armacost's "high-profile cost cutter," he would be given considerable power and exposure—dangerous toys. But Cooper fitted Adizes's theories that no one man can do the job alone. Armacost was being perceived by some—unfairly, Adizes believed—"not to be decisive, not to be active." A CEO must choose a team that complements his strengths. Armacost, the great integrator, needed Cooper, the administrator. But Adizes urged Armacost to have Cooper agree to one condition: "that he would not change what we had built so hard for two years." Because he was confined to BAPS, his opportunities for dismantling seemed limited.

"It was Sam who called me at home and asked me to consider coming here," Cooper said. There were compelling family reasons to say no. Cooper's commitment to restructuring the industry had driven him, since the 1960s, to a dedication that made him, he admitted, "the world's lousiest father and husband." San Francisco would be a chance to reform. "We have a very strong family—six children. My wife is a marvelous traditional wife. I made a commitment to her that I wouldn't go through what I had been through the last ten years of our life. I was not going to be on the board. I was not going to be public when I came here. I wouldn't interview with anybody. Typical PR announcements were not done." He would "just keep my head down and do my work." There were clear agreements on the limits to his power. "We brought him in to do the BAPS job. There were no promises," says Armacost. Nor, Cooper confirms, were there any expectations. "I came here with no intent whatsoever to vie for the presidency or any other aspect of this company. There probably aren't three people other than my wife who believe that." If there were no promises of power, there was promise of profits. The current pay for prophets with a sharp sword, it appeared, would be close to $500,000 a year.

Cooper had interviewed well, although Max Hopper, who had run the interviews, sensed "a Messiah complex." But he was coming across as decisive and intelligent. His thick head of brown hair, neat-cut and side-brushed, gave a boyish look to his forty-eight years. There was a cleft in the chin of an attractive, somewhat round face whose suggestion of sensuousness was masked by academic rimmed glasses, and a style of workmanlike shirtsleeves and body actions that bespoke sincerity. Cooper kept his elbows up on the table, hands clasped or in prayer position, fingers splayed and gold wedding band very evident. His experience of East Coast industrial decline and financial shocks had taught survival lessons about being lean, mean, and cost-efficient. "One of the best things that happened to the East Coast banker was the bankruptcy of New York City, the decline of the Northeast urban areas, and the Herstatt failure," he stated, lecturing on the dangers and delusions of Lotus Land.

The West, Cooper reminded, "had nothing but continued growth. You can believe eventually that you're as good as your profits if you don't have economic pressures." You can believe your success is the result of good judgments rather than lack of competition, as the U.S. oil, steel, and automobile industries had for so long.

B of A was a bank with "a marvelous heritage, but . . . a culture which was much more . . . self-satisfied and confident of its own criteria for success as opposed to the market criteria for success"—a failing that had led the bank from "that leading-edge mentality in the late fifties to absolutely a follower." In this self-focused place, skewed judgments had been made: "Continuing to

invest in branches . . . was just as bad a decision as *not* to invest in technology."
A pioneer in reducing the overhead of branches with automation, Cooper said,
"I'd visit the West in the late seventies and be amazed to see them still opening
branches, when, at Girard, I'd closed fifty branches and gained market share."

But he had not come to lecture. He had come to cut. And to do it swiftly. "I
can't underscore enough how much I felt a sense of urgency. Time was not on
our side." He believed there would "probably only be a relatively few—not
more than a couple of handsful—of truly dominant global banks. They will be
the ones who are highly capital-intensive, highly technology-oriented . . . and
there really isn't catch-up time in that kind of a business. . . .

"When I arrived here, I thought that Mr. Armacost had done an excellent
job of identifying the issues that had to be addressed." But there were alarming
problems Cooper had not been shown. "I was basically told that the loan
problem was now under control." Clearly it was not. Preoccupation with loans,
though, "had caused the public and many in-place managers to miss the
fundamental other problems in this company": archaic operating systems.
Management information didn't exist. There was no integration of loan accounting. You had delivery problems. You had 1,250 branches, "which you
had to get down to nine hundred," and a desperate lack of capital, which
reduced the flexibility to close branches. Closing branches was vital—and
"very expensive."

Cooper quickly became known, he knew, as the eastern gunslinger. "Even
though it might be painful to me and my personal image," Cooper says,
corporate image makers cast him from day one as Armacost's hatchet man; it
was not surprising that factions and conflicts built around him. He prodded
BankAmerican sensitivities to harsh truths by calling the bank's process "a
turnaround," rather than the gentler "transition." And his presence put Max
Hopper on edge. Hopper had expected to bring BAPS into his systems empire,
as part of Armacost's half-promised plan to unify all the computer systems under one division and one man, presumably Hopper. As head of BAPS Cooper
would thwart that hope. Cooper did not believe in its concept. A realist, he
operated BAPS, but did not think the conglomerate of units pulled from their
natural homes worked. Credit cards. Travelers cheques. Wholesale payments.
Cash management. The units had been brought together to get them under tight
management control. He was doing that. But as soon as he had forged them into
efficient units, he would unbundle BAPS and send the various payment units
back to where he believed they could serve the customer more directly.

Hopper observed ambitions in Cooper that Armacost did not see. "He was
no team player. He was against Sam from day one. . . . And he wanted retail
immediately."

Adizes saw disturbing signs that his theory of the need for a Cooper might be backfiring. Joining the team as the cry for cost cutting was becoming a scream, Cooper was not enhancing Armacost's image, as Adizes had hoped. His decisiveness was making Armacost look more ineffectual. Cooper's comment that "when you're in a restructuring, you need to be decisive; you can't work through consensus" was reassuring analysts, shareholders, and the press; Armacost, the man of consensus, was being perceived, increasingly, as a man who was not in control. And perception was everything.

The systems people watched Cooper closely as he came in. He's a "very formidable enterer of rooms. It's like watching George C. Scott do Patton." Katherine Neville smiled as Cooper arrived for his first meeting with the travelers cheque group. "He marched in like a general, with a vice-president at either arm, and every time he'd think of something, he'd say, 'Take a note on that!' He was steely-eyed. More militant than Sam. He asked some intelligent questions, and as he left, the guys were going, 'Wow! How about that. What a management style.' " The message went through the bank "like wildfire, presented with formal hoopla, dog-and-pony acts" that Cooper's mandate in BAPS was to clean out the paper-crunching back-room operations in every branch. There would be "no more of the brick-and-mortar, storefront, branch-type stuff" that was killing the bank with its redundancies and extravagant fixed costs. "We would deliver sophisticated electronic products." Neville hoped there was as much substance as form.

She was optimistic as Cooper revived James Cerruti's float product that made money for the bank by extending the float period in travelers cheques. It had been killed in December 1983, after Armacost's approval had brought it near to on-line status. To Neville, the killing of the product by a committee on which Wiesler and Miscoll served had been more distressing evidence of the persisting power of the old guard and its resistance to new products. In April Neville heard that when one of the tenacious champions of Cerruti's product had shown it to Cooper, he'd said, "Why aren't we doing this? It's great," and supported its implementation. The product was being rushed to market. When it went on-line, Cerruti would get his $50,000 award.

IT WAS A MORE cynical banker Neville reached by phone in 1985 in Miami, where Cerruti was now stationed with other BankAmericans in the strategic retreat out of Latin America. Assigned to the Latin American Division in March 1984, he had taken the job in Caracas, then the divisional headquarters, completely disillusioned by the killing of his product. The job intrigued him: to help design and implement a new banking strategy for South America, one which would determine which markets the bank should remain in or exit. It was not how he had hoped to go abroad as an international banker. He was an ocean away from Greece, flying into a semitropical oil boomtown "as part of the rescue crew." The debt crisis had become epidemic since Mexico, two years earlier, and South America was now a morass of trouble unprecedented in any banker's experience. The shock of the Mexican debt crisis had halted the lending boom and signaled a wave of economic crises in neighboring countries. Debt restructuring had turned South America into a vast negotiating table.

Many levels removed from line bankers like Cerruti, the restructuring ritual played on. Lord of the Latin American workout, Citibank's Bill Rhodes hopscotched the Andes and led marathon rounds of negotiating sessions in New York, trying to save over $240 billion in commercial bank loans to Latin America. Emerging nations throughout the world were caught in the trauma. But the fear of a debtor cartel in the Southern Hemisphere—and the sheer magnitude of its debt—brought the focus to Latin America. Argentina had been saved from the brink of default on $2.5 billion in overdue interest payments by an emergency loan package. Rhodes was leading the ongoing Brazilian restructuring through economic and political volatility that would keep banks on a roller coaster through the 1980s. On September 7, 1984, Mexico and the banks announced agreement on the rescheduling of $48.5 billion of debt—the largest debt accord in history. The major Latin American debtors huddled in summits in Quito, Ecuador, and Mar del Plata, Argentina, searching out solutions to the common nightmare.

"The divisional headquarters in Caracas was essentially gutted. There were only about forty or fifty people left out of a staff of four or five hundred," Cerruti found. As staff trudged dispiritedly north to the new base in Miami, there was "a terrible phobia in everyone's mind about Latin America."

In those final twilight months in Caracas, he tasted the style of international banking Al Rice had known in the mid-seventies. He enjoyed the life-style of cooks, maids, and gardeners, of golf clubs and swim clubs, and savored the excellent restaurants that had opened during the years before the 1982 decline in oil prices when Caracas had been a dynamic international entrepôt. He had surveyed "the most beautiful women I've ever seen in my life" at the Miss Punta del Este beauty pageant, where the competitors were the impeccably bred daughters of the Argentine aristocracy who vacation at the exclusive beach resort. Touring the bank's customer countries, he was feted at elegant dinner parties and discussed economics at the desks of finance ministers as representative of "the bank I took pride in."

But as he did his evaluations of the stay-or-leave status of each country,

Cerruti found himself a war correspondent surveying the effects of a distant battle whose damage has not yet been fully reported back home. These were the graveyards of BankAmerica's failed judgments over the last fifteen years.

All the banks were suffering, of course. But the failures Cerruti was seeing were Bank of America-specific. He winced every time he saw a bottle of Polar beer, knowing that Polar, with close to 85 percent of the Venezuelan beer market, was financed by Citibank, while Bank of America financed its almost insignificant competitor, the money-losing Cervesa Nacionale. Bank of America had arrived late again and been left with the second-class risks in the private sector.

In the Chilean port town of Valparaiso, "it was a horror to see a branch of the Bank of America run-down and dismal. Curtains torn, carpets stained, files strewn about—a disaster area in contrast to the new Citibank branch, beautiful with a really high tech banking strategy." It was more evidence that Citibank "was pursuing a very expensive electronic-based strategy throughout Latin America," while this dismal slum of a branch sat as victim of the bank's technology lag. Even more shocking was his discovery, in his tour of the retail bank in Argentina, that "in literally half the branches, the latest technology is the hand-crank adding machine."

And there was the controversial Argentinian bank "causing huge losses. . . . It wasn't just the cost of amortizing the 'goodwill.' It was the operating costs of running sixty-six branches in an economy that was over-banked."

As Cerruti summarized his findings, he came to the reluctant conclusion that "Bank of America was just completely off cycle."

Sitting in World Banking's luxurious second-floor headquarters armed with the arrogance of youth and a prestigious master's degree in international finance, Cerruti had found it easy to critique Clausen's and Prussia's failure "to look beyond the next quarter to the future" or "to have the tools in place." In San Francisco bad news from the front had been filtered through thick carpets and hushed executive offices, diluted by gentle manners and cover-ups, and polished by Corporate Communications. Here, on site, was the reality. The blood pouring from loan portfolios. "I was astounded. There was only a seven-billion-dollar portfolio. But over half was in questionable loans." And no one yet knew how deep the damage went.

He was witnessing the painful death of the Golden Age of Lending. The dénouement of Clausen's boldest change: the decentralizing of foreign operations, in 1974, to the four autonomous empires, each vying with the others for profits and customers. Armacost still believed that Clausen's "putting people in the field close to customers developed business much more effectively" and had made B of A one of the few multinational banks to grow "a good indigenous business" abroad. But Clausen's chairman, Chauncey Medberry, had been heard saying that Clausen's dispersal of authority without the structures and systems to back it up was "*the* major tactical error, a . . . dilution of credit discipline."

Cerruti saw the country managers trapped by internal conflicts. They were suffering the impact of their bad loans directly; reserves for loan losses were taken out of each country operation's earnings. "They couldn't sweep it under the carpet anymore. They felt terribly threatened." Yet they were driven by a mind-set of "growing their assets"—making more loans. It is all they had ever done as bankers. Cerruti found himself "in conflict not only with management in Venezuela but with my boss, who was married to a Venezuelan and had perhaps lived there too long." Although Cerruti had urged shrinkage of the loan portfolios, he had finally capitulated when the Venezuelan manager had blazed at him, "We're going to have to *grow* it!" Cerruti was vindicated when Armacost rejected the growth strategy during review of the country, but he felt like a wimp for having given in.

But out of the battlefield of South America, the bank's most troubled foreign sector, he was seeing a new rational strategy emerge, led by division chief Bill Young. In the countries where B of A remained, it would largely abandon retail and refocus on the large multinational customers. On wholesale banking. The portfolios of sovereign loans would shrink.

Cerruti felt the emotional import of the change he was helping impose. "To say, 'We will not be a full-service California bank everywhere in the world because we can't afford it,' was one of the most difficult internal cultural dilemmas that the bank has faced," he said, feeling a certain poignancy.

Would the strategy's momentum carry the day in San Francisco? Young had brought the vision of a predominantly wholesale international bank from Europe, where, away from headquarters politics, new ideas and leaders had often flourished. Al Rice, Armacost, and Mont McMillen all had fanned the sparks of more sophisticated systems and credit controls. Young had joined the bank in 1966, part of the same class of young officers as Armacost and McMillen; the three had worked together in Europe. Young had been promoted from head of Eastern Europe operations to head up Latin America in 1981, as Bolin had been bumped to head of World Banking.

"We knew in our minds that if Bill was successful and it worked in Latin America, eventually it would for the world." It challenged Bill Bolin's way of "build, build, build," as he had through the seventies. But before he retired as head of World Banking in March 1984, Bolin, too, had become "a champion of the strategy. He saw we had to change," says Cerruti. Rising like the phoenix from the ashes of B of A's Latin American debt disaster was new hope for the bank. It would not be a long-term solution to the bank's third world debt problem, but it would enable B of A to halt the bleeding and carve out a more realistic banking profile abroad. One that would bring Armacost more bad surprises in the short run, but might help save the bank. As Cerruti joined the retreat to Miami, Young was still delivering bad news with the good. So far Armacost had not shot the messenger.

Chapter Fourteen

MOTHERBANK'S HABIT of sticking her neck out when her pride was assaulted was irrepressible. A hubris that had grown over decades of having her superiority echoed back from every side and corner of her universe showed in *Wellenkamp,* in the bank's overbid for the Argentine bank, in the bank's lawsuit against its insurers over NMEC. And now in the Cory case, which promised to drag on forever, another drain on the bank's resources and good reputation. Since the late 1970s the bank had been wrangling over how much B of A owed the state of California in repayment of interest on dormant deposit accounts that should have been forwarded to the state to hold in trust for the owners. All the California banks had been caught. The rest had settled. But B of A had challenged, inviting a test in court. It had lost the first round in 1981 and been ordered to pay $26 million. The bank had appealed, driving the state to demand an amount nearly three times that of the original $26 million. Now, as 1985 began, the state appeals court came out with a mixed decision that would still require the bank to pay an as yet undefined sum. With the heels of both bank and state controller dug in, the "escheat" issue, as it was known, would go on interminably, Armacost feared, while Controller Kenneth Cory gained political mileage by wringing more and more dollars from the bank.

If hubris was the cause of self-imposed damage, the regulators' weapons—reserves and capital—had become the great threat from outside the bank by the spring of 1985.

And yet the momentum of Armacost's revolution seemed to be holding against it. The April 26 management forum in the downstairs auditorium at world headquarters had been very upbeat, Steve McLin noted, a promising sign for his acquisitions strategy. There had been a setback in March. The Comptroller of the Currency had rejected the bank's proposal to open a string of out-of-state nonbank banks, part of the bank's positioning for interstate banking. But it was not a vital part of the strategy. Not the best entry vehicle for interstate banking, McLin and Armacost had concluded. Nor was Finance-America, the two-hundred-branch nationwide consumer credit subsidiary that was rising to the top of a list of assets they might sell. "In retail banking you've got to make a big enough acquisition on the ground to have some impact in the marketplace and to carry your flag," said Armacost. "Orbanco is the way. And so is Seafirst." Seafirst had moved back from the cliff edge of failure to modest profitability by the end of '84. Orbanco, in Portland, was a failing bank that would expand their access to the Northwest and tie together the West Coast regional strategy, if they could buy it. McLin was opening negotiations for Orbanco.

With the regulators en garde, McLin must try to negotiate from strength. The first quarter of 1985 looked good. The bank had taken the $95 million NMEC hit in the last quarter of 1984. Put it behind them. McLin had heard that Gillis would be reporting earnings of $118 million, a small but positive upward trend after the steady earnings declines since 1981, and in early April he asked Gillis for a 1985 earnings forecast. He would never forget Gillis's response: "Oh, we'll make between four hundred and five hundred million dollars this year." "You're sure about that," McLin pressed. "We're on track," Gillis reassured him. On April 15 the first-quarter earnings were confirmed, McLin caught a plane to Portland, and at five-thirty on April 17, the deal with Orbanco was cut. The definitive agreement would be made public in May. He and Armacost were hopeful they would get regulatory approval. At a cost of roughly $60 million to buy $1 billion in assets, it would be an insignificant drain on the bank's resources yet an important strategic move.

But the rejection of the nonbank banks in March, added to the humiliating pledge to raise reserves in November, were disquieting signs of the regulators' deepening intrusion into the bank's business. "These guys increasingly wanted to be making major tactical, strategic type of decisions . . . having an impact without being accountable for it," Armacost said fretfully. He admitted that "because of the ravages of unrestrained growth during the seventies, we were an accident waiting to happen in the eighties." But since Continental Illinois, the examiners had been "covering their butts" excessively, he felt. B of A's traditional disdain for regulators firmed into hostile resentment as the "SWAT team" arrived.

Mike LaRusso and his squad moved into the bank in April. "We did some very careful checking when we knew LaRusso was going to be the examiner on our account. We talked to the banks he had examined directly, and we had absolutely zero good comments," Armacost reports. Gillis was getting feedback that he was a "pretty tough cookie." Worse, a trusted friend of Armacost, someone close to the regulatory process, reported an alarming rumor: LaRusso was coming in with the overt mission of making a change in management—Armacost. "We were all on our guard after that."

He was harboring the enemy, Armacost felt, one looking for weak lines. Those were not hard to find. Harvey Gillis had been astounded to find, when he arrived in early 1985, that the bank still relied for loan reviews on the old "circulars" system—photocopies sent out to the divisions and branches requesting data on their loan portfolios, usually only a few weeks before the end of every quarter. They were sent out by Al Rice's nemesis, Ken Martin, who had assumed a new role as senior credit administrator, and his staff. "Circulars were so stupid," Gillis scoffed. In asking branches to report their own portfolios, "they'd send out a letter to the very fox that was trying to get in the chicken coop." Other banks he'd experienced had computer tracking of loan quality. At Security Pacific's headquarters in Los Angeles the CEO could punch up the credit status on loans anywhere in the world, instantly, on his computer terminal. In B of A, at the highest level, credit quality was in the hands of the old guard with nothing to gain by revealing a pattern of shoddy credit quality on its watch. Many of the new guard felt that the bank's senior credit officer Lloyd Sugaski would have to retire early if Armacost were to transform the credit process and break down resistance to baring problems.

From 1983, when the red flags went up in Armacost's mind that B of A was not recovering from recession as its peer banks were, he had been trying to reform the credit discipline. It was a formidable task. Loan portfolios were still being checked on a sampling basis. "We pulled the credits out of the branches and were aghast at the dollar amounts and number of bad loans we found. . . . Most of the rocks we turned over for ourselves, and the examiners just validated the findings," says Armacost. "If we had left those loans in the branch system out there, they would have come through the process much more slowly." But it was painstaking, still full of surprises. "You're never sure when you hit bottom until after you've hit it." What he *had* hit, he would later see, was "the crux of the problem that would unendingly frustrate the board and senior management: As we intensified our efforts to identify and declare problem credits, the flood gates opened, lashed on by the new credit team I'd charged to get it right and by examiners who saw safety in excessive charge-offs."

His critics would see it differently. Here it was, mid-1985, four years into his tenure, and the full scope of the loan mess was just being revealed. Why hadn't Armacost been more "proactive" from day one in declaring the past as Clausen's burden and hired a tough credit man from outside the incestuous system, instead of waiting for "surprises"? Why wasn't he firing more of the people directly responsible? It was the question, more than any other, that would gnaw at his credibility.

By late May it was clear that the bad loans being tallied by Mike LaRusso's team surpassed Armacost's worst nightmares. The American economy was stumbling through an erratic recovery from the Fed-induced recession, with industries like agriculture still not bottoming out. With banks' loan portfolios often the last to feel the blows, it made predicting losses a game of Russian roulette. ICERC had just "classified" a Latin American debtor nation, rumored to be Bolivia, automatically requiring Bank of America, as a major creditor bank, to increase its reserves against potential write-offs and take them from capital. Half a dozen other countries would go "classified," more time bombs for the banks.

Gillis's optimistic forecast for the year was beginning to seem just that—optimistic. Armacost was facing the imperative of huge additions to his second-quarter loan loss reserves. Numbers must be released by mid-July. The examiners would not tell the bank what reserves they wanted to see on the balance sheet; that decision was up to the bank. But if they reserved too little, the examiners could order an increase. A damaging event.

Armacost had been increasing his reserves for several quarters, more aggressively than most peer banks. But "every dollar I added decreased earnings," he says, "and diminished our chances for another positive quarter." B of A still had some weeks before the new figures had to be announced. But it was becoming clear that the numbers were going to be so large that they would have that "material impact" on the bank that required a public announcement. As he heard the news at the June board meeting, Schwab urged a strong statement. "We should tell the public what it's going to be—*a break-even quarter.*"

The memo Armacost released to the board and to staff on June 3, and to the press the next day, scarcely hinted at the magnitude of the bad news. Second-quarter net income would fall to "near the break-even point" because of higher loan loss reserves and overseas write-offs—"a blow to our collective pride." It was more than that. This was the moment when surprises could no longer be seen as aberrations, but as clues to systemic problems of still-unfathomed depth and magnitude. Armacost was now dealing with a steady running tide that could sweep away his gains as it washed over him.

The memo set off an alarm in the market, as BAC became the most actively traded stock on the New York Stock Exchange and dropped $1.875 to $19.875.

"IT'S JUST GOING to drift and drift." Chuck Schwab anguished. Between June 13 and June 26 he and his wife sold 307,500 of 1 million shares he received when he sold to BankAmerica. He sold his stock now at an average price of $18.75. On July 1, 1985, he hired Deloitte, Haskins & Sells, one of the Big Eight accounting firms "to educate me and guide me through an analysis." Using public information and comparisons with B of A's peer banks, Deloitte would do an independent analysis to root out the true condition of the bank's reserves, as he had been urging the board to do. His concern was increased by a special board meeting in July at which Armacost announced that the examiners were going to force B of A to create a special reserve. As if from a hat, Schwab felt, the number $500 million was chosen and announced that day. Was it the right number? Schwab wondered. How did they know?

THE WALL STREET JOURNAL'S managing editor, Norman Pearlstine, was monitoring events from New York. NMEC had aroused his interest. There had been a flurry of little stories before and after NMEC. San Francisco–based Mike Tharp filed a story on Armacost on June 3, warning of lower income with the headline BANKAMERICA'S PROFIT TO PLUNGE FOR 2ND QUARTER. There was no clear shape to emerging events. But Pearlstine smelled a big story. Dallas deputy bureau chief G. Christian Hill was scheduled to be moved to San Francisco in July. Specializing in financial institutions since 1979, Hill had learned during his first four years in Los Angeles "how vulnerable the banks are" as he covered the collapse of U.S. National Bank of San Diego. From the front lines in Texas, he had watched the savings and loan industry go down. He and colleague Richard B. Schmitt had covered the industry-shaking Midland National Bank crisis in Midland, Texas. He had earned more combat medals covering Continental Illinois. It was still a hunch. But Pearlstine moved Greg Hill to San Francisco two months early, in May.

Hill left his family in Dallas and for four weeks worked full-time reporting, and then two weeks writing, a major feature story on Bank of America. He conducted a blitz of thirty-five interviews with senior officers. Worked up his sources. He found Armacost the most accessible CEO he had met in his fifteen years with the *Journal*. Twice Armacost drove Hill home in his limousine to San Mateo; Armacost lived in the next town, exclusive Hillsborough. "You know he's trying to charm you and co-opt you, and you're alert to that. But he wants to make sure we hear about the positive things that are happening. He knows we'll get the bad news," Hill mused. Hill and Mike Tharp filed their by-line story on July 11—a seven-column story, more than a full page—and it sat in New York.

THE DAY before Hill filed his story, Armacost, Prussia, Gillis, and auditor Mac Nelson flew to Phoenix, Arizona, for a secret meeting at a resort hotel with acting Comptroller of the Currency Joe Selby, Patriarca, and LaRusso. The comptroller was having a retreat with his examiners and had reluctantly agreed to meet the BankAmericans. Armacost suspected Selby perceived it as an attempt to go over the head of his on-site examiner, LaRusso. The examiners had not yet released the results of their examination, and B of A urgently needed to get some perspective on the size of the reserves the bank was planning to add in its second-quarter results. The numbers must be released in a week. Armacost was very quiet. "He doesn't show his highs and lows like most people," says Gillis, "as a good CEO should not." But inside, Armacost was upset over the form the meeting was taking. "It was almost a setup. Nelson had prepared a big, thick dossier of all our notions. We thought we were having a very small meeting with Joe Selby and a couple of the examiners to go through our capital plan and our strategy. We found a very large group of examiners, including LaRusso. And I got the distinct impression it was very much a show by Joe Selby to show how macho he was. . . ." The environment, Armacost perceived, was "very hostile."

After Armacost and Prussia had gone through their presentation, trying to persuade Selby of the strength of their strategy, Selby told Armacost bluntly, "Sam, I've got to tell you, Mike LaRusso knows what he's doing. We back him to the hilt. We trust him and he's qualified." Selby didn't seem to be hearing the plan. Or want his men to give any clues to the reserve they would like to see. He pressed: "You have to give me some kind of an estimate. Because we're coming up with our own conclusions." LaRusso finally said, "Listen, Sam, after seeing all these surprises, I would add to the reserves hundreds of millions of dollars." Armacost looked at him and said, "You're crazy. It's not that bad."

The real numbers didn't come up until an eleventh-hour meeting in San Francisco just before the earnings release on July 17. LaRusso was being rather gentlemanly, knowledgeable and fair, Gillis thought. In fact, he thought Armacost tended to overstate LaRusso's "tough guy" behavior. But Armacost, Lloyd Sugaski, and Gillis blanched as LaRusso told them, "I would add at least five hundred million dollars to the reserves." Added to the reserves already committed to cover write-offs, it would be a $928 million hit. Nearly a billion dollars. When it was subtracted from earnings, *the bank would have to declare a loss for the first time.* The red ink at the bottom of the balance sheet would be $338 million. *The second-largest quarterly loss in banking history.*

On Thursday, July 16, Armacost told the board. He waited until after the market had closed, hoping to prevent more dumping of stock, like Schwab's. The press release went out on the wire on July 17. B of A could not contain the impact. Analysts would cry doom. The stock would drop. Armacost braced himself; the press "will feed like sharks."

He was seething. The bank was not failing. But the huge loss had branded the bank as the same kind of calamity as Penn Square or Continental Illinois. The regulators, he fumed, had made an example of Bank of America, singled it out "as being on the weaker side of the spectrum." If all the banks had raised their reserves dramatically against their losses then, as they did two years later, "when the game of third world debt was being played a lot differently, it would have been a nonevent—a virtue even," Armacost has reflected. Analysts might even have applauded his prudence, he suspects, as they later did John Reed's for taking his $3 billion hit—more than three times Armacost's—in May 1987.

Instead, the stock dropped again at the news. Moody's lowered its rating from C to C/D. Bank of America became the most sensational banking story in the nation. Greg Hill had only to change the lead and the headline of the story he had filed a week earlier, and on July 18 the *Journal* broke with a front-page story and the entire page 16. BIG QUARTERLY DEFICIT STUNS BANK-AMERICA, ADDS PRESSURE ON CHIEF . . . LOAN LOSSES HELP TO PUSH RED INK TO $338 MILLION; A BATTLE WITH EXAMINERS. And, in smaller print as the third subhead: SETBACK MASKS SOME GAINS. "Continental Illinois had been the biggest banking story since the depression. But Continental, LDCs, thrifts—all paled compared to Bank of America," says Hill.

Hill imported Rick Schmitt from Dallas to work the story with him and began documentation of "a great morality play, a tormenting saga of a CEO surviving hit after hit." On another level it was a story told in the tersest terms by the stock price: As Hill's story ran, it was at a low of $8, down from its all-time high of $76. Even allowing for the stock split, it was a massive drop.

Media would now be as relentless as the regulators. The *Journal* saw the *New York Times* as its prime rival. But the San Francisco papers and the *L.A. Times* also claimed B of A as their turf. The *L.A. Times*'s John Broder had two by-line stories the same day as Hill's, July 18. Both of Broder's stories speculated on Armacost's shaky position, planting seeds about his vulnerability. Although Hill, too, had posed the possibility that Armacost's crown was shaky, he had balanced that with news of the gains.

"We called it the *L.A. Times* rebuttal," Katherine Neville said of the videotape Armacost filmed and showed to all middle and senior management. "The format was a faked-up interview situation. The interviewer asks him about the *L.A. Times* story, and Sam says, 'Well, frankly, I was pissed off,' " as Neville recalled it. She sensed a change in Armacost as she read the series of memos he sent out to the staff. The tone of hurt had changed to frustration and a sense of betrayal. "Somewhere in that time frame he had come to believe that he and the bank were one and the same. That to betray him was to betray the bank," says Neville. McLin had picked up the same tone at the August 1 management forum. The message McLin heard was: "I depend on you, guys, and you're letting me down."

CHUCK SCHWAB came to the August board meeting determined to get action. Deloitte, Haskins had finished its analysis of public records, and his briefcase bulged with documentation to support the two proposals he urgently hoped the board would accept. He would propose a resolution to have an independent audit done of the bank's reserves adequacy, just as he had done, and to have a subcommittee of the board set up to review loan loss reserves. His findings showed that even with the $928 million increase in reserves, "we were *still* underreserved." He had reviewed Deloitte's report. "Christ, it was even worse than I thought!" The tension at the meeting was heightened by the presence of the examiners. Earlier Schwab had chatted with Mike Patriarca, LaRusso's boss, to try to learn more about the process, and he felt now, as he read Deloitte's report, that the examiners' concerns had been *tame*. His concern was that the board was not grasping that while nonperforming loans had climbed, reserves had stayed flat.

While Schwab challenged the board, shareholders and class action attorneys were formulating the very serious idea that the bank might have overstated its earnings—that by shortcutting on needed reserves, it might have kept earnings misleadingly high—it might have misrepresented, the stuff of lawsuits.

How could Ernst & Whinney—the outside auditors who had lived with the bank's books for years—not have known the true condition of the bank's loan portfolios? disgruntled shareholders were asking. Auditors, too, for Continental Illinois, Ernst & Whinney had been sued by shareholders in that debacle; the case was pending. Was it possible that the handful in that charmed circle of banks that were "too big to fail" were perceived as "so big and so important to national policy and the community that auditors went along with it because the impact would be so devastating"?, one asked.

Schwab laid his evidence of the need for an audit before the board and made his proposal. But he had no ally set to support him. He had not lobbied the board. He had hoped his work product would be so powerful that it could not be denied. There was no vote. His motion was not even seconded.

He was down, but not for the count. He had also come to challenge the continued payment of dividends. Dividends were sacrosanct. But they, too, came from earnings, and the bank could no longer afford to pay them. He pulled more stacks of papers from his briefcase and argued for "a *total* renaissance program—a crisis management approach." The bank must trim employment by 12 to 14 percent, trim expenses by such means as selling the corporate jet, raise up to $300 million capital in the market with a special discounted rights offering, cut executive pay, rescind the recent directors' fees increase, reassess the loan management system—and kill the dividend. As the largest shareholder he had the most to lose by the loss of dividends. "But we're paying out eighty to ninety percent of earnings!" They couldn't afford it. A vote was taken around the table. Schwab's initiative lost, five to eight. There would be a dividend cut, 47 percent, or 20 cents a share, a small sop to the need, he felt. But the split vote revealed an unprecedented change. It was a divided board.

"In hindsight, I should have lobbied," he says. "What a naive, dumb guy I was to think I could persuade an institution like that to do anything." He did not want to drive a wedge into that divided board. He wanted Armacost to act. "But I'm not going to drop this thing," he determined. Looking for support for his proposal on reserves, he flew to see three directors, had meetings in Washington. Wanting a second opinion, he had several of Deloitte's senior partners review the findings he'd presented to the board. While his handsome face smiled out daily from the *Journal,* he was becoming consumed with trying to rattle and shake the bank to grasp and act on the desperate issues they faced. His vibrant baby was trapped in this troubled institution.

On July 19 the first class-action suit was filed, charging the board and senior management and the auditors Ernst & Whinney with "conspiracy" to give "false and misleading" information on the bank's true financial condition. The *Zarowitz* case was filed by a lawyer whose high-profile advocacy of shareholder litigation cases was about to earn him a profile on the front page of the

Wall Street Journal, Dick Greenfield, from Haverford, Pennsylvania. He had recently won $3.5 million for stockholders of Crocker Bank over losses in 1983.

On August 30 Schwab, too, was sued, the complaint charging him with selling his stock while in possession of "material information not available to the public"—a charge of insider trading. His spokesman Hugo Quakenbush quickly denied the charge, claiming that Schwab had acted on the same information the public read in the papers on June 4.

The lawsuits, gradually consolidating in tall stacks of files in the basement of the federal courthouse in Los Angeles, were the beginning of a new stage for the bank, a phase of threat and harassment no prestigious bank, its board, or senior management could have imagined would be its daily fare a decade earlier. The moments of terror would grow to a relentless barrage.

As the examiners turned the screw on the balance sheet, Schwab became the embodiment of the growing pressures for faster—and in Armacost's view, unrealistic—change.

It frustrated Adizes. It was Schwab who had introduced him to Bank of America. He admired him as the archetypal entrepreneur. But Schwab didn't understand the complexities Armacost was dealing with, Adizes believed. " 'Let's fire five thousand people.' That was Chuck Schwab's motto. It is peanuts when you compare it to the bad loans. You're talking about *billions.* And Sam *was* firing. By attrition." Armacost was also dealing with a subtle issue Schwab did not understand, Adizes argued. "Banking is based on reputation. If you destroy that, people are going to run for their money, pull their deposits out. You're very vulnerable. You have to maintain some appearance of control and self-respect."

"Adolescent" is how some on the board were beginning to view Schwab. Armacost met and talked to Schwab regularly, but Armacost was getting impatient with him, too. "He was the pure classic go-go entrepreneur. Too simplistic. Too impatient." He wanted everything changed at the speed of light. "Unwilling to admit to the complexities of a gigantic enterprise . . . I think Chuck always felt that he had sold his company too cheap. He would never acknowledge that it was the bank's purchase of Schwab that had increased its value," Armacost felt.

Adizes sensed that there had been a turning point in Armacost's safety since the big loan losses were uncovered during the spring, that he was now vulnerable. Adizes's own continued presence in the bank depended, more than ever, on Armacost's strength. "After every board meeting, I asked, 'Is the board behind you?' Every month I checked it. The one who was giving him a hard time was Chuck."

Whom could he count on? Armacost wondered. Schwab was clearly a problem and may have gained McNamara as his ally. If that were true, perhaps Wally Haas, who had been McNamara's roommate at Berkeley, was in that camp too. An early and persisting rumor was that Richard Cooley, Seafirst CEO, had ambitions to sit in Armacost's chair. "He saw himself as the natural alternative," a board member states.

Armacost knew it was tough for his board. "You get in the club, and all your pals read the articles, and they're giving you a little gig while you're putting on your golf shoes," urging you to take the easy way out, change management, and get the pain off your back. "It takes courage to say, 'We believe in the program. It's taking longer than we thought. But we're willing to take the abuse,' " as he believed the loyal stalwarts did.

"They're absolutely behind me," Armacost reassured Adizes each month, a confidence Greg Hill of the *Journal* confirms. In eighteen years of business writing, he had never seen such board support. Replacement of bad management was a board's principal function. Considering the deteriorating news, Hill found the board's unswerving support of Armacost remarkable.

ARMACOST DID HAVE a lot on his plate. The board, he perceived, was legitimately concerned about how he was going to get it all done. "We've hired a lot of good people to help execute the strategy," he told them in his rapid-fire summations. To reassure the board that the old order indeed changeth, Armacost and Bob Beck had prepared a summary of senior management changes that laid out the dramatic number of new players he had brought to the team he had inherited from Clausen. It was a telling document: Of eighty senior vice-presidents in the bank when Armacost took over, thirty-eight were gone. Few old faces remained in the California Division, where the old culture was most entrenched. Armacost's discreet and measured way of removing them satisfied his distaste for "public executions" of loyal senior managers guilty of no crime more heinous than that of coping badly with change. But it would keep him from getting credit for the almost total overhaul of upper management, he would ultimately see.

As the old guard departed, it was showered with a list of epithets that seemed to apply to almost all who had risen in the Golden Age: "gentleman"; "great people person"; "good credit man"; "just a wonderful guy." "There were a lot of wonderful guys in the bank who were incompetent," says Steve McLin.

Mont McMillen had been removed in January from the North American Division and sent to languish in the half-life of an administrative post in World Banking in San Francisco. It had been painful for Armacost to cut the man who had raced the fast track with him since 1966. But caught in insoluble in-house battles, McMillen knew he had lost the respect of the managers below him "because I was unable to deliver a solution." Armacost suspected that "at a certain stage of the game, it doesn't matter whether you're a good manager or a bad manager if your credibility is lost in the street." Cooper forced Frick to tell McMillen to tender his resignation next March. Frick drove over to the East Bay to tell him over lunch on a weekend. "I've never seen a guy so uncomfortable. He was a very soft guy," recalls McMillen.

World Banking's Bill Bolin, tarred with the Argentina debacle, was taking early retirement. Lloyd Sugaski, chief credit officer, was retiring in the fall. His predecessor, Iver Iversen, had despaired from the sidelines as he watched Sugaski's dismantling of the General Loan Committee, and he had finally written Armacost on August 17, 1985, urging that he root out the causes of the terrible loan losses and that he reverse decentralization of credit authority. Sugaski had lost his credibility with the examiners, Armacost admitted. As a longtime colleague of Sugaski said, "He could make a commercial loan better than anybody. But he wasn't good at managing the credit process—nor did he ever want to."

Sugaski's replacement as chief credit officer, Glenhall Taylor, arrived on September 11, 1985—a move that should have been made four years earlier. He was the first of the "implants" from Wells Fargo. At the time Wells was just one of several strong companies B of A was hiring from to build the new team—Citibank, American Express. But of the peer California bankers, senior Wells men were coups. Wells was just coming off a virtuoso job of successfully digesting Crocker Bank, the largest bank merger in history. Wells's CEO, Carl Reichardt, was admired as a western Walter Wriston, and its ratios were beautiful; it had become the analysts' pet.

Taylor had been lured to Seafirst by his former colleague at Wells, Dick Cooley. Called out of early retirement from Seafirst, Glenhall Taylor had checked out, Armacost says, as "a tough, knowledgeable, highly respected credit officer who could restore credibility." Taylor had built a reputation at Wells Fargo as one of the most rigorous and successful bad loan hunters in the industry. He was the first of a small flood of Wells-trained executives who would be hired to help out in the emergency. A. P. Giannini would have bellowed indignantly at the existence of a Wells Mafia within the gates.

Bob Beck had discovered that as Wells refocused on western retail banking, a treasure trove of highly regarded corporate and international bankers was now available, made redundant by the changes. Others, at the top tier of power within the bank, were loaded for bear after the triumphant Crocker merger and looking for new challenges. In B of A, credit and lending men rose through the bank on separate, and even adversarial, tracks; Wells men were trained in both. Rare for a CEO, Reichardt was a credit man who was still called in on the biggest, toss-of-the-dime loan decisions to make judgments. Lewis Coleman, joining the flow from Wells just seven months after Taylor, jokes, "They say loans made in heaven—in the office of the CEO—are always bad. It just happens that at Wells, God is a credit man!" With the addition of Coleman, one of Wells's most admired international credit men, the Wells presence at B of A threatened to grow so large and powerful that Armacost, fearing a political "implant problem," put an embargo on any more Wells hires.

But with the hiring of Taylor, Armacost had already made the move that, as much as any other, would determine his personal destiny. He knew that, to save the bank and his place in history, the bad loans had to be dug out of the portfolios even more vigorously. Nothing would escape Glenhall Taylor's X-ray eyes. But risk lay in Taylor's relentlessness. An outsider with nothing to lose, he had nothing to restrain him from rooting out the worst, even if it meant baring monumental losses that would cripple Armacost's reputation. It was the essence of Armacost's "proaction"—of intervening to prevent possible future negative events. It had to be done.

As he scanned the personnel changes by late summer '85, Armacost felt heartened that "we'd added good people at all levels, not just at the top. For every Talbott, Hopper, and Cooper, we had ten good new middle-management guys."

BUT THERE WAS growing frustration among some of the new team. Talbott brought his frustrations to Armacost. "You're great at saying, 'Go do it, Pete.' The problem is at Citicorp I could turn to my next level and have sixteen guys who could execute. Here I ain't got anybody who can execute." Armacost responded: "That's exactly why you're here. Go hire the next three levels down." Talking out the frustrations with his wife, Judy, at night, Talbott mused, "When I came, I wondered how McLin could be here eight years and not get things cleaned up. But I'm beginning to think it would take twenty Pete Talbotts to do the job." He and Judy had not been automatically integrated into San Francisco society, as they had been in London and St. Louis with Citibank. With Talbott preoccupied with his job, Judy was getting restless to return to New York.

Harvey Gillis was getting nervous about lawsuits. As financial controller he knew that BankAmerica would be one of the first targets of shareholder class actions that were erupting around troubled banks. He was already included in a shareholder action that named him in Seafirst's financial collapse, an irony, he thought, recalling his opposition to the cavalier lending by Seafirst's energy division. He was being scouted by a Seattle venture capitalist, Sam Stroum, and that possibility was looking increasingly attractive. He tried to resign in the late summer but was urged to stay until the end of the year. Gillis resisted the bank's offer to make him chief financial officer and left in December 1985, to be chief operating manager of Samuel Stroum Enterprises.

Max Hopper was bristling over Tom Cooper. "He's cutting the muscle, not just the fat," he railed as conflict built between the two. "He's not delivering on his commitments to reduce employees for '85, although he continues to suggest that others reduce theirs." Hopper felt ready to run BAPS as well as BASE. But Armacost feared BASE's independence as a technology server for the whole bank might be undermined by BAPS. "I wasn't ready at that stage of the game to hammer the payment flows, a line function, and the technology guys, a supply function, together again," he says. "Sure, the battle of the barons between Cooper and Hopper was going on under the surface. They were both strong-willed guys. But I took that as a signal that we had finally arrived." Armacost cheered that. "We had big, strong-willed, successful, competent managers willing to argue with each other over business issues. That had not been apparent in the B of A structure ever in my lifetime. It was 'positive contention'!"

But Hopper was frustrated that Armacost was building Cooper's power, while Cooper, he saw, was "undermining Sam, talking about Sam's lack of decision . . . to all of us. Cooper was against him from day one. But Sam trusted him." Fashioning a bigger role for Cooper in his mind, Armacost claims, "I had Cooper in BAPS as a testing ground." Hopper steamed. The fair-haired boy was creating unhealthy factions, "and I was not on his team," Hopper believed. "Positive contention" was hardening into a steely schism between the two. American Airlines Chairman Robert Crandall had suggested early in the year that Hopper return to the airlines. Hopper's wife, Jo, loved living in San Francisco, but she did miss Texas.

Armacost was risking his new team. Underlying the specific complaints was a classic failure of leadership. Disaffection from below comes not when a tyrant rules with an iron hand but when lack of clearly defined power leaves people in a limbo—when they don't know precisely what their authority and rights are. This ambiguity is what underlay the restlessness. The new stars had expected flux. But Armacost was giving bold mandates, then not clarifying the lines of command needed to achieve them.

* * *

PETE TALBOTT spent a number of sleepless nights deciding to make the break. In late summer he talked to Armacost. Told him that Judy was unhappy and had threatened to go back to New York without him. He hated to leave the job unfinished. But because he was burdened with more of the old guard in retail than other divisions, the frustrations seemed insoluble. First Boston had made a superb offer. Talbott had phrased his words very carefully, leaving Armacost room to ask him to stay, perhaps for a better compensation package. Having opened the discussion, he waited. At this point at Citicorp, "John Reed would have said, 'What the hell, you can't leave. What'll make you happy?' He would have put up a fight." But nothing happened. Armacost told him how sorry he was, how much he hated to lose him, that he understood. Judy did want to go. "But I could have been persuaded to stay."

Talbott left Bank of America on September 1, 1985. "That set my strategy with Wiesler back six months," says Armacost. Pressure to replace Wiesler was continuing. Talbott had been his backup. "I didn't have a ready replacement, and I didn't want to say 'go' to Jim and have a rudderless ship." Armacost was "developing a counterstrategy; I was thinking about taking Cooper out of BAPS and putting him in the retail bank to give him some experience, before I chose a COO." That would have soothed Max Hopper, too. But Armacost didn't act. In the 1985 annual report published six months later, Wiesler was still listed among the top five in the bank's hierarchy.

MAX HOPPER resigned in October. Just months earlier he had been a hero as BASE was unveiled. But as the bad loans popped in the spring, blame focused on Adizes's big-budget, years-long projects, of which Hopper was a major part. The climate of hope that had surrounded him "reverted like a rubber band, and I became a lightning rod." Early tensions between Hopper and Tom Cooper broke into open warfare. The conflict was really one of "competing visions," Hopper saw, as he and Cooper were thrust onto a five-man committee Armacost had appointed to draw up and prioritize a list of possible "non-strategic" asset sales as losses mounted in mid-1985—the "Gang of Five," as it was informally known. Hopper's strategy for asset sales was to "crank it down every year so that you maintained revenues. You couldn't hit the muscle. Tom's was major surgery. The salami sausage approach—just lopping off parts." Liquidation! "That's when I began to think of leaving." Cooper saw ideological conflict with Hopper, felt Hopper wanted to lead in *creating* technology, while Cooper wanted to lead in *using* technology—in using what was there. B of A couldn't afford to be a Bell Labs *and* an IBM. It was not "creation of basic technology in any form" he supported, says Hopper, but the *use* of new technology as no banks had used it before, if B of A were to leapfrog the competition; "Mr. Cooper," he says archly, "wanted to set *both* the technology direction and the direction of his own area."

Adizes was there, in Armacost's office, at the showdown. "Max told Sam he was willing to stay if he got BAPS as well as systems engineering." Hopper made his demands believing that "Sam was willing to give me BAPS and give Tom retail. I didn't think I'd taken systems engineering far enough and asked Sam if I could run both." Adizes stood, stunned, as Armacost said no.

Armacost didn't plead with him to stay. Hopper had done "a marvelous job." He had consolidated the Balkanized technology side of the bank and put the bank back in the game. He had been a sufficiently tough cost cutter to have lived up to the early nickname Max the Ax among the computer people. But Armacost had a backup. He had hired Lou Mertes, a strong technology man at Seafirst who was "much higher-geared than Seafirst needs." Armacost claims he hired Mertes "so that if we ever lost Max for any reason, we had a replacement." But it appears Armacost was ready to permit Hopper to be "lost." "Mertes was a combination of a man who understood technology, but a real tough manager in terms of getting costs down. I could say to Mertes, 'Get me a hundred million out of there.' He'd do it."

Armacost's readiness to let Hopper go for a man with a bigger ax suggests that something had been lost in the summer of '85. "His vision shrunk with the shock of those loan losses," Hopper reflected as he moved back to Dallas. Returning to American Airlines, Hopper was given command of the airline's entire technological effort, a far more powerful role than he had had as head of SABRE, the reservations system.

ARMACOST WAS FIGHTING defection now, as well as earnings declines and loan losses. The pressure was taking a shocking toll, Katherine Neville thought. In early October, before Max Hopper left, he and Armacost came over to Travelers Cheques to award several Eagle Pins for exceptional performance. For months word had been flying through the rumor mill that Armacost's days were numbered, that he would be replaced by Seafirst's CEO, Dick Cooley. The rumor mill, Neville had found, was "surgically accurate," and by the time Armacost arrived for the pin ceremony, "his epitaph had already been carved." She still had hope but had been increasingly distressed by the tone of hurt and recrimination that had crept into his memos and videotapes, the incessant football metaphors. Now, gathered with just a few people in an office, she was seeing him at closer range than she had since that first speech when she had been so enchanted by his virtuoso performance and the promise of strong leadership.

She could scarcely believe it was the same man. "He looked exhausted, his hair was thinning, and he looked fifteen years older. He was pitching *Visions, Values and Strategies* like an ice-cream man. He only had three or four pins to give, and he couldn't remember the names of the people; he kept having to look at cards. And he stammered, he literally stammered, through the speech. This was a guy that was suffering badly."

FEW WOULD SEE it as Neville had. Those who saw him regularly didn't notice the change as much. He continued to function by Adizes's "duck theory"—"very poised and unflustered above the surface, but paddling like hell underwater." Publicly he exuded confidence and stated that he had no intention of giving up the president's chair.

But circling predators smelled blood and were preparing to dive on the weakened prey.

Chapter Fifteen

THE STORY OF MAX HOPPER'S resignation in October '85 was charged with significance for banker William Sudmann, reading it in his fifty-ninth floor office on the executive floor of First Interstate's Los Angeles skyscraper—a tower that, symbolically, looks down on Bank of America. "It's an indication good people are leaving," he excitedly told the tiny group of people who, since July, had been working on a project so secret that not even the most tenacious of the media would smell it out for another four months. Joe Pinola's tight inside team was working on the ultimate dream: a merger with Bank of America.

Bill Sudmann, a former lawyer at B of A, was one of the Bank of America alumni Joe Pinola had gathered around him to run First Interstate; at the most senior level, they represented 120 years of B of A experience. He had always thought the drama of Giannini and the forced unbundling from Transamerica of the chain of banks that became First Interstate was "a fabulous story." For Pinola's team, the legend came with the territory: how the archipelago of western banks the dynamic Pinola now commanded had been wrenched from its parent by the Federal Reserve, thwarting the Giannini dream of nationwide branch banking—but leaving them blessed by a golden twelve-state banking franchise. Ranging from its flagship bank, First Interstate Bank of California, to a small-town bank in Kalispell, Montana, Pinola served his territory with twenty-two banks and nearly a thousand branches. A merger with Bank of America would create, Keefe, Bruyette analyst Don Crowley would soon claim, a financial behemoth "with absolute dominance in the West" and resources rivaling Citicorp's.

Affection as well as ambition drove the dream. "Because of so many of us coming from the Bank of America, there was this special affinity to B of A, a feeling of kinship with the organization," says Sudmann. "It's hard to convey accurately the immense pride you felt," confirms Pinola's chief financial officer, Don Griffith, a former Citibanker and BankAmerican. "Here was something on a world scale that had been built by, truly, a great man. Few have equaled what he's done. There was huge pride in belonging to what he had created," especially if you came from California, as Griffith did. "The problem is that it became a blind pride, unable to see the difference between the past and the future," says Griffith, trying to explain why he and others left in the late seventies as the banking revolution galloped toward them. "In 1979 I said no to being head of credit for Latin America for Bank of America." Griffith had joined the expatriate flood at First Interstate.

"The idea of a merger must have floated among all the B of A people," Griffith admits. "It was a very ethereal idea—kind of a vision that had not yet formed," says Sudmann. But in April 1983, while Griffith waited for a reporter from *Forbes* in a suite in the Fairmont Hotel in San Francisco, he looked out the window at the Bank of America headquarters down the hill and said to Paul Minch, the bank's corporate communications chief, "You know, there ought to be some way to put our two companies together." Minch remembered the words "just as clear as a bell."

The next step had been taken on the afternoon of July 16, 1985, when Sudmann and Griffith sat in the conference room on First Interstate's executive floor and listened to a provocative proposal from San Francisco–based Robert A. Huret and J. Richard Fredericks. Senior consultant and research analyst respectively in the area of banks and financial institutions at Montgomery Securities, an active West Coast investment banking firm that was trying to move into major deal making, they had been picking up rumors from their contacts within Bank of America. Sam Armacost was vulnerable, they reported. The Comptroller of the Currency's examiners were putting pressure on management and on the company to raise capital, and Armacost, they perceived, was on the ropes. Would First Interstate be interested?

Griffith and Sudmann exchanged glances. They would have to be terribly discreet. "We didn't want to be out there, visible. It was presumptuous of us."

First Interstate was a $50 billion bank, the nation's ninth-largest bank holding company; Bank of America, now number two, had resources of $113 billion. Griffith and Sudmann sent Huret and Fredericks back to San Francisco encouraged to explore the idea in a very preliminary way, "but absolutely not on behalf of First Interstate. They were *not* representing us."

The next morning they huddled with Pinola. The arguments for a merger were powerful. Pinola had built a strong reputation as head of First Interstate. But the dominance of his corporate tower, the highest in Los Angeles and second-tallest west of Chicago, was not being matched in the balance sheet. In the tier below B of A, he was competing boldly with his California peers, Wells Fargo and Security Pacific. But not well enough for Pinola's ambitious nature. His earnings and profit ratios were coming in a little lower. "This is the best retail banking state in the nation. Of all the places where you want to have the greater piece of the pie, it's the state of California. Security now has six hundred and eighty-five branches, Wells has five hundred . . . six hundred. With three hundred twenty-five California branches, we sit number four. I don't like to be number four in any market."

Bank of America was unquestionably the Queen of California. And though troubled and retracting, her international network was still one of the most pervasive of the American banks. Although Pinola might profess, "Our goal in life is to become a national provider of a wide range of financial services," he was a man who also "yearns to strut upon a global stage," as the *L.A. Times*'s John Broder described his ambitions. First Interstate was too small, now, to compete effectively in the global arena; Pinola was currently trying to reduce its foreign debt exposure. To reign in either market, "You need a breadth of product and a massive business. And you must be the lowest-cost provider to that mass."

But the banking environment had become a minefield. "How do you manage inside an envelope that changes so dramatically in such a short period of time—five years, ten years?" As he watched an ambivalent Congress swing from more to fewer powers for banks, with no clear champions for banking on the Hill, "it is not impossible to think that we may even *re*regulate." He could not even count on the support of California's senators in Washington. Pete Wilson was a friend to banks, but Alan Cranston canceled him out. It was ludicrous, but he could score more points by sharing a barstool in Washington with a senator from Montana or Wyoming. "Life ain't simple; it's enormously difficult to manage in this day and age."

Pinola also felt the urgency of time. He was sixty, within a few years of retirement. First Interstate was swiftly losing its interstate advantage. It was being eroded by the invasion of the territory through all the loopholes that permitted financial hybrids to flourish where banks could not and by the building of reciprocal interstate banking regions in several parts of the country. On June 11, just a few months earlier, the Supreme Court had ruled that regional interstate banking zones were constitutional, giving birth to a prospering new breed of bank, the superregional. The franchising of banks he had devised as a means of expanding the territory and pushing his products without the expense of building or buying banks was moving too slowly, as oil and agriculture-dependent states fell into depression and created a bleak north-south corridor that blocked natural migration of franchising eastward through contiguous states. If he was to leave a legacy of industry leadership, he must find a bolder, faster way than the gradual spread of his network through franchising or buying up collapsing banks through the FDIC.

B of A would be a quantum leap. The combined banks would make A.P.'s babies again the nation's largest bank and give unsurpassed positioning for nationwide interstate banking. They would blanket the western states with branches, plus Schwab. Pinola loved Schwab! What a delivery system the combined banks would be. He would still have a lot of brick and mortar—a heavy cost for Pinola to maintain—but he'd be pushing much more product through them.

And what delicious satisfaction to come back to the Bank of America as commander in chief. It was assumed among his team that Pinola would displace Armacost as CEO. Armacost had reported to Pinola in the North American Division; Pinola had called him back from London to open the Chicago office. He already made more money than Armacost; Pinola's 1985 salary was over $900,000. To be the instrument of reunification of the two banks—to have that on a banker's epitaph—would be a satisfaction beyond money or title. But if he tried and failed, "we could look like a paper tiger," he feared.

Since Continental Illinois, Bank of America might be "too big to fail." But was it too big to be the target of a corporate takeover? There was a whispered assumption in San Francisco—as the city watched Crown Zellerbach devoured by James Goldsmith, the Kaiser empire dismembered, and Safeway escape raids by buying itself back in a leveraged buyout, then sell off profitable big chunks from the chain of supermarkets to pay down the debt—that Washington would put up regulatory barriers if anyone tried. A Japanese takeover, especially, would rouse such xenophobia that "it would *never* be permitted," B of A's corporate communications chief, Ron Rhody, claimed. But other impregnable giants had been attacked. Some had fallen. Powerful national symbols, CBS and TWA, were under siege. A psychological threshold had been passed when San Francisco's Chevron swallowed Gulf Oil and Gulf vanished from Pittsburgh. Corporations, no matter how large and powerful, were not protected by divine right. It was a shock to corporate America and to a society that took certain institutions for granted, like the church and the presidency. Bank of America would test the sacredness of a corporation like no other.

This climate helped Pinola and his team think the unthinkable. They couldn't help being struck by the enormity of it. They would explore it only on friendly grounds. Goodwill, and access to the books before you bought a bank as large as B of A, were so vital that bank mergers could be done only on friendly terms, they believed. Banks were standing aloof from the hostile takeovers that raged across America. Phone calls and meetings began with Montgomery Securities. And the project received a secret code name, Operation Snowflake.

Through the summer Huret and Fredericks sparred delicately with Steve McLin, on the B of A side, and reported that the bank seemed "not uninterested." As discussions picked up, Pinola's team augmented its negotiating clout by hiring Goldman, Sachs, one of Wall Street's most successful deal makers, but always—and *only*—in friendly deals. Montgomery had brought First Interstate the deal and would continue to explore it. But if it developed, Pinola would need heavier hitters from Wall Street as well. "There's no conflict of interest. We're available," said Geoffrey Boisi, the Goldman superstar who had found himself in the middle of the most contentious takeover in history as deal maker for Getty Oil in its acquisition by Texaco. Pinola's team gave Goldman permission to say it was "acting on our behalf." Montgomery and Goldman knew the other was on the deal, "and it set up some competition between them. It's like having two surgeons at surgery," said Minch.

Bank of America brought in its New York investment bankers, Salomon Brothers, with its president and senior partner, John Gutfreund, personally involved. Martin Lipton, of Wachtell, Lipton, Rosen & Katz, one of New York's two most powerful takeover lawyers, was put on call, while First Interstate called Joseph H. Flom of Skadden, Arps, Slate, Meagher & Flom, Lipton's archrival. Friendly, perhaps. But the inchoate event shaping in California was taking on the look of a major struggle for corporate control, "with the investment bankers doing most of the talking to each other," Pinola observed.

In the preliminary sparring one of the first things to be discussed was the "social issue"—the question of who would run the merged firm. "There was never any question in our minds that Joe would be at the helm," says Sudmann. But how would Armacost feel being pushed out to, perhaps, the chairmanship? After all, Pinola would be gone in a few years, and Armacost was only forty-six. They assumed that McLin must be talking to, and for, Armacost. In broad terms, they discussed the most obvious themes: the name of the bank; location of its headquarters; management structure. It became clear that whatever name the surviving entity might have—Bank of America or First Interstate—technically First Interstate would have to acquire Bank of America to preserve First Interstate's precious inherited interstate charter. Remarkably, B of A seemed not to be balking at these sensitive issues. But it was still all very tentative. Sam Armacost kept his cards down even with those closest to him. But the idea of a merger had not been rebuffed out of hand.

On September 1 Pete Talbott's departure was reported in the press. Defections were beginning. Pinola's team was sent a copy of Armacost's schedule and, seeing he was leaving for Asia in late September, had an urgent desire to have him meet, face-to-face, with someone from First Interstate before he left. Boisi got on the phone and talked to Armacost, who was initially guarded. He just listened. But he suggested that a representative from both banks should meet and designated McLin as the contact person for B of A.

McLin and Griffith met in a suite at the Fairmont Hotel on September 26, the first direct meeting of the principals. The Montgomery Securities pair had met with McLin just three days earlier and discussed five themes: the vision of putting the family back together, the obstacles, timing, pricing, and due diligence, which dealt with the issue of "How would we go about getting a look at each other's books?" Now McLin and Griffith added a few new areas to the growing dialogue: regulatory approval; board integration; the assets that would have to be sold off in a merger. And they broached some of the philosophical and cultural questions. How would a decentralized network like First Interstate operate with a more centralized power structure like Bank of America's? Progress in the talks was oiled by the powerful attraction both sides felt toward the vision of "a real western strategy"—not to mention the banking history—the merger would create. It would put MotherBank back on the list of the world's ten largest banks.

When McLin had talked his way into being Armacost's strategic planning chief in 1981, he had not envisioned merger strategies for the entire bank. But this incredible thing was taking shape and gathering momentum. However, the hand he held grew weaker daily. Although he brought the nation's most desirable deposit base to the bargaining table, he also brought a sickly stock price. B of A's stock was selling at $22 a share; First Interstate's, at about $48. He and Griffith discussed a straightforward deal in which market value would be merged with market value—B of A's $3 billion with First Interstate's $2 billion, creating an institution with total capital of $5 billion. It appealed to McLin. B of A's flag would still fly. "The name would have been retained, and B of A shareholders would have come out on top in terms of economic value. As Griffith and I originally worked it out, they would have ended up with sixty percent of the combined entity," says McLin. As the meeting ended, the two men hadn't agreed to anything. But they hadn't disagreed.

For Pinola, the deal's viability hinged, increasingly, on "the magic of purchase accounting"—an accounting technique that would let him rid the merged balance sheet of billions of Bank of America's greatest drag: its bad loans, "a pouch, we figure, that's about $13 billion in total." Purchase accounting would allow him, during that brief window of opportunity during a merger or acquisition, to mark undervalued assets *up* to their market value on the balance sheet, mark overvalued assets like bad loans *down* to market value, and offset one against the other, coming up with a new valuation of everything—a fresh start. In the case of the Bank of America it would increase the value of assets to $5 billion. With the press of a computer key, he could write that amount off against the bad loans, reducing the pouch substantially. "Just think of the two headquarters buildings, the Italian bank, and all those places where you have things carried on your book that you acquired at low value!" he mused, eyes flashing at the possibilities. "You get rid of the junk. It's magic. It's fantastic!"

But it would be destroyed if B of A sold off high-value assets like the headquarters building, as it was trying to do.

On September 30, 1985, B of A's headquarters building was sold to San Francisco developer Walter H. Shorenstein for $660 million. Trying to raise capital, Armacost had ordered McLin to speed the divestment process. On October 8 Chrysler bought FinanceAmerica for $434 million. Those two sales gave Armacost a nearly half-billion-dollar pretax gain. But it was not good news to Pinola. But there were still empires of real estate—all the branches, real property, several dozen subsidiaries. And Schwab was still there. "The asset I wanted more than any other asset was Schwab, because it has a million and a half accounts across the country and I'm trying to spread myself across the country. It would be *great* with continued deregulation, because you could sell mutual funds and other products through Schwab. And if you were reregulated, it might have even greater value because it would be grandfathered in, and you'd have something nobody else could *get*. There is no downside to acquiring Schwab!" Pinola said exultantly.

As the dream took on more substance, Pinola's team began to grasp what they had set in motion. "There was no fire yet," Paul Minch observed, "but a definite glow in the belly." As rumors persisted that Armacost was indeed vulnerable, Pinola's team joined the new game of speculating on who the board might put in in his place. Citicorp's number two man, Tom Theobald, was an obvious choice. Paul Volcker? A long shot. As they got into the game, a member of Pinola's team ran Clausen's name up the pole. "Never, *never*" was the bemused consensus. "He's part of the problem."

"But B of A stock started to run down in that autumn period, to sixteen dollars; it lost a billion in market value," says McLin, "and First Interstate stock ran up to about fifty-five dollars. All of a sudden you had a fifty-fifty deal." Armacost pressed McLin. "What about this First Interstate thing? I'm getting calls from the board." McLin replied: "You could make a case for the sixty-forty B of A cut. But look at the numbers, Sam. I just don't think you can support this deal with us at sixteen dollars and them at fifty-four or fifty-five dollars." He discussed it with Salomon and Wachtell, Lipton. The lower B of A stock fell, the harder it would be to cut a merger deal that would favor the B of A shareholders, McLin's prime obligation in any merger. In McLin's mind, "Pinola had been effectively rebuffed" by the growing distance between the two stock prices.

Trying to read the tone of McLin's voice for signs in a phone call on October 17, Pinola's team thought it sensed a cooling. Armacost was just back from Asia. Perhaps he had fully grasped that he would no longer be CEO, the Pinola people speculated. Or perhaps the sale of the headquarters building and FinanceAmerica, even though they were just one-time infusions of capital, had made him feel stronger. And yet B of A's bargaining position was eroding daily. By December the stock had fallen to $12. Pinola's people delicately shifted from the idea of merging at market value to placing a value of $18 a share on B of A stock in a merger—a 50 percent premium over market. In the minds of Pinola's team, B of A's image was gradually shifting from partner to target. McLin interpreted the $18 offer as a dramatic change in the tone of the discussions, a shift away from a friendly negotiated merger toward that terror of terrors—hostile takeover. Pinola flexing his muscles. "With that premium, they think we'll feel compelled to take it, they'll be the acquirer, and there will be no friendly discussions about who ends up where," McLin mused.

First Interstate heard rumors that its proposals had been brought to the November board meeting and that no decision had been taken. But it was just rumor. It had put nothing on paper. No letter or tender offer that required an answer. It had not put the bank "in play." The Pinola team wondered how much the board had been told. Then word came back that Armacost had been strongly reaffirmed by the board at the December meeting, even though 1985 would end with a loss for the year in excess of $300 million. First Interstate was sparring with shadows. Operation Snowflake had always been fragile, and now the whole impossible dream seemed to have lost its momentum and, by Christmas, to be fading away.

As 1986 BROKE, Pinola's premium offer, which had looked compelling when Bank of America's stock was trading at $12, suddenly looked less strong. For in late January, like a brush fire, B of A's stock flared up, died back, then flared again. There had been no breath of a leak about Pinola's plans. "The stock was running up," observed McLin, pleased but puzzled, "and it wasn't because of Sam's good looks."

There was no obvious news about the bank to account for the surge in the stock. There was good news for critics of Armacost's loyalty to the old guard; in January it was announced that Jim Wiesler would be retiring in June, under sub rosa pressure from Armacost after he had failed to clean up a mess in the branches—a failure to report large cash transactions to the Treasury Department—that had drawn the ire of the examiners. But allowing Wiesler to linger until June, Armacost saw later, was a "critical" mistake, for it gave more ammunition to those pushing for faster change.

No, Wiesler's slow-motion departure was no more likely to be the source of market excitement than Checking Plus.

In fact, most hard news breaking around the bank was so bad that it could only drive the stock down. On January 21 Armacost declared 1985's results: the first annual loss since 1932, a chilling $337 million. Dividends, already reduced, were now suspended. North in Yuba City, farmer Bob Stanghellini, his aunt, and his mother had filed a $50 million lawsuit against B of A. Keefe, Bruyette had lowered its ratings on B of A's preferred stock, and the bank was fined $4.75 million on the mess Wiesler was to have cleaned up.

IT WAS TAKEOVER rumors that were affecting the stock. But not Pinola's. The Street had picked up threads of a rumor that Sandy Weill was on the march again and was moving on Bank of America. Founder of what became one of the nation's dominant investment banking firms, Shearson Lehman Hutton, just resigned as president of American Express, Weill was known to be searching for a vehicle on which to build his next financial empire. Although Weill's interest would remain an elusive rumor until late February when the story broke in the press, one of Wall Street's most successful financiers had sniffed out vulnerability, too. Under a cloak of secrecy equaling Pinola's, he had initiated his own dialogue with the bank. Unknown to each other or anyone outside their secret circles of bankers and lawyers, two suitors were now circling the great corporate organism soon to be dubbed by First Nationwide's Tony Frank "the greatest prize of capitalism."

Weill's was not a household face, like Chuck Schwab's. With bags under his eyes giving him a hangdog look in repose, his presence lacked the electric charge of Pinola's. The trim waist of the former junior Davis Cup champion was gradually falling before the great restaurants of Manhattan and vintage Haut-Brions from his Westchester County estate wine cellar; of average

height, he moved with the low-key manner and slightly apologetic slouch of
Peter Falk's Columbo. He had an engaging smile that invited hugs, not fear.
Although he had commuted to San Francisco through most of 1983 performing a virtuoso turnaround of Fireman's Fund Insurance, an American Express
subsidiary, most San Franciscans would ask, "Sandy who?" if they heard the
name. But Sanford I. Weill was perceived by the Street as one of the seminal
architects of the seventies' and eighties' sea change on Wall Street, when
deregulation, electronic technology, and globalization of the financial markets
converged to trigger a shakeout that continues to remake the Street. It has
dethroned the clubby "white shoe" establishment and made men like Weill,
the entrepreneurial son of garment industry immigrants from Poland, lords of
a new elite.

Like Schwab and John Reed, Weill saw before the herd that the future lay
with a high tech back office that could handle the exponentially increasing
volumes and velocity of transactions that were coming with the electronic age,
that firms with state-of-the-art operations would inherit the earth. It came to
pass. With shrewd instincts, the most efficient back office operation on Wall
Street, and a breathtaking series of annexations of weakened companies, he
and his early partners forged Shearson Loeb Rhoades. Moving in "like pirates"
to board and save sinking brokerage houses, as Weill protégé Peter Cohen
describes it, they grew it, under Weill's command, to the nation's second-
largest retail brokerage house, behind Merrill Lynch, at the time of its 1981
merger with American Express. As Amex, already an upscale global leader in
the exploding financial services field, bought Shearson, Weill assumed the
presidency of American Express, which had moved to the top tier of the
diversified financial giants that had suddenly become commercial banks' most
aggressive competitors. A trend launched by the merger of Prudential and
Bache and now a galaxy that included Sears, Ford, and Merrill Lynch, these
corporate combines were powerhouses of innovative products, capital, and
global "distribution systems." Operating outside commercial banking's sti-
fling regulatory environment, American Express seemed, in the mid-1980s,
the new financial age incarnate.

Weill seemed to have reached the apex of corporate success. As president of
the merged company, Weill saw Shearson/American Express acquire the
venerable Lehman Brothers Kuhn Loeb, an event that sent Shearson's assets
ballooning from $2 billion to $54 billion, making Weill's baby the most
profitable investment house on Wall Street. Weill became a hero to thousands
who watched their stock escalate from $2 in 1974 to a value of $350 in
American Express stock by 1986. He had achieved all the trappings of
corporate power. He jetted to Twentieth Century-Fox board meetings with

fellow directors Henry Kissinger and former President Gerald Ford. On weekends with the Kissingers, Henry asked *him* for advice and counted Weill as "one of my very favorite people." Weill had made the *Esquire* cover as "Man at His Best" and had had an intimate gem of a concert hall in the refurbished Carnegie Hall named for him and his wife Joan.

But frustrated with playing number two to CEO Jim Robinson at American Express, he suddenly dropped from the scene in early 1985, shocking Wall Street. "The long and short of it is that Sandy can't work for anybody else," Cohen claims. Forsaking his half-acre corner office with fireplace on the 102d floor atop the World Trade Center, Weill had holed up for a year in an unpretentious 33rd-floor office in the Seagram Building, making the Four Seasons his cafeteria, and searching for his next challenge. He scanned his Quotron, researching every candidate in the financial services industry. Analysts and investors were watching, waiting; every time Weill was seen lunching with someone, rumors started.

Weill and his dashing young assistant, Jamie Dimon, his loyal Sancho Panza through the quest for a new challenge, had looked at Bank of America and kept coming back to it. "What a great vehicle it would be. A fantastic branch system in California. A worldwide name that couldn't be beat. A growing name in international capital markets. And Schwab's discount brokerage—fantastic," he said to Dimon, unleashing the slow-spreading Weill smile. "There were twenty or thirty billion dollars of problems to be resolved, so that a good part of our energy would be working on problems from the past and trying to put out the fires and meet the risks. But Bank of America would be a fantastic base for what we want to create," Weill was increasingly convinced. In the second quarter of 1985, as the bank announced its bad earnings, Weill started getting serious.

By late September 1985 "Bank of America was a large part of our conversation every day." He and Dimon started talking constantly to analysts—to Shearson's, William Weiant at First Boston, others. "Could I add value?" he'd ask Dimon. He decided he could, and developed a scheme. A very brash scheme: He would offer to raise a billion dollars in capital—and to run the bank himself as CEO. A risk-averse man who cannot bear rejection, Weill played from a confidence built by a career of success as "the mouse attacking an elephant," as a 1979 *New York Times* story described his pattern of acquisitions.

Weill first showed his hand to Peter Cohen, by then chairman of Shearson Lehman Hutton, when the two spotted each other at the U.S. Open tennis matches in Queens in late September. "I got an idea," he said to Cohen, unfolding the scheme. Cohen had responded cautiously: "Sandy, unless you can convince people you've got the right kind of local support, it's a no-do." He feared that Weill, with his big cigars and New York borough accent, would not be accepted by Bank of America's board or management. As with American Express's southern gentlemanly board, Cohen suspected that "stylistically, Sandy was not the kind of person the Bank of America board was going to feel comfortable with running the company." With its polished, WASPy bankers at the top—the Chauncey Medberrys, the Armacosts, McMillens, and Mis-colls—and with San Francisco's haughty disdain for anything from New York or Los Angeles, it would be difficult. But Cohen's own wealth and power at the age of forty-two, product of his association with Weill, were proof that riding Weill's coattails could be highly profitable. The two could get into raging fights, but Cohen never took a Sandy Weill idea lightly.

Weill studied Bank of America's numbers through the fall. He was hearing rumblings that the board was upset. Well-placed friends on the Federal Reserve Board had quietly encouraged him to act. When regulators told him the bank was unlikely to do the needed things itself, it got his attention. He watched "that terrific reputation in the retail market, wasted away." He noted Max Hopper's exit in late October. And though cynics might sneer, Weill began to feel stirrings he can only ascribe to patriotism. "If it was the Bank of Podunk, I wouldn't have felt the same. The Bank of America was a symbol of our national credibility internationally."

In November rumored board dissent over leadership was confirmed to him by a Bank of America board member, reportedly Robert McNamara. In coming weeks "more than two" board members brought the same message. Adrenaline pumped. Weill called Marty Lipton, who had become very close as his adviser during the painful machinations that preceded his leaving American Express, and told Lipton his idea. Lipton had been one of Bank of America's outside counsels, but freed himself to work with Weill. Lipton knew people in San Francisco who could help carry Weill's message to the board and to the city's corporate and political establishment. Lipton put Weill in touch with old friends who had just founded a "boutique" investment banking firm in San Francisco, Tully Friedman and Warren Hellman. The two had burst impressively into the game by engineering the leveraged buyout of Levi Strauss for the Haas family; Hellman had called on Lipton to help him with that and was ripe for more mergers and acquisitions opportunities.

But it was Hellman's special connection to the city that could make him helpful to Weill. His great-great-grandfather was Isaias Hellman, founder of Wells Fargo and A. P. Giannini's old rival. As part of San Francisco's Jewish establishment he was old friends with Wally Haas, Jr., a B of A board member.

"Jesus, that's an interesting idea . . . an *outstanding* idea," Hellman thought as he listened. A former wunderkind president of Lehman Brothers in New York, he had known of Weill "forever. I was a big Lehman snob, and I thought they were kind of pushy, aggressive people who would go someplace, but not very far. But it was astonishing to me that each time he acquired a firm, it was five times the size of the business he had and that any of these people would even talk to him. But I watched earnings go up, the companies work better, and as Sandy acquired each firm, he really stressed the strengths of the other firm." Hellman had been a reluctant convert. But as his old firm, Lehman, was smoothly merged into Shearson in April '84, he had been forced to come around to viewing Weill "as one of those rare individuals who is both a hands-on manager and a visionary conceptualist."

But there was risk for Hellman in taking an advocacy role for Weill. San Francisco was his town, and it could be seen as betrayal of the city's preeminent corporate resident. He knew that "people would say, 'Gee, isn't it going to hurt your business?' or 'That sanctimonious son of a bitch.' " But the call had triggered emotion and reflection on the bank's, and his own, attachment to the city. "Our family has been here for a hundred years. We've been contributors to the community." The museums, hospitals, opera, ballet, schools—his family had supported them all. His sister was the new president of the symphony. "And if I want to have an opinion on the B of A, God damn it, I'm entitled to it." But he was thinking, too, about "the fabric of what makes a city a great place. The B of A probably is not more important than Hewlett-Packard, Silicon Valley, Levi Strauss. But somehow it is. This bank is the linchpin of this community." He had watched several dozen corporate headquarters flee the city since he returned to San Francisco, most for Los Angeles. "I happen to have a business here. If the city continues to go backwards from a business standpoint, if the Bank of America goes down, that's the end." He was clear about several things: "San Francisco needs the B of A to be headquartered here, and any trade-off for that isn't satisfactory. The *worst* thing would be to lose the B of A; the second worst would be to have a *crippled* B of A." Whatever he did, Hellman determined, would be "with the purpose of strengthening the bank and keeping it here."

Hellman was attracted, too, because of his personal history, which made deep-rooted rivalry with B of A part of his birthright. "We always think we bailed them out in the thirties. Supposedly my great-grandfather felt that he had saved the Bank of America," says Hellman, tossing oil onto flames. Claire Hoffman was spraying the current hiring of senior Wells people with venom, declaring, "My father hated everything Wells Fargo stood for, which was serving the wealthy and privileged. He fought with the people at that bank all his life." The schism, Hellman believes, is based partly on the fact that A.P.

and Isaias "took different roads. My grandfather was more of a corporate banker. You didn't have any branches. You dealt with large customers. You were what would be called today a wholesale bank. To our family, when A.P. started opening all those branches, we said, 'That man's going to get in trouble.' But we were always faced with seeing him being apparently right."

Like Citicorp and B of A years later, the two banks had always been in a size race, with Bank of Italy "nosing out" Hellman's Wells Fargo Nevada National, only to be one-upped in assets by Hellman's merger of Wells with the Union Trust. Bank of America's official history paints a picture of Isaias as a hide-bound elitist turning a deaf ear to A.P.'s pleas to make loans to the little customer when both Hellman and A.P. were on the board of Columbus Savings in 1904. "Had Hellman given a friendly ear to the reforms Giannini wished to institute in the Columbus Savings and Loan Society, the Bank of Italy might never have existed," says the book, savoring the irony that the Hellmans brought the competition on themselves.

Although Hellman claims that "after the depression the skepticism turned into real admiration," that in spite of the rivalry, "there was always a feeling that A.P. and the Gianninis were a great man and a great family," the two families had lived in different social worlds, compounding the tension between them. The Gianninis might have felt snubbed as Italians, but they knew nothing of the prejudice the Hellmans had felt as Jews. "My grandfather, father, and uncles drove by the Pacific Union and Olympic every day but knew they could never belong." Hellman had been raised with the displays of wealth Claire Giannini had ached for. Summers and holidays had been spent at the great Hellman houses at Tahoe, Oakland, and San Francisco. At the end of a day of lifeguarding during college summers, he had sat on the porch of "granny's" antebellum mansion in San Francisco and sipped frozen daiquiris served by a butler in tails.

At Tahoe, the chauffeur drove the water-ski boat, and everyone dressed for dinner. But the Hellmans could never join A.P. and Mario at their camps at the Bohemian Grove. Dark-haired, with sharp, sensitive features, Warren Hellman has the lean and hungry look of a marathon runner. His obsessive athleticism had been motivated, partly, by knowing he could get into the Olympic Club only if he qualified for its swim team. Hellman's sisters had broken the Semitism barrier in the 1950s, becoming the first Jewish girls to come out at the Cotillion, where—with a little reluctant massaging of the Cotillion committee by Claire—Anne and Virginia Giannini had made their debuts. Even though San Francisco had currently returned to the tolerance of its cosmopolitan gold rush era, Hellman felt, it was impossible for a Hellman not to savor tweaking the Bank of America.

Weill flew to San Francisco and met in Hellman's half-finished new offices with Hellman, Friedman, and power-brokering lawyer William Coblentz, who looked around the room and cracked, "How is this going to sit with them? They could call us 'the Jewish cabal.' " Aligning himself with Weill was a risk for Coblentz in his hometown, too, but he was drawn to the drama, like Hellman, by a sense of civic duty to "keep the B of A a viable institution, and keep it here." Clearly, Coblentz would be helpful. A close adviser to Mayor Dianne Feinstein, Coblentz was Lee Prussia's lawyer and knew a number of board members. Haas. Franklin D. Murphy. Philip M. Hawley. Prentis C. Hale. Coblentz felt confident that "if we could show 'Here we are, with long, old ties to San Francisco, we support this and here's why,' that would be sufficient. I didn't have any doubts that we could persuade the media that way, too." As they settled in to talk, Weill lit up a huge cigar—appalling Hellman, a health nut—and said with a sly smile, "You owe me one." He was reminding Hellman that when Hellman was still at Lehman, he had once bypassed Shearson to give Salomon a piece of business.

It would not be a hostile deal. "It was either going to be friendly through the board of directors, or it wouldn't go at all," says Coblentz, stating the consensus view. Weill said, "It's very difficult to do a hostile takeover in the financial business because so much of what a company does, or can do, is based on credibility. It's a fragile kind of thing, and if it gets destroyed—or if good people decide to go someplace else—in a fight, you don't end up with the human asset." The human asset was all-important to Weill. "There was no intention to displace Sam," says Dimon. "Sandy would have the senior operating role, but Sam could have stayed or not." Hellman saw the two as complementing each other superbly: "Sam Armacost was an absolutely first-class outside person—a very smart, creative, investment banker type of banker. And Sandy is the absolute archetypal inside person." A match Adizes should see as made in heaven.

By the time the men had completed their initial meeting in Hellman's office, "I actually thought I would be doing the board a substantial favor," says Hellman. "I thought they ought to be looking for a CEO. And my reaction was that Sandy would have been an ideal CEO for the Bank of America. It couldn't have started out more constructive."

Quietly Hellman and Coblentz began to open doors and sound people out. They called board members and influential San Franciscans, lined up meetings with Weill and the mayor's husband, entrepreneur Dick Blum. As Prussia got wind of the daring enterprise, word came back from him that he would not meet with Weill because "Sam won't allow it." Weill called Chuck Schwab. The two had several meetings at the small round table in Schwab's sleek office at 101 Montgomery Street, his new headquarters tower, its distance of several blocks from MotherBank's headquarters a pointed statement of independence. Schwab's maverick role as critic of the board and of Armacost had spread from the privacy of the boardroom to common gossip on the Street, and he now risked damage to himself and his company by any alliance with Weill. He was a senior Bank of America executive, his revenues had increased fourfold since association with the bank, and to directors used to peaceable consensus, his actions were verging on insurrection. The board had the power to fire Schwab and throw him out of his company and off the board; the bank held the right to use the company name, Charles Schwab & Co.; McLin had made sure of that in the marriage contract. The practical reality was that the more alienated he was from the board, the less able Schwab was to win the board's support for the program of change he still hoped it would institute.

Schwab took an equivocal stance. "He was pro change, but he never said he was pro Sandy," as Hellman remembers his words. "He absolutely said, 'You do not have my support. You do not have my opposition either. But something has to happen. I want to know who *is* available to run this bank. I'm glad that Sandy is. He might be excellent. I'd like to know who else is. What I want is a *change*.' "

"The best thing would be to go direct to Armacost with your plans," Schwab recommended to Weill. "But we never really talked about . . . where he would be the CEO. I probably would have guided him otherwise—to come in with some kind of advisory role or to at least have some representation on the board," says Schwab. "I would have advised, 'Come in a little bit more softly. Then shoot for the heart.' "

As Schwab and Weill talked, Schwab was even considering mounting his own takeover bid. "I had a large following of people out there that thought maybe we could add something to it. This floundering thing was something I was part of, and I would have done anything reasonable to try to correct it. But it would have been very divisive, very expensive, very messy. That's not my style." And not his main objective. Breaking free of the bank was beginning to supplant action by the board as Schwab's consuming goal.

It wasn't just the bank's sick state that distressed him. Being owned by a bank holding company, his company was hamstrung by banking's regulatory restraints. "There were Glass-Steagall confinements and the Regulation Y thing that really restricted some new areas that we wanted to get into. I'd thought they would die faster. But they didn't, and they were a terrible handicap to growing and competing with other brokerages." The entrepreneur was rankling, as Adizes knew he would. As the bank developed the list of assets it planned to sell, Schwab had met with Armacost in November to propose adding Schwab to that list. Armacost had seemed to understand, to know "some of the handicaps I was under," had seemed "empathetic."

But, a master at disguising his real thoughts, Armacost did not let Schwab see how vital he believed Schwab's company was to the larger strategy. "Sam did not want to sell Schwab," Ichak Adizes knew. "He said, 'I don't want to be the Massey-Ferguson [the tractor company that sold all its good divisions to protect its bad] of the banking industry. The direction we want to go is financial services—why should I sell it?' " To Schwab's frustration, his meetings with Armacost were leading to little beyond "empathy." Armacost was cogitating while the troops were looking for direction, in Schwab's view.

THE IMMEDIATE GOAL of Weill's team was to have Armacost and Weill meet. Hellman called Armacost. "He wasn't thrilled, but he talked to me—kind of." Tentative meetings were set but never happened. Hellman, who knew Armacost casually, was not able to arrange a personal meeting with Armacost.

By late January they were getting urgent messages from the board member insiders say was McNamara to act, to send a letter. You could play games on the telephone or in meetings. But a letter would make Weill's proposals a fact to which the board must respond.

On February 22, William Wolff, head of Shearson's Financial Institutions Group, got a call in his office from Peter Cohen, Shearson CEO. "Come on up. Now." A squad of fifteen from corporate finance, capital markets, and marketing rushed to Cohen's 102nd-floor office in the World Trade Center in lower Manhattan. "Sandy wants a letter from us pledging to raise one billion dollars," Cohen told them. The job at hand was to do, in hours, "a very quick and dirty analysis of Bank of America to see if a billion was enough." They'd be meeting Weill in Pebble Beach for breakfast next morning, with the letter. Weill and Robinson were scheduled to play in the Crosby golf tournament, renamed the AT&T, a safe, informal cover for this top secret deal—Project Bingo. "This was very highly sensitive," says Rick Wolff. The team met for forty-five intense minutes, dispersed to stuff any information they had on Bank of America into their briefcases, and raced to La Guardia to catch American Express's Gulfstream. On the five-hour flight they worked steadily, crunching numbers, talking scenarios. "Our quick assumption was that a billion would be the low end of enough. But it basically confirmed to us that the bank had a good underlying business and that the problems were concentrated in asset quality and overhead," says Wolff.

Out of the crucible of the cross-country flight came a letter that not only committed Shearson to raising a billion in the market but pledged it to using its own corporate resources if the money could not be raised. The men on the Shearson team were dumped in Monterey at three-thirty, got a few hours' sleep in a motel, shaved, put on their suits, and headed for the Del Monte Lodge in Carmel.

When the men converged on the Del Monte, Hellman glimpsed Weill's residual power. As the group marched through the breakfast room to their small glass-walled room at the back, "Jim Robinson and Sandy are dressed to play in the Crosby. There's this Shearson guy, John Maher, an establishment Los Angeles investment banker with his braided elephant-hair bracelets, and Peter Cohen and his guys in their New York suits and briefcases, looking like the Politburo." As Weill walked through the breakfasting crowd of corporate movers and shakers, men were calling out, "Hi, Sandy." Former Secretary of Defense Melvin Laird leaped up to say hello. "Here he is a member of the establishment," Hellman saw, embraced as Weill probably never would be in San Francisco.

The letter that emerged from the breakfast meeting was "the strongest letter of commitment I've ever seen an investment banking firm give," says Hellman. "Basically, what Peter Cohen said is, 'If it can't be underwritten, we'll buy it.' " The group had decided that the proper approach was through Armacost. One of the directors called and said, "Do it now!" The letter would force Weill onto the agenda of the board meeting that Monday.

Hellman called Armacost, and after the weeks of waffling, "he was very amenable to having a meeting with us." Armacost agreed to meet Weill in San Francisco the next day, Friday, January 31. Weill canceled out playing in the AT&T, and that afternoon he and his wife, Joan, caught a "puddle jumper" to San Francisco, while the exhausted Shearson team returned to New York. The Weills checked into an elegant hotel on Union Square, Campton Place. As Weill primed for his meeting, his team was daring to feel the excitement Pinola's group had felt a few months earlier.

Next morning, hours before the meeting, Armacost called and canceled. "It was almost like he was sitting with a script in front of him," said the frustrated Hellman. "Sam was very tense. Kept saying one sentence, and the more I pressed him, the more heatedly he said it. Basically he said, 'I have too much on my agenda to meet with you today.' I said, 'I can't believe anything is a whole lot more important than *this*.' " Hellman pressed: "What about tomorrow?" Armacost said, "No, too busy." "What are you doing next November?" Hellman asked, exasperated. What had happened? Who had got to Armacost? Hellman and others suspected the bank's senior counsel, George Coombe. Hellman reported the failure to Weill. Weill sent the Shearson letter, hoping it would still assure his proposal's reaching the boardroom on Monday.

Weill, Joan, and Dimon, buoyed by the shared intensity of the past few days, dined with the Hellmans and Friedmans, drove to Stinson Beach to see Hellman's beach house, and talked and talked the deal at Hellman's offices, where Weill was assigned his own cigar room. The wives took Joan Weill around to see some houses, the informal launch of house hunting.

WEILL'S PEOPLE waited nervously while the board met on February 3 in San Francisco. From what they could glean from their board contacts, the Weill issue had been brought up late in the afternoon, to a tired board checking watches and airline schedules, and rejection had been ramrodded through. "This was the worst piece of corporate manipulation," says Hellman. It was also reported that the orchestrator *had* been Coombe, who had come armed with opinions by the bank's investment advisers, Salomon and First Boston, that "if capital was needed, they could raise it—but it wasn't needed." Weill was convinced that it was capital, above all, that was needed—and that a billion probably wasn't nearly enough. The board sent a message to Weill saying, as Dimon paraphrases it, "Thank you, but no, thank you." Tossed out. The tone of the response, Weill's team thought, was haughty and hostile. That killed it for Weill, who had said from the start, "If they didn't agree with what we were thinking about after we had a chance to express it, we'd go away and God bless 'em and good luck." They hadn't really had that chance, Dimon argued, eager to try again. But rejected—the thing he hated—Weill flew to Puerto Rico with Joan to lick his wounds and play some golf and some craps in the evening.

Chapter Sixteen

BOTH THE WEILL AND THE PINOLA bids now sat in limbo.

But Project Bingo would not be allowed to die that easily. On February 21, 1986, Dimon called Weill to tell him that the story was in the *Wall Street Journal.* BANKAMERICA SAYS WEILL SOUGHT POST AS CHIEF BUT BOARD WASN'T INTERESTED was the headline. BankAmerica had released a statement confirming Weill's approach "about the possibility of becoming chief executive officer"; the bank, it said, "wasn't interested in his ideas." Secrecy was blown. Weill's team was convinced the bank had leaked the news, feeding street gossip that linked Weill's name with that of the most notorious corporate raider of the moment, Carl Icahn, and triggering extremely heavy trading in the bank's stock in the five trading days prior to the *Journal's* story. The bank had needed to make the public statement to calm the market, but Hellman feared it would turn the private rebuff Weill had just received into "a holy war."

As the news spread, Weill found himself the butt of the Wall Street brand of the Polish joke. The Shearson letter to the B of A board spurred the wit of First Boston's mergers and acquisitions superstar Joe Perella, who christened Weill's bid "the 22 cent takeover—the cost of the postage stamp to mail the letter." It was, "with due regard to Sandy, a job application for Sandy Weill," went another joke. Granted, First Boston and Salomon Brothers might have raised capital with the same ease as Shearson. As investment houses went public or sold out to rich financial services giants, they were better capitalized than ever before; Perella's powerful corporate finance group was increasingly pledging First Boston's own capital to deals. But it was the flip denial that capital was needed—the arrogant refusal to give someone of his stature a hearing—that made Weill's supporters fume. "They treated it as a ridiculous effort. The investment bankers should have been advising the board about the true condition of the bank—that they indeed needed capital—rather than make a big joke of it to protect Sam's job. It was absolutely disgraceful," says Dimon.

For a man who cannot tolerate rejection, there was instant affirmation for Weill as the announcement raced through the Street. "That's when the phone started ripping off the wall, with thirty-five people wanting to put some money in." Donald Trump was the first to call, offering capital. B of A stock began to climb. "It went from twelve dollars to seventeen dollars—a five-dollar gain," says Dimon, frustrated that it was Weill's presence that was raising Bank of America's market value.

For Weill was known as a consummate manager at a time when the need for management was being rediscovered. Vice-Chairman of Merrill Lynch Capital Markets John Heimann, today one of the most "connected" financial theorists in the western banking system, says of Weill, "If Sandy's a superstar, it's not because of doing the biggest deal in town or creating the newest financial instrument. He's a *management* superstar, and we don't have many like that in the financial community." As Tom Cooper explained the need for more Sandy Weills, "There is virtually no reward for fixing the long-term problems. The reward is in the *transaction*."

Lost, also, in the contemptuous giggles that swept the Bankers Club atop the B of A headquarters was an extraordinary cultural compatibility between Weill and A. P. Giannini. Both had built giant corporations based on a "family" culture. Even as his hustling little brokerage grew to a sophisticated international empire, Weill had stuck with a style of management-by-extended-family that would have warmed A.P.'s heart—a benevolent patriarchy that kept the layers of bureaucracy that blocked contact between CEO and line salesman to a minimum. He embraced every employee and subsidiary as "family," prized loyalty, promoted nepotism, and took defections personally. Could you make management-by-extended-family work in the competitive electronic world of financial services—and with great size? critics asked. "In Shearson we did it. It's still thriving and doing beautifully," said Weill before the '87 crash. "The culture now has become so deeply rooted that it perpetuates itself because we trained people to function as I did and to instill this in their people."

Weill had been dramatically more successful than Bank of America, however, in combining a "family" culture with the development of the efficient operating systems of New Age banking, underpinning to survival. It was the stage Bank of America had largely skipped in the 1970s, the missing link that, in the opinion of many insiders, had brought the bank to its knees. Weill's emphasis on corporate "family" was more than a management style; it answered a psychological need to be constantly reassured by the loyalty that only family will give. He hired all his relatives. But he also suffered all the pain and emotion of real family. He counted heads at "family" gatherings and was as wounded as an abandoned lover if all members didn't show. He and Peter Cohen still had the kind of love/hate screaming matches only those bound by family ties can survive. Yet for Weill, it worked. His corporate babies thrived as evolutionary successes; Bank of America did not. A.P. had not left a team of disciples to teach that a warm fuzzy family culture is a luxury a company can afford only if it also cares about the back office. If the implications of Weill as a messenger of change were missed, it would be at the bank's peril.

With the deal made public on February 21, there was fresh fuel on the fires. Weill's team reconvened in New York, soul-searched, and decided to push again for a hearing. Dimon was eager to keep charging. Weill was concerned that the bank's "fantastic franchise of trust and respect" could be destroyed as his letter was transformed by the bank, and by press coverage, into a hostile cause célèbre. Weill had been quoted as having a business plan for the bank. He didn't. The specifics hadn't gone far beyond the initial broad judgments Weill had made, as Dimon identifies them, to "raise capital, take your losses in some areas and build in others, bring in good people, and strengthen the board." He would build retail. Raise capital. Dramatically reduce expenses. Build capital markets and merchant banking. But Weill was feeling more confident; he interpreted the climb in B of A's stock to a vote of confidence by the market. The market was buzzing about his alleged proposal. He decided to prepare one before the board's next meeting in Los Angeles on March 3.

Weill sent another letter to Armacost asking for a full hearing of the proposal at that time. The Shearson team went into a four-day, round-the-clock blitz that at times involved forty or fifty people. The essential proposals—to emphasize retail and technology and to deemphasize international—were developed. And a five-year plan that would start with a "one-shot fix" to clean up the asset problem—a $1 billion reserve that would lower the bank's capital. It would be replaced with the billion dollars raised in the market, most of it common equity—new stock sold to investors. The plan, backed by graphs, numbers, and charts showing peer-group comparisons, was compiled in shiny white binders, with display cards and a speech for presentation by Weill; it was hoped he would be invited to address the board.

His influential friends got on the phone to urge a fair hearing. Jim Robinson called "people in the B of A orbit. I told them he could do a very interesting turnaround job at the bank, that we could definitely raise equity capital without diluting the shareholders, and that it was a very legitimate option for the board of directors to consider." Robinson believed that "if you could get Sandy's interest, his ego, and his money all lined up, you had one hell of a force for change."

The tension was becoming too much for the vivacious Joan Weill. She called her daughter Jessica, a Wall Street money manager, and said, "Come with Mommy. We are going on a trip," and flew to the Golden Door, the exclusive Southern California spa.

As Weill sat tight in New York waiting for the call to fly to California to address the board, B of A's stock climbed again on word that Weill's plan was ready to be presented to the bank. The team was elated. "The market has already started rewarding Sandy's announced intention to try to restructure the company," said Jamie Dimon. It was getting increasingly difficult for any board that didn't want to be sued to deny him a hearing.

Weill practiced his delivery: ". . . My intention is to assist BAC in its recovery, not to create disruption or provoke debate. . . ." He would list a withering litany of troubles: regulators forcing the bank to a higher capital ratio than that of its peer banks. Rating agencies making it almost impossible for BAC to access capital markets at the same cost as competitors. Business clients drifting away. Loss in market share. Stockholder suits multiplying. And, sure to make the board squirm, the lack of normal insurance protection for the directors—a trauma Weill had already remedied with a letter of commitment for D&D coverage from an insurer. "The right outsider can alleviate those pressures," he planned to tell board members as he drove home the impact an outsider, he himself, had already had on shareholder value: "Since the publicity began, BAC's common stock is up forty percent, outperforming S & P 500 money center banks, which rose six and three percent. . . ."

With only a letter, so far, Weill had enriched the stock value by nearly a billion dollars. Word came back. The board would not see Weill. But his letter would be dealt with at the board meeting.

SCHWAB WAS EN ROUTE to a Young Presidents' meeting in New Delhi. He had got as far as Bangkok with Helen and several friends when he learned of the special board meeting being called in L.A. to discuss the Weill issue on Sunday night, the day before the regular meeting. The board had dismissed Weill wrongly in February, he felt. It should, at the very least, have formed a committee to study Weill's proposal, an idea initiated by McNamara and picked up by Schwab. He determined he would try to push that through; he and Helen flew back to California.

OPERATION SNOWFLAKE had been languishing since December. But in Los Angeles Joe Pinola had been encouraged by announcements early in '86 that a merger was in the works between Wells Fargo and Crocker Bank. "The Feds are going to permit a rather *large* intrastate transaction," Sudmann noted, jubilant. Although a merger of B of A and First Interstate, with their overlapping branch network, held more antitrust implications than Wells and Crocker, it did not seem insurmountable. Sudmann and Griffith met in Goldman's offices in New York early in February to review all the issues and plan the next step. They had no idea that B of A's silence was caused partly by its preoccupation with a competing suitor, Sandy Weill.

And then the Weill story broke, buoying them more. Rumors flew. Armacost had panicked when he got Weill's letter, they heard. Weill's presence could put Pinola in a powerful position as a potential "white knight" for Armacost, offering to merge to save him from the interloper from New York. "And our deal made more sense. B of A needed more than a billion dollars and a new CEO. More than one man and money!" an insider cracked. On Pinola's behalf, Goldman's Geoff Boisi moved to exploit the moment.

Deciding to use the threat of a letter as a weapon to push for the elusive meeting between Armacost and Pinola, Boisi called Steve McLin: "If Sam won't meet with us, we're going to send a letter to your board." McLin knew Armacost wanted to postpone any meeting with First Interstate until after the board had dealt with Weill. But Boisi was getting aggressive, McLin saw, saying, in effect, "Our hand is in the mailbox, down the chute, if you guys don't talk to us."

Armacost consented to meet with Pinola that Saturday in San Francisco, the day before the March board meeting in Los Angeles that would address the Weill issue. In preparation, a Goldman and First Interstate team would meet with Armacost and McLin two days earlier, on Thursday afternoon, to lay the groundwork for the most important meeting yet in Pinola's bid for the Bank of America.

"THEY'RE MY *FRIENDS*," said Armacost to a close colleague, dismayed at Goldman's sudden aggressiveness. Armacost was responding to takeover threats the same way he was responding to the bad "surprises" from the loan portfolios: with a tone of hurt and personal betrayal. He had shown hurt when

Weill first showed his hand; he had played golf with Sandy Weill. "It's hard to believe that Sandy Weill is my friend," Armacost had said, the colleague recalls. On all sides friends were attacking. First Schwab. Then Pinola and Goldman, Warren Hellman and Tully Friedman. And Jim Robinson. "God, *he's* my friend!" Armacost had some difficulty, a colleague felt, "realizing that what Weill did, or what Pinola did, was not a personal thing against Sam Armacost, the man." Jamie Dimon says, "He took it personally." The struggle for corporate control was revealing Armacost to be bound, still, by the gentlemanly code of the old culture.

Hurt feelings had no place in this arena. The bank's destiny, in terms of independence and leadership, could be determined in the coming weekend. All the forces playing on the bank were converging. At the board meeting Armacost would not only be testing the board's loyalty under the pressure of the first real threat to his leadership and confronting the Pinola challenge face-to-face but would also be making management changes at the highest level, promotions and demotions that risked creating powerful new enemies and rivals. He had some surprises on the agenda that were sure to enrage Schwab and destroy any hope of keeping him peaceably in the fold.

Coming to the testing ground, too, was the bank's persisting pattern of making bad judgments under pressure. Apparently unaltered by experience of the real world, Bank of America's primordial brain had proven itself capable, time and again, of making monumentally out-of-sync decisions. The bank was the product of nearly forty years of operating as a closed system, savoring its grandeur in splendid isolation from competitive realities. Would its capacity to respond to change now be too crippled for it to function soundly as it faced a threat to its independence? For all his intelligence, will, and vision, Armacost was about to prove himself, when the chips were down, a BankAmerican—like Clausen, an instrument of a culture whose skewed survival responses now seemed imprinted in its genes.

Armacost planned to propose Tom Cooper as president and chief operating officer (COO) of the bank at the meeting, just a year after being hired. If the board voted Cooper in, as it was sure to, Armacost would relinquish his own post as president of the bank to Cooper, retain the presidency of the corporation, and take Prussia's role as chairman of the bank. Although Prussia would still be chairman of the mother ship, he would be displaced from the number two position he had held since 1981. Prussia had shown signs of what some interpreted as depression as bad news was dumped on the bank in 1985. He also carried the stigma of the old guard, and voices urging Prussia's removal had been rising. As chairman he had taken much of the flak, with diminishing authority to effect change. Now Cooper's star was about to rise at Prussia's expense. A man who knows Prussia "probably better than anyone" says, "He's not a prima donna. He's an unpretentious, good human being. He didn't want to fight. But there were some divisive things, and he was being stripped of authority. He could feel the pressures on him building."

In handing Cooper more power, Armacost would seem to be building a rival more threatening than Prussia. People were coming to Armacost, warning that Cooper was creating factions of " 'Cooper's guys' and 'Armacost's guys,' trying to create the momentum for himself to be the heir apparent." Cooper's image of decisiveness was continuing to erode Armacost's credibility. But the strategy he kept close to his chest required that he keep Cooper, just as it required him to keep the old guard beyond its time. Armacost still needed Cooper as a symbol of cost cutting, as "a visual catalyst. I had to have somebody as my champion of the budget, purely and simply. He was doing exactly the job I put him in to do. He had become my strategy." Cooper's first challenge had been to turn BAPS's $100 million annual loss into a profit. Cooper was proud that "we were able to, in one year's time, get rid of a hundred-million-dollar loss and turn the business around."

Cooper was still professing to be a team player. "He was sending me notes saying, to the effect, 'Gosh, I know by inference that you think I'm out for your job. I'm not. I have no interest in that. I'll leave now,' " says Armacost. Cooper confirms, "We had discussions about . . . my desire to be CEO, and I made it clear to him that I did not have that as my personal goal. The last thing in the world I needed was to take any credit away from any member of the management committee or Sam." Working long hours alone in his office as the storm rose around him, Cooper was arriving "at the conclusion that I probably would have to leave the company. Whether they were right or wrong, the kinds of decisions and actions I had to participate in taking were of a *curing* but not of a *healing* nature. I felt that it was highly likely that a person with a different background and exposure would have to come in and administer the company going forward."

Cooper knew that he was suffering from the one-dimensional image that had built around him since the day he arrived, that he had become "a product of the thing called a public relations department. . . . I don't think I had messages that were popular to be spoken, and I had a sense of urgency and a personality which caused my communication to be less sensitive" than it might have been, he admits. He had not "communicated well in public . . . the unspoken reasons why I was such a big advocate of selling off investments, consolidating B of A, and getting out of the international scene—*especially in a company that didn't have the capital.*" But there was a pro-Cooper faction, he sensed; there was "really an undeserved amount of loyalty, commitment, and risk taking shown to me by people at the senior and executive vice-president level." As well, "those persons on the board that I talked to indicated to me—and went out of their way to tell me—that they wanted me to participate on the team."

In hindsight, some feel, Armacost should have listened more carefully to the critics who told him he had to be very careful. But he felt confident that Cooper's appointment as COO would give healthy emphasis to the cost-cutting program. Observers claim "it was widely understood by the board that it was not approving a CEO, but a cost-cutter." Schwab agreed that although he had voted for Cooper as "a good COO dollars-and-cents kind of guy, I'd want a different person for CEO. He lacked grace in the social things and didn't make people feel at ease." Says Cooper of the possibility of sitting in Armacost's chair: "I didn't believe that would occur."

Adizes was profoundly concerned. He had supported hiring Cooper. Armacost had needed a hatchet man, and still did. By his theory, the two should complement each other, the cutter and the statesman. But Adizes was seeing Cooper go beyond implementing strategy already in place to forge his own platform of programs—"the thing he promised he would not do." He was gaining the power to dismantle Adizes's creations. The idea of appointing a COO had been one of Adizes's favored strategies for buying time to get the job done: If Armacost were kept in the wings while a day-to-day strongman turned the boat around, "we would have the captain ready. The statesman. One idea was to hire somebody sixty years old who doesn't threaten any of the young guys coming up, who will take the heat for three years, then Sam finishes the job. But Sam said, 'Why should we bring in somebody for just three years?' "

"Tom is going to undo you," Adizes had thundered at Armacost. "If that happens, that will happen," Armacost said. "Ichak, I'm not at stake. The bank is at stake. If I have to pay the price, I have to pay the price."

"That's why I have such respect for the guy," says Adizes, his emotion barely contained. "He could stand pressure. . . . He has his ears to the rails, could hear the tomtom almost better than anybody else." He knew the dangers. "But he wouldn't compromise." It was in these confrontations that Adizes saw the complex balances Armacost was trying to keep, a side of Armacost that would be lost in the cry for more simplistic, short-term solutions focused on by the press.

"I can't underscore enough how much I felt a sense of urgency. Time was not on our side," says Cooper. "But if you make some very hurried moves, you might damage the reputation of the bank," Adizes argued. "Sam *had* a plan for selling these properties. But you don't announce to the world, 'I'm going broke. The sale of the season is on us.' "

They were running out of time. With everyone screaming for his pound of flesh from Armacost, Adizes began to urge, " 'Sam, fire! Saving your reputation is valuable if you're going to finish the job. . . .' But he would not do artificial things just to appease the newspapers. To appease the pressures." Finally, Armacost declared to Adizes, "Ichak, hell, if I had those options, I'd do them. But they *ain't there*. The bank has run out of gas. There are no short-term decisions that can be taken to put any life into the bank's future. That was all done in the seventies. Every single short-term profit-making device of that kind that raped the future of the institution had already been done."

THE FLYWAYS between San Francisco and Los Angeles, and the B of A elevator banks, were filled with conspiratorial pods of bankers and lawyers in the preamble to the Armacost-Pinola meeting on March 1. With Goldman's offices in the B of A building, but on a different bank of elevators, the inside team was shuttling steadily on Thursday, Friday, and Saturday, when the key meeting would take place. On Thursday Armacost and McLin had huddled with Boisi, while the rest waited nervously in Goldman's offices, like prospective fathers. Several calls came down, wanting information. How old was Joe? They must be discussing the social issue. Boisi reported back; everything was on track for Saturday. There would be more meetings next day between Goldman's and Salomon's biggest deal makers, Boisi and Jay Higgins. Sudmann and Griffith raced to catch the late flight home to L.A. to report to Pinola. Next morning, in an antiseptic chrome-and-vinyl meeting room off the sixth-floor employees cafeteria, Pinola gathered his full team together for a strategy review over breakfast. The battle was about to begin.

Meeting with McLin in San Francisco on Friday, Goldman's bankers were getting intimate glimpses of Armacost's preparations for the Sunday pre-board meeting that would deal with Weill. Aides were coming and going in McLin's office, obviously preparing a financial report for presentation to the board. The visitors got the sense Armacost was trying to say, "We can do it on our own; we don't need Sandy Weill." They got the sense that Armacost was discounting Weill. It was heartening that Weill was not about to be embraced as savior. On the other hand, part of the fragile strength of First Interstate's revived bid was Armacost's possible need for an alternative to Weill. A white knight. If Weill were dispatched too quickly, it could undercut that role.

That afternoon the First Interstate team moved north in corporate style, Griffith and Sudmann flying in FiCal's turboprop King Air, and Pinola taking the corporation's nine-place Jetstar. Secrecy was vital. The market would go wild, runs could start, if there were a leak that Pinola and Armacost were meeting. They checked into the Stanford Court on Nob Hill, three steep blocks above the Bank of America. Dining discreetly in a private dining room at L'Étoile a block away, they talked cool merger jargon—takeover premiums and the need for good primary capital numbers for the combined entity. For the Goldman group it was just another deal. But excitement was building explosively in Pinola's team. They knew that Greg Hill, in the *Journal*'s offices just six blocks away, would kill to be privy to what was happening up the hill as he headed home to San Mateo for the weekend. But the press still had no inkling of Operation Snowflake.

Next morning events took on the cloak-and-dagger flavor that is one of takeover's attractions to the deal makers. They must sneak Pinola into the B of A building. Joe Pinola is not a pale gray banker; his white hair and presence radiate like a beacon blocks away. Leaving the Stanford Court with banker suits and briefcases, they broke into twos and threes so as not to look like a platoon for the short walk down California Street. Because it was Saturday, they had to sign in with the security guards. With several of his team hovering close, trying to hide him, Pinola mumbled something about going to Goldman Sachs and scrawled his name illegibly. Flanked by Boisi, he vanished into the elevators for the fortieth floor, where Armacost awaited him.

Armacost felt even more readiness to merge than he disclosed to Pinola. "You work for your shareholders," he said later, describing the thoughts he brought to the meeting, "and if somebody puts an offer on the table which is compulsive, you've got to look at it and understand it. You may have deep reasons why you think those offers, no matter what dollar amounts are attached, are inadequate. But I don't think you can ever get yourself in a close-minded point of view that a company must always stay independent, regardless of shareholder interests."

Armacost was open to giving up the CEO's position to Pinola and to working with him. "I would willingly sublimate my ego if the price for my shareholders was in the right ranges," he said privately. "I don't think there is any doubt that we could work together personally, since we had before." He could see how it could work. "I think it would not have been a very difficult thing to rationalize because the units that were mutually intertwined were so few in number. There were some basic issues—their Oregon versus Bank of Oregon, their Washington versus our Washington. Their California being absorbed, sold, or broken up in parts. Those were the only really difficult ones. The rest of the issues were all nonevents. They didn't have any foreign to speak of; they had a little tiny merchant bank that was a nonstarter. Their foreign business could either have been sold or absorbed. It was a very easy integration in terms of potential merger issues. I think the integration of the two institutions might have been fantastic."

Armacost and McLin had even discussed, on a number of occasions, launching their own takeover of First Interstate. "If we had been a little stronger, I would have certainly launched a Pac-Man strategy. But we just weren't in that capital position," says Armacost.

Nor was FIB as a suitor for B of A, Armacost grasped with some impatience as the two men sparred cautiously through the meeting. "Joe *refused* to talk prices—about what was in it for B of A's shareholders. But they were clearly thinking about numbers that were far too low. They were just not big enough to buy the Bank of America."

First Interstate's team waited in Goldman's offices on the thirty-first floor, wild with speculation, as the two men met for an hour in Armacost's office. When Pinola came back, he was noncommittal. Yet he gave the distinct impression that there was continued receptivity. There had been much parrying and jousting, discussion about the differences between the two cultures, where people could be placed. The deal was clearly not dead. Armacost had told Pinola there were board meetings in Los Angeles Sunday and Monday, which the eavesdropping Goldman men had already reported. About to catch the corporate jet for Los Angeles, Armacost called Pinola next morning in his hotel room to say, "You'll be hearing from us after the Monday meeting." As a tingling First Interstate team loaded aboard their jets, Operation Snowflake seemed alive again.

As HE FLEW to Los Angeles, Chuck Schwab was still drained by jet lag after his long flight back from Bangkok. Scanning the agenda, he saw that the Sunday gathering of the board would be followed by cocktails and a dinner meeting, with the formal board meeting to be held on Monday morning.

AN UNACCUSTOMED CLIMATE of sensationalism and publicity surrounded the directors as they arrived in Los Angeles for the meetings, heightening the tension as they prepared to confront the Weill issue. "Takeover bids . . . are probably the worst thing in modern times that boards can go through," confirmed Walter Wriston in an interview in *Directors and Boards* magazine. This board was without adequate insurance if it was sued for irresponsible decisions. The press, especially the *L.A. Times*, had its ear to the boardroom door, its horror stories feeding the board's fears.

From the first symptoms of trouble in the early eighties, the board had had the option, the obligation, to question, to act, to intervene. It had not. It had given Armacost unqualified support, as it had Clausen. With Clausen at the helm, board meetings had been a happy pattern of "Oh, fine, earnings up eighteen percent. Let's break for lunch," as a close observer describes the mood of unquestioned confidence in management. Why fix what ain't broke? went the maxim. Like California, this board had known only good times. Would the fear level now rouse it from passivity? Armacost was concerned that "we had too many retirees, too many older guys sitting there who . . . really weren't comfortable with a lot of the wild rough-and-tumble gyrations in a business that had been cautious, conservative, and untroubled for so long, during most of their tenure." It is hard to cast as naive men like Bob McNamara, who ran the Ford Motor Company, John Kennedy's Defense Department, and the World Bank for two terms, but Armacost feared that twenty years out of the active business world might have stripped even the sharpest executive of the hands-on "feel" of today's violently deregulating environment. As directors had retired, Armacost had made a decision that would hurt him now: He had chosen to go to a smaller board, instead of padding it with his own appointees. "I cut it down from twenty-six to fourteen. In the next couple of years I could have nominated most of the board." But, as it converged on Los Angeles, it was still Clausen's board.

Armacost was getting disquieting information that some on the board were beginning to panic. Associates had been bringing him intelligence concerning Weill's and Schwab's contacts with the board. Hurt was turning to spiteful criticism as he learned of directors bypassing the board. "As a member of a board you don't *do* those things. You keep a channel through management."

For Armacost, the final innings were coming. He had the right team, the right strategy, and recovery under way, he would argue to the board, as he had before. But this time he had prepared a thirty-one-page report, a five-year forecast that detailed his projections. It was the report whose urgent preparation in McLin's office Pinola's team had glimpsed as they had prepared for the Armacost-Pinola meeting a few days earlier. It would be the centerpiece of his report to the board Monday morning. "Sam kept wanting better numbers," says McLin of his feverish efforts to ramp up the earnings and ratchet down the expenses for a report designed, says Armacost, "to comfort the board and tell them why they should sit tight in their chairs," a report that "in the context of Weill and Pinola, any CEO threatened like this would present." Having flown to Los Angeles to continue reworking the numbers with Tom Cooper, searching for another $100 million in cuts and new income for Armacost until the final hours before the Monday board meeting, McLin was worried that his wife's labor might begin while he was gone. Armacost tried to allay his anxiety by keeping a bank airplane ready to fly him back to San Francisco.

On Sunday afternoon, with the turmoil disguised under the civilized ritual of MotherBank's best manners and clubby jokes, the leaders and advisers of a tormented colossus began the schedule of meetings of the full board and committees that would lead into cocktails and a dinner meeting. But fears, rumor, positioning, and testiness ran through like an electric current. Rivals Salomon and First Boston found themselves both there as investment banking advisers. Salomon's CEO John Gutfreund bristled as it was revealed that a more elaborate proposal for raising capital was expected—more numbers—than he had come from New York prepared, or willing, without more analysis, to give.

Schwab tried to raise the issue that had brought him rushing back from Bangkok—a board committee to deal with Weill as recommended by McNamara—but he could get no discussion going. "Not even McNamara chimed back." In the corridors and in spontaneously assembled submeetings, invisible to Schwab, Gutfreund was opposing the notion of a special committee, which had made its way to Coombe's list of motions for next day's board meeting.

As the Sunday meetings broke up and directors met for cocktails, Franklin Murphy, powerful chairman of the *L.A. Times* and the board's Executive Committee, came up to Schwab and surprised him by asking, "Chuck, as a personal favor to me, will you please go along with the plan tonight to separate the board meeting into two meetings?" Schwab was to join Prussia, Cooley, and Cooper, while Armacost dined with the rest of the board. It was not a "real" meeting tonight, Murphy said, to appease him. That's tomorrow. To Schwab this "bifurcation" smelled wrong. As cocktails were winding down, Murphy came up to Schwab again and asked, "Will you *please,* after cocktails, go into this room." "This man looks you in the eye so pleadingly, and he's near the end of his career, and what can you do?" Schwab shrugged. It was, after all, just a dinner. They were not going to talk heavy things or hammer out the bank's destiny, he reassured himself. But Armacost was controlling this badly, he thought, to cut out Prussia, his chairman! Talk about trying to create a gulf. Sam's lost this little power dance—he's lost Lee's allegiance. Schwab complied with Murphy's request and joined the little band of insulted men.

As Schwab read the *Journal* the next morning on his way to the Monday board meeting, he saw his face not only smiling out from his ad on the inside back page, but sketched in a story on page three. SCHWAB RUNS RISKS IN BACKING MOVE TO OUST ARMACOST . . . BANKAMERICA'S CHAIRMAN'S ADVISERS SAY DISSENT MAY COST BROKER HIS POST. He was a "disgruntled director," "a loose cannon." He was "the one most likely to make a motion this morning to appoint a special committee of outside directors and . . . counsel to consider Mr. Weill's plan." His job as chairman of Schwab & Co. was in jeopardy, Greg Hill's story reported. This was clearly a leak by the bank, his team thought. Armacost, Schwab feared, had thrown down the gauntlet, undercutting him with an already nervous board. The board would have the *Journal* story fresh in their minds at the meeting.

SCHWAB WAS "LOADED FOR BEAR" as he headed for the boardroom for the 10 A.M. meeting in the BankAmerica tower on Flower Street. There was no question in his mind that the bank needed capital or that Shearson, with its muscle, could raise it, as Weill had offered. Or that Weill as a CEO candidate was not "a joke" as the bank was painting it, but was "real." It made absolute sense to have the Executive Committee appoint a committee of four outside directors, independent of management, to study the Weill situation and report back to the board. Schwab had been diverted from making the proposal yesterday. He would not be diverted today. But "conflict is not one of his things," says longtime colleague Bill Pearson. "Oh, he's tough. He'll stand up. I've seen him mad. But he gets mad at events, not at people." "Firing people with a pistol in my hand is not my style," Schwab admits. A shootout with the board of the Bank of America was absolutely not his style.

THE BOARDROOM DOORS, like the Golden Gate Bridge, never ceased to impress. As Schwab approached the grand bronze doors of the fifty-first-floor boardroom that Monday morning he was struck again by how they represented "the sense of grandeur the bank has about itself." Each end of the boardroom was guarded by a matched pair of doors more than twelve feet high, the gleaming golden bronze carved in high relief with classical gods and god-desses that evoked Ghiberti's Renaissance Florentine Gates of Paradise. As Schwab came within twenty feet of the doors, they automatically opened toward him with a regal *swooooosh,* then closed behind him with a solid, muffled thud. The room itself looked as long as a basketball court. Paved with deep Chinese red carpeting, the gold velvet wall panels framed by burnished wood paneling, the room was centered on a thirty-foot oval table of mahogany and bartiki wood, subtly lit from an elaborately coffered ceiling. Schwab approached his high-backed brown leather chair, his seat in the home cave of MotherBank.

At each director's place was a copy of Armacost's report; another copy had been circulated at dawn that morning. Working from the report, well marked with his own emphatic doodles and notes, Armacost "walked them through" a summary of events that swept compellingly through the causes of the bank's malaise, the corrections being wrought by implementation of "the strategy," and a financial forecast through 1990. Diagnosis, treatment, and cure. Pulling the bandages off the wounds, he forced the directors to look once again at the distasteful litany of ills triggered, Armacost claimed, by deregulation, recession, and mismanagement in past decades: the mismatch; languishing technology; dismal capital ratios; deterioration of the bedrock of California lending— car financing, agriculture, real estate; the archaic branch system; and the bank's still-high cost of delivering services.

But recovery was coming swiftly. Loan problems were easing. He had beaten the mismatch down from $7 billion to $2 billion and had doubled capital. Excessive reserves being taken now would accrue later. Earnings would be rebuilt largely through consumer and ag loans in California and the West; staff numbers and expenses were being driven down. The bank was moving at last from a paper environment to computers; the ATM network and Max Hopper's successful statewide item processing system had moved B of A's technology to within respectable range of its competition. And there was a huge wholesale market to be rewon: the mid-size and large corporations now lost to the bank. He would attract entrepreneurs and wealthy individuals. "There's no place in the bank now where the entrepreneur can feel comfortable," Armacost said. His new target was not A.P.'s "little fellow"; it was upscale private banking and the top third of the agricultural market.

Finally, with his indefatigable glibness, he presented the numbers for his five-year plan. They were breathtaking. With implementation of his program, the bank would sweep over 1985's loss of $337 million to seize and secure a series of ever more profitable years: $415 million net operating earnings in 1986, $574 in '87, $711 in '88, $867 in '89 and—the final triumph—over a billion dollars in 1990. Within a year, as the bank announced a half-billion-dollar loss for '86, his words would sound hollow. Three years later, as profits climbed to within a few million of his goals, they would make him a prophet. But at the time he hoped his words had achieved what they must if he was to survive to complete the resurrection of the bank. They must comfort the board. Give them the confidence to sit tight in their chairs.

SCHWAB WAS ALERT as the Weill issue moved toward them next on the agenda. Schwab had consulted with his lawyers and was ready to fight any efforts to oust him today. As he searched for an opening to the special committee issue, it became clear that Weill would be dealt with not by a committee but in the boardroom, now. The blood was being drained from Weill's bid as it was split into two separate issues: the need for capital and Weill as CEO. As the morning's *Journal* had already told the world, Armacost would tell directors the bank had ready access to capital, should it be needed, and would have its advisers, First Boston and Salomon Brothers—and a letter from Merrill Lynch—on hand to confirm that fact. A participant who had observed Gutfreund, on Sunday, playing "a major role in trying to reassure the bank that it could raise a billion dollars without Weill," felt that now, "when push came to shove, Gutfreund was evasive about what price and in what amounts he could raise the money." Schwab knew it was needed, and suspected Gutfreund knew that with the turmoil in the bank—with the loan losses and uncertainty—the market could not absorb a billion in B of A stock right now, even at the substantial discount Gutfreund had told the board would be required. For his part, Gutfreund was testy at being suddenly pushed for details that required intensive analysis. But his "waffling" was seen by one observer as a display of "the eternal conflict investment bankers deal with—greed and ethics. He knows he can't raise the money, but he doesn't want to lose the account."

As for Weill as CEO, his offer was still being treated as a joke, Schwab fretted; the dramatic rise in B of A stock triggered by Weill's presence was being dismissed as a flash in the pan that could be sustained only through consistent earnings. If new management was needed, it would not be Sandy Weill, advisers confirmed. But this delicate issue was reserved for "executive session." Murphy suddenly announced that with such "sensitive matters relating to management" about to be discussed, it would be appropriate for inside directors to . . ." To *leave*, Schwab grasped. He had endured "bifurcation" the night before, at dinner. Even now, it might be all right if it were a simple pay raise for me, Schwab thought, indignation rising, but when it was something to do with the future of the bank! "I had an enormous stake in the outcome of their deliberations—I had been voted in by 150,000 shareholders. I was the largest single shareholder, and a major profit center for the bank. I *knew* I should be there."

The board watched, riveted, as Schwab stood and stated his case for staying. He challenged Coombe: "My lawyers say this is *not* appropriate, and we have a right to be here." Coombe leaped up and snapped back at Schwab, "Your lawyer's *wrong.*" In the electric silence that followed, Schwab waited for murmurs of support, discussion, "*anything*" from the table. There were at least two or three men he was sure shared his view. It was common knowledge that Cooley, Haas, and McNamara were dissident spirits. "But not one other board member raised a voice to say anything. They just sank down in their chairs and stayed absolutely silent." Schwab was revved up, contained but ready to explode.

But the grandeur, the silence, the disdain he felt focusing on him suddenly overwhelmed Schwab's instinct to fight. The power of the setting—a certain standard of behavior that seemed mandatory there—came over him and made him feel "like a jerk." Schwab let his challenge sputter out.

He and the other insiders rose and left the table, Cooley walking with Schwab toward the south exit, Armacost and Prussia to the north. Steaming with anger and frustration, Schwab just wanted to get out. After four years of fighting, he felt outraged, and finally resigned, that he could not save the Bank of America from itself. Exiting with him was the last shred of hope that the marriage could work. That hope had been replaced with the determination to win the battle for liberation.

In the executive session, with Schwab and the others waiting in the ante-rooms, Armacost was given a reprieve. For the first time the possibility of changing management was raised at a board meeting. Gutfreund advised the board that if it believed Armacost's projections, it should stay with him.

After waiting outside for more than an hour, the inside directors were called back in for a voice vote on the Weill issue. Distressed that consideration of Weill's bid had deteriorated into a charade, Schwab abstained. No special committee would be appointed. Weill would be told "thank you, but no thank you." His bid was dead.

After the vote, Murphy was directed to send a letter to Weill telling him that the board unanimously agreed that it was "not desirous of making a management change" and had "no intention of considering you as a candidate for the chief executive officer's position." An accompanying letter from Armacost declined Shearson's offer to raise a billion. But he asked to see a copy of Weill's plans, a cautious move that demonstrated he was doing his fiduciary duty by the shareholders, examining all proposals. He must also have been eager to see Weill's strategy for a turnaround. Weill lit a cigar, savored the moment, and refused.

WHILE THE WEILL DRAMA went on in the boardroom, Tom Cooper sat with another senior officer in the anteroom, waiting for his call to be presented to the board as president-elect and COO of Bank of America, another arrow in Armacost's quiver on this pivotal day. At one point Lee Prussia was recalled into the boardroom where he was presiding for the last time as chairman before he was displaced by the title shifting that would boost Cooper's stature. As Prussia walked past Cooper, the man sitting next to Cooper whispered, "He's going to eat Sam for lunch." Prussia was offended, he felt. Embarrassed. "Your loyal lapdog, all of a sudden *out*." Prussia might not be the strongest manager, but at least "Prussia talks about business; Armacost talks about bullshit," the officer observed. "Sam's a great salesman but never engages in business kinds of things" at board meetings.

Prussia did not have Sam for lunch that day; as Cooper was voted in, he handled the demotion with poise. But he took from the boardroom a smoldering hurt that would break out as a fire storm several months later.

ON MARCH 5 Sandy Weill withdrew his bid and turned back to his Quotron, renewing his search for the right vehicle.

Armacost had taken Weill's bid seriously "because it was another round of negative publicity. But Sandy Weill was nothing more than a sham . . . a swashbuckling attempt for a guy to find a job publicly." And the Shearson commitment letter? "It was Peter Cohen's new theory of investment banking, that you get a guy in place who's friendly to you, and then he switches all the investment banking to Shearson. But our ongoing advisers just laughed," said Armacost, joining the amused chorus. As if talking of a bothersome mosquito, he said, "Sandy Weill was never anything other than a nuisance."

The Weill camp was shocked by the arrogance. "They heap contempt on a guy with an unblemished record of success and applaud themselves for what can't even be vaguely described as a mediocre record," said Hellman, feeling some bitterness. The outcome confirmed Hellman's deep concerns about American boards, and B of A's board in particular. Believing the board had been "flummoxed" and "manipulated," he was distressed that "the board permitted the management to paint this as a hostile takeover. In a sort of personal shoot-out at the O.K. Corral, Armacost won. But Sandy never had the intention of making it that; he's never done an unfriendly takeover in his life. The *crime* is that an individual's interests were equated with the interests of the institution."

AS ARMACOST had promised, he and Joe Pinola talked by phone on March 4, the day after the second L.A. meeting. He couldn't have been more gracious. But the energy had dropped out of his voice. Pinola's ideas were good, but Armacost wanted to focus currently on the short-term future and outlook of B of A, he said. Armacost was leaving for the Far East again. Would be back March 17. Further talks now, he told Pinola, would not be productive.

"I think the deal is dead," Boisi reportedly told the team. With the immediacy of the Weill bid dissipated, there was no longer the pressure for a white knight—a presumptuous illusion, scoffs Armacost, claiming he never welcomed Pinola as a white knight. Operation Snowflake went dark again.

IT HAD BEEN a historic weekend. Armacost had driven Weill back to the Seagram Building, where Weill would soon put his energies into turning around a stuffy old Baltimore-based consumer credit company, Commercial Credit, hoping, as he took it public on the New York Stock Exchange, to make it the staging point for his next financial empire. Pinola was curbed for now. Schwab was effectively isolated. Cooper had been handed great power, and Prussia was seething. To the *Journal* writers, Armacost's survival had "dramatized the sort of clubbiness of the board" whose stubborn support of Armacost they continued to find "pretty amazing." He had won the day. But with the inexorability of Greek tragedy, he had set in place all the elements of his downfall.

ABOUT ELEVEN ON March 4, the night after the critical meeting in Los Angeles, Greg Hill got a call at his San Mateo home, an hour south of the city, from a Bank of America officer, who was chuckling. "Well, Greg, you better go out and look at your *New York Times*. It's too late for you to do anything about it, but it's something you'd be interested in." The caller knew how competitive they were, the *Times* and the *Journal*, and he was hinting that the *Times* had some scoop. Greg leaped out of bed and ran out to his lawn to pick up the *Times*'s early edition. He scanned the business page. Nothing there about the B of A. Relieved, he called the banker back. "What are you cackling about?"

"There should be a Bob Cole story tomorrow on First Interstate having made an attempt to acquire Bank of America," he told the stunned *Journal* writer. "God damn it, son of a bitch," thought Greg, going back to bed. The story was in the morning edition. A monumental scoop by Cole! He couldn't believe it. "First Interstate had come this close to a historic merger—the largest in history by many magnitudes—and no one ever knew about it. It was a nifty piece of deduction," he had to admit, as he pieced together Cole's skillful sleuthing, apparently triggered by the Weill story and by Goldman's refusing to comment on whether it was defending the Bank of America, a longtime Goldman client, against Weill. If it was not, why not? Cole must have sniffed out, Hill guessed, that First Interstate was also an old Goldman client and that something was up.

The only consolation for Hill was that the First Interstate bid was dead as

Cole wrote it; it wasn't a story that was happening. But it put a fire under Hill. "I admire Bob's work," he said, "but I hate to get beat on anything." If he allowed more than two or three such scoops on the biggest bank story since the 1930s, it would be the greatest embarrassment. Hill determined that that would be the last time he would "get beat" on the B of A story; to even the score, he would have to counter-scoop. Another takeover attack on B of A was no longer a matter of *if,* he felt. It was a matter of "where was it going to come from? Because things were getting worse, not better."

Chapter Seventeen

"IF SOMEBODY'S GOT YOUR BALLS in their hand and they ask you to turn around, you don't try to fight them. You say, 'Which way?' " one of Armacost's closest associates quipped, using the most compelling locker room metaphor he could conjure up to convince Armacost of the power the examiners held over him. Warning signs of rising charge-offs in the loan portfolios were mounting alarmingly in early June 1986, putting stress on the issue of reserves, which must be resolved before second-quarter results could be announced in July. Steve McLin was experiencing an ominous déjà vu. As he watched Armacost's resentment of Mike LaRusso's presence grow into testiness and stubborn resistance, he saw that "the national bank examiners were to Sam as Ken Martin had been to Al Rice." In both cases the need to play ball was absolute. Rice had not, and Martin had won.

The year had started with promise. The first quarter had shown a small profit of $63 million. Through April and May, predictions to analysts and investors continued upbeat; the second quarter, too, should be "modestly profitable." Armacost and McLin were clearly not expecting any serious surprises. Keefe, Bruyette's Don Crowley, however, put the prospect of even modest gains into perspective: "Analyzing or investing in BankAmerica Corporation is like cohabiting with a two-ton rhinoceros: When it's good, it's not very good, and when it's bad, it's really beastly."

The historic conjunction of deregulation and global recession was still painting a ghastly landscape for bankers, more ghastly for Armacost than for most. It was now seven years since the turning off of the money supply, four years since the Fed had eased money in 1982, beginning the recovery that had moved the economy steadily back toward health. Yet the worldwide deflationary impact was continuing to pummel Bank of America's loan portfolios. Volcker's mighty boot had stamped out inflation, but the great experiment with manipulation of the money supply that had achieved it still reverberated through the global economy in fitful surges, with lags and aftershocks, teaching Americans lessons about the invidious chain of worldwide cause and effect that, in milliseconds, could alter their personal lives—their net worth; debt; the value of homes, cars; the safety of savings. By 1986 America sat on a quagmire of debt.

Banks were, at last, feeling the full effects of deflation. It had wiped out the value of real assets, the homes, farms, oil rigs, and reserves that had appreciated steadily since World War II—the reliable source of consumers' and companies' ability to pay back interest and principal on their loans.

"Losses roll out of a bank typically after the bottom of a recession because it takes time for them to be discovered," explains University National Bank's Carl Schmitt. "Companies don't want to die. They writhe and go through this horrible period, trying to protect themselves. And much of that is holding the banker at bay. . . . Also, banking is a service business . . . and bankers probably go along with problems much longer than they should."

Armacost was not facing these lingering aftershocks of recession alone. In 1985, 120 American banks had gone into bankruptcy, the largest number since the Great Depression. The number would grow to 145 in 1986, and 203 in 1987. Most were smaller banks hit by collapse of their regional and local economies—the Texas and Oklahoma oil patch, midwestern ag banks. The savings and loan banks, dependent, mostly, on home mortgages and construction, had been so badly hit that they stood threatened as an industry. In Texas and the Southwest, failed thrifts were also found to be a cesspool of fraud and corruption. The resources of the FSLIC, the government insurer, were so drained, paying off depositors of failed S&Ls, that it risked bankruptcy if Congress did not grant it more funds—a bailout some estimated would take $100 billion of taxpayers' money.

B of A had its great, deep deposit base shoring it up. But it also had huge portfolio holdings, across the board, in all the suffering sectors.

As Armacost looked out from his desk in the early summer of 1986, he viewed a bleak landscape. Commander of the largest "farm bank" in the world, he watched agricultural land values, his "belt-and-suspenders" fallback collateral, lose $149 billion in the United States in three years. "It hasn't really been since the depression that farm credit has been in trouble in California," he observed. But for the five and one-half years he`had been in charge, "farm incomes declined every year. Farm values dropped forty, fifty, sixty percent. They never really reached bottom. . . . We had thousands of customers go bankrupt. Ag. Real estate," says Armacost.

Gritting his teeth as he continued to claim that Volcker "didn't have any choice," Armacost had watched oil prices collapse at the end of 1985, drop-ping from $22 to $12 a barrel. But instead of invigorating the economy as lower-cost oil was expected to do, it was wreaking devastation on oil-producing states and countries as they lost vital foreign exchange income. It was pushing more Mexican, Venezuelan, and Indonesian loans to nonperforming status. Bringing the bank's loans to real estate developments—office buildings, ho-tels, homes—in Texas and Oklahoma, California and Colorado to bankruptcy. The workout of LDC loans was still horrendous, but it was up-front and shared by a thousand banks and all developed nations. In California Armacost felt other, indirect shock waves from the foreign debt problem. His loans to California's middle-market companies were proving to be "a lagging indicator of problems that have already manifested themselves elsewhere. The manufac-turer who finds out he can't sell to Mexico because there's not enough credit to finance the sale of his product may be in fine financial condition for the next year and a half without those orders," Armacost explains. "But a year and a half later he has suddenly run out of other things that kept the exporting company propped up, and that's the point in time when it becomes a bad loan." "The same credit disciplines that had seemed to serve the bank so well for so long were totally inadequate in this environment," he lamented.

Well and good. But Armacost's California peers, and most of his big multinational competitors, had been riding the same storm far better than Bank of America. Wells Fargo, apparently swallowing Crocker with little indiges-tion, had moved its stock price up a stunning 56 percent since the beginning of the year to $99, while B of A's stock had declined 17 percent. As the third quarter unfolded daily, Bank of America was losing 4 percent of its deposit customers and nearly 2 percent of its market share of core deposits—its most prized possessions—to Wells Fargo, which would gain more than a billion in new deposits for the quarter, an increase of 4.5 percent. The pulsing blood-stream of the bank was being systematically drained by the competition. "Wells's foreign risk is minuscule; they can just walk away from third world debt," he claimed, implying that little Wells didn't *know* the troubles of the big boys. But Wells was divesting its foreign assets by choice, committing to a "back to basics" focus on California retail banking with the marketing energy Citicorp had brought to its rediscovery of the consumer in the mid-seventies. And Wells was a merciless cost cutter. Armacost continued to see the tiny new service-based banks—like Carl Schmitt's University National in Palo Alto saying its thank-yous to customers with gifts of gourmet Walla Walla onions and hiring string orchestras for Christmas parties—as an even more dangerous competitor for market share.

Of his multinational competitors, only Manufacturers Hanover, the New York money center bank whose vital signs were lagging, was suffering as much. But it was more than bad performance that was hurting Armacost; a credibility gap was growing between his optimistic rhetoric and reality. The evoking of cosmic economic events as cause was losing its magical effect. The patience of the local press was thinning, goaded by visiting writer Ken Auletta's amazement at the mannerly treatment Armacost had received. "With such a six-year record, why have there been no City Hall press conferences or editorials demanding Armacost's scalp? . . . In a comparable metropolis—New York, Los Angeles, Chicago—politicians would have screeched from podiums. Newspaper editorials would have thundered. And the corporation's board of directors would have ordered the CEO to yank the cord on his golden parachute."

THE INCREDIBLE SHRINKING BANK. McLin hated the headline. He had become the eliminator. The facilitator of asset sales that had shrunk the bank by roughly $16 billion in the past three years. He could feel the momentum of acquisitions that were key to new kinds of business and a stronger territorial position slowing. And the growing gap between earnings expectations and the quarterly shocks was throwing both strategies—sales and acquisitions—into a limbo of uncertainty. He needed earnings forecasts for negotiations. "I couldn't do the earnings forecast myself. I was kind of a-reeling and a-rocking from all these lousy forecasts. As Sam was. And it was very difficult for me to execute strategy without . . . even basic weather information, if you will . . . trying to figure out what the climate was." Since the disastrous loss declared last summer, they were hanging at the cliff edge each quarter, trying to fathom the depth of the nonperforming loans that were being dug up, trying to estimate what reserves to place against them; earnings would shrink or grow depending on the size of the reserves.

Riding this roller coaster, McLin had been trying desperately to hold to strategy. He'd been keeping the Orbanco acquisition negotiations going for nearly a year. It was a small bank. But Orbanco was a symbol that Bank of America was aggressively positioning itself in the West for interstate banking, that it was in the game with Citicorp, Security Pacific, Wells, First Interstate.

But the regulators were looking less and less favorably on B of A's buying anything until it got its capital ratios up to prudent levels. Of the three ways to increase capital—by earnings, by selling stock in the market, or by shrinking assets so that the capital you have becomes a larger ratio of your assets—shrinking assets was the only viable option. With McLin's asset sales, the bank had added a billion in capital and moved capital ratios up to nearer the industry average, but it wasn't there yet. It was powerfully tempting to sell Seafirst. Its $8 billion in assets would boost the equity-to-assets ratio back up to levels that would satisfy the regulators. But the more you sold, the less earning power you had. He and Armacost were holding Schwab and Seafirst, no matter what the pressures.

It was the bank's responsibility to decide on the final size of the loan loss reserves each quarter. But LaRusso could force larger reserves. Or put pressure on the board to change management. There were rumors through the spring that the examiners had written a list of potential CEOs—names like Tom Theobald, Cooper, Beckett, Pinola, Bill Simon. Guessing games about Armacost's successor were becoming the Street's parlor sport. Mike Patriarca claims that the examiners would never write such a list. A spokesperson for the Office of the Comptroller of the Currency backs him up: "Decisions on management are the responsibility of the board. We do not make them." Both admit, however, that if a board presented a list of potential CEOs to the OCC, "we could look at that list and would certainly say something if we knew someone had not performed well in a management position."

As Armacost refused to attend a meeting the examiners had asked him to attend, McLin and Adizes began to plead. "McLin was telling Sam, 'Bow your head to the Comptroller of the Currency. Those guys in Washington have the power to fire you.' I was telling him, 'Sam, please bow. Kiss their ass, if that's what needs to be done. Bend!' He would not bend," says Adizes, who shared breakfast with Armacost each time he visited the bank in San Francisco, gaining rare access to Armacost during these tense days. Armacost retorted, "The day the bank examiners are running the bank is the end of the capitalist system. And I will not allow Washington to tell—" Adizes begged, "Then let *me* talk to these guys." Again Adizes was in the position of admiring the integrity of Armacost's stand, while hating its suicidal bullheadedness.

THIS WAS ALMOST the last of Adizes's cautions. He was fired in May. Armacost called him in and told him that the basic work he'd been hired to do was largely done, "that they had reached the point of diminishing returns. There was no animosity," Armacost recalls. Adizes had known "there was continuous opposition to me from the first day. I went through hell. But it was underground. I never knew who was fighting me." There had been a scurrilous playlet written and circulated, casting Adizes as the man who deserts a sinking, dying bank to catch his plane and escape to a house in Monte Carlo bought at the expense of the bank. He could see the end coming. "I became a political liability because people wanted my head. I made so much change, and somebody had to pay the price." Adizes knew, too, that his own grand projects at the bank were taking more time and money than that environment of panic could tolerate. "Cooper was saying, 'We're not moving fast enough. We should be firing, cutting. The bank's not going to make it.' "

Although Adizes saw Tom Cooper "as instrumental," it was Armacost who removed him. Adizes understood, and continued to see Armacost as "a wonderful, warm, bright individual" who represents "the understanding, statesmanship, long-range view, indecisive, friendly old-time B of A." Armacost had been making changes "so quietly, so elegantly," Adizes would continue to argue in Armacost's defense. As Armacost would argue in Adizes's defense. "It was *not* voodoo, *not* a touchy-feely kind of Esalen thing," Armacost responds to Adizes's critics. "Ichak was hard-nosed, knew business well, and was able to allow three or four levels of management to come up with organizational solutions and get it done." The derision and anger that swirled around Adizes were, he says, "part of the strategy. Ichak focused hostility toward change on himself, *not* on the CEO. He allowed people to be aggressive to him. It was the price he knew he had to pay."

Adizes would not get the three years he believed he needed to complete the most dramatic assignment for a consultant—or "*in*sultant," as he preferred —in corporate history. He heard that Cooper swiftly began dismantling his projects. "I'm wounded, and I'm a professional," he admitted later. "Wounded means that people did not understand the bigness, the strength, the magnitude of the change that Sam, Lee, and myself were going to do." But in the rise and fall of consultants, CEOs, or presidential candidates, "with nations or the Bank of America," Adizes believed, "what we are voting for is what we deep down subconsciously believe we need."

"FOR ME, BAPS was not an icon," says Cooper, who had, indeed, dismantled the payments system that was one of Adizes's proudest products. The unbundling had been planned before hiring Cooper, says Armacost. "But decentralizing BAPS was *not* dismantling the dream," Armacost insists. "The payments functions had been pulled together into BAPS so that we could get a handle on them, bring managerial discipline and market focus to a neglected group of bank units, then unbundle and send them back to the operational departments where they could best meet customers' needs," Cooper explains. Bundled or unbundled, Armacost saw BAPS's potential as a profit center as *"tremendous*—five percent of U.S. checks run through B of A." He had seen it as international. But the vision of a great global utility had been too grandiose—an expression, perhaps, of the bank's need to refurbish the tarnished image of its own greatness. Created in a deteriorating earnings environment, BAPS "had been publicly touted far beyond its potential," Cooper believed. As J. C. Penney's, Sears's, and ARCO's payment systems claimed domestic market share, as international payments giants like American Express and VISA (owned by 21,000 banks in 185 countries) swelled the competition, and as consortiums of banks and multinational information networks seized control of the electronic clearinghouses which were the key to payments dominance, Cooper doubted that one bank could control anything in which "the marketplace is so dynamic, alternatives so plentiful."

THE URGENT NEED, now, was to create a perception that the bank's bloated expenses—the problem that nagged even more than bad loans—were being decisively addressed. The largest cost was still staff. It was very hard for a bank known as a loyal birth-to-grave employer, almost Japanese in its paternal benevolence, to boast of having slashed its staff from 82,700 to 77,950 in the four years from 1981 to 1985. Harder still to admit was the fact that while staff levels had declined, staff costs had risen 42 percent!

Cooper was needed more than ever, a bold knight in crisp white shirtsleeves and glasses who would swiftly dispatch the ten-headed hydra, staff costs. He was perfect casting, as action images became more vital to the bank's tenuous hold on credibility. His power had grown exponentially since Armacost made him COO in March. By June Cooper had control of the bank's two major operating divisions: the California retail bank and the World Banking Division. World Banking's Bob Frick reported to him. Cooper himself took over as temporary head of the retail bank as Wiesler left. Systems, the whole computer side of the bank, also reported to him. Cooper had risen on a track faster than any of the other new stars and was rumored to be favored as the new leader if Armacost was to be removed. Palace gossip had been warning Armacost for many months. Journalists, too, were beginning to describe Cooper as "destabilizing" to Armacost's power.

In June 1986 Cooper dismantled the thing no one had dared touch, the major structural achievement of the Clausen regime: the 1974 division of the globe into four parts. The centralized model developed by Bill Young in Latin America was now migrated home to headquarters to become the pattern for a new international structure, the World Banking Group. The world was now redivided into two, rather than four, parts: the United States and Canada, and the rest of the world. Young was migrated home, too, to run the international side, a triumph of the tough strategies he had imposed on Latin America, where he had pulled the bank out of eight countries, out of most retail banking, and out of the middle-market private lending that had proved such a nightmare. The focus was now on serving the big multinational customers and entering the international capital markets more aggressively.

COOPER'S BLADE CUT into credit quality, too. A member of the newly created Credit Policy Committee, which assigned high-level executives to credit scrutiny, as president he now personally examined every nonperforming loan over $1 million. Glenhall Taylor scarcely needed help. The former Wells man recruited as Armacost's chief credit officer was leading as rigorous a hunt for loan problems as the bank had ever seen. "Federal examiners had never gone out to the branches," says Armacost. Now portfolios were pulled from the branches into the thirty-five regional centers and every loan was scrutinized. As the bad loans gushed up, Armacost was trapped in the catch-22 inherent in hiring Taylor: The more bad loans he found, the worse Armacost looked. "I was well aware I would not survive the changes I was making," said Armacost later with a shrug.

Had Armacost applied a theory "so obvious you feel like a moron for even enunciating it," banker Anthony Frank later postulated, Armacost's personal fate might have taken a very different turn: "When you're the new CEO of a troubled situation, you immediately set up reserves—make it clear that the problems are not yours but rather those of your predecessor." If you don't disown the bad loans already in the portfolio and start with a tabula rasa, "then after a while, what happens is that they're no longer Tom's loans, they're your loans. And when Sam, with full justice says, in '85 and '86, 'Hey, there are a lot of bad loans. I'm setting up reserves. I inherited all that,' everybody says, 'You've been there five years. Those are your loans.' And they weren't. They weren't his loans."

Since March Taylor's old Wells colleague Lewis Coleman had been digging out the mess in World Banking as its new chief of credit quality, trying to plumb the depths of the bank's third world disaster. He had found "a classic credit system. A credit system is known by the level at which the credit and loan functions come together and judgments are made. At B of A it was at a very high level." The credit and loan functions were still on separate tracks, "with wars between them," and with the loan men in the field feeling isolated from the decisions at headquarters on the loans they originated.

With time running out and blood pouring from the portfolios, Coleman left B of A's structure in place but imposed emergency measures to make the existing system work better. He stripped loan officers of lending limits if they didn't report accurately on the status of loans. "You know at least a year ahead what trends are," he claims. There shouldn't be "surprises." He raised bonuses for performance. Made decisions on the tough loan calls himself, keeping a balance between deciding for credit, or the field, to defuse the competition and hostility between them. He visited the countries; he was unprecedentedly hands-on for a credit man.

By the end of June Taylor and his team had uncovered so many nonaccrual loans, particularly in the real estate portfolios, that it would be almost impossible to hold reserves where they were. Debate raged, as always, over how big a hit to take. A worst-case scenario that was shaping could tear Armacost's reputation apart: *taking a loss in excess of half a billion dollars.*

Armacost was in China as the numbers came clear. "Get him back here, the balls are rolling down the hill," McLin said urgently to Cooper, on the eve of declaration of a loss so large that it would destroy any vestigial shred of a positive image. It would be the second-largest quarter loss in history, second only to Continental Illinois's. Unless they could avert it. "Cooper tried to get Sam to come back to deal with the problem. I know he had several conversations. Prussia may have called Sam, too," says McLin. "For whatever reasons, Sam didn't come back. But from my perspective, there was a bona fide attempt on Cooper's part to get Sam to come back from China."

Armacost did come back a little early to face the crisis of nonaccruing loans—and indications from LaRusso that he would like to see reserves moved up to more than $2 billion, increasing them by almost a third. "I wouldn't say I didn't have any arguments about it. LaRusso enjoys inflicting pain," says Armacost. "We had in mind a much smaller number. But at the end of the day we decided to err on the side of excess." A colleague concurs: "The second-quarter reserve probably didn't have to be as big as it was." It would be $600 million, taken from the bank's capital—a number so large that it reportedly surprised even the examiners.

On July 21 Armacost held a news conference, with Cooper by his side. He announced a $640 million loss for the quarter. Continuing to "paddle like hell" under the unruffled exterior, Armacost delivered the usual upbeat message: "The corporation's fundamental strategic program is functioning effectively, and the decisions taken during the quarter will accelerate our progress along the sometimes volatile road to recovery." Cooper played his role deftly, giving details on the expense reductions and on the five thousand projected staff cuts for the year—an annual saving of $180 million.

The day after the announcement a group of six reporters rolled their eyes when Armacost told them, "The loss because of the increased reserves actually strengthens the bank rather than weakens it," sending them back to their offices to write stories that led analyst Don Crowley to say, "The local press, which had been rather tolerant in the past, has become increasingly hostile. . . ."

And Crowley's predictions for the bank turned bleak: a 40 percent probability of a change in management and a 30 percent probability of the bank's changing hands or receiving a capital injection.

EVENTS WERE CONVERGING on Armacost and the bank. But this time Armacost was helpless to control them.

In the hours and days after the announcement of the $640 million loss, Greg Hill kept checking with his foreign exchange trading contacts in Tokyo and London. Nobody was dumping B of A CDs. This shock was not starting an electronic run, like Continental Illinois. The deposit base in California was still standing fast like the Rock of Gibraltar. Rick Schmitt wrote up the loss, a page two story, injecting the standard jab Armacost hated about the tenuousness of his survival in the subhead, TENURE OF PRESIDENT QUESTIONED. Then the two became preoccupied with the bank's vulnerability, combing their sources for credible scenarios. Three days later, July 21, "we pieced together a story that the acquirer would offer a special preferred issue and that the tender offer would consist of a combination of its own stock, cash, and a 'special preferred'— using, ironically, the model that McLin developed to take over Seafirst. First Interstate had used it first in their acquisition of the IntraWest Bank in Denver," says Hill. They had used only sources that had proven themselves to be "extraordinarily prescient—the smartest men we know in the industry." Hill and Schmitt had laid out a blueprint not for a friendly merger but for takeover.

"Hey, you're inviting a bid by writing a story about how it could happen, how it would work," was the gist of the complaints Hill would get from Ron Rhody or John Keane, who, Hill knew, thought they were being "shopped around by the *Journal.*" Rhody, the *Journal* men sensed, suspected "hidden agendas" and was trying to deflect stories he feared could become self-fulfilling prophecies.

"We don't care whether B of A is bought or sold or broken up," Hill responded. "It's just that the people who we consider the wise men in the industry, or in investment banking . . . all are voicing the same theme: that B of

A's franchise is enormously valuable, that different parts of it can be sold, that these are hidden unrealized values, and that you can use accounting techniques to really pay for a bunch of charge-offs. . . . If you think it's going to invite a bid, all I can say is, only the fundamentals will dictate that. No one's going to spend two and a half billion dollars just on my say-so."

IN FACT, the bank itself invited takeover speculation when news of a secret move made at the August board meeting was revealed two months later. Word of golden parachutes for Armacost and other senior executives broke in early October, sending the stock up nearly a point. Assuring Armacost of $1.7 million in severance pay, the parachutes were to be deployed only in the event that officers lost their jobs in a takeover, suggesting that the board was moving into a mind-set that permitted the possibility of a change in corporate control—good news for the market. The parachutes had been passed without approval of shareholders. Not a word had leaked out at the time.

Chuck Schwab had come to the August meeting looking for signs of change, not for golden parachutes, which he saw as symbols of greed and defensiveness. He made one last fitful effort to rouse the board to listen to his program of change. Hoping to break through the isolation and gain their respect and attention, he gave the board members a summary of the whizbang results and plans of the Schwab subsidiary. He got no response. Like Claire Hoffman, he had become background noise, no longer heard.

He went home that night deeply frustrated by "my total inability to impact events." For several nights he slept fitfully. On August 13 he woke up and told his wife, Helen, "I'm going to resign." She encouraged him. "Chuck, you're spending sixty percent of your time negatively worrying about this. You better do the thing you feel." There were risks for his company. He was still married to the Bank of America, locked in as the chief executive of a subsidiary. "I would lose my so-called power position in respect to protecting the Schwab organization. It would leave us naked." But Schwab's only goal was to get his company back. He was convinced Armacost would never let him go. A number of times he had asked Armacost for "a friendly, amicable separation. 'I'm just a thorn in your side, and that's not my style,' I'd tell Sam." But to sell Schwab would be to abandon the heart of "the strategy."

He wrote a letter of resignation to Prussia, wished management luck in turning the company around, and flew to his condo in Hawaii. "It was a great liberating thing to be free from the bank's problems. It left me free . . . to take the next step to liberate this firm." He felt the exhilaration soldiers feel when a decisive campaign is about to begin.

His act was "most disruptive." Particularly now, just two days after John Poelker had quit. The chief financial officer, hired less than six months earlier, had had enough. His leaving had been clouded by confusion, as an analysts' meeting in New York had been scheduled, then canceled, as the bank drew a curtain over the Poelker drama. Armacost stormed when he read Schwab's letter. "What I do find reprehensible is the way in which he executed his own singular self-interest late in the stages, at great expense to the institution he was supposed to be serving as a director. . . ." Schwab had first received a call from Jack Beckett, the new chairman of the Executive Committee, asking him not to make his resignation effective until the end of August. Schwab told him, "I'll change the date, but not the decision." Armacost called Schwab in Hawaii, trying to persuade him not to take action. "The timing is bad," he said. "Sam, I've just got to do it," Chuck replied.

The *New York Times* reported: "Reacting to the resignation Wednesday of Charles R. Schwab from the board of directors, the stock of BankAmerica Corporation yesterday moved in fits and starts among heavy trading. As the sixth most actively traded stock on the NYSE, BAC closed at 12.375, unchanged, after trading as high as 12.75 and as low as 12." At the end of the day the Golden Boy from the Sacramento Valley had not moved the market, but he had given Bank of America's stock a hell of a good rattling.

Immediately, Schwab called together a small war party of aides, lawyers, and investment bankers to lay plans for the buyback campaign.

IF THERE WAS a time when Adizes should have been there to warn Armacost to beware the Ides of March, it was as Armacost approached the Los Angeles boardroom doors for the September board meeting. But it was not Cooper, as Adizes had predicted, but Prussia who would undo him. Every meeting now was held in a climate of tension. This meeting, so far, was on track. With his usual voluble articulateness, Armacost had made a presentation to the board of a proposal for a supremely sensitive asset sale. The Italian bank. The big retail bank that A.P. had bought in 1919 and that Al Rice had turned into an important profit source in the 1970s. A tie to the bank's Italian heritage, its very name, Banca d'America e d'Italia, was loaded with emotion and strongly held feelings. Armacost had invited First Boston to come armed with a full-dress proposal for the sale, with numbers and rationales. The presentation had gone smoothly.

Unknown to Armacost, Prussia had written his own scenario, "his own view of the world of the future," which, an observer remarked, "is always very negative." Prussia had taken hold of the meeting and, "out of left field," attacked the plan to sell the Italian bank. It had been discussed many times in the Managing Committee. Consensus had been reached. Dissension among management at a board meeting was taboo. Suddenly the chairman, who had been part of the leadership duo with Armacost since '81, was telling the board that the decision to sell the Italian bank might be flawed. That it might well be a crown jewel. Adizes had seen that "Prussia was even more clear and strong in his vision than Armacost." But to speak his vision at this time and place was nothing short of sabotage. Armacost was aghast.

Prussia had gone on to argue that there should be changes in the board, even if it meant that he, too, must go. The comment could only mean Armacost. "We were flabbergasted. Nonplussed. We just couldn't believe it," says a member of the management team at the meeting. Despite Prussia's growing aggressiveness at Managing Committee meetings, Schwab had observed in the past that "Prussia knew that his position was subservient to Sam and made absolutely certain that he never crossed the line. He was a fine gentleman." His outburst was also "extraordinarily embarrassing" to the investment advisers who had presented a range of options based on the scenario previously discussed and agreed on by top management. More than most senior management, Armacost and Prussia had been perceived as a tight, cooperative team. Prussia had revealed to the board a divided management.

As he listened to Prussia's unprecedented defection from the management line, Armacost suspected that Prussia had finally reached an attitude of "By God, if I'm to go in all this controversy, we're both going." The irony for Armacost was that Prussia was still there only because of Armacost's tolerant ear for the arguments of several board members—in the face of a strident chorus of calls for Prussia's removal—that the timing was bad for ousting the chairman.

A former board member who talked to Prussia after the September meeting believes that Prussia's behavior was the explosion of a man who felt "that Sam had violated his loyalty and trust," a resentment that had begun to surface when Cooper was made president. To many who observed him during those days, Prussia was despondent, testy, a man in depression.

But the immediate triggering event for Prussia's decision to act may have been a secret showdown just a month earlier, when Armacost had finally told him he would have to leave. There had been overt demands from many in executive management and from some board members to remove him, complaints that he was contributing nothing and was pulling Armacost down. Armacost had resisted. It was hard to break the BankAmerican code of loyalty, to disconnect, even though Prussia was losing credibility with the line officers. At the midsummer meeting with Prussia, Bob Beck and Armacost told Prussia he would be offered a graceful exit. Prussia showed no interest in the proposal, but in subsequent discussions it was made clear to him that he would have to find something else to do and retire. Prussia's behavior was observed to have become even more aggressive after that meeting. And now Prussia, the loyal team player, had butchered Armacost at the September meeting. He would follow up later that month, meeting privately with Jack Beckett to restate his concerns.

Prussia's stunning behavior at the September meeting was, a colleague believes, "very key in the breaking of the dike—of Armacost's dike." That split view of management, Armacost later came to believe, had been the event, more than any specific bad news, that finally shattered the stubborn support from the board through five years of precipitous decline. Its support had been loyal through the shrinkage of the bank from first to third biggest in the United States, through loss of top-ten ranking worldwide, and through losses that now approached a billion dollars. Prussia's was the knife that cut the fragile thread of confidence and galvanized a beleaguered and uncertain board into one with the will to say "go."

THE RUMORS started overseas. In London and Tokyo. No news had leaked about events at the September meeting. But the market was intuitively picking up the rising tension within the bank. By September 13 rumors that the bank was "on the verge of bankruptcy" and Armacost about to be ousted began to fly. The stock started to slide. It reached its new low, $9\frac{1}{2}$, the day the rumors started. It was the preamble to a run, if it was not halted. For Corporate Communications, a new theater of war had opened. Ron Rhody created a task force. Emergency task forces were becoming a way of life for his huge staff.

"Preposterous, irresponsible and absolutely groundless in fact," the *San Francisco Chronicle* quoted as Corporate Communications ground out denials. Regulators confirmed it: no emergency. In a check of the Euromarkets, it was clear that the institutional investors were not dumping the stock. But the rumors persisted. There was urgent debate within the bank. And Armacost took to the airwaves. The bank bought time on California radio stations, and Armacost reassured the state that the Bank of America was strong and stable.

By September 24 the terror of Rumor Week, as Corporate Communications christened it, had been contained. That day Bank of America announced it had dropped its bid for Orbanco. Armacost had fought for it, but the Fed had refused to let him buy Orbanco. "It was a tactical, strategic play that would have given the world a view of continuing forward motion," said a deeply disappointed Armacost.

Five weeks later, on November 4, Bank of America, wearing the humiliation of its deep capital poverty, would wince as Security Pacific announced that it would march down the aisle with Orbanco. It was also acquiring Rainier in Seattle, the bank Bob Truex had made such a success. The deal strengthened Security Pacific's regional positioning for interstate banking and thrust Truex into position, like Pinola, to challenge the bank that had spit him out.

GOLDMAN'S KATHY SHARP arrived at San Francisco International Airport, rented a compact car, and drove swiftly to the Bank of America headquarters. She looked like just another good-looking suit-wearing New York investment banker lady carrying a briefcase. But in her case was a letter she was hand-carrying to Sam Armacost. And a copy for each of the board members. She was rushing to deliver the thick stack of letters before office closing on Friday afternoon, October 3, 1986, so that Armacost and the board could read them and raise the issue at the board meeting Monday morning. The letter was from Joe Pinola.

"Piles of stuff always arrive just at closing time," complained the reception-ist as Sharp piled the letters on the counter. No, Mr. Armacost was not in. Wishing she could tell the woman that this was *not* just another letter, Sharp left the letters and reported back to the Goldman offices on the thirty-first floor. Phone calls flew to Los Angeles, where Pinola's team could not believe Armacost had not been there. He knew the letter was coming; he had been notified. Through their contacts they heard that he was playing golf with football star Daryl Lamonica. "Joe would be there. And so would we. *Nobody* would be on the golf course," said one of his aides with amazement and no little contempt for such casual behavior by a CEO under these conditions. Contained in the letter was a formal proposal for First Interstate to acquire Bank of America.

Golf! A.P. hated it. Clausen had no use for it. Both saw it as a moral curse. As Pinola's letter arrived, Armacost's golf clubs had become damaging weapons in his own destruction. He was a man perceived as having the time to golf while the company crashed.

"It's fanciful folklore! I *wasn't* playing golf," says Armacost, annoyed that the story "tended to portray Nero fiddling while Rome burned. We were prepared for the letter. We didn't know when they'd send it; we hoped they wouldn't. But we had all our lawyers ready." But jokes were building about Armacost's golf. "He used golf as a business tool," said McLin in defense. "If he hadn't been such a *good* golfer, nobody would have noticed as much."

During the months when Operation Snowflake had been in hiatus, Pinola had been laying his groundwork and keeping the idea visible. By coincidence Tony Bennett had been hired to sing "I Left My Heart in San Francisco" on the eve of First Interstate's annual meeting. Pinola was the subject of a major profile in the Sunday *New York Times* business section on June 8 headlined BANKAMERICA'S AUDACIOUS PURSUER, a story laced with quotes from his former boss, Tom Clausen: "Mr. Pinola would have been a strong contender for the top job" had he stayed with Bank of America. Pinola displayed to the *Times* the worldly banker to whom "a '61 Latour . . . is pretty close to the ultimate." But the visceral image that leaped from the page was of the scrappy "football end from the Pennsylvania coal fields."

B of A's huge loss the following month, July 1986, had put Pinola back on alert. During the summer he had paid "courtesy calls" on Volcker and the FDIC's Isaac, the heads of the regulatory agencies whose approval he would have to have. "I kept them informed of what was happening. They were very concerned about Bank of America." On September 17 Griffith and Sudmann had met in New York with the bank's investment bankers, Salomon Brothers, at the height of Rumor Week. B of A, Salomon had reported, was still interested. Two weeks later the two had met again with Goldman in New York to decide what to do. The mood was optimistic. It would still be a friendly overture; both Goldman and Pinola were firm on that. There had been growing feeling that a letter should be sent. The First Interstate team respected Armacost's political skills and suspected that he might be keeping the talking going to avoid getting a Weill type of letter that would have to be taken to the board. The letter had been written and rushed to San Francisco by Kathy Sharp the next day, October 3.

On Monday, October 6, Joe Pinola was in Oklahoma City shaking hands deep in the reception line at the party celebrating First Interstate's acquisition and renaming of the First National Bank & Trust there. Pinola spotted an urgent high sign from Paul Minch across the room. He smiled and chatted his way out of the crowd, as Minch whispered, "Bank of America has just released part of our letter." There had been a B of A board meeting that day, and the board had released it at 4:00 P.M., as the market closed. It was 6:00 P.M. in Oklahoma City. After more than a year of drift the deal was engaged. Pinola could feel it. As they got details, it was clear that Armacost's response had been ambivalent; Armacost wanted Pinola to withdraw because the bank would be releasing its own restructuring plan in January. But he had not *rejected* the offer. Pinola made his speech to twelve hundred people and flew back immediately to Los Angeles, as Edward M. Carson, his chairman, flew out to pick up the festivities next morning. Not a beat would be missed in Oklahoma City.

*　*　*

No one knew except the Bank of America board, and Sam and Mary Jane Armacost, that as Pinola got the high sign in Oklahoma City, Armacost had just been given the pink slip in San Francisco.

A board member had warned Armacost that since Prussia's statements at the September meeting, there were several "disruptive" directors who could give him trouble at the October meeting and had recommended that he present a very specific, clear view of how problems were being resolved—the strategy speech he had given so often. But Armacost did not go to the meeting with any sense of an impending coup. The board had Pinola's offer to deal with, "and a lot of people assumed you would not . . . unhorse your CEO in the middle of a takeover battle," says Armacost. Another threat had surfaced just that day: a letter offering capital from corporate turnaround specialist Stan Hiller, a man of such stature and success in turnarounds that Warren Hellman, who was shepherding Hiller's attempt to gain a board seat as he had shepherded Weill's bid, said exultantly, "Why wouldn't any board *kill* to have him on its board?"

Armacost also had the happy announcement that in that reservoir of talent within Wells Fargo, B of A had found a superb new chief financial officer, Frank Newman, who would be starting work next day, filling the gap left by Poelker. Newman's reputation was so strong that Armacost had lifted his embargo on Wells people to hire him. The meeting's principal issue would be how to respond to Pinola's letter. Most of these men knew Pinola. With A.P.'s legacy and a very large bank behind him, he could not be treated as lightly as Weill had been. Armacost sensed that the Pinola letter was "crystallizing a lot of emotions in the board over independence," allowing the most unsettling question of all to creep into the minds of the directors: *Is there a price at which the Bank of America might lose its independence?*

The "trouble" Armacost had been warned of had not come at the meeting, and he returned to his office, "still in a 'draft a response, pull our internal valuation together' " posture on the Pinola bid. He was still not sure that Pinola was going to be able "to put a number on the table that he could afford that we could afford to take." He'd placed a call to Pinola's aides.

But the board had not disbanded after Armacost left. The outside directors remained in the boardroom, and in an emotional closed session, those he had counted as his champions—Hawley, Peterson, and Beckett—rose against him and voted for a change at the top of the Bank of America. As chairman of the Executive Personnel and Compensation Committee, Hawley had been in the hot seat. The room was charged as Sam Armacost was voted out of power. Tom

Clausen, who had already let his willingness be known—who had, some suspected, "engineered his own return by letting them know he'd sacrifice himself to come back"—would be asked to return. The eleven outside directors, board member Andrew Brimmer later said, had decided that Clausen was the only hope to restore credibility.

Jack Beckett appeared in Armacost's office a few hours after he had left the meeting and told him he had come to ask for his resignation. For Armacost, "it was almost anticlimactic. . . . I'd taken a rather fatalistic view of my own tenure for months. There comes a time on boards when issues kind of take on a life of their own. At a certain stage you become an inanimate object. You become a symbol that needs to get changed to make the pain go away." He didn't hold it against the board. "They really couldn't see their way through the web." He had told the press on several occasions that he'd fully expected it to happen earlier "just based upon guys wearing out."

He called Mary Jane. She was relieved. "She was tired of all this nonsense going on in the bank. I think she felt that it was no way to live in that environment. Life is too short. She felt the bank wasn't deserving of that degree of devotion and commitment. It wasn't giving anything in return." Mary Jane told her husband, "That's great. It's the best news I've heard in a long time."

THAT SAME EVENING Tom Clausen and his wife were having a dinner party for eight at their apartment in Washington, and just "as we were going to go into the dining room, the phone rang." Clausen was intensely proud of his wife's gourmet cooking, and took much pleasure in matching wines from his wine cellar to her food. He excused himself and took the call. It was a conference call from Jack Beckett and Rudy Peterson, "calling on behalf of the board." Beckett told Clausen what had happened that day. Armacost was out, and they wanted him back. "It had hurt me no end, sitting in Washington, reading about it," says Clausen. But the risks were daunting. First Interstate's bid was turning the screw on near-terminal losses and ratios. "My whole career has been winning. . . . We're used to playing from the top of the mountain." To come back when the bank was at the bottom, pride and confidence in disarray, and the world watching like a vulture, was to lay himself open to the first failure of his career. They talked for an hour and a half. When he returned to his guests, dinner was almost over. "Kind of a long phone call, wasn't it, Tom?" Peggy commented. "Yes, I'm sorry," said Clausen, taking two bites of his dessert before the phone rang for him again. He left the table. "I was really taken aback. . . . But when the right people ask, it's not a difficult choice. I said, 'Okay, if you want me to come back, I'll agree to come back.' "

His guests were gone when he finished the call. He didn't tell Peggy that night. "I could not. And did not. I was so tired. . . . In a state of shock. I begged off helping clean up," as he would normally have done, and went to bed. In the morning, as he told her, she said "in good humor, 'I've known you for thirty-nine years. I've been married to you for thirty-six years and always suspected you weren't very bright. But I didn't think it was quite this bad.' "

THE *JOURNAL* WOULD DENY Armacost a dignified resignation. By Thursday, October 9, Hill and Schmitt had wind of the secret events going on at the bank and pressed every source they had to confirm the resignation and to confirm an incredible rumor about his successor. They ran the story, highly qualified, in the first edition on Friday, pressing the bank for more and more facts. By the three-star edition, they had it cold: BANKAMERICA'S BOARD TO REQUEST THAT ARMACOST QUIT, SOURCES SAY. The subhead held the blockbuster: SPECIAL MEETING SAID SLATED SUNDAY; POSSIBLE RETURN OF A. W. CLAUSEN IS SEEN. Prussia would leave with Armacost, retiring voluntarily, they reported. They still couldn't believe it. Clausen. Only a small handful, even in the bank, knew it yet. Other papers could only follow next day with unconfirmed stories. It had been a hell of a week, but Hill and Schmitt drove home happy. They'd scooped everybody, including Bob Cole.

ON WALL STREET, BankAmerica's stock closed Friday at $15, up from $14.25, after the morning announcement. The rise and fall of Sam Armacost had been summed up by the Street in a market move of 75 cents upward, a small, exhausted cheer.

"JUST TWO more years," groaned Adizes as he absorbed the news that Armacost was out. "He would have been a hero. The new Iacocca. He could have been the president of the United States!"

THE EVENING Armacost's resignation was announced, Claire Hoffman was watching KQED, San Francisco's PBS television station. She had given hours of her time and mountains of memories and opinions to interviewers who had come twice to Seven Oaks for a story on the problems at Bank of America. It was being screened tonight. As she watched the program, she grew furious. The news about Armacost's resignation had swept almost anything else away. There was only one brief picture of Claire. And most infuriating, Angelo Scampini—the lawyer Scamp, who had been the firebrand orator for her father during the Transamerica proxy battle and who, she believed, had later betrayed her father's trust—was on camera at great length, while A.P.'s daughter was cut out. She felt hurt and cranky most of the time now, as the distress and worry destroyed her sleep. And now "the Führer" was back.

THE IRONY DID NOT GO unnoticed that had Al Rice taken over from Clausen, he would have been hit with the same inherited problems and global economy. No matter how brilliantly or badly he had handled them, the era would have been hell, as it had been for all bank chiefs. Rice, now sixty-four and still seeking a business opportunity as satisfying as B of A had been, would have been moving into the twilight of his tenure, preparing to hand the scepter to Sam Armacost, who, by the end of the decade, would have been a seasoned veteran of deregulation taking over a bank ready, after the revolution of the eighties, for the statesman Adizes believed him to be. Armacost would have been barely fifty. Reflecting on his ouster three years later, Armacost would say, "Perhaps my timing was the mismatch."

As he heard of Armacost's sudden exit, Rice reflected on what might have been if he had grasped the brass ring in 1981, and said the same thing he had felt when he'd been denied in 1978: "Gosh, it would have been such *fun.*"

THE SPECIAL BOARD MEETING on Sunday, two days after the announcement of Armacost's ouster, was a painful requirement of the bylaws. The current president must preside over the appointment of the new president to make the transfer of power official. There were no farewells to the troops, no oratory of appreciation. The directors did not want to see Armacost's face any more than he wanted to see theirs. Everybody was "just so embarrassed," says Armacost, who performed his duty and left as quickly as he could. He guessed Clausen must be sitting in the anteroom, waiting to rejoin his old friends in the boardroom.

"It was just like a high school reunion," insiders reported of Clausen's return to the boardroom that day. He had scheduled his first management meeting next morning, "eager to get back to work."

PART FOUR

Chapter Eighteen

IT WAS AN ELECTRIC WEEKEND for American banking. Within the past two weeks Clausen had been reconstructed as leader of Bank of America and Pinola's offer sat on his desk awaiting an answer. As ten thousand bankers descended on San Francisco for the annual American Bankers Association convention October 25 to 29, 1986, those two events rose above all other issues, dominating the dozens of cocktail parties and dinners.

The dynamic ebb and flow of California banking power were expressed at the hors d'oeuvres tables. Within one block on Saturday afternoon, bankers and their wives strolled among Bank of America's, Wells Fargo's, and Security Pacific's gala welcoming receptions. Chauffeurs lounged against black limousines that lined the curbs flanking California and Montgomery streets. What last year had been simply elegant parties seemed, this year, shrewdly crafted challenges and statements. Wells Fargo, basking in the success of its Crocker merger and its emerging role as training ground for Bank of America's new ruling class, greeted guests with a costumed banjoist sitting atop the Wells Fargo wagon in the ground-floor museum, a reminder of western roots that went back beyond the Bank of Italy's. Greeting guests to the most lavish party of the afternoon upstairs in the corporate penthouse, CEO Carl Reichardt and

President Paul Hazen seemed to be taunting the troubled giant that could ill afford a toothpick.

Hosting in its main branch in San Francisco, Security Pacific—which would soon announce the widening of its already broad door on the Pacific Rim's financial action with the acquisition of Seattle's Rainier—laid out its California banquet of breads, cheeses, and fresh crab in the classic-columned banking halls that had been A.P.'s last headquarters at California and Montgomery.

Bank of America's party, lording it over the carpetbagging Los Angeles banks from the fifty-second-floor Carnelian Room, was a voyeur's paradise for bankers come to see the historic oddity of a CEO returned to the scene of the crime.

But the central action for bank watchers was First Interstate's brunch next day at the World Trade Center in the old Ferry Building on the docks—where Pinola stood aloof from the competitive partying downtown on the second floor of a building dwarfed by skyscrapers. A red carpet led from the curb, past the Diego Rivera murals lining the ramps up to the club. The food was not the main event; it was a down-home brunch Pinola might have brought with him from Pennsylvania coal country: biscuits, scrambled eggs, and smoke-cured hams. Eyes on eagle alert as he scanned the scene, Pinola focused briefly but with ferocious intensity on each of the bankers who waited with his well-groomed wife for a chat and a handshake. "No comment," he said with a smile when asked by reporters about Bank of America.

Reporters trailing him like a comet's tail, John Reed was trying to stay unobtrusive. It was Pinola's party. With neatly brushed brown hair and tweed sports coat over a slim, wiry build, Citicorp's CEO tried to fend off questions, saying quietly, "I have no intention at this time of bidding for Bank of America," but admitted, "I do have interest in some divisions." He politely moved away, saying, "Come on, fellows, I'm here to talk with people. This isn't the time for an interview."

In shock like the rest of the banking and financial community when he got word of Clausen's return, Pinola had called to congratulate his old comrade. With his offer caught in the crossfire of explosive events, Pinola had wanted to reaffirm the friendly nature of the proposal delivered October 3. Clausen had told him it would take a little time to get things sorted out and deal with the proposal; Pinola hated being put on hold. Listening in on the call in Pinola's office, Bill Sudmann had got the distinct impression that Clausen had not returned to work for Joe Pinola.

On Monday morning, the day after his party at the Trade Center, as bankers attended speeches and seminars, Pinola met quietly with his board at a special meeting in San Francisco and gained its approval to make a move to force Clausen to respond. Next day he sent a sweetened bid to Clausen, raising the value of his offer to $22 a share—a claim supported by an elaborate financial analysis that was packaged and sent to all the analysts.

"Mongrel securities" was how B of A's new chief financial officer, Frank Newman, condemned them in his response to Pinola's new offer. Pinola's team traces the beginning of the bank's hardening stance "to Newman's . . . comments back in October about our 'mongrel securities.' " He released his insult to the press for all the conventioneering bankers to read, angering Pinola.

A. Winship Clausen had come back to a bank under attack by an old comrade. He and his senior staff had been forced by Pinola's bid to do a swift and rigorous evaluation of B of A, "to look at what the company's prospects were as a stand-alone entity," says Newman, who joined the bank a week before Armacost was fired, "in order to be able to say to the shareholders either, 'We believe that it is in the best interests of the shareholders to talk with FIB [First Interstate Bank] and take this offer more seriously,' or, 'We think . . . the company has better prospects independently.' " Recovery was under way, they were persuaded, but, Clausen later told his shareholders, "When I returned in October, it was clear we needed to make a major effort to step up the pace of our recovery . . . the return to profitability." Why should they share that momentum with First Interstate's shareholders? From this accelerated self-examination came the conclusion that the bank would be better off without Pinola. Armed with this conclusion, Clausen put up his fists to any interloper who dared to threaten the sovereign and sacred independence of the Bank of America.

Appointed head of the task force formed to deal with FIB, Newman seemed the least likely combatant. He was a thin wraith of a man with reddish hair and mustache and a mild, academic manner. But he was known by his old team at Wells Fargo as brilliant, sound, and strong when he had to be. They had often had to wait for an answer, but "when it came, it worked." As chief financial officer at Wells Fargo until Armacost hired him away, a man voted best bank CFO in the nation, Newman arrived wearing the laurels of Wells's virtuoso integration of Crocker, the largest bank merger to date. Wells's reputation for management and profitability stood at a zenith that made it the darling of the analysts and the market—"the Citicorp of the West," said institutional investor Sam Marchese. Starting work the day after the board received Pinola's proposal, the week Armacost was fired, Newman arrived without clear orders. He and Armacost had had to dance around the details of the bank's condition and strategies in their interviews, for Newman was a very senior man in a competitor bank, and he might, or might not, join B of A. There was no time to study or analyze. He would have to earn his spurs in battle.

*   *   *

A WAR COULD BE very useful to Clausen. It could gather up diffused fear within the bank, the board, and the city of San Francisco and galvanize it into the will to beat a common enemy. It could divert attention from other problems. It would give him the opportunity to establish his own decisive posture, distinct from Armacost's, right at the start; he swiftly renamed the Armacost-initiated recovery strategies "our restructuring program." The big institutional shareholders were getting restive, as they sat with holdings of B of A stock selling at $16, while Pinola had offered $22. Clausen and Transamerica's Jack Beckett, one of his last appointees to the board, were back in harness together; they called Joe Pinola on November 3, in response to his sweetened package, and, in a very cautious call—well scripted by lawyers, Pinola's aides were sure—read Pinola a press release the board had just issued and asked him to read it with care. It snapped at Pinola for creating "an unnecessary impediment to the bank's progress," promised evaluation of his proposal, and, in the most equivocal of lawyer language, stated that "we aren't rejecting the First Interstate or any other proposal at this time." In the meantime, Clausen urged First Interstate to "withdraw its takeover bid." One of the team saw "Clausen was pushing Joe back." The Armacost days of "let's keep talking" were clearly over.

Next day, when the media picked up the press release, Clausen opened to the world what had been essentially a private dialogue. By revealing it, and asking Pinola to withdraw, Clausen had made First Interstate seem the aggressor simply by having its bid out there. A corporate communications officer who was at the front line from the day of Clausen's return says, "We had to go through the charade of saying that the board of directors had to weigh the offers, and so forth. In reality, from the first second, it was a defense in everyone's mind. . . . The whole process was fundamentally driven by lawyers."

Clausen's tactics came clear a day later, November 5, when the bank announced that it would sell Schwab. Clausen had called Schwab the same day he called Pinola to tell him the bank was trying to decide whether his discount brokerage was, in fact, a "core business"—the new term for any division it decided not to dump. For the bank's mission had been clarified during the urgent soul-searching of the first few weeks. Although Clausen claimed, "The globe is our market," he announced, "We will focus on the basic banking business which has been the cornerstone of this institution for more than eighty years." B of A would shrink its global presence and concentrate on the rich western market, targeting retail, middle market, and wholesale. And it would sell off all assets that were not part of the "core business." "We'd identified the California bank as our core business in '83, '84," says Armacost; he and McLin had already been aggressively divesting assets to feed regulators' demands for more capital. But shrewdly seizing the momentum, Clausen effectively made it his own.

"The capital ratio is what the regulators were looking at," he explained later. "We couldn't raise it in the market; with our stock so low, nobody'd buy it. We couldn't get it through earnings; we were losing money. So we looked at the other side of the equation—the asset side of the ratio. If you shrink your assets, you raise your capital ratio." He went at it relentlessly. Within two months, he would have shrunk the bank by $9 billion, then another $5 billion.

Asset dumping also served another purpose. It would make the bank less attractive to Pinola. The announcement of the Schwab sale was a declaration of war, a statement that Clausen was prepared to start selling crown jewels to beat Pinola. McLin lamented the sale of Schwab. It was "the first new thing that the bank had done since Giannini—maybe since credit cards." It was the prize Pinola wanted above all others. "I would not have sold Schwab," says Armacost.

The next barrage came from Cooper, giving a speech and press conference in London, a week after the press release. Now the instrument for Clausen's war machine, Cooper announced another five thousand jobs to be cut. And that the bank would sell Banca d'America e d'Italia, the Italian subsidiary, already in the works before Clausen returned. That divestment *did* fit the new foreign strategy to exit retail operations and concentrate on serving multinationals abroad—the strategy that had migrated from Latin America to become World Banking's worldwide strategy.

BUT IT DEEPENED the almost daily stabs to the heart being felt by Claire Hoffman and, now, by Russ Smith, A.P.'s first internationalist. A.P. had taken sixteen-year-old Claire out of Rosemary Hall to take her to Italy in 1919, when he bought the Italian retail bank that became Banca d'America e d'Italia. "I sold my stock when they announced they were selling it. I made a small fortune. It was very profitable," said Claire, emphasizing how valuable an asset was being dumped.

"I'm sorry they felt it necessary to sell the banking operations in Italy. . . . I thought they ought to put up a fight to keep it," said Russ Smith as he read of the continuing dispersal of the empire he had helped hold together in the great proxy fight. The bank was allowing the regulators to swing it by the tail as A.P. would never have allowed, Smith felt. "When it got right down to a case of survival, he was ready to fight to the last breath. And did."

* * *

THE DAY AFTER the November 5 announcement that the bank would sell Schwab, Steve McLin faced a barrage of phone calls from potential buyers. "The phones were literally ringing off the hook. Transamerica was very interested. Chrysler Financial. Ford." The Ford Motor Company, which had become one of the nation's financial services giants, had been a 20 percent owner of Schwab through its savings and loan subsidiary, First Nationwide. First Nationwide's Tony Frank had sold Ford's stake in Schwab at the time B of A acquired Schwab, and Frank was eager to ride with Schwab's fortunes again. Citicorp and Security Pacific were sniffing around. By early December there had been forty inquiries.

The buyback of his company Schwab had been planning since his resignation from the board now moved into high gear. Through communication with the bank Schwab had learned, to his horror, that "they wanted to put the company up for auction. With disclosure, everything we had would be laid out to the world. It would have put us at a competitive disadvantage for years. There was *no way* it was going to auction." There were two statements he wished to make, loud and clear, to Bank of America: "Let Chuck buy his company back and, second, *he will fight you tooth and nail.*" He proceeded to compose "my greatest symphony."

First forging a team of lawyers, he would put three kinds of pressure on the bank: peacemakers to negotiate for a friendly buyback, litigators to explore creative weaponry to back up the diplomatic effort, and a third team to structure the deal. The peacemakers would be Ronald L. Jacobson and Frank D. "Sandy" Tatum, Jr., of Cooley Godward Castro Huddleson & Tatum, Schwab's personal lawyers. Bartlett A. Jackson of Jackson Tufts Cole & Black would run the litigation path. To put a businesslike deal together, Schwab called on Lawrence B. Rabkin of Howard Rice Nemerovski Canady Robertson & Falk.

Hugo Quackenbush laughs. "As usual, we had no money, no assets. Service was all we had to sell." Schwab called in all his chips. His father-in-law, Joe O'Neil, and his good friend George Roberts, the leveraged buyout specialist, put in some cash. Schwab's senior staff contributed $16 million gleaned from a long-term incentive program, repayable at the buyback. And he turned to two legends in the restructuring of corporate America.

Junk bond king Michael Milken, since indicted on criminal charges of racketeering for securities fraud and insider trading at Drexel Burnham, flew up from Los Angeles. Milken was, Quackenbush says, "an absolute genius in understanding how to put value on *the customer as asset.* Our one million active customers were, in fact, our only asset."

But it was Roberts, the San Francisco–based partner in Kohlberg, Kravis,

Roberts and Company, the nation's most successful leveraged buyout (LBO) firm, who was hired. KKR had made LBOs—buyouts by a corporation's own management—an increasingly important restructuring technique; Schwab's would be, in effect, a management buyout. It was Roberts who came up with a "unique financing structure," which would prove more compelling to Schwab and more convincing to Bank of America than Milken's junk bonds. It gave B of A a 15 percent interest in the future appreciation of Schwab stock—the divorce would not be complete. This plan paid the bank a price, on paper, high enough to meet the "fairness" test, yet gave Schwab a cash flow of $47 million a year from depreciation of his assets over seven years and attractive stock warrants for all his shareholders, of which he was the largest.

As the structure—a thing of irresistible beauty in the eyes of Schwab's war team—took shape, the question was, would the bank buy it? In excited strategy sessions, Schwab's options, his leverage, were examined and reexamined. He even toyed with the idea of launching his own takeover assault, one scenario the *Journal* seemed to have overlooked. As a solution, Schwab knew, it was remote.

How much was his face worth? "They can sell the company, but they can't sell me," he said, guessing that without his face and persona, the bank would be selling an empty shell. No one knew how powerful a bargaining chip it was. Pinola's bid gave him another trump card, for it added urgency to selling Schwab as a "crown jewel defense," but it did not assure that Schwab would be sold to Schwab. He must position himself as the only buyer.

Out of the deep secrecy of the strategy meetings emerged the ultimate negotiating lever, a lawsuit against Bank of America that could damage the bank more than any defaulting LDC loans and could tie up any other suitor's bid, perhaps for years—a rescission suit that would seek to rescind and dissolve the original Schwab deal with the bank on the grounds that the bank had misrepresented its financial condition to Schwab. It was a harsh accusation, one that had already been made in shareholder lawsuits filed against the bank in federal court in 1985. Schwab drew the idea from his own painful experience. It had been a rescission order in Texas that had struck him such a devastating blow in the early seventies. Whether Schwab won or lost, if his lawsuit went ahead, defending it could consume such enormous resources and do such image damage that it could be incapacitating to the already wounded bank. "It's the last thing I want to do, to sue the bank," Schwab says, anguished. He estimated it would cost him at least a million dollars from his own pocket. "It was a minnow taking on a whale. But I was prepared to go to the wall on it," he says.

He quietly asked Tony Frank if, as a former shareholder, Nationwide Savings would join the suit. Frank ran it past Ford, Nationwide's owners. " 'Do you want to be part of the undoing of one of the major banks in this country?' I asked. They said, 'I think we'll pass on that,' " as rumors of Schwab's top secret rescission suit swept Montgomery Street's gossip mill.

The suit had not been filed. It existed only in draft. But through the old boy network the bank learned that Schwab was serious. On a weekend golfing date with George Coombe, Sandy Tatum discreetly let Coombe know that neither the rumors, nor Schwab, were to be taken lightly.

The suit that never was, says Quackenbush, was "the pawn the other side didn't see that put the king in check." But what won the game, he believes, was "the financing and the structure to complete the checkmate" that stood behind the threat.

The bank could fire him over the rescission suit. Through the fall of 1986, as Schwab's "greatest symphony" built to a crescendo, "it was incredibly tense. I was at maximum risk at all times. I knew I held *some* of the cards." He held his breath and made an offer to the bank.

STEVE MCLIN wanted to get away to Hawaii for his first real vacation in three years. He had decided to leave B of A, and wanted time to mull over options. Instead, he found himself in a crisis meeting on the Schwab issue. Roughly a dozen lawyers, investment bankers, regulatory specialists, and strategic planners had gathered that November to plan implementation of Clausen's orders to sell Schwab. Some had managed to rationalize selling Schwab as serving the higher purpose of keeping the bank out of the hands of Joe Pinola. McLin was not happy about being involved, "but when it went on the sell side, I tried to facilitate it." Bidders were pounding at the door. Bidding packages had been prepared and must be sent out to the bidders. But Schwab had reportedly threatened to sue once the bank started to solicit bids. What to do?

There was a faction, reportedly led by George Coombe and Frank Newman, that, some thought, gave off a message of willingness to sell Schwab "no matter how much of a licking we take." Newman, in command of the task force, clearly wanted his quarterly earnings to be as strong as possible as defense against Pinola. George Coombe, the bank's chief counsel, seemed to want Schwab gone to avoid any more embarrassment with the board. "George really hates Schwab. He sees himself as the protector of the board. Chuck was very disruptive, and I think George took it personally," says a participant.

Coombe, who appeared to have taken a lead role in expelling Schwab from the Weill board meetings, was all for suing Schwab, for launching a preemptive strike. The kind of macho response that had backfired so disastrously in the past, it would have put the board and the bank in even greater jeopardy. Coombe's idea was killed.

A growing faction favored selling Schwab to Schwab. As long as the rescission suit threatened, it could scare off buyers; it would have to be disclosed in marketing materials. And if Schwab filed his suit, "everybody's gonna get hurt," McLin reportedly said. "I think the way we get out of this sticky wicket is to give Chuck a chance to bid. As long as Salomon will render a fairness opinion on the competitiveness of Chuck's bid, we can avoid the bloodshed of a lawsuit." Give him a window to come up with a deal, an exclusive for a few weeks.

Schwab was tossed around the room like a hand grenade. He'd been trouble for so long. Finally, the group agreed to get rid of him. To sell Schwab to Schwab. The price would be critical. If it were too low, shareholders would scream that they had been sold out, and sue. Yet Schwab held some powerful bargaining chips.

McLin could not bear to go through the negotiations. He left them in the hands of an associate and took his wife on vacation. When he returned to his office in early December, he surveyed the trophies of the companies he had bagged, or sold, for the bank. On his desk and shelves sat a group of small plastic-encased tombstone ads from the *Journal* and SEC prospectuses, a graveyard commemorating the twenty-seven divestments and acquisitions he had made since Armacost gave him the job in 1981. FinanceAmerica to Chrysler. Decimus Corporation to General Electric Credit Corporation, April 22, 1985. A piece of BankAmerica Trust Company of New York to Security Pacific Corp., 1986. Epitaphs to the most sensational shrinkage in banking history. Monuments to capital ratios. Expedients to survival. To McLin, they were the sellout of Armacost's vision. With Schwab, and the loss of Orbanco to Security Pacific, the strategy was being compromised. His prized neutrality had been breached by being so visible a member of Armacost's palace guard, he feared; his critics saw his "little Switzerland" as the pose of a Teflon politician to whom his leader's problems had never stuck. He came back from vacation knowing he would have to leave or be forced out. "He saw the writing on the wall," says a colleague.

He had two final asset sales to complete before he left. On December 9 the bank announced it was selling a large chunk of its trust portfolio to Wells Fargo. As McLin met with Joe Perella to work out First Boston's handling of the sale of the Italian bank to Germany's Deutsche Bank, he told Perella, "Banca d'Italia is my last deal." A black leather notepaper holder engraved "BankAmerica Corp has sold Banca d'America e d'Italia to Deutsche

Bank AG. The First Boston Corp. December 1986" joined his collection of tombstones. When his resignation was announced January 13, 1987, he encompassed six years of high drama in a limp statement to the press: "BankAmerica's recovery along an independent path is well under way, and I have accomplished the personal goals and objectives that I established for myself."

McLin joined an old friend as president of America First Financial Corp—two floors above B of A's fortieth floor, where the past years' drama had played out—and set about raising $400 million in equity capital to buy two Northern California S&Ls, sating the appetite for acquisition frustrated at B of A.

JOE PINOLA was about to ruin Tom Clausen's Christmas. Angered by the rude dismissal of his proposal package as "mongrel securities" and feeling the urgency of the announced sale of Schwab, Pinola had asked his board on November 17 for approval to make an aggressive move: to file his tender offer with the SEC. Consensus among the Pinola team was that "the fact that we were going to file an S-4 with the SEC . . . was a hostile move. But we never intended to have the hostile move be the ultimate winner. We wanted to have the hostile method bring them to the table and then strike a friendly deal."

Pinola assigned his chairman, Edward Carson, to run First Interstate day to day, for he knew that he would be spending all his time from now on huddling in war rooms in New York, Los Angeles, and San Francisco. On December 15 First Interstate filed a registration statement with the SEC offering to buy 100 percent of the Bank of America. Pinola had launched a tender offer, the least tender act in the business world; he invited shareholders to sell their Bank of America shares to him, paying what First Interstate valued at $22 a share. With Bank of America stock selling at $12, the offer could not be ignored. It must be taken to the board and possibly to the shareholders. Four days later the Fed notified Pinola it would delay its decision on approval until April because of a technical concern over interstate banking. Delay or not, the clock was ticking.

FOR THE CONSUMMATE cost cutter, giving James Cerruti his $50,000 award for his product idea must have been painful. But on May 25, 1986, after a three-year struggle to keep his float product alive and have it implemented,

Cerruti had been flown to headquarters from Miami and presented by Tom Cooper with a certificate and a blown-up surrogate of his check. It was in character and somewhat ungracious, Cerruti thought, that Cooper cracked as he made the presentation, "I guess I'm going to have to give you the real thing, aren't I?"

It was the highest employee award the bank could give. But three months later Cerruti was gone, and was in Washington, D.C., job hunting. He had been resigned for some time that in a sick and shrinking bank, the hope of an assignment to the Athens branch that had drawn him to the bank eight years earlier was dead. But he had hoped to be rewarded for his product, and for the implementation of Young's strategy in South America, with the offer of at least an interesting and well-paid job. He was offered a job in New York that would have paid him "barely enough to feed the cockroaches." And he quit, subtly forced out by being relegated to limbo, like so many before him. His friend and ally Katherine Neville had left, too. They were only two of thousands leaving voluntarily or by force during the exodus. But the loss of Cerruti and Neville was a symptom that the bank was still unable to digest the creative maverick. And that, at all levels, good people were still leaving.

COOPER WAS KEEPING his head bent over his desk, hunting for more assets to sell and costs to cut. At first, Tom Cooper's role seemed stronger on Clausen's return. He was made president of the corporation, BankAmerica, the day Clausen was made CEO, another jewel in the coronet he already wore as president and COO of Bank of America. He sat on the two powerful committees that ran the bank: the Managing Committee and Money and Loan Policy Committee, which now held only two old BankAmericans, Bob Frick and Jim Miscoll. The bank was still in a hell of a mess. Clausen knew it. He had been brought back to do the decisive things Armacost was perceived not to have done. Like Armacost, Clausen still needed Cooper to do the radical surgery and shed the blood neither Armacost nor Clausen wanted directly on his hands. And yet the image Clausen was trying to promote was one of "healing." Cooper still believed that he was going to be redundant as soon as the "curing" process shifted to "healing"—from "turnaround" to "recovery." He went to Clausen and said, "Bring in your own team. Get your own plan. I'll help in any way I possibly can. But for goodness' sakes, whether it's today or any other day, we just don't have time for any politeness." The same kind of statement he'd made to Armacost.

But those close to the two men could see that Cooper's position was becoming undermined. Newman seemed to be getting closer to the throne, strengthening the Wells Fargo lock on top-tier power. Keeping their ears to the ground, Pinola's people concluded that "there's only one leader when Clausen's around, and that's Clausen. There was probably antagonism between the two. We heard soon after Clausen showed up that Cooper was going to be a scapegoat." They watched for signs or rumors of any erosion of Cooper's powerful mandate. Cooper had boldly restructured the World Banking Division, Clausen's creation. Cooper controlled the two most important operating divisions, retail and international, and the all-important computer systems reported to him. BAPS, the payments system, was still under his control, and he was following Armacost's strategy as he dismantled it. "There's no way Tom Clausen is going to allow anybody else to have that kind of power. He'll get it in his own hands," said a colleague.

The threat of takeover that colored every act and thought from December 15 revealed a fundamental difference between Cooper and Clausen in their attitudes toward corporations and corporate survival. To Cooper, it was not the name on the flag, or the heritage, or the shape and structure of the bank that were sacred; by whatever name, it was a corporate entity's ability to serve its constituencies well and to be efficient, profitable, and competitive. Cooper did not deal in emotional words like *shrink, decline,* or *butcher.* He saw the president of B of A not as a California Sun King, but as a player in the dynamic competitive process of shifting the management of corporate assets from weaker to stronger hands. He was a manager of assets, a deployer of resources, not a defender of the corporate faith. He did not care whether the architecture was marble columns or a computer terminal—or even if it was called a bank.

Clausen's defense of Bank of America would reveal a man who had made preservation of the bank's independence his sacred trust at a time when the crucible of corporate restructuring had made independence, per se, indefensible as a manager's goal. Armacost had showed that he understood that in his openness to merging with First Interstate, at the price of losing the president's seat. The bank's grand old man, Rudy Peterson, still influential as a nonvoting member of the board, echoed the "independence" theme: "Keeping Bank of America independent is what we're prepared to do." Pinola was highly "irritated" as he read in the *L.A. Times* Clausen's statement to the *Times*'s editorial board "that he was going to keep the bank independent at all costs. That's none of his damn business. That's a shareholder's business." Clausen's vow of independence came partly from his team's analysis that a stand-alone bank would be better for the shareholders. Mont McMillen, who had analyzed his mother's holdings in both First Interstate and B of A stock and concluded that a merger was in her best interests, believes the blocking of a merger served the self-interest of Clausen and his team trying to save their jobs. Clausen's statements and actions suggest motives that lay deep in psychic needs and feelings. They were the motives of a true BankAmerican, a man who claimed, "My whole life has been given to the bank. I'm a product of the bank." Much of his identity—his chance of redemption, his reputation in history—lay within it. To sell the bank, or see it broken up, would be like burning down his own house. The bank had always given loyalty. He would give it in return.

The two men, Cooper and Clausen, could not long coexist.

"Yet Clausen had tremendous respect for Cooper," says an observer who watched both at close range. "He thought that, of any voice on the Managing Committee, Cooper's was the most intelligent and the most *like* his. Clausen thought they were only different in small ways. And I think he . . . wanted him to stay badly. But Clausen knew he had a problem." As the wounded animal crawled back to its home den, the California branches, Clausen needed a new head of the retail bank. He was rumored to have identified Richard M. Rosenberg, already part of the B of A family in Seattle as president and COO of Seafirst, a well-regarded star of Wells Fargo's galaxy, and a legend in marketing lore. Most Californians knew Rosenberg's innovations, if not his name. Attacking the deposit drain caused by banks' low regulated interest on checking and savings accounts in the early seventies, he had issued a prestigious-looking gold card to customers, their passport to a "bundled" package of convenient services for which he charged a flat fee—the Gold Account. Looking at the plain and lowly checkbook as a marketing opportunity, he invented the scenic check sporting Wells's romantic stagecoach. Rosenberg was the "marketing genius" who stole 3 percent of California's consumer market share in nine months for Wells in 1973 by moving the passbook savings interest rate up to 5 percent—when other banks paid $4\frac{1}{2}$ percent.

When Armacost hired Rosenberg from Wells Fargo, part of the lure was the promise that he would have a crack at the top—at succeeding Cooley at Seafirst or running the California bank at B of A.

As an associate saw it, "Clausen's conundrum was: If I bring Rosenberg on with the things that Rosenberg wants, if I strike a deal with Rosenberg, this is going to put my relationship with Cooper at risk. I think Clausen was betting that Cooper would stay. . . . He knew Tom was the only one in the bank that had any kind of broad-based managerial capabilities in systems, marketing, and operations on the lending side. Clausen knew, 'I'm going to have to give him more money. I'm going to have to give him strategic planning. . . .' "

Cooper felt confident that he had earned "an undeserved amount of loyalty at the senior and executive vice-president level." But he was not sure he had done "a great job with the in-place brass." He had made enemies among those whose ankles he had nipped on his fast trip to the top, those who felt threatened. Whether from jealousy, the need for a scapegoat, or a political power play, the subtle process of isolating Cooper from power began.

ON JANUARY 5, 1987, Bank of America's board met and voted unanimously to reject First Interstate's merger proposal "after thorough and intensive review." It was the bank's official rejection, part of the ritual of grand struggles for corporate control. On January 6, Clausen called Pinola and said, as Pinola recounted it to his team, "Joe, I don't want to fight. Please go away. You're distracting us from our restructuring." He had issued fair warning.

The same day, Clausen unleashed his defense. Wearing a "FIB-busters" button, he took the stage of the Giannini Auditorium and, before three hundred employees, led a pep rally. In a delivery that was something less than Churchillian, he declared, "I'm going to wear this from here on out until they go away. The gloves are off." What his stolid delivery lacked was more than compensated for by the compelling imagery of his message: the historic rivalry between San Francisco and Los Angeles, growing more sensitive as Los Angeles undercut San Francisco's ambitions to be gateway to the Pacific Rim and hub of the West. He evoked the role of the bank in the history of San Francisco—as generous supporter of the community, as employer, as backbone of the city's economy. Pinola had repeatedly claimed that he would keep Bank of America headquartered in San Francisco. But fears lingered in San Francisco, a declining city's fears of domination by outsiders, of the city's talent and power being siphoned off to L.A. Clausen's cry to turn back the invader invoked BankAmerican values of loyalty, service, and patriotism, memories of the earthquake and of A.P.'s funding of the Golden Gate Bridge. It was the beginning of a campaign so well choreographed that Pinola's team would shake their heads and whistle with admiration.

But underneath the public bluster and buttons, the cheers and photo opportunities, the pep rally revealed Clausen's internal political strategy. An event full of jockeying and uncertainty for his senior staff, the rally was a clear statement by Clausen that he was in sole control of the ship. He took the stage alone and left his team to scramble for positions in the audience, letting rivalries sort themselves out. "It's a team defense. He ought to have his senior managers onstage. He's not the Lone Ranger," thought an observing vice-president.

It was now widely known within the bank that Dick Rosenberg would be the new head of retail, displacing Cooper in that important arm of the bank.

Rosenberg was still in Seattle and would not arrive until mid-April. But his presence in absentia raised the tension levels in the room. A close Cooper supporter felt near to panic. As Clausen entered the hall, there was Frank Newman at his heel; word flew that he had "finagled" to come down the elevator with Clausen. A group of executive vice-presidents was hovering close to Clausen, trying to stand within the circle of power. And there was Cooper, unobtrusively taking a seat in about Row 18, where a BAPS person had saved him a seat. As the hall began to fill up, the public relations officer assigned to Cooper asked Rhody, "Where shall Tom go?" Rhody, busy orchestrating the event, snapped, "Anywhere." Clausen was Rhody's assignment.

Over the next few months, Cooper, the ex-Methodist minister, devoted his pulpit oratory to the bank's holy cause with a fervor that rivaled Scamp's orations in the Transamerica proxy fight. But by January 6, at the pep rally, months before the press saw the signs, Cooper had been removed from the center of power.

Clausen's campaign was planned to look like a spontaneous ground swell of support for the bank. It was not. Rhody assigned the task force to identify all the constituencies that could help or that owed the bank a favor. Led by one of Clausen's old compatriots, George Skogland, retired head of personnel, the army of senior retirees who fill California's communities became the foot soldiers. They were gathered in for a rally, given specific assignments, and supplied with a flow of material from Corporate Communications. They would rouse other retired employees to talk up the Bank of America in their communities. They would remind mayors and supervisors of what a generous corporate citizen the bank had been, with documentation on the dollars spent on cultural and human services. "The suggestion was that if the FIB bid goes through, all of this is going to go away," said a member of the Corporate Communications staff. The campaign's goal was letters and public statements of support, local rallies, voting for the bank by doing business at B of A— anything that would focus public attention on the need to keep the Bank of America in San Francisco, and independent. One idea that almost made it was to have every retiree send a "Go home" postcard to Joe Pinola; they would smother Pinola under a mountain of sixty thousand postcards. The idea was dropped.

The bank's task force members searched history for press opportunities that would let them celebrate the bank and talk up the cause. Ah, they found a nugget that might have been overlooked in more peaceful times. The sixtieth anniversary of A.P.'s consolidation of the 175 branches of the Giannini-owned Liberty Bank of America with the Bank of Italy, the event that made Bank of Italy the third-largest bank in the United States and California's first statewide bank. The birth of statewide banking! Celebrations were planned for both Los Angeles and San Francisco, and resolutions designating February 19, 1987, as "Bank of America Appreciation Day" were presented by the two mayors, Tom Bradley in the south and Dianne Feinstein in the north. Celebrating the resolution in Los Angeles, the bank's "Mr. L.A.," Jim Miscoll, was in his element. In San Francisco, at a ceremony at A. P. Giannini Plaza beside the black "banker's heart" sculpture, Dianne Feinstein disarmed the task force with a rousing speech asking support of the bank as a gesture of appreciation for the support the bank had given the city over the years. A vivacious and forceful speaker, she cited a few specifics: $12 million in contributions to civic causes and $7 billion in city bonds and notes underwritten by B of A.

She had not been asked to say it. The mayor had been supplied with informational material before her speech, but she was responding spontaneously. Calculatedly or intuitively, Rhody's task force had found the right chord to play at this time in the city's history. Feinstein had made many trips to Asia during her two terms as mayor and understood well that California sat as fulcrum to Pacific Rim trade and finance, and that her city's position in that future was increasingly uncertain. She had appointed Clausen to a blue-ribbon committee formed to study ways to regain economic vigor. Her husband, entrepreneur Dick Blum, even made a gallant offer to try to raise a billion dollars for the bank, an idea dreamed up by the Blums' worrying at home one night about the plight of the bank. An initiative that was made and rebuffed within a week, Blum's gesture was an act of family solidarity that revealed a strengthening feeling of protective concern for the bank. The bank's internal polls were showing that nearly half of all Californians refused to do business with the bank. But as the campaign gathered steam, Bank of America was being transmuted from a for-profit financial enterprise founded by a hard-headed capitalist into a local, national, and even international treasure. It had briefly transcended the negative to become metaphor for a city fighting for a viable place in the twenty-first century.

A JAPANESE NEWS AGENCY broke the rumor. Clausen had unofficially asked for "financial assistance from Japanese banks," reports said. Raising capital in Japan was potentially a far more explosive issue than any merger with Joe Pinola, for it suggested the loss of control of the bank to the nation fast surpassing the Red Menace as America's perceived threat beyond the gates. But with public attention focused on saving the bank from Los Angeles, the item passed without a ripple as Clausen extended his anti-FIB message, carrying it to the editorial board of the *L.A. Times*. Finally reversing his stubborn denials that the bank needed any capital beyond that generated by asset sales and its own earnings, Clausen had "strongly hinted that a portion would be raised overseas." But he all but denied it would come from Japan.

If the Japanese proved reluctant, it could also be deeply humiliating for the bank whose Tokyo office and industrial loans in the wake of World War II had led the international banking community in support of Japan's reconstruction.

Clausen's planned trip to Japan in the late spring had nothing to do with raising capital, affirmed his spokesmen. Clausen had an award to receive. More anniversaries to celebrate. Above all, he had a war to fight back home.

PINOLA WAS FIGHTING back with his own public relations campaign. He admired Feinstein for standing up for a major corporate citizen. "I would hope Tom Bradley would support First Interstate in that kind of situation." He met with the editorial boards of both newspapers in San Francisco, received a polite hearing from Mayor Feinstein. And, to everyone, emphasized that he would keep the headquarters in San Francisco. He had his own history and heritage to promote: the old Transamerica connection; the bonding again of sibling banks. The great strength the merged entity—and San Francisco— would have.

But some of his maneuvers were being repulsed. It was hard to gain shareholder support. "A.P. was so smart," said a First Interstate officer, "when he sold stock, he never wanted to have his stock go into concentrated hands. He wanted to have the little person out there have stock ownership in his company. It's a very effective way to disperse power." As a result, B of A is two-thirds retail-owned—that is, individual owners—and one-third institutional, the investors whose huge blocks of pension fund stock can be manipulated. Pinola had commitments from most of the institutional investors who saw a nice run-up of the stock with a Pinola takeover. But the small shareholders who held two-thirds—an unprecedented ratio in today's market—were loyal to the bank. Bank of America's campaign was aimed at solidifying that loyalty, so that they would not sell to Pinola. It would be almost impossible to break them free and win control in a proxy contest.

There were events in Sacramento that suggested to Pinola's team the long arm of Citicorp entering the game. Powerful speaker of the State Assembly, Willie Brown, under attack by a group of his fellow assemblymen for flagrant abuse of his power, had brought to the Assembly on November 11 an emergency bill that, as the *Wall Street Journal* described it, "will push emergency state legislation to allow Citicorp and other large institutions to bypass existing interstate banking bans and bid on B of A." Intelligence Pinola's team was getting informed it that Brown had been royally hosted and partied in New York by the big banks, including Citicorp. And regulators had discreetly leaked to the press that if B of A were to be merged, they would prefer its partner to be a larger, better capitalized bank than First Interstate.

The market was not responding well. First Interstate's stock had tumbled from $67 in early 1986 to as low as $50 at the end of the year. It had risen since the December SEC filing, and had bounced between $52 and $61 in early 1987, as Bank of America's investment advisers fanned debate over the real worth of the securities Pinola would be offering.

Pinola had been angered when Clausen said about First Interstate, "I'm not impressed with their management." Pinola had tough skin, but dare to attack his team! "I got mad at Tom when he said things like that about our people," he says. "We taught some of the First Interstate managers everything *they* know. But we didn't teach them everything *we* know," Clausen had said in L.A. "Thank God," Pinola snapped back to his associates, a line that would be incorporated into a videotape for his employees explaining his merger plans. But what Pinola found "reprehensible" was Clausen's flip comment to a reporter who asked why B of A had sold the Banca d'America e d'Italia when it made $36 million a year: "Well, it doesn't take a genius. . . . In 45 seconds, I can tell you how I could make $36 million by investing [the money] at 6%." Pinola says, "What he doesn't tell you is that the profit that you make on the sale of an asset is capital and that capital in our business is leveraged. You leverage it eighteen, nineteen, or twenty times. He cannot leverage it. He needs it to support that pile of junk loans. . . ."

Pinola was a smart banker and knew Clausen's stubbornness well. He may have sensed that Clausen's resolve to fight was hardening with every day. For as '87 began, there were the first traces of what, by the end of the first quarter, would be contained excitement among Clausen's inside circle that the bank was going to make it. "I never felt overwhelmed," says CFO Frank Newman, "but my sense that 'this bank is manageable' started to emerge in early 1987. If you just read the printed profit and loss, it was very difficult to tell what was happening in the underlying trends, but we could start to see it. The company was still losing money, but losing *less* money." With Clausen lecturing his team "not to overpromise, but maybe overdeliver. Hell hath no fury like an analyst misled," Newman began, cautiously, to articulate the fragile sense of progress to analysts and the press. Analysts were still jumpy; the press was still locked on to the drama of decline. "But," says Newman, "I got an increasing sense of confidence that the trend was going to, in not too long a period of time, cross the curb from the red into the black"—an event that would indeed occur within the year.

At a board meeting in San Francisco on January 20, Pinola told his board that things were not going well and that he might exit at some point.

"They're selling bits and pieces of the company, and it's becoming less and less attractive to us, because rather than cutting out the cancer, they're cutting out the muscle."

The last straw was the sale of Schwab. On February 1, Schwab announced that he had succeeded in buying back his company, ending a campaign Quackenbush would remember as "more exciting than anything I've ever read about in corporate history books." Having suddenly become B of A's "crown jewel defense" against Pinola had speeded negotiations for the buyback. There had been a handshake by Christmas. A written document was ready by the end of January; it would be signed March 31, 1987, an even greater day for Schwab than the day he went on line. He had struck a price of $230 million—or $280 million, depending on how one interpreted the conditions of the deal—roughly five times what he'd been paid, but far lower than many analysts thought Schwab & Co. was worth. In real terms, he had paid only $190 million for the buyback. Those who knew of the rescission suit speculated that the threat of that suit had let him lever the price down. Schwab got the remedies of his lawsuit through an artificially low price, observed banker Carl Schmitt in Palo Alto.

That was it for Pinola. Schwab was the asset he wanted most. His secret weapon, purchase accounting, had been seriously undermined by the asset sales. He had watched as Wells Fargo used the device with brilliant success in its merger with Crocker, raising net margins and improving earnings. Pinola triggered his exit strategy.

Early on February 9, Sudmann and Griffith flew to San Francisco Airport, met the head of the S.F. Fed, Bob Perry, in the United Airlines Red Carpet Lounge, and told him they were dropping their bid. Then they flew back to Los Angeles in time for a 10:00 A.M. special board meeting. Pinola told his board, and then the press, "We didn't run. We exited." It was the most painful moment of his thirty-eight-year career in banking. "The easiest thing to remember was the hardest thing I had to do. And that was exit. . . . We had worked very, very hard."

"I'm one manager who wants to win the war, and not every battle," Clausen had said. "My whole career has been winning." He had won the war.

THERE WAS A personal war Pinola still wanted to win. On April 9, his black limousine pulled up to the corner of Columbus and Green streets in San Francisco's North Beach neighborhood, hallowed ground for the Bank of America. A.P.'s original bank had stood just two blocks away. Accompanied only by his PR aide, Paul Minch, Pinola entered one of the surviving bastions of the Italian community, the Fior d'Italia restaurant; he moved purposefully through the animated lunchtime crowd to a private dining room and slipped into his place at the head of the table. This was the monthly lunch of Il Cenacolo, a club of Italian men founded in 1928 by Giannini and his cronies. Most of the members are lawyers, small businessmen, doctors, and bankers. But a few are living links with A.P.; to this day, Bank of America's CEO is an honorary member.

As petrale sole and veal sausages were washed down with Louis Martini's cabernet, eighty-nine-year-old Salvatore Reina breathed life into the 1931 Transamerica proxy fight, telling his tablemates, "When Walker was trying to liquidate the whole banking empire built up by A.P., a call went out which everybody in North Beach heard. I was in my pharmacy that morning, and I grabbed my friend and went down to Montgomery Street to the third floor of the bank. There was A.P. at his desk, right out in the open, and he said, 'How can I help you gentlemen?' and I said, 'What can we do to help you?' He told us, 'There's a meeting on downstairs right now. Get to it!' " Reina had fought at the heart of the proxy fight, put to work by Angelo Scampini—the famous Scamp, now eighty-eight, and still a regular at Il Cenacolo's lunches.

Il Cenacolo's president, attorney David T. Giannini, tapped his spoon on his glass, taming the noise. It was time for the speech. Pinola's eyes darted over the group like a warrior's taking measure of the enemy before he engages them in battle. He was deep in Giannini territory. He—an Italian, a BankAmerican—had defected and attacked MotherBank. Building his story with care and wit, he set the scene of battle, giving the men a breathtaking gallop through the minefield of deregulated banking. He flattered a Giannini family member, and exchanged spirited barbs with a Wells Fargo man, turning a rival into a delighted straight man. Then he cut to the heart of the story they had come to hear: "The merger of the two banks would have created a stronger B of A. It would have given B of A, rather than a California presence, a multistate presence, extending the tradition and life goal of A. P. Giannini, who fought for interstate banking until he died." "If we had merged," he added, as chests swelled, "the flag of Bank of America would have flown over eighteen states."

"But our bid was treated as a joke," he said, socking the bank with a velvet glove. "I didn't want this to be a hostile fight. . . . But they did a brilliant job of PR—brilliant! They made the whole city feel as if the survival of the city depended on the survival of this bank." Seizing the warm sentiment that rolled toward him, Pinola declared in his commanding baritone, "This is where the bank's home, the bank's roots, are. *We would not have moved the bank from San Francisco!*"

He closed with a disarming admission of defeat. "There was a man called A. P. Giannini who believed in branch banking . . . and there was a man called Pinola, also an Italian, who believed in branch banking. But he didn't fare so well." Not one hostile question followed his speech. As the final question came—"Is the deal still there?"—Pinola responded with an enigmatic smile and left as unobtrusively as he had come. He had won the war in North Beach.

But, as if punishing him for daring to mess with MotherBank, the next few years would be a time of trial for Pinola. His soaring headquarters in downtown Los Angeles was swept by a spectacular fire; Pinola stood on the sidewalk and watched his bank burn like the building in *The Towering Inferno*, the movie that had used B of A's headquarters in San Francisco as its model. He rented temporary space in an office tower that still looked down on B of A, shoring up an ego under assault. Don Griffith left. Paul Minch died. Pinola's hastily acquired Texas bank, Allied Bancshares, was suffering grim losses. Analysts' impatience with First Interstate's lackluster performance increased. Pinola still commanded the eighth largest bank holding company in the United States, but he seemed unable to realize the potential of his incomparable banking franchise. As time beat toward his retirement in June 1990, Pinola's hopes of leaving the imprint of a giant on his page in banking history faded. But where Clausen, in 1981, had polished the numbers to add luster to his legacy, Pinola proceeded to bite the bullet. He sold the bad Texas loans, taking losses. He raised capital in the market, risking the ire of shareholders by diluting the stock. He did costly restructuring to position his team to achieve his own failed dreams. Pinola, a man of legendary ego, would leave banking without arrogance.

THE KISS OF DEATH for Cooper was a major profile in the *Wall Street Journal* on April 30, telling a nation of *Journal* readers: BANKAMERICA'S COOPER UNDER PRESSURE. Relentlessly describing the erosion of Cooper's power, it was a story that illustrated the perception-shaping power of the press. The decision to go with a major story on Cooper on his way out was made, finally, because the story was, by all the evidence, irrefutably there to report. But blazed across the daily profile page, the story reinforced itself.

Cooper resigned within two weeks of the *Journal*'s obituary. His presence lingered on in publications that were in the works before he left, too late to stop. Clausen would name him, in the 1987 annual report, as one of the "key executives who are directing BankAmerica's turnaround." In the first-quarter 1987 *BankAmerican*, he had a by-line story on the "securitization" of loans, a technique pioneered by BankAmerica in the late seventies, when it packaged mortgages and credit card receivables into tradable securities and sold them. It was a revolution in lending, moving banks "from the traditional role of originating loans and holding them to maturity to a new role of originating loans, packaging them, and selling them in various forms to other investors in new markets," said Cooper.

As the momentum of securitizing gripped third world loans, Lew Coleman, World Banking's credit chief, cautioned, "I think that selling off your loans is the right thing to do for your shareholder and the wrong thing to do for the country. . . . Our shareholders no longer have the overhang, but somebody else still owns the debt, and the country still owes a hundred cents on the dollar to the new holder of the debt. The problem hasn't gone away for the country."

But in securitization Cooper had found a welcome new source of capital for the bank. It freed banks' money from being tied up in loans, gave banks unprecedented liquidity. It was the kind of redeployment of assets that was the essence of Cooper's sense of himself as a manager.

Those who think Clausen wanted Cooper to stay are in the minority, but an associate who watched the final drama at close range believes that Cooper's quitting was a "misjudgment" on Clausen's part—that Clausen had believed he could keep Cooper running the operations side of the bank. Cooper left the Bank of America with dignity; he did not hurl bitter epithets behind him as he closed the door. He left the same way he had left the ministry in 1964: "I had no job. Simply resigned." Departing without a severance package, he left with something of the aura of the ascetic forsaking worldly goods to wander off in quest of his next calling, a calling that now commanded $500,000 a year. He surprised bankers by bypassing an expected appointment to a major bank, perhaps the Mellon Bank he had left, to enter the trenches of the financial revolution. On July 1 Cooper became chairman of the board and CEO of ISFA Corporation in Tampa, Florida, a company that operates "a full-service brokerage program for banks."

For the first time since Beise and Peterson shifted the fast track to corporate "wholesale" banking in the 1960s, the highest prestige reigned in B of A's California bank. The retail bank had been such a dead end that Clausen had not permitted his two protégés, Rice and Armacost, to run it as both had wanted to do. Following the lead of Wells Fargo, Clausen was betting the bank on making California and western regional retail banking the "core business," with international operations diminished. The bank's "global network," celebrated two years earlier, was being downplayed as the strictly wholesale, tightly targeted market strategy replaced it. It was part of the shakedown occurring among the large regional banks, as they were faced with two choices: concentrating their resources on dominance in the rich regional markets or becoming as big and omnipotent internationally as an American Express or Citicorp.

Achieving the latter would be daunting. The cost of success in capital markets and electronic services internationally was so high that the Treasury Department had concluded that America may need to create a new breed of "megabanks—giant banks in combination with large industrial companies"— to hold its own against Japan. Paul Volcker, however, told Congress, "No, we're a long way from that. . . . We do not have to go out and deliberately create something called 'megabanks.' "

With one of the old guard, Bob Frick, running World Banking, and the dynamic Rosenberg in retail, a change had come to MotherBank. Talent, which had been pulled from the branches since the early sixties, was now being focused there. No matter how successful Clausen's recovery, it would be years, if ever, before a grand global presence would be more than a dream for B of A. Coleman was working effectively within World Banking on the job of credit quality. But the biggest bank in the world was finally biting the bullet of pride; it would join the ranks of the superregionals where the best returns on assets, and relative freedom from the albatross of third world debt, lay.

Chapter Nineteen

"WHAT DO I THINK of Dick Rosenberg?" Mellon Bank Corporation CEO Frank Cahouet said. "The day he went to B of A, I bought the bank's stock."

Any last illusions that branch officers were still traditional bankers would fall quickly under this powerful marketing-oriented executive. Rosenberg would run the retail bank with a very different style from Jim Miscoll, who had passed through as commander of the retail bank in 1983 and '84, the days when Miscoll fought back blossoming troubles by declaring, "Watch out, everybody. MotherBank is back!"

From Los Angeles, he gloried in the bank's "rebirthing"—his lyrical term for the anticipated turnaround. Yet it was clearly the old values Miscoll personified. Miscoll had been sent south by Sam Armacost in late January 1985, and his appointment as executive officer–Southern California had been a superb eleventh-hour solution to the conundrum of how to respond to Miscoll's critics without losing his incredible style. "I am the missing link," Miscoll said, laughing.

On the afternoon of May 12, 1987, just two weeks before the annual meeting, the job at hand for Miscoll was to squire Dick Rosenberg around the fifty-first floor. Rosenberg was here on his first get-acquainted visit since taking over retail operations in mid-April. He was also a leading contender for Clausen's throne. In the ruling clique Clausen was creating, the only Bank-American within striking distance was Bob Frick—and Frick was hung with the image of indecisiveness. Newman, Coleman, and Taylor, the rest of the Wells team, all were gaining strength. But the man who would stand at Clausen's left shoulder in the 1987 annual report portrait was Rosenberg.

Guided by Miscoll, Rosenberg moved confidently through the rich carpets and Asian antiques, shook hands graciously, eyes alert and engaged. He carried a briefcase and wore a discreet dark suit. But he had more the style and look of a ring-wise boxer. His compact body, broad face, and short, spring-curly hair bespoke a package of contained energy, ready to explode at the bell. He was known for delivering aggressive marketing strategies, not aphorisms, Miscoll's specialty. The differences in styles of the two men was a striking summation of the revolution in cultures that had taken place within the bank.

In a setting of tapestried wing chairs, emerald green velvet settees, and leather-bound classics, Miscoll was a grace note in the L.A. glitz. Balding, with a round, sensuous face, and dressed like an ad for *Gentlemen's Quarterly,* Miscoll came as close to jaunty as dignity would allow. Entertaining important clients and foreign visitors with courtly charm, he brought ebullience and erudition to his task. "These are my friends," he says, of the six-foot shelf of Great Books that sat on his office bookshelf; he carries them "up here" when he travels, he says, pointing to his head. He kept extra copies of the collected sayings of A. P. Giannini at hand and recited them verbatim. Jesuit-schooled and a Bank of America history buff, he has framed on his wall the resolution from the city of Los Angeles and the state of California honoring the sixtieth anniversary of "the formation of California's first statewide system of branch banking," the resolution that had given Miscoll a classic opportunity to celebrate MotherBank in the midst of the First Interstate battle. A rough translation of the word *renaissance,* "rebirthing" is a word far more befitting this man than Clausen's word *recovery,* with its implications of surgery and strong medicine, or the efficiency-driven, buzzwordy *restructuring.* Rebirthing was a process going on not just in Bank of America but across corporate America, Miscoll claimed, "but we've been doing it for six years. We're almost *finished.* Others like GM and IBM are just starting their rebirth—we're way ahead!" Supporting the Clausen party line with the fervor of a true believer, he said, "What we have to do is get back to the core business the bank was founded on. Some of these young managers came in and took us out in other directions." Issuing a pointed caution to fallen leaders perceived to have violated the founding ethic, he recited his favorite aphorism, said by A.P. in 1928 to the *San Francisco Examiner:* "Golf may be all right in its right place for the man who enjoys it. But I contend the man who leaves his office twice or three times a week at two o'clock to spend five hours on the links is creating an astonishing economic burden." Miscoll looked up, eyes twinkling mischievously, and smiled. "Isn't it amazing? I just happened to open to that page."

THE ANNUAL MEETING offered the world a snapshot of the new hierarchy, as Clausen and his senior team took their seats on the podium of the Masonic Auditorium on May 28. Unlike the pep rally, here he would face the anger of the shareholders with Frick, Glenhall Taylor, Newman, and Rosenberg at his side. All except Frick were from Wells Fargo; at the next year's meeting Frick would be gone, replaced as head of the World Banking Group by Lew Coleman, leaving the Wells Fargo group in command at the tier below the leader. There had been a flush of gossip as Rosenberg was leapfrogged over Frank Newman to be made vice-chairman and a new member of the board. Although still very visible and a rumored candidate in the race to succeed Clausen, Newman had not been put on the board. Rosenberg's prominence confirmed that, fourteen years after Wriston had "looked in the mirror and seen the future," as Armacost had praised Wriston's pursuit of the American consumer, Clausen had rediscovered him, too.

But events of the past few months had forced Clausen to lift his eyes abroad. On February 20, 1987, Brazil blindsided the banks by declaring a moratorium on interest payments on its foreign debt. The banks termed it a "temporary moratorium," but there was no promise of a date when payments would resume. The act was unprecedented. Smaller, less developed countries had declared moratoriums in the past, but a moratorium by "a country of that stature, a wealthy country, a country that in the last thirty years has achieved a growth that in GNP terms, in *real* terms, of six and a half percent—*more than any other country in the world*," as Clausen saw Brazil—was unprecedented. A complex of global and domestic economic factors had sent Brazil's inflation rate out of control and the country into acute financial crisis. Austerity programs imposed by the International Monetary Fund in the past were so hated that any Brazilian government that tried to impose the IMF's or its own invited collapse. Finance Minister Dilson Funaro's Cruzado Plan had just failed; Funaro risked being ousted.

For the bankers, the fear was that ICERC, the three-agency regulatory group that examines the creditworthiness of foreign debtors, might, at its next twice-yearly meeting, declare Brazil "classified," forcing the Comptroller of the Currency to intervene and order the banks to raise their reserves to a level that would wipe out Bank of America's capital. This potential touched on one of the most dangerous aspects of the Latin debt: Among the nine money center banks, debt exposure equaled far more than 100 percent of the banks' primary capital—their capital *plus* reserves. With all the banks building their capital as well as reserves, the ratio had been reduced from a high of 209 percent in 1983 to 147 percent by the end of 1986. But it still meant that even Citicorp—rich enough to take a $3 billion hit—would, with its foreign loans valued at 137 percent of its primary capital, be wiped out of capital and declared insolvent if the worst should occur—a default of, say, two or three of its largest debtors.

Sam Armacost had been steadily raising capital and reserves and had reduced that gaping ratio more than any other of the major banks; by the end of 1986 B of A's loans were 108 percent of its primary capital, compared with Chase's 125 percent, for example. But if Mexico, alone, were to default, B of A would lose nearly 40 percent of its primary capital. The fear was that one default would start a chain reaction.

On May 19, just a week before B of A's annual meeting, Citicorp's John Reed declared his $3 billion loan loss reserve, taking a massive hit to his balance sheet. Now the herd must follow. A week later Chase Manhattan pledged a $1.6 billion reserve.

THE PRESSURE on Clausen to raise his reserves was explosive as he faced the aggressive and hostile questions of press and shareholders when the annual meeting convened. "This is how the Christians must have felt when they were getting ready to go into the colosseum," Clausen cracked as he opened his press conference just before the meeting, getting no laughs at all. Anticipating questions about Chase's announcement the day before that it would take a hit, he repeated "that our reserves are adequate." He was testy about Brazil when KCBS radio asked, "If I didn't pay back my debts, you'd take my house. What are you going to do to Brazil?" Clausen said with grim imperiousness, "I am unaware, sir, that Brazil is contemplating defaulting on its obligations. To the contrary, Brazil officials . . . have not in the slightest way indicated a default on its obligations." But, he admitted, "perception also drives actions in the real world. . . . And there has been a conceptual change, principally caused by the very fact that Citicorp and Chase have made these moves." That is why, he said, B of A had been steadily increasing its reserves. And, obviously, why, while denying that his upcoming "strictly ceremonial" trip to Japan had anything to do with raising capital, he told the reporters that he would not be distressed if "there should be some interest" in a B of A stock issue.

Anticipating the brouhaha awaiting Clausen in the auditorium, John Broder of the *L.A. Times* asked, "What are you going to tell shareholders whose stock is trading around eleven or twelve dollars today when they ask you why you turned down First Interstate's offer, which they claim was worth twenty-one or twenty-two dollars a share?" Clausen chose his words carefully, knowing that that decision, too, was already the stuff of lawsuits. "It was determined that it's in the best interests of our shareholders to reject that offer when our book value is much higher than our market value. And furthermore, the so-called merger First Interstate was proposing was absolutely dependent upon the turnaround of B of A. And why give up, say, sixty percent of the benefit of that turnaround to First Interstate's shareholders? It's *our* shareholders who've been taking the beating."

The reporters' straightforward questions were gentle barbs compared with the unsheathed swords he would face in the meeting. Moving with his entourage from the press conference toward the restless crowd in the auditorium, he said, "Just remember, no shooting." He had prepared himself for the assault as best he could. "Having read the transcript of the two previous shareholder meetings, I recognized that there had to be a tremendous amount of frustration. So let the frustration come out rather than try to chop it off," he had decided. But he wasn't looking forward to it. "I don't like to be attacked. But I know the buck has to stop somewhere. . . . And so the chairman has got to take the punishment, for whatever reason."

He delivered an earnest stump speech to shareholders, then unleashed the questions from the floor. Anne McWilliams, who had held her B of A stock while Claire Hoffman sold hers, had kept her chin in her hands, looking skeptical, as Clausen spoke. But as the bombardment of criticism was lobbed from the floor, she began to twist her hands and worry her gold necklace. Claire had not come, and Anne—tanned and tawny-haired, wearing a red silk dress and high black heels—was a handsome representative of the family. But her nervous hands revealed the pain of being a Giannini at this time.

Clausen was put on notice by Emil Rossi, a hardware store owner and leader of the Eight Balls rube band that plays each year at the Mendocino County Fair in rural Boonville a hundred miles north of San Francisco, that he and the board had best prepare for a long session. "Last year they tried to close the meeting while there were still people who wanted to talk. Your obligation is to stay and hear every shareholder. They own the company. For one short afternoon it behooves them to stay." Today shareholders would have their first chance to vent rage at the man they suspected of fathering many of the problems.

Clausen was assailed for turning down the First Interstate bid without giving shareholders a chance to bid. He was damned for selling the consumer trusts, for dumping assets, and for permitting the lavish severance package paid to

Armacost. "You're rewarding *lack* of success instead of rewarding success" was followed by cheers and applause. "If you're worth a darn as our leader, you must prove it to us. Mr. Clausen, you will work for fifty thousand dollars a year until you restore earnings growth and dividends," said Emil Rossi's son, Nick, as even louder cheers rang through the hall.

"The severance packages to which you allude are not abnormal for the industry," Clausen responded, to boos, "and there is *no* severance for Mr. Cooper."

There were rumbles over the proposal to be voted on that would guarantee board members immunity from responsibility for their actions. "They want protection so they won't be *sued,*" shouted a shareholder, fed up that "coming here every year is like getting brainwashed. 'Boy, do we have a plan for you.' *Please,* don't give us any more help!"

Clausen held his temper, fielding the questions with mannerly answers. But his efforts at striking a friendly bond failed. "I'm a shareholder, too," he said with a chuckle at one point, "and I came back."

"Why *did* you come back!" was yelled from the floor.

A Berkeley shareholder probed the larger issue, "In the seventies you went outside your basic lending experience. You knew your customers, and they knew you. What role did you play in leading the bank away from its loan experience? It seems to me that's where the bank went astray."

Clausen tried to set his actions in context: "As an international institution, part of our future was moving capital around the world; it's a tremendous market for the future."

But in the emotion of the meeting, few shareholders grasped that what Clausen next went on to describe was a stunning shrinkage of the bank's vision of itself from those great days of the seventies. It was stark abandonment of the boasts and promises that had beguiled shareholders each year in his, and Armacost's, glossy reports. In his last report in 1980 Clausen had delivered record results with the projection that Armacost, his successor, "will lead this corporation to new and higher levels of achievement in the decades ahead." Armacost had continued to claim in 1985's report: "We will be the leader among the world's financial institutions." Yet Armacost had also understood and argued the thing Clausen now admitted to the shareholders as he officially declared Bank of America's long self-delusion extinct: "*We can no longer be all things to all people all over the world.*"

Clausen had let the anger flow, and by four o'clock, energy was spent, the balcony was nearly empty, and the last harangues had been heard. His final attempt to rouse excitement over the goals of "recovery" at the end of the question period sounded canned and unconvincing. "It's so easy to see the blood and the red ink. But there's nothing wrong with the B of A that can't be fixed. We are taking steps . . . to return to preeminence once again." He went out with a whimper after a terrible afternoon and turned to the voting.

When the votes were cast, the board and all its proposals were over-whelmingly approved. The deep reservoir of loyalty had flooded over and drowned out the voices of dissenters. It had been an awful meeting. But the vote had revealed that the persisting need for the B of A myth was still so strong that shareholders would close their eyes and suspend reality rather than give it up—as the Stanghellini sisters and the city of San Francisco had. If "recovery" was rooted in rebuilding the California constituency, the power of the mythic image was still a powerful weapon.

On June 8 Clausen made an announcement that tested loyalty even further: Bank of America would add a $1.1 billion allowance for credit losses. He was taking the hit. The corporation was drained of salable assets. He *must* raise capital.

CLAUSEN HAD CALLED even ninety-three-year-old Russ Smith from retire-ment for the trip to Japan a week after the meeting. The trip had several official ceremonial purposes. Clausen would be honored for contributions to Japan with Japan's highest award to foreigners, the Grand Cordon of the Order of the Sacred Treasure, although the award would be presented by the Japanese ambassador in Washington in November. And the fortieth anniversary of the Tokyo branch Smith had opened would be celebrated. The trip had been coordinated with Mayor Feinstein's trade and goodwill trip, an effort to lure Japanese business to the Bay Area; the mayor's presence at Clausen's reception for six hundred customers in a ballroom of the Okura Hotel would lend a stamp of civic support.

But as with the LDC restructuring rituals, ceremony was a shield for desperation. Clausen's business meetings with government, bank, and indus-trial figures were at the heart of the journey. Although his public relations people continued to insist he was going strictly on a ceremonial visit, as he departed by jet with his entourage, Clausen was turning to the world's biggest pool of capital.

Within a week of Clausen's visit, Frank Newman flew to Japan, meeting with bankers, the first of two trips that early summer. Raising capital in Japan would become the bog Armacost had feared. Japan would make Clausen dance for months with the samurai sword of confiscatory interest rates at his throat before agreeing to lend him the emergency capital he must have. In October, five humbling months after Clausen's Japan junket, and after world-publicized reluctance on the part of Japanese banks, Bank of America would manage to raise only $350 million from a consortium of nine banks that consented to buy BankAmerica's stock and notes. The bank would be forced to pay premiums on interest rates so much higher than its competitors that one of Clausen's senior officers says, "It is so expensive that I cannot imagine we would ever do this again." It was a clear view of where the once-biggest bank in the world sat in the twilight of the decade.

WHILE CLAUSEN JUNKETED, Al Rice teed off at the Del Monte Lodge with Peter Ueberroth and Clint Eastwood at the Swallows golf tournament. Sam Armacost, soon to join Merrill Lynch Capital Markets, was supposed to have joined Rice in the tournament, but had some social conflict and had to cancel. In red sweater and gray slacks, looking a generation younger than his years, Rice felt buoyant. After a turbulent few years as CEO of Imperial Bancorp in Los Angeles, things had gone well at American Interstate, a small independent bank in Newport Beach, since he took over in October. Reversing four years of losses, he had returned the bank to profitability in February 1987 and had been increasing profits a little each month. They were not Bank of America numbers. But as he rode a golf cart around the course with California's corporate establishment on June 6, he was entering a month that would show an $81,000 profit—"a very fine accomplishment," he felt. He had achieved it not with exotic transcontinental deals but mostly by nuts-and-bolts cost cutting in operations, the "simple little day-to-day things" that could eat a company alive. The financing to recapitalize the bank was coming from his old friend Joe Duffel, the man with whom real estate dealings nine years earlier had destroyed Rice at B of A. Within three weeks, on June 26, Duffel would be delivering his $4 million, gaining control with 51 percent of the bank's stock, confirming Rice's position as president and CEO.

On June 22 Duffel attended an American Interstate board meeting in New-port Beach and reaffirmed that the money would be there on June 26. Rice checked with his old pal the day before; everything was set. But the next day the money did not arrive. Rice called Duffel. Could not reach him. Duffel did not return his calls. Rice called Duffel's lawyer and was told that—for reasons the lawyer would not disclose and Rice never learned—the money would not be coming. Duffel had backed out, without a word to Rice. "We were *good* friends . . . I thought," says Rice, of the man who suddenly appeared to have taken Rice for a soaring ride, then cut the engines.

It was all over in a day. The bank board met that evening and decided that without Duffel's infusion of capital, it could not afford a pricey CEO like Rice.

Rice had lost his champion. He was fired. The board chairman, seeing the speed and apparent ease with which Rice had turned it around, decided to run the bank himself. For the second time in Rice's career, association with Duffel had led to catastrophe.

Rice claimed not to feel hurt about Duffel and American Interstate. His son, Ted, says, "He hides his feelings well." With the irrepressible Rice smile, Al Rice shrugged and said, "Things like that happen. I am more disappointed . . . more disturbed about throwing the opportunity away than anything else. Like the Bank of America. A classic opportunity to do something great, and to have it deteriorate into a bank that is always referred to as the 'problem bank' is just a terrible lack of business opportunity."

What if he were asked tomorrow to go in as CEO of the Bank of America? At the question Rice loosed a roar of laughter while he pulled an answer together. "Oh, you'd almost have to do it. You couldn't resist trying, just to see what would happen," he mused. "When the bank got into difficulty, I was always the one they thought of to go save it." Memorex and the European/ Middle East/Africa assignment flashed to mind. "But that's not going to happen, so I'm not going to worry about *that*."

SAN FRANCISCO had risen to protect the bank from attack out of its own self-interest. But to Claire Hoffman's distress, it seemed to have forgotten her father. As preparations for the fiftieth birthday party of the Golden Gate Bridge—the bridge her father had made possible by buying the bonds to finance it—she had received no invitation to any ceremony. Guarding her father's memory against the cascade of disasters damaging the bank's image, she monitored every scrap of relevant news. She got disheartening word that "Hibernia Bank loaned them half a million dollars for the celebration and said, 'We want to be the official bank.' " She was told, further, that the bridge authorities had taken their accounts out of the Bank of America out of deference to Hibernia. "Yes, *yes!*" she railed, shocked. "It's not only petty. It's worse than childish!" As publicity about plans for the celebration filled the press, she saw with disbelief that her father, and she as his surrogate, were to be invisible at the event.

She read about a big civic lunch for the bridge to be held at the Fairmont Hotel. "I went and bought two tickets . . . because I wanted to patronize it. And I walked into the luncheon just like any old Tom, Dick, and Harry—which I am—and sat down at any table where I could find a spare seat." She should have been at the head table, she felt, as in the past, "when we were invited to every official bridge thing. Even when Armacost was president, he and I went." Someone spotted her, the MC announced her presence, but she refused to stand. The only redeeming part of "that horrible lunch" was "the two delightful workmen" at her table, men who had helped build the bridge. At the lunch "they gave the official group gold hard hats and the workmen white hats. I think it should have been the other way around." She, of course, had received no hat, had been sent a gold one later by an embarrassed official, City Attorney Louise Renne, and was now determined that it should crown the "little fellow," as her father would have wished. She had made it her personal quest to find the workmen's names so that she could send them her own hard hat as a memento.

Eight hundred thousand people poured onto the bridge before sunup on May 24, 1987, filling it to gridlock. Like Bank of America, the bridge had become a potent amulet holding the city's power. With power draining from San Francisco, it couldn't hurt to honor the bridge gods. Among the balloons and parkas, Citicorp T-shirts were even more evident than Hibernia's. That evening the mayor pushed a button to bathe the rust red Art Deco towers in light, and a waterfall of fireworks spilled from the entire length of the span, climax of the most festive event in San Francisco memory. "Bank of America was cut out, and so was A. P. Giannini. There was no mention of him the whole celebration." Claire didn't care about the bank so much. The bank had indeed financed the bridge. "But it was A.P.'s decision."

It was a bad time for the bank to be seen spending money on a party to applaud itself. In the prevailing spirit of austerity, it had planned its own discreet ceremony for July 1—the unveiling of a bronze plaque honoring A.P. and the bridge's engineer, Joseph Strauss, the stubborn visionary who had persuaded A.P. to buy the bonds. Claire was invited to share the unveiling with Strauss's son and agreed to go "for my father, of course, not for any other reason." She arranged to be taken by Mike Paioni, manager of the A. P. Giannini branch in San Mateo, just around the corner from Seven Oaks. She would arrive on the arm of a true BankAmerican.

It was a morning when low cloud and sea fog merged into spitting mist, and the cautious wore light raincoats. In advance, corporate communications people were preparing the ceremony site, corseting folding chairs and a modest podium into a small clearing in the center of a miniature flower garden that bloomed, out of sight of the traffic rolling through the toll booths, at the edge of the parking lot just below the city-side entrance to the bridge. Blue drapery cloaked the chunk of rough-cut granite on which the plaque had been embedded. The monument stood against a spectacular backdrop; a brilliant bed of nasturtiums, lilies, lobelia, and rhododendrons encircled and splashed the base of a steep bluff that, before the bridge was built, would have given the garrison at old Fort Point, just below, a strategic view of the harbor. Beyond, the first bridge tower soared, and the cliffs of the Marin headlands rose steeply from one of the world's most beautiful harbor entrances. As sun tentatively filtered through cloud, coloring the bay blue and shafting light onto the headlands just as guests began to arrive, the city's effervescent chief of protocol, red-suited Charlotte Mailliard, glanced with relief at the incomparable view and laughed. "Whew, I just got that set painted and in place in time."

Small knots of people began gathering and strolling toward the clearing. Strauss and his wife, who had flown up from Los Angeles for the day, were greeted and introduced. Mario's girls, Anne and Virginia, arrived with their husbands. The A. P. Giannini Middle School band, tucked at the end of the paved walk that curled around the left flank of the hillock, was warming up with "San Francisco, Open Your Golden Gate" when Claire appeared, flanked by Paioni. Several other old banker friends immediately hovered around and trailed her as she moved. In a deep red wool coat lined with sheared fur, straight-backed, fully upholstered, hair parted in the middle and pulled back in a classic knot, and chin high, she was an imposing emissary for A.P.

It was an occasion that seemed to endow every act and comment with significance. "Are the girls here?" she asked someone, and when told yes, said, "Oh, I'm surprised." She had never met Strauss's son. And as photographers documented their handshake, she said warmly to Strauss, "We were blessed with two fathers of wisdom and foresight." A slight and dignified elderly man wearing a dark topcoat that looked a little too big around the neck—a sign of the frailty and shrinkage of age—greeted her. It was Clark Beise, successor to Carl Wente as president, the bank's leader through the 1950s. "You're a darling. You're always so faithful," Claire said, gripping the hands of the man who had put the bank at the leading edge in technology and been her mentor and friend after her father's death. A big, full-faced man with a shock of white hair and look of power joined the little group. Towering over Beise was Clarence Baumhefner, the fearsome cashier who had kept the bank's books in his head, intimidating even Clausen, legend had it. "I long for the old days," said Beise as they reminisced, two years before his death at ninety-one.

Minutes before eleven a group of dark-suited men walked in together: Clausen and his senior officers and about twenty others. As whispers and waves revealed the cast of characters, it became evident that this was an extraordinary moment. This understated event was a rare parade of the bank's past and present. The men's tenure spanned nearly seventy years of the bank's history. Russ Smith, a spry ninety-three and using a cane more for effect than need, had been with A.P. since the early twenties and had been "given the world" by A.P. just after the war. There was Rudy Peterson, the president who had transformed an oversized regional bank into a global force in the sixties, a Swedish farm boy who, at eighty-five, still had the most worldly presence of anyone there. Tall, with a distinguished head of satin silver hair and with red silk at the breast pocket of his elegant suit, he had that rare style of the prince who can bend to casual chitchat without condescension or loss of presidential aura. Wearing a corduroy sport coat, Al Zipf wore the unbankerly garments of the computer pioneer who had revolutionized check handling and put the bank ahead of the pack in the mid-fifties and who now lived for fishing in Alaska. Beside him was a man who had started his rise to executive status, in classic Giannini style, as a janitor at the Half Moon Bay branch.

With the colorful prose and ruddy-faced good humor that had made him a legend, too, as the bank's chief counsel, Sam Stewart was chuckling as he retold the story of how he'd told designer Walter Landor, as Landor had proposed an endless feast of creative design solutions for the bank's new logo in the early seventies, "Just make sure it's got two letters—a *B* and an *A*."

And there was "Jake" Fischer, who had raced to Santa Rosa with sacks of cash to calm depositors and prevent a bank run in 1921 and, on the eve of the bank holiday of 1933, had joined Russ Smith in a rush to Sacramento by airplane and limousine with more millions of cash Smith had borrowed from the Federal Reserve and other banks to meet rumored runs as panic spread across the nation. The two had celebrated with A.P. the bank's surviving in good health the nation's most severe economic emergency, a time when Roosevelt's inaugural words seemed vindication of the values that drove Giannini's bank. Fischer and Smith had stood proud as the president excoriated Wall Street's "unscrupulous money changers . . . indicted in the court of public opinion. . . . They only know the rules of a generation of self-seekers. They have no vision, and where there is no vision the people perish."

Being paraded before the straggle of tourists who happened by was a scene that hardly seemed worthy of a photograph. But they were witnessing a requiem to the passing of an age. A pin-striped pageant of the rise, the glory, and the decline of Bank of America. It carried the import, if not the glittering panoply, of the funeral procession at the death of British King Edward VII on the eve of World War I, which marked the transition of dominance from the British Empire to America—the last gathering of the crowned heads of a Europe that would no longer run the world with kings and imperial hegemony. The somber suits lacked the pomp and ceremony, the state carriages and bemedaled splendor, of that earlier procession. But assembled here like the ghosts of profits and stature past was the power structure of the greatest assemblage of commercial banking wealth since modern banking began in the early Renaissance. Beise, Peterson, and Clausen—backed by the military might and coffers of the globe's dominant nation—had bestridden the banking world for three decades, the leaders through that era when the bank had seemed exquisitely in sync with the society it served. They had bankrolled gratification of America's dream—and the dreams of any country that had come knocking at the doors of the granite tower on California Street.

They had come, officially, to honor the vision of their founder and wish a bridge happy birthday. But in a climate of decline and uncertainty over the destiny of this bank, of the banking industry, and of American power, this parade of bankers marked, more eloquently than the most elaborate LDC debt restructuring, the passing of the Golden Age into an age of sobered recognition that supremacy of the sort they had known might never be their bank's, their industry's, nor perhaps their nation's again.

It was a moment as tantalizing as the moment at the Silverado retreat when Sam Armacost had held in his hands all the bank's problems, written on two hundred small file cards. For these men held the secrets of failure, as well as of success. On the positive side, they represented the massed experience and collective wisdom of Bank of America, the distilled essence of the bank's strengths—its integrity, civility, loyalty, sense of family, pride, tradition, service, humanitarian instincts, and, if not at the level of A.P.'s genius, intelligence. Beise, Peterson, Smith—they were models for the composite BankAmerican who inspired tens of thousands of expatriates to the "immense pride" the First Interstate team had felt. They were of that breed of banker that had brought the same qualities of stability and trust to America's dynamic young communities as the country doctor—men whose own impeccability had given the paying of interest a good name for the first time in history. They had had grace, if not the efficiency of New Age bankers like Tom Cooper and John Reed. Something had been lost in their retreat before the juggernaut of bloodless transactional banking. And yet if all their experience could be fitted together into a great mosaic, it would be a telling portrait of decline, a blueprint for the drift from greatness.

After a welcome by Clausen, a grease-painted A.P. and Joe Strauss, with stiff collars and gold watch fobs, leaped into their parts as the famous scene between the two men was played out by two hired actors. It promised to be cloying propaganda. Strauss, gripping furled bridge plans in his hand, popped to his feet at the top of the bluff, pointed toward the bridge, and proclaimed the words of a dreamer: "Fellow citizens, hear me. The world revolves around things which at one time couldn't be done because they were supposedly beyond the limits of human endeavor. San Francisco has often done the impossible . . . can again do the impossible . . . to become the great city she is destined to be. *It can be done.*" The corporate communications staff, acting as a muttering crowd of disbelievers, chanted dissent: "The tides will rip it away . . . earthquake will knock it down . . . enemies will bomb it and bottle up the whole Pacific fleet . . . worst eyesore ever created by man. *It can't be done.*"

Of course, it was melodrama. But the attention of this partisan audience—and even of casual bystanders—was becoming engaged. The small group huddled in the chill went silent as the actors approached the famous scene. Having fought back twenty-three hundred lawsuits against the building of the bridge, an idea all the more unpopular in the economic devastation of the 1929 stock market crash, Strauss had finally carried "the vision that burned in his eyes, his mind, and his heart" to the desk of A. P. Giannini, his lender of last resort, and pleaded his case. The rolling thunder of traffic seemed to fall away as A.P. said the words. "San Francisco needs this bridge. *I'll* buy the bonds."

It was the low-budget production of a troubled bank. But it stirred the same pride in the achievements of giants as the great costumed pageants that had flanked A.P.'s death at mid-century. Claire the Indomitable sat straight and poised through the play, but as the group broke into rousing applause, there were glints of tears in the heavy-lidded eyes she had inherited from her father. Stirred, Russ Smith remembered the moment when A.P. had called him over and told his cashier he'd committed to a $6 million bond issue for a bridge—a decision that, as much as any A.P. made, displayed his sound and visionary judgment. The bridge would become the beloved symbol of a city throughout the world. But sadness hung in a fact that could not go unobserved in this company: that the bridge stood strong, its global image untarnished, while the lifework of the giant who had empowered it had fallen low.

Claire and Strauss pulled the white tassels that unveiled the plaque. Clausen joined them for a picture session. Claire and Clausen, the man she had called "the Führer," had been treating each other with careful politeness. But as he motioned to her to come over and pose for another picture, she looked rather fiercely at him and said, "I'm tired of this. I don't like having my picture taken," and turned away. Clausen was making a real effort at affability. For just a moment, though, when he turned and unexpectedly faced a writer who mentioned her upcoming interview with him—an interview he clearly knew nothing about—a sudden pall fell over his face, and the suspicious and fearful look seen in the past flashed in his eyes—the old flaring of insecurity that apparently still lingered, even after the exposure at the World Bank and his return to the throne room in the carnelian tower. Was the same old Clausen—the man whose self-esteem had fed on size and dazzling quarterly numbers—still there inside the born-again banker? If so, it was cause for alarm for the Bank of America. But as waiters in black tie served flutes of champagne and boxed sandwiches, Clausen regained his composure and showered gracious attention on his two Japanese guests.

Clausen and Peterson strolled away from the ceremony together, as the old boys climbed aboard a bus for the ride back to the bank, where Clausen was hosting lunch in his private dining room. On the drive back to Seven Oaks after the luncheon, Claire found herself thinking, "I think he's softened a lot." For Clausen had done proper honor to A.P. and to his daughter. Redeemed some of the dishonor of the last few years. Time would tell. But if he had won Claire Hoffman's goodwill, he would have bought himself a little peace for the recovery he knew had already begun under the daunting loss that would be declared for the year—the recovery on which so much depended for them all. Bank of America was still sixteen years short of the life span of the Medici Bank.

Chapter Twenty

BY THE LAST QUARTER of 1988, America, a nation that loves the under-dog, was being treated to the spectacle of "the greatest recovery ever wit-nessed in the U.S. banking industry," as an analyst termed it. B of A's "recovery" was surprising the banking world as profoundly as Clausen's return two years earlier had. But, by God, it was happening. By the end of the year, Clausen was presiding from his blue velvet chair over a bank that had been returned to "sustained operating profitability," as he had vowed. The sick bank had passed its life crisis and was now breathing comfortably. It was in the black. Clausen was proudly saying, "My greatest accomplishment was to stop the red ink—to reverse directions." He and his recovery team were just beginning to know the luxury of lifting their heads and looking farther ahead than the next morning. As he produced fourth-quarter earnings for '88 that were "a record for the corporation" and net earnings for the year of $726 million—"the third best year in our history"—the villain of a year ago was receiving the kind of adulation from analysts and media he had known ten years earlier when he had led B of A into the 1980s as "the first and only private institution in the nation to record earnings of more than $600 million."

It had taken time for perceptions to change. Clausen had reported a profit as early as the fourth quarter of 1986, but the bank was still masking losses under the hoopla of one-time asset sales. "We were still selling the furniture," Clausen says. The magic moment—the return to honest operating profitability—had come in the third quarter of 1987, when CFO Frank Newman reported, "Our recovery is being written solidly in black ink." Those gains had been lost in the horror of the total loss for the year of $955 million, the loss forced by Citicorp's stunning decision in May to pledge $3 billion in reserves against its Brazil loans. "But by December, I knew things were going to work," says Clausen. Earnings moved steadily up each quarter through 1988.

Though the good news was still overwhelmed by the problems of the last three years, professional bank watchers were beginning to pick up the signs of life. Across the bay in Walnut Creek, Sam Marchese, tracking bank stocks for the SIFE Trust Fund, had started buying back into B of A stock six days before the May 1988 annual meeting, after dumping all his B of A stock in disgust in 1986. Marchese had identified B of A as being "on the comeback trail when it realized it had to downsize itself," he says of the company he had watched drive its assets from the $113.8 billion at Clausen's return down to $94.6 billion by the end of 1988—to third rank in the United States. BankAmerica's flag would now fly from only forty-two posts abroad, reduced from four hundred; assets in Europe were slashed in half. "Shrinking your assets does wonders for your capital ratio," said a jubilant Clausen. By the end of 1988, BankAmerica's risk-based capital ratio stood at 8.12 percent, surpassing the 8 percent required by regulators by 1992; it would stand at 9.1 percent a year later. B of A's reserves ratios had moved up, too, to 33 percent of the value of its third world loans, "close to the industry average," Clausen claimed.

And he was driving expenses down. Even though it still cost BankAmerica fifteen cents more than it cost Wells Fargo to make a dollar, the effort to puncture the bloated expense balloon—Armacost's nemesis—was pervasive throughout the bank. Marchese bought more stock as he saw fat being cut; staff had been reduced from 86,104 to 54,800 by September 1988. Clausen's loan makers were booking higher-yielding loans while shrinking the number of loans not paying interest, widening the spread that was still "our largest single source of revenue," as Clausen said—the net interest margin. It swelled 25.6 percent in 1988. But "perhaps the outstanding feature . . . was the improvement of credit quality," said a Salomon Brothers report, citing the factor that, more than any other, had brought the bank down.

As the news got steadily better, Ron Rhody judiciously stepped up the pace of media interviews with Clausen. By early fall, perceptions had begun to change. *Business Week* put Clausen on its list of America's corporate elite and dubbed him "one tough banker," a term that made Clausen beam, a colleague reports. Citicorp's John Reed was simultaneously being named fourth best CEO of all Fortune 500 corporations. But to the market that was a yawn compared to Clausen's sensational turnaround story.

The stock price responded, soaring from its low of near $6 to $19^{1}/_{8}$ by November, making it the world's best-performing bank stock of 1988. DO NOT GET OFF THE BANDWAGON NOW, urged a Salomon Brothers report, recommending the stock as a buy; the resurrection of A. W. Clausen was rolling. Even bank analyst George Salem, a doubter, finally capitulated, admitting that "the turnaround seems real."

Under Dick Rosenberg, the retail bank had set out to rewin the West. B of A had been close-mouthed about the loss of market share in the California territory it had "owned," but the numbers in just one flourishing community, Napa Valley, revealed the scope of Rosenberg's challenge. In June 1981, as Armacost took over, B of A had held over 46 percent of Napa Valley's deposits; a new local bank, Napa Valley Bank, was a pale second with $14^{1}/_{2}$ percent. By the end of 1986, with Clausen back, the two banks were neck and neck, Napa Valley Bank having inched ahead to a shade over 30 percent. Even in recovery, B of A's market share had continued to erode. Other local banks—Napa National and Vintage Bank—and Wells were carving into the territory; by the end of '88, Napa Valley Bank's deposit share had shrunk to 22 percent and B of A's to its lowest yet—*less than 15 percent.* Yet deposits were one of the keys to recovery, the captive source of cheap money that had always assured Bank of America a wider spread than market-funded banks.

Now, spurring salesmen's hustle in the branches, Rosenberg was turning the retail side into "combat banking." With war cries from the new chief of branches, Thomas Peterson, to "kill and crush" competitors and with merciless perform-or-starve pay incentives, B of A's genteel bankers were being whipped into a pack of pit bulls.

At the asset end, Rosenberg pushed high-yielding, old-fashioned home and car loans and middle-market commercial loans. At the deposit end, he drove new products, trying to attract checking accounts. The Alpha Account was a stunning success. It was not an innovation; it was little more than a clone of the Gold Account Rosenberg had created sixteen years earlier for Wells Fargo— checking and savings Alpha linked and packaged with a few conveniences and sold for a healthy fee.

But whether by accident or design, the Alpha proved psychologically potent. Alpha's advertising symbol was a small wooden sphere. It looked like a globe you could hold in your hand. It was the overblown, bureaucratic, world-girdling bank returning to a human scale, returning home to California. It offered a focus for Californians' residual affection for the bank. Like the Stanghellinis, Californians had felt personally betrayed when the bank failed their needs and their trust. Alpha's warm, wooden sphere on TV, on billboards—and eating two-thirds of the bank's entire advertising budget for 1988—was the route back into the bank for thousands who were eager to end the estrangement. In six months, B of A had gained 350,000 Alpha Accounts, 40 percent of them won over from the competition.

The only promise Clausen had not kept by year-end was to restore the dividend. But 1988's balance sheet had been given a powerful boost, a shot of $351 million as Brazil resumed its interest payments. With his hand thus strengthened, Clausen, on February 6, 1989, declared a dividend, an act that "assures our loyal customers that BankAmerica has put behind a very difficult chapter in its history." It seemed like the right time for him to reveal his long-range vision for the bank. Instead he named a workmanlike goal: a 1 percent return on assets—"the benchmark of an excellent bank." He determined to join "the small group of highly regarded 100-basis-point ROA banks"—banks that earned one dollar after taxes for every hundred dollars of assets. By mid-1989 Clausen would sweep past his goal to a 1.26 ROA, joining the rarefied elite.

Still, some monumental gaffes did get through all the new safeguards, past the Wells Fargo watchdogs. The computer systems for the bank's trusts, a smoldering problem for several years, became a debacle, costing the bank its $60 million investment and costing Max Hopper's successor, Lou Mertes, his job as the bank found scapegoats. Then, in April, Citicorp and several other major foreign banks sued Bank of America for $650 million for failing, as trustee, to monitor and prevent a massive loss in student loan portfolios. It was potentially far worse than NMEC, the mortgage fraud that had cost the bank a $95 million loss and revealed its appalling lack of systems to monitor and control risk. It was not yet known whether these were aberrations, or if systemic disorders still coursed through the culture.

Foreign debts were still a wild card. Clausen sharply rebuked a journalist for citing the *New York Times* headline THIRD WORLD LOANS NO LONGER A THREAT, claiming that "No one said that. No one could say that. That problem will be with us for a very long time."

Yet at the annual meeting in May 1989 at the Los Angeles Airport Marriott, the accolades outnumbered the taunts, and Clausen was cheered as a hero.

WATCHING CLAUSEN'S TRIUMPH from his modest fourteenth-floor office at Merrill Lynch Capital Markets, Sam Armacost claimed, "I've lost no respect or friends." Yet for Armacost, the crowning of Tom Clausen as the bank's savior was clearly a blow. The two men had run into each other at a dinner party aboard Malcolm Forbes's yacht in San Francisco Bay—the yacht from which Armacost, as CEO, had golfed and fished in Florida each winter. In fact, the two ran into each other frequently. They stayed "distant" and never discussed the bank. "But when they claimed credit for cutting expenses . . . when clearly, the expense numbers had turned, clearly" during his tenure, Armacost called Ron Rhody from his office a few blocks from B of A headquarters and said, "Hey, Ron, I'm partly amused and partly annoyed. You know what we accomplished. . . . We brought the expense line down to zero." Clausen, Armacost believed, was "riding the momentum curve we created" and reaping the rewards.

As he saw Clausen continue to downsize, sell assets to raise capital, and reduce expenses, Armacost recited his achievements in a seamless rush. "What people don't understand is that in the five years that our team was there, we increased our operating earnings before loan losses four of those five years. Our margins went up four years in a row." He and McLin had reduced what Clausen termed "the overburden" of assets by nearly $30 billion. "We actually put a billion dollars of capital in the institution through asset sales— we doubled our capital," he said, scanning the glossy 1988 annual report. "Our recovery was precisely on track. . . . We told the board in '86 that the bank would make a billion dollars by 1990. We predicted earnings in '88 of $711 million." There on page two, opposite the smiling faces of Clausen and his senior management team, were the 1988 earnings numbers: $726 million—within $15 million of the target Armacost had told the board they would achieve. By mid-1989 the bank's earnings would be over half a billion dollars, well on their way to the one billion earnings he had forecast in 1986.

He found it "a bit ironic that the large reserves that caused a lot of dark stuff to fall on us from the analytical community" in '85 and '86 now largely explained Clausen's spectacularly swift "recovery." Armacost sketched a graph with his pencil: credit losses declining—because of the rigor of Glenhall Taylor, his hire. Recoveries on loan losses improving—as he knew they would, once losses bottomed out. And a pool of reserves so big that you could pull some of them back into earnings tax free on the balance sheet. "Hell, it wasn't Alpha that saved the bank," he declared. From Los Angeles, Joe Pinola supports Armacost's thesis: "Tom's success lies in the *huge* amount of reserves taken in the mid-eighties. They were overreserved for domestic loans and have excess reserves *now* supporting their LDCs."

Every significant asset sale, except Schwab, was already done or was in the pipeline before he resigned, Armacost claimed, "and I'd never have sold Schwab." He said, "We'd focused on the California core business by '83, '84," and had defined, during the soul searching of the early eighties, the "customer-driven" philosophy Clausen now claimed as his own. "We'd tried to do an Alpha, but we didn't have the systems to deliver the product." It was California Data Network, built and operated by BASE—his, Adizes's, Hopper's pride—that had given Rosenberg the tools to put Alpha on line, Armacost stated, and that powered the state-of-the-art global banking system driven forward by Armacost and now coming on-line under Clausen.

And personnel! Armacost had hired the Wells team that was leading the recovery. Rosenberg. Coleman. Taylor. Newman. And Bob Beck, the human resources chief from IBM who had attracted so much talent to the bank.

The defeat of Pinola at First Interstate was Clausen's achievement. But Armacost still believed that had Pinola been willing to talk a rational price, a merger would have forged "an incredible product distribution network"—a bank unbeatable in the West at a time when the superregional was the best game in town.

Armacost denied that the precipitous decline he had hosted was as historic, unique, or desperate as the media had painted it. "What went on from '81 to '86 was the restructuring of a major American enterprise that was ill equipped to face the rigors of deregulation and competition. . . . We were ahead of the trend line. . . . Without the credit situation, we would have been given credit for having managed very well. In any other environment, we would have done great," he said, then added with a droll smile, "and I'd be sitting there instead of here."

Armacost replayed events endlessly, discussed them with friends. If the recession hadn't hit . . . if they hadn't had the loan losses. What might he have done differently? "I blame myself for one glaring faux pas. I should have stood up the day after I came and said, 'This is a roaring disaster.' I should have. But what credibility would I have had?" He identified another "biggest mistake—not firing Prussia a year earlier."

Armacost knew the bad loans had not been an uninvited plague ravaging a healthy bank, as members of the old guard seemed to believe. He had understood the real disease. He had not lacked vision. He had seen clearly where the bank had to go. But he had been trapped within his own Bank-American skin, too concerned about bruising the culture—and perhaps too bound by Burlingame Country Club manners—to move the bank fast enough, decisively enough to satisfy the cries for blood. Torn between being a conservator and an instrument of violent change, he had, in hindsight, not been tough enough. Armacost recalled sitting around with his longtime colleague Bob Frick after desperate days of bad news, consoling Frick instead of firing him. The times had required ruthless surgical strikes against old comrades—a sad loss for the bank's human touch, but fatal for Armacost to have ignored.

In the short term, Armacost would probably be held more responsible than Clausen for the bank's travails; most of the disasters broke on his watch, and the market's view of history is myopic. Armacost felt about his own fall, as he had about Mont McMillen's, that "at a certain stage of the game, it doesn't matter whether you're a good manager or a bad manager if your credibility is lost in the Street. I'm sure that's how I found myself on the street."

IN SUTTER BASIN, Bob Stanghellini harvested four varieties of beans and prepared the land for winter wheat while waiting for the bank's appeal of his $50 million jury award to grind through the state's Appellate Court. "We're going all the way with it," he said, heaving sacks of beans ready for delivery to the Sutter Valley Co-Operative. "If they want to settle, we're in the ball game, but they have to settle right." For the past three years, he'd been farming without the bank's loans. Taking small crop loans from the local Tri-Counties Bank, he'd paid back all his suppliers—fertilizer, equipment, repairs, seed— and had made close to a $50,000 profit in 1987. With drought shrinking his yield in '89, he'd just break even, even though prices were strong. He had cut back his farming to about half of his previous 2,500 acres. But he'd been able to buy a new $120,000 Case International axial-flow harvester, a single machine that did the work of four machines. "This does it all," he grinned, pleased as could be to be making it without Bank of America.

His attorney, Dick Murphy, was now handling thirteen lawsuits against Bank of America; the two men had delighted in slapping a lien against B of A in every county in the state "on everything they owned in the State of California. You should have heard them holler," Stanghellini laughed. The lien was dismissed, "but we wanted people to know that there's a jury verdict out there. The judge upheld it, every cent of it."

Under angry questioning about the Stanghellini case at the 1987 annual meeting, Clausen had tried to reassure shareholders that "agriculture has been on our agenda since 1913," but he admitted that "we've reduced our penetration and exposure." He revealed that since Wells's merger with Crocker, B of A was no longer number one in agricultural loans. But ag loans were "going to continue, careful, across the board." After the drain on his mother and aunt, who were now eighty-six and eighty-five, Stanghellini cared not a whit for Clausen's words and eyed the recovery cynically. "It's just a paper recovery. They're just getting in shape to sell out to a Japanese bank."

YET THE STREET was alive with rumors that MotherBank was about to take over its recent adversary, First Interstate Bancorp. Keefe, Bruyette analyst Don Crowley had sent First Interstate's stock soaring with his June 6, 1989, report headlined FIRST INTERSTATE: WANTED DEAD OR ALIVE. Painting a number of scenarios—takeover by Wells Fargo, Security Pacific, or BankAmerica, the breakup of the company, or self-reform—Crowley saw the bank's stock as a "win-win" investment.

Bristling at Crowley's comments, Pinola said, "I find a great deal that is objectionable. It will be fun now for writers to speculate that B of A is successful enough to take us over." But Crowley spoke some truths. Joe Pinola had still not translated his extraordinary interstate advantage into the kind of profits and stock price the market demanded. Crowley did grant that Pinola had "ended the fiefdom era," unifying his twelve banks under a common name, replacing old management, networking with computers. But he was moving at too slow a pace, Crowley claimed, in breaking down the still-independent operations and spirit that had thwarted efforts to shrink the overhead and create efficiencies of scale to overcome the cost of all that brick and mortar. "You don't just walk into Idaho or Nevada and have a revolution—they have a century of history behind them," a senior bank officer retorted. "You have to do it in a slow, humanistic way. Pinola came in when the giant was asleep, and he did the best he could." Fanning takeover rumors to flames, Crowley ended his report with the caution that if First Interstate did not reward stockholders, eliminate the elaborate hierarchy of individual banks, and cut costs, "another management will."

"First Interstate still represents the best territory in the nation," affirmed Pinola from his Los Angeles headquarters. But therein lay the problem. He was vulnerable to the economies of each state. First Interstate's setbacks "have *not* stopped our objective of being a national player," he said, "but it seems to me that if you own banks in fifteen states and four are in depression, wouldn't it be nice to own banks in *thirty* states, to spread the risk?" As if keeping news of his ambitions from regulators, he said in a stage whisper, "What we need is *massive expansion*"—expansion still restrained by the McFadden Act.

A takeover of First Interstate by one of its California peers—or, after 1991, by a Citicorp—might well be "win-win" for A.P.'s creation, the string of banks spun off from Transamerica. To a child of the banking revolution like Tom Cooper, the name First Interstate was expendable; it had been born yesterday.

369

By whatever name, the bank would not only have survived but would have been catapulted by merger with Wells, B of A, the Japanese or whomever—from eighth largest bank holding company in the United States to first or second, and to absolute dominance in the West. Pinola would have left a formidable legacy to Californian and American banking.

But to Pinola personally it would be devastating on the eve of his retirement to see his bank, his alter ego, merge like money or sand into the stream of change. That was not what he had come from the coal fields to oversee.

BEFORE HE DIED in August 1988, Bob Truex had secured his banking legacy. His sale of Seattle's Rainier Bancorporation to Security Pacific a year earlier had been an act of brilliant positioning for both banks; it put Security Pacific into the second rank in asset size of the nation's superregionals. During his last year Truex suffered from emphysema so severe that he carried a tank of oxygen at all times—carrying it with such casual aplomb that it might have been an ivory-headed cane. He remained as chairman, savoring the sight of the merged banks setting up a formidable challenge to B of A, the bank that had rejected him, in the western states and Asia. He watched his long-time dream become reality as Rainier dramatically extended its reach into the Pacific Rim.

BUT THE GLAMOUR had moved to local banking, to the branches. America's banks, like America itself, seemed content to regroup in the home cave, where lavish profits were being harvested and stocks were strong. "Shareholder value is the buzzword," says Armacost. In the wake of the foreign debt disaster and the shrinking of multinational corporate business, the best-performing bank stocks were not those putting their necks on the line abroad, like Citicorp. Having shed most of his LDC loans, Pinola expressed the mood. "I'm not going to be the first guy back in," even though he knew that "we're all much too short-term-oriented in LDC to see that those countries are huge customers for our products. Money must flow into them." Pinola, the competitive animal, noted that the four top U.S. banks in market capitalization—the value of stock owned by shareholders—were all superregionals. Echoing Pinola, Armacost said, "It's the superregionals, not the global banks, that are making the incredible profits—3 percent ROAs! It's the local boutique banks who've been eating our lunch. With credit cards, people don't *need* an international bank."

Banking had finally caught up with Al Rice. Ever since corporate banking had pulled prestige and talent from the branches in the 1960s, Rice had argued that the branches were banking's front line. Rice had picked himself up from the Duffel disaster in Newport Beach, and by the end of the summer of 1988 had joined a Washington, D.C.–based venture capital group, Federal Bancorp Systems, as managing director. He was scouting troubled California banks, looking for acquisition candidates for the chain the group hoped to buy and have Rice manage back to profitability. When the CEO of one of the banks he'd rounded up resigned, Rice took over and ran the First National Bank of Marin in suburban San Rafael, across the Golden Gate Bridge from B of A's headquarters. In October he and a partner bought control; he was now chairman and president of his own unit bank, negotiating for two more.

It was a little jewel of a bank, a cozy throwback with tall Corinthian columns, antique brass teller's windows, and deep green carpeting. The computers, which Rice believed were the key to achieving lower costs than the big banks, were artfully disguised in a setting that made customers feel they had walked in off Nye Street to a serene, pampering oasis.

"Since it was founded five years ago, this bank had never had a profitable quarter, or year. In the eight months that I've been here, we've had two quarters of profitability," Rice reported. He had reduced expenses. And he had increased earnings by playing to Marin County's upscale prosperity, marketing to the large medical/dental community, lending to custom home builders, and promoting a specialized credit card. He was still tweaking Bank of America. Although Clausen's recent words still rung: "We're growing tall people in the branches. We're bringing judgment back to the interface with customers," the fact was that B of A had pulled all its loan-making authority out of the branches. Rice chuckled. "People want to deal face to face with decision makers—they don't like curtains. By taking high-powered decision makers out of the branches, they're making it easy for a bank like us to succeed. All we have to do is stand in front of B of A and say, 'There's a decision maker just around the corner!' "

Rice's critics saw the persistence of a style that pushed the edges of flamboyance as football hero Joe Montana sued Rice's bank for mentioning Montana in its ads without permission. But the incident gave his bank headlines on the business page. Al Rice was having a ball. As he left the bank on a Friday evening and revved up his bright-red high-performance Porsche 928 S4 for the drive to his Tahoe condo, he thought of Tom Clausen in his limousine, pulling sedately away from the carnelian tower for the drive to the stately pomposity of Hillsborough, and laughed his great room-filling laugh. "Who do *you* think won?"

CHUCK SCHWAB still sought to keep the human touch in the computerized transactional operations of Charles Schwab & Co. by using his own face in his ads, even though the new format of the *Journal* had forced him to relinquish the choice inside back page. Marketing had never been more vital to him. With the stock market crash of October 1987, life had not been a bed of roses since the buyback. Just as his staff had begun to relax and revel in the time they assumed they had before Schwab's next big push, he told them, "We're going public right away." Schwab took his company public just three weeks before the crash. It had been a ravaging experience, with just one customer, a Hong Kong investor, Teh Huel "Ted" Wang, skewering Schwab with a $22 million loss on put options. "He had to cover overnight. But liquidity had died. He couldn't trade out of his position," Schwab reported.

He faced a potential loss of $98 million, larger than B of A's NMEC loss. It could be wipeout time again in the entrepreneur's tumultuous career. But Schwab had learned some lessons about delegation of authority. As his team ran doomsday scenarios, he said, "You guys are *going* to do it. We are *going* to be successful. I'm going home now." Working through the night and for the next fevered week, they tied up Ted Wang's assets with a restraining order so that he could not write a check, and they urgently tried to negotiate a settlement with Wang. By the night of October 28, Quackenbush had written two press releases, had had the public relations firm Hill and Knowlton reserve a conference room at the Ramada Renaissance Hotel, and was waiting for the 4 A.M. phone call from Hong Kong that would tell them whether Wang had signed the agreement to pay back the loss, now reduced to $40 million before taxes, $22 million after. As Quackenbush shepherded Schwab to the microphones through a mob of TV cameras and reporters, he handed him the press release. Wang had signed. He would also pay.

But in the climate of fear, "investors pulled in their horns. Volumes dropped drastically. In 1988 our volume was down thirty-five to forty percent," says Schwab. He cut back, laid off some people.

Yet Schwab, the irrepressible optimist, saw "very clear signs right after the November election—volumes were up. It was a vote of confidence." Demographics were, he believed, still on the side of the discount broker and diversified financial services. "It's the graying of America. All those baby boomers are going to live longer, save more, prepare for the future. Social Security won't do it. That's our market over the next ten to fifteen years." He had thirty-five products, "and we'll expand." Twenty-seven thousand customers now ran their financial affairs from their home computers through Schwab's Equalizer. "They're still small numbers. Personal computers are not quite there yet. They have to be as easy as stepping into a car." Then, he believed, the life-style that futurists had been predicting for decades would take off.

His stock had dropped as low as $5.75 before moving back up to $8, down from the $16.50 it had started at when he went public. Within two years of the crash his stock had regained lost ground; profits surged 155 percent in 1989. The harassed and capital-hungry entrepreneur had finally gained stature. On the podium of a University of California, Berkeley, symposium, seated between two of the most impressive banking CEOs in California, Security Pacific's Robert H. Smith and Tom Clausen, Schwab got roars from an audience of a thousand with his wry opener, "Indeed, I am deeply indebted to these two men. . . . I owe Security Pacific $150 million and Bank of America $106 million."

Schwab flew to San Francisco on June 22 from his ranch in Montana to receive a Golden Plate Award from the American Academy of Achievement, along with Beverly Sills, Kareem Abdul-Jabbar, Ernest and Julio Gallo, Jesse Jackson, Oprah Winfrey, various industrial giants, and half a dozen Nobel Prize–winning scientists and scholars. While his teen-aged children marveled at the massing of celebrities, he listened alertly to the short speech each inductee gave over the four-day meeting. And it struck him that "there is one common denominator in them all. A passion for what they do. Giannini had it. But, damn it, it's that *passion* the bank's leaders lost."

SCHWAB MET Sandy Weill again in July, this time on national television, on PBS's "Wall Street Week." Since his aborted run at Bank of America, Weill had been on the march, empire building as he had in the 1970s. With Baltimore-based Commercial Credit as his cornerstone, he bought the high-profile financial services company Primerica and, abandoning the stolid image of Commercial Credit, made Primerica his new corporate name. With the company he acquired a gilt-edged carriage-trade broker, Smith Barney, expanding his distribution network. He moved his headquarters from Baltimore to a building on East 55th Street in New York, and built a thirty-five-foot-high fireplace on the top floor. He gathered in family, rehiring a protégé from Shearson when his old "baby" faced financial crisis in early 1990, and tried to merge Shearson into his new corporate fold. For a man whose very name had sent B of A's stock price soaring, his own stock was "a little disappointing," his chief financial officer, Jamie Dimon, admitted, as it floated around $24. "This is a marathon we're in. But we're running it in hundred-yard dashes," he reassured his team. Another gem he'd acquired with Primerica was A. L. Williams, a hot young firm that marketed life insurance and mutual funds direct to middle America, "the real America" that Weill saw as his major market.

"What's our niche? It's direct customer contact," says Dimon. Weill was not buying corporate logos or brick and mortar. He was buying product distribution systems.

*   *   *

BY TOM COOPER'S TERMS, Weill was a "third wave" thinker. Those managers who "regarded themselves as the keepers of the flame in an era of laser beams" would not survive, Cooper warned, speaking out as an articulate preacher for the banking revolution he had imposed with such fervor and conflict at Bank of America.

That crucible had only strengthened his conviction that at a time when Americans were no longer in awe of or intimidated by banks, the "second wave" dinosaurs who continued to focus "on the needs of the institution, rather than on the needs of the individual," as Bank of America had when he arrived, would perish. The arrogant notion that "the marketplace exists to serve the needs of banks" must be "turned around and upside down."

BAPS had been the perfect example. Cooper's critics still mourned his dismantling of BAPS, the embodiment of Adizes's dream of a vast, computerized payments system that would turn B of A into an indispensable global utility. But to Cooper, BAPS was the embodiment of bank-driven market strategies. "The idea that BAPS could become a global payments utility grew from an inward, bank perspective rather than an outward, marketplace perspective. This vision was founded on the belief that simply because banks had always controlled payments in the past, they always would control payments in the future."

Cooper had moved twice since leaving B of A. He had spent nearly two years in Florida, improving the performance of INVEST, a financial services company that sold its packaged financial products from five hundred INVEST Centers in commercial and savings banks. In the spring of 1989, Cooper moved to Buffalo, New York, to heal Goldome, a $15 billion savings bank wounded by bad loans and low capital. But he did not have his ego or identity invested in Goldome's marble-columned, dome-roofed mausoleum architecture, or in its name. They were simply shells to be cast off, if necessary, to get competitively positioned for the future.

"The creation and maintenance of organizational structure should not be the objective of a business; meeting customer needs is the proper goal," Cooper preached from corporate pulpits. "Organizations are not sacrosanct."

Epilogue

AND NO LONGER sacrosanct, it seemed, was the global patchwork of power balances bankers had known for forty years.

"What's coming . . . what's coming over the horizon three to five years from now—that's what Ed and I are solving on the way home every night," said Clausen, of his daily hour-long drive back to Hillsborough, when he looked to the perspective and judgment of his chauffeur, Ed, "one of my best friends," to help solve the more cosmic issues of banking. For most of the first year after his return, he had been "putting out fires, manning the water buckets. The adrenaline was going. . . . But when the pressure eased after ten or eleven months, that was our thrust"—looking ahead.

Clausen had launched his recovery into an international environment that made the domestic struggles over deregulation and California market share seem almost trivial. It made the old bipolar face-offs between the United States and the Soviet Union seem as simplistically black and white as western range wars. As the last year of the decade began, Clausen speculated, "We're going to see more change in the next ten years than we've seen in the last thirty, forty years. It's like *whoosh*! I don't know what form or shape it's going to take."

Winds of change swirled over the globe with the velocity of time-lapse films of weather patterns, shifting power, reshaping the world order. A year and a half after the Golden Gate Bridge ceremony, the funeral of Emperor Hirohito slowed, for one minute's silence, the frantic financial markets of the small, resource-poor nation that now stood at the threshold of what might well be the Japanese Century—or Quarter Century, given the competitive clamor snapping at the heels of even the Japanese economic "miracle."

In China, in Latin America, in Eastern Europe, the wind of democracy and capitalism blew, while in capitalism's North American bastion its force was subsiding. Even as they watched the stunning collapse of communism's dreams in the breaching of the Berlin Wall later that year, Americans found themselves in the disquieting position of being not only participants in but also observers of their decline as the dominant world power, engaged in agitated debate over its speed and degree, and the possibilities of reversal. The decline was being measured in banker's terms—national debt, relative size of American and Japanese banks, imbalance of trade flows. In the inextricably interdependent global marketplace that was emerging, it was questionable whether any one nation would inherit the mantle, as new economic power blocs formed in Europe, the Americas, and Asia, where China's presence swelled. In May the wind that had blown China toward what the *New York Times* termed "the free market of ideas as well as of commodities" suddenly died with the massacre of students in Tiananmen Square, as China again turned its reactionary face to the world.

Just as the concept of globalization had been beaten into the parochial brains of American bankers, just as "Pacific Rim" had established itself as a cohesive concept, a competing vision of the world was evolving, one that saw it subdividing into regional blocs. Influential minds within the financial community joined the debate. "If we have one world anywhere, it is in the financial system," stated former Comptroller of the Currency John Heimann, now with Merrill Lynch Capital Markets in New York. The flow of capital was clearly global, honoring no borders and no sovereign power. The world's three mightiest central banks—the Federal Reserve, Deutsche Bundesbank, and the Bank of Japan—met with only fitful success as they tried to drive down the dollar by massive coordination of the buying and selling of dollars in the international markets. Of this attempt to reverse America's trade deficit, Koei Narusawa, chief economist of the Bank of Tokyo, observed, "There is so much momentum in the market that it can't be reversed or stopped by monetary authorities. Capital itself has its own logic, its own selfish purposes: The money flows to the country where one can expect to get the highest yield with the highest degree of safety . . . be it the U.S., Europe, Egypt, or Japan."

Confirming that thesis was the exodus from Latin America of billions of dollars of flight capital; reversing that debilitating drain would "be like trying to reverse the law of gravity," a Mexican businessman told the *Wall Street Journal*.

Political scientist Jeffry Frieden at UCLA fired back: "Modern electronics since 1960 have magnified the impact global markets have. . . . But there is no international economy in the abstract, no economic no man's land in which world trade and payments take place. The international economy is simply the sum of many national economies, and each national economy is subject to powerful domestic political pressures."

As the *Wall Street Journal*'s series on changing world power helped shatter the "myth of an Asian trading bloc," B of A's new head of World Banking, Lew Coleman, concluded that "the globalization of the world's financial markets is a figment of what appears on a Reuters screen. . . . All you're looking at is the ability of the world to *communicate* between regional markets."

Trying to translate the winds of change into practical strategies, Coleman was shrinking the great European barony Rice and Armacost had run in the 1970s, predicting that the 1992 economic union of Europe would be "a consumer play," no longer B of A's game abroad—a strategy expressed in the sale of the Italian retail bank. He was aggressively shifting personnel and resources to Asia, since Clausen had determined that the bank would "take a role second to none . . . in finance and trade within the Pacific Basin." As China's tumult threw into confusion the bank's business strategies there, Coleman mused, "I'm beginning to sense that what we need to do in the Pacific Rim is deal much more directly with the three or four regions that exist there as regions. I don't know where they're going to regionalize . . . but we've got to make sure . . . we can move with their markets very rapidly."

DID TOM CLAUSEN truly understand the nature of the changes he claims would come "like *whoosh*" over the next ten or twenty years? Was he positioning the bank for the year 2000 at a time when it was not at all clear that banks, per se, would survive into the twenty-first century? It would be at least half a decade before the quality of his current decisions could be measured.

What could be measured now was his timing, which in both leaving and returning, had been spectacular. An associate close to both Armacost and Clausen says, "In my heart of hearts, I believe Tom left knowing what was coming. . . . And I believe he engineered his own return. He clearly knew what he was doing. He's a great game player." Steve McLin tends to concur.

"Anybody coming after Clausen would have got the dip, and anyone coming in after Sam would have got the uptick."

Some uptick. As the third anniversary of Clausen's return approached, his balance sheet delighted the analysts and institutional investors, a small (36 percent) but formidable ratio of B of A's shareholders. "Maybe I'm not as dumb as people thought," Clausen told the *Journal* as, in early October, B of A stock traded at an all-time high of $36 and the bank prepared to post the largest net income in its history. By mid-year Clausen had surpassed his goal of a 1 percent ROA, sweeping to 1.26. And soon the $50 million award to Stanghellini would be overturned on appeal, the second major ag case reversed in the bank's favor. The bank would post the first $1 billion-plus earnings in its history for 1989, a year ahead of Armacost's projection.

But Clausen's vision had not yet been tested. He had focused on damage control, discipline in credit and expenses and execution of the tightly focused market strategies being followed by successful peer banks, mainly Wells Fargo. His dazzling performance partially propped up by the bounty of reserves and tax credits he had inherited, he still relied on the earnings stream from net interest margin, that slim profit margin, the spread, that is metaphor for traditional banking. While Security Pacific installed Spanish-language ATMs, targeting the Hispanics who would be one-third of California's population by the year 2000, Clausen and his power team had not yet revealed that bold commitment to forward-looking strategies that had made Citi the leader among big banks. Where Reed, and Wriston before him, always seemed able to perch, omniscient, above the myopic imperatives of quarterly performance to get a broad view of banking, Clausen's stunning results of the moment held no clear proof that he was doing the same.

Yet a strategy for the future based on conventional banking was becoming suicidal as the shape of the bank of tomorrow changed with alarming speed. What would differentiate banks from other financial institutions twenty years from now? Deposit taking might be one difference, Wriston suspects. "And the payments mechanism will always be there. The problem of taking care of the mortgage on your house, car, or sending your kids to school. . . . And underwriting the bonds for the sewers of the world, states, federal government— that's always going to be there." But will banks get the business, as gas stations and discount stores develop competing payment systems? The Federal Reserve will stand firm behind commercial banks, Wriston believes, for "the central banks love to have control of deposits. They control the money supply through that mechanism." The Fed also has an interest in the survival of bank holding companies, for by regulating them it has the power to move into areas other than banking. Yet sustained decline in the dollar's value would make deposits—B of A's enduring strength—worth less, and therefore less important as a basis of banking power.

Will the lending skills that were the BankAmericans' greatest pride atrophy as fee-based services grow as a profit source and as entrepreneurial product salesmen and capital marketeers inherit the earth? Although the basic function of banks is still the financing of commercial enterprises and private needs, the bad real estate loans wreaking havoc on some of New England's strongest banks reveal the risks of continuing to rely on loans' thin and fragile spreads. And yet financial author Martin Mayer suggests that as the securitizing, or selling off, of loans becomes standard practice, good lending judgment may become more important than ever. With investors detached from any means of monitoring the loans they buy, the quality of the initial loan judgment becomes vital; the trading value of the securitized loans, and thus the investor's return, depends on it. The great days of lending may still be ahead, but only for more sophisticated bankers than those that sat like an assembly of the gods around B of A's legendary loan review table.

And will any American banks survive in the international arena? With the current bold trend to interstate banking, "the U.S. could have *massive* national banks that could compete with the Japanese banks," says Frank Newman, as opposed to the current 12,706 commercial banks. "We have a banking system based on the *states*—in essence, fifty separate banking systems rather than one unified one. Can we have truly global banks without having *national* banks in the U.S.?" asks Dr. H. Robert Heller, the former Federal Reserve Board governor and senior international economist for B of A.

Interstate banking, a vital evolutionary step toward a national banking system, and the deregulating spirit that drove it through the 1980s may be "dramatically slowed," Joe Pinola fears, by the loss of deregulation's champion, Ronald Reagan, and by the savings and loan disaster, which hangs like a Damoclean sword over the nation and its banks. By the end of 1989, American taxpayers faced a potential cost of $200 billion to try to save an industry brought to disgrace and bankruptcy by profligate management and fraud, compounded by recessions in real estate and energy. Many believe the savings and loan industry—its simple functions largely usurped by "real" banks— will be merged into the commercial banking system and vanish as an entity. Pinola says, "*No* one knows what will happen when hundreds of billions of defaulted real estate are dropped on the economy. But the crisis will slow the dreams of national banking and continue to erode our financial system, especially vis-à-vis Japan, not just for Joe Pinola, but for American banking."

Scanning the dismal statistics he keeps at hand in his desk drawer, he says, "Not one U.S. bank is in the top twenty in the world as far as deposits. Citi was number twenty-eight at the end of 1989." Bank of America was forty-fifth. A nation of savers, the Japanese have built a deposit base that gives its banks unparalleled buying and lending power. Twenty-five percent of California banking assets are now owned by the Japanese. With bags full of low-cost capital, they are able to underprice American competitors on commercial loans and still show a profit. As for asset size, Japanese banks now sweep the world's top ten. Citibank ranked twenty-second, and Bank of America languished at forty-ninth at year-end 1989, though Citicorp clung to tenth in total assets. Japanese banks, permitted mammoth mergers that are prohibited in the United States because of the old fear of financial monopolies, only grow larger.

Yet size, supposedly, is no longer the measure of banking success. Like Silicon Valley ten years ago, U.S. banks still hold the innovative edge in products and services over Japan's giants Dai-Ichi Kangyo, Sumitomo, Fuji, Sanwa, and Mitsubishi. Citibank was the world's most *profitable* bank, while the world's biggest, Dai-Ichi Kangyo, ranked seventy-seventh in return on equity. But, as in computer chips, Japanese banks are beginning to go beyond the high-volume, cheap-price strategy that led to Japanese domination of such "American" industries as autos and electronics. They are beginning to *invent*, to innovate. They may close the performance gap.

"The game now *is* performance—the bottom line," Pinola muses. "But size will always be something analogous to power."

MOTHERBANK suffers from an identity crisis. She is widely perceived as a money center bank, one of the dozen prestigious U.S. banks that dominate commercial and international banking. Yet her role as a retail bank—and her shrinkage—put her on *American Banker* magazine's list as an also-ran among the superregionals. BankAmerica still has a powerful international network. But its future role is unknown as the bank focuses its effort very selectively on corporate wholesale banking abroad. It has pulled back from Europe just as Eastern Europe's mighty surge toward "the free market of ideas as well as commodities" (a surge at least temporarily suppressed in China), opens dynamic business potential—as West Germany's Deutsche Bank positions itself to dominate European banking in the early nineties. B of A's withdrawal, and its abandonment of the dream of dominating global payments, suggests an acceptance of something more modest than global leader. "There will always be a relative handful of global players. Citicorp will be one of them," Armacost believes. "Our international network is our most important competitive advantage," Wriston confirms.

Yet viewed through the close-up lens of quarterly performance, this appears to be B of A's moment. As the new decade began, BAC inched a few cents ahead of Citi's stock price on the New York Stock Exchange. Armacost says, "The bank that's going to look the best in the next downturn is B of A—they've been through the trenches." "I think Citicorp is a casualty of changing times," says SIFE Trust Fund's Sam Marchese, as analysts found the performance of America's largest bank "dismal and disappointing." "Right now, if I had to make a choice between buying the stock of Citi or B of A, it would clearly be B of A," says Marchese. "Citicorp's heavy involvement in worriesome LBO lendings" was depressing its stock, says analyst George Salem, as B of A stood with less than one-quarter of Citi's portfolio holdings of HLTs (highly leveraged transactions) and largely purged of bad domestic loans by the hawk-eyed vigilance of Glenhall Taylor. Citicorp's scattered empire of savings and loans, a sly means of positioning for interstate banking, was suffering the doldrums of the thrift industry. Retrenchments overseas had recently cost nearly half a billion. Citi's huge investment in building the information business was, Wriston observed, an essential long-term investment. "We'll do it in less than the seven years it took to build the consumer business." But analysts disliked its drag on earnings, as they had disliked the clobbering Citi took when it flooded the country with unsolicited credit cards to build its card business. As the 1990s began, Citicorp's stock was being further bruised by the bankruptcy of the Campeau Corporation, whose junk-bond-based retail empire had been financed with $2.34 billion from a Citi-led banking syndicate, and by Reed taking another massive hit of $1 billion in reserves against "possible LDC credit losses."

Citibank is a symbol of the conundrum of American banking. Here is the behemoth that in 1988 had more global power, more resources, more profits—$1.86 billion—than any American bank in history (its 1989 profits were shrunk to $498 million by that $1 billion provision). Citi brags in its television ads that it is "$200 billion strong" (its total assets are, in fact, $230 billion). As B of A withdrew, Citi's global consumer business "grew" its profits 35 percent in 1989. It leads the world in foreign currency transactions. With the pulse of a computer key, it can mobilize the services and resources of its entire network for any customer anywhere in the world in any currency—a grand global extension of the power of Giannini's branch bank system to shift resources, flexibly and swiftly, to wherever they were needed. Citi is pushing toward owning 10 percent of the nation's mortgage market; it owns the Quotron on every banker's desk; and it has 30 million credit card customers. It claims to make more money in investment banking than Goldman Sachs, and it straddles the globe with more than 2,000 branches and affiliates. Its leader is not a lending officer but a nimble-minded, computer-savvy operational man who has no psychological barriers to thinking of a bank as a retail store or of the globe as his back yard.

In a revolution built on loopholes, Citi is still the most creative end runner in the industry. Thwarted in New York, it entered the securities market through its Delaware subsidiary. It found a vehicle for reentering corporate business in the financing of corporate acquisitions and leveraged buyouts—the "deal" market. Barred from nationwide expansion by the McFadden Act, it has used its continent-straddling credit card and its network of nonbanks and thrifts to position itself to become the first great national bank, Giannini's long desire.

But with deregulation having freed markets faster than it has freed banks, the game is still a frustrating one. Citi cannot compete with the vast deposit base of Japanese banks because it cannot do the national banking needed to suck in great pools of capital. Nor can it affiliate with huge industrial corporations, as can Japanese and European banks. Although automotive and retail giants Ford and Sears have pioneered the concept of industrial/financial combines on the thrift side, it is unlikely that commercial banks will be permitted anytime soon to emulate powerful corporate linkages like Germany's Deutsche Bank and Daimler Benz. Until 1991 Citi cannot move into California and buy a bank, as foreigners who are not yet in other states are permitted to do; it has had to enter the succulent California market through the back door. Although lobbying hard for new securities powers, Citi cannot now fully compete in investment banking as American Express can through its subsidiary, Shearson Lehman Hutton. It must go abroad, to the Euromarket, to enjoy these freedoms. In 1989 Citi was stretched thin abroad with a $15 billion LDC exposure—the largest of any bank—while powerful regional banks, with virtually no foreign debt and with rich captive interstate franchises, outstrip the performance of the New York giant. Citi sees Morgan Guaranty, jewel of the "boutiques," smugly continuing in its corporate niche, eschewing the consumer and the array of diversification on which Citi stakes its future.

That diversity, however, may be its strength. "Citi is so well diversified, playing in every possible market, that it can overcome specific weaknesses in certain market segments," says a banking economist, explaining its profitability. Yet Citi's greatest strength, its most valuable lesson for U.S. banking, may be its willingness to endure barbs and forgo instant gratification to invest in the future. "It may not be called Citibank twenty years from now. It may not look the same. But it will be a survivor," says former BankAmerican Mont McMillen, who is now doing real estate for the Japanese-owned developer Haseko, Inc.

"By whatever name, who does the business is going to depend on who's awake that morning," says Wriston, summing up the bank of tomorrow.

BANK OF AMERICA'S response to the wake-up call would depend in part on Clausen's response, in his remaining time at the helm, to three issues. Would he allow strongmen to remain at his elbow, as he has not done in the past? Would he, at sixty-six, respond to change with the flexibility and sensitivity required by a complex world? Where Wriston says, "Laws and regulations are not sacred. They are there to be changed," Clausen claims, "A rule is a rule is a rule." Finally, had he gained the confidence and statesmanship to raise his eyes from the security of numbers to view his universe with real vision—would he dare to sacrifice quarterly profits for investment in long-term strategies? And to choose a successor of breadth and vision.

As for the human touch, some saw a mellowing. "Tom fully realizes his mistakes," says Clausen-hired technology chief Michael Simmons of Clausen's overdue but aggressive support of computer systems. "He can be hard, gruff, and sarcastic, but he's always *fair* and says 'thank you.' " Clausen loves to say, "I'm the nicest guy I know," and boasts of a collegial, close-knit team. But he had not been able to sustain Claire Hoffman's goodwill, nor to break into the Wells Fargo "club," claimed executive-floor observers as they watched alienation and resentment grow between Rosenberg and Clausen.

Yet Charles Schwab had developed "a very good rapport" with Clausen since Clausen's return, "the kind of rapport that didn't develop with Sam." Finding Clausen "quite warm and straightforward" at their first lunch together in the president's dining room on the fifty-first floor, Schwab said, "Tom, I can't believe what the press has made you into." Clausen responded, "My son says so, too."

But in Clausen there was, apparently, still a dichotomy between the man who can praise his beloved wife, Peggy, for teaching him "egalitarianism—she's the same with queens or cleaning ladies," and the autocrat who, in the next breath, seizes a visitor's questions and hurls them back like a boomerang, attacking queries about his management record by attacking the questioner and dismissing his critics by snapping, "They're *wrong*!" "Tom's back to his old tricks, calling people out," a former member of his team said, as he received reports of the old style of intimidation.

"I'm a corporate man. I started in the vaults. I'm a product of the University of Bank of America," said Clausen recently. He said it with a kind of fierce resignation, as if helpless to escape the Promethean burden of dedication and abuse he must shoulder for the good of the institution he has loved and served for most of his adult life—a burden only he and Peggy fully understand, one that explains and justifies his style. "I'm a *corporate man*," he repeated.

BEFORE CHRISTMAS of 1988, Clausen had brought the two cultures together at a luncheon gathering of the board, the Big Four from Wells, and the old guard—Beise, Peterson, Baumhefner, Russ Smith, Zipf, and the new retirees, Prussia and Frick. "The really successful teams combine the best of the old and the new, and emerge winners," he said. "We are building a new Bank of America now, not resurrecting the old . . . an organization which combines the best of our traditional strengths and values with the best of the strengths and values brought to us by those who have joined us from other cultures . . . an organization that can, and will, be . . . *the best in the business again.*"

The drama lay not in the words that tried to bridge the gap between two cultures but in the ghosts that filled that gap. Clausen stood alone, the only survivor in the field of bright young men who had traveled the fast track with him. The absent figures of Rice, Truex, Pinola, Armacost, McMillen, and the new wave—Cooper, Hopper, Schwab, and others—vibrated in the chasm between the old guard and the Wells team. "The tragedy is that all those good and talented guys were cut to pieces," says a former BankAmerican who had watched the exodus. "MotherBank devoured her own children."

The new BankAmerica would be shaped partly by external events. But as always the people within it would determine how successfully it rode the larger waves. "The bank was too humanistic for many years," says Steve McLin of the years when "the human touch" was distorted to mean job security and softness in the areas of innovation and banking discipline. "Now," he says, "it's crossed the line too far on the other side. Making money may be all that shareholders want." If not, if the bank can find a way to combine the best of the old values—the "humanity and credibility" Armacost knew a great branch manager brought—with the unforgiving, profit-minded style of Citi and Wells Fargo, the culture forged could be a model for the 1990s. If Clausen can blend the "relationship" with the "transactional" banker, as John Reed, too, struggles to do, it would be a greater legacy to his beloved bank, and to banking, than a 100-basis-point return on assets. He might then have earned a statue.

The human touch of the Wells team was still an unknown quantity, although their former bank, run like a Swiss watch by hard-nosed credit man Carl Reichardt, is known to breed ruthless managers. But it is possible—and it would be profoundly ironic, given A.P.'s distaste for Wells Fargo—that in its Wells implants, the bank may finally have rediscovered the "old bank" in the best sense. There appear to be no giants on the scale of Giannini among them. But some of the elusive essence of the "real" A. P. Giannini seems to reside in Lew Coleman, for one. "I don't know if I'm a BankAmerican," says Coleman. But A.P. would boom approval of his words: "I find it helpful to manage with a little force of personality rather than force of paper, or policy. I don't write lots of memos. I like to be hands on, verbal, face to face." "I want my managers to make things happen as opposed to letting them happen. I like people who are willing to risk trying new things . . . people who set high standards for performance."

And yet Coleman's "human touch" does not seem to have compromised his toughness. He wielded the sword that slashed Wells's foreign operations. After watching Coleman in action in World Banking meetings, a former B of A senior officer saw a decisiveness Coleman's predecessor, longtime BankAmerican Bob Frick, did not have. "Coleman makes a decision, bang! and it's done.

It is possible that the inertial power of B of A's culture is still so strong that even Wells's tough warriors will be co-opted by it. For example, when he arrived, Coleman found a hierarchical credit system in World Banking in which credit and lending decisions did not converge until several levels removed from the field. Instead of changing the system, he left it in place and patched it with incentives, performance-measuring tools, and harsh discipline for those who disguised low-quality loans. It bears watching.

It seems more likely, however, that Wells's costs-and-margins culture will be imposed with a sledgehammer. "They're trying to wreck the old culture and make it WellsAmerica—just another plastic, soulless corporation that will be swallowed in the next downturn," said a middle manager as, by late 1989, Dick Rosenberg emerged as heir apparent. A man whose drive and discipline can be measured by the M.B.A. and law degrees he earned at night school from Golden Gate University, he is a marketer extraordinaire; if the bank's focus remained on the consumer market in the West, the brass ring might well be his. But if Clausen became restless to climb out of the superregional category and set his sights on returning B of A to global preeminence, Coleman would be the logical general for that war. Rosenberg lacks foreign exposure vital to the nineties and was nicknamed "Ricochet Dick" for his bouncing from product to product with no long-range strategy. Coleman has never run a retail bank. An old Wells colleague of both men says Rosenberg carries a force field of energy that inspires, but Coleman has the best balance of managerial gifts of any of the Wells "implants." As results for the final quarter of 1989 were released in mid-January 1990, the numbers were read for signs of the relative strength of the two men. Rosenberg seemed strengthened by Clausen's claim that 1989's record $1.1 billion earnings had been aided by "particularly strong growth in domestic consumer loans and residential mortgage loans." Yet Coleman was regaining profits for corporate banking. Clausen was not revealing his choice, nor the date of his next retirement. But as he basked in "an excellent finish to a turbulent decade for the corporation"—as *Forbes* named B of A "the financial services company best positioned for the 1990s" and *Fortune* ranked its corporate reputation "most improved"—the assumption grew that Clausen would make 1989 his closing page in banking history and name his successor at or before the annual meeting on May 24. Disabled by a knee smashed during the October earthquake, two years past mandatory retirement age, and his workaholism worrying Peggy, he must retire soon. Coleman, more than a decade younger than the fifty-nine-year-old Rosenberg, had gallantly told his rival, "I hope you get it." "Tom will make his own choice, and it will be the right one," said old friend Eugene Trefethen. But Clausen had no options. He must name a successor, and there was really only one candidate. The contest was a charade, for Coleman's lack of retail experience disqualified him for now with the board. And Rosenberg held a trump card that added urgency to the decision: an $800,000 golden parachute that would trigger if he resigned during 1989 or '90, an event that would ravage Clausen's last balance sheet and tarnish the glow of recovery. "It had the force of blackmail," says an insider.

As the clock ticked toward year-end, Rosenberg met quietly with directors. Tension "you could cut with a knife" gripped the Managing Committee through mid-December. Then, suddenly, it ceased. The decision would remain secret until February. But Rosenberg had won. Coleman would probably have won A.P.'s vote. Unlike that train of BankAmericans who paid lip service to change while clinging to false icons of the past, Coleman seems to speak from the heart: "If you don't change, you're dead."

THAT IMPERATIVE should be emblazoned on the banner of every banker locked in combat with the third world debt crisis. For where recession and deregulation have been the testing grounds at home, the debt crisis has become, for B of A as for all American banks, the test that will reveal whether they can successfully graze the global pastures in the coming years. It will reveal the dinosaurs. Even as events pull the fickle public eye to Eastern Europe and the apparent triumph of the Western economic system, the debt crisis sits like toxic waste, menacing the future.

By the early months of 1989, tensions over third world debt had built to a climax. Citicorp's Bill Rhodes, the bankers' restructuring king, had scarcely returned from the inauguration of Venezuela's new president, a gala "corona-tion" attended by Vice-President Dan Quayle and Fidel Castro, when riots exploded in that country. Three hundred dead and thousands of wounded were pulled from the streets of Caracas, Maracaibo, San Cristobal, and Puerto la Cruz after guns sprayed mobs who had burned and overturned cars and buses, blockaded streets, smashed windows, and looted stores. Violence had been triggered by the raising of fuel and transportation prices by President Carlos Andrés Perez, who had ruled Venezuela through the 1970s oil boom. But the riots were rooted in the country's $33 billion foreign debt. The hated price increases were part of a package of economic reforms Perez had imposed to win emergency and long-term loans from the IMF, World Bank, banks, and governments as the last of the oil dollars that had kept Venezuela's economy beating drained away.

Still sitting on rich oil reserves, Venezuela was far from bankrupt by Wriston's definition. But as "debt fatigue" escalated to bloody insurrection, as bitter rumblings grew in the other three major Latin American debtor nations—Mexico, Brazil, and Argentina—that old argument turned hollow. Although Brazil had ended its moratorium and returned to international re-spectability by signing a debt package in September 1988, that nation had swiftly regressed into crisis; its inflation ran at an incomprehensible 2,000 percent a year, as Peru's soon would. Its debt was trading on the secondary market at 29 cents on the dollar—junk! Argentina's debt had sunk to 18 cents on the dollar, and its debt went unpaid for five months as its economy went into a death spiral; by May, Buenos Aires residents were shooting and looting for food, and Peronistas were being called back to power. In Colombia, drug lords launched a murderous reign of terror, driving the nation close to anarchy and casting doubt on Colombia's continuing capacity to pay its debt.

In Europe, Poland picked up the cry. As Venezuela bled, labor hero Lech Walesa met with the Polish president in Warsaw, drafting a demand to the world's financial community to find relief for the crushing foreign debt. In Hungary, soldiers cut down the barbed-wire iron curtain on its Austrian border to signify the Eastern bloc's surge toward participation in the thriving Euro-pean Economic Community.

The crucible of debt had ruthlessly pushed countries into two camps, "those that make it and those that don't," a Federal Reserve Board governor ob-served. "Korea is blazing along with an embarrassment of riches. Chile's making it and, maybe, Mexico, if it carries out its domestic reforms. But Peru and Argentina are the worst." The brutal facts were that with all the reschedul-ings since the 1982 Mexican debt crisis, Latin America's total debt had not shrunk, but had grown from $323 billion to $414 billion.

Foreign debt was not the sole cause of the chaos, however. Flight capital—the money drained off as nations' own citizens cut and ran with their personal riches instead of investing and paying taxes on them at home—also undermined economic recovery. By 1989, $84 billion had escaped from Mexico alone. And bankers pointed out that Latin America's huge internal debt posed an even greater threat in Mexico and Brazil than their foreign debt. But as Brazil's desperate peasants burned and cut the Amazonian rainforests for fuel, cattle, and crops—compounding the threat to the ozone layer—as Brazil's government, under pressure from the community of industrialized nations, proposed swapping some of its foreign debt for investment in land trusts to protect the vanishing forests, bankers found not only the future of the third world but responsibility for the very survival of life on earth laid at their feet.

"A year ago, the banking world probably had enough reserves to solve the problem, but we didn't figure out how to deliver the benefit of those reserves to the countries," admitted World Banking Group's Coleman, searching for the roots of the inflexibility that, in leaving the countries too poor to grow and trade, had harmed the banks' own interests. "Why," he asked, "if I'm going to sell a hundred million dollars of my Brazil loans to Deutsche Bank at, say, fifty cents on the dollar—and take a fifty-cent write-off—would I not be better off and accomplish the same thing if I went to Brazil and said, 'I've got a deal for you. Just repay half your debt'? Somehow, I'm unwilling to do that because, by God, everybody pays their debt."

There was something more than conventional thinking at the root of the intransigence, Coleman believed. "Never, in the previous debt crises, have commercial bankers been the lenders, and central governments the debtors—the two most ill-suited parties that have ever been put in a room to negotiate anything!" he said. "The bankers are insisting that the last dime gets paid, and the central governments, who are basically politicians, are absolutely insisting that 'if I reduce the real-wage growth another 40 percent in Mexico I'm going to lose my office.' " "The problem for bankers," he speculated, "is that we don't have a 'final event.' Bankers always need a final event. A company goes away, files bankruptcy, is liquidated, you lose or get your money. There's an end. But a country doesn't go away. It doesn't file bankruptcy. It's going to sit there and stare at you forever. Your grandkids are going to be there and see the country."

The mind-set had to change. They had all collaborated in creating the mess. The banks' greed and naiveté had been matched, dollar for dollar, by the debtor countries' financial profligacy, mismanagement, and resistance to economic reform. Eventually, they all must share the pain. "But," says Coleman, "most bankers don't want to deal with that yet."

After six years of dogged restructuring, the foreign debt problem had swelled into one of the two most challenging issues for the Bush administration, along with the national deficit. Yet by the end of February 1989, the president's promised solution had not appeared, fanning frustration and unrest in the third world.

THE DEBTOR COUNTRIES bled, but the commercial banking system had survived the debt crisis. DEBT CRISIS FOR BANKS SAID TO END . . . THIRD WORLD LOANS NO LONGER A THREAT, the *New York Times* had announced in early January 1989, paraphrasing regulators' testimony to a congressional banking committee in Washington. The first international regulatory standards had just been established by the Cooke Committee, which represented the key banking nations of the world, setting capital guidelines for creditor banks based on the "risk" rating of their foreign loans—a hopeful discipline for bankers who might again be gripped by lending euphoria. Brazil's moratorium had been declared a failure, and interest payments resumed in December.

Bill Rhodes, ringmaster for Brazil's record $82 billion rescheduling package, signed September 22, 1988, was optimistic that the Brazil agreement would prove to be the "next step, a new phase" in solving the debt crisis for the debtor countries as well. The agreement provided some new money, which was vital to growth, all agreed, but which only exacerbated the load of debt. Embedded in the package was the key, Rhodes believed, to the ultimate solution. *Not* forced debt forgiveness, never! But some voluntary debt reduction that would ease the burden on Brazil, reducing the capital and interest payments. But the reduction would be gradual, at a pace that would not imperil the banks or shut the countries off from the capital flows they needed for future growth. It was the heresy bankers had not wanted to hear. Rhodes had received a congratulatory call from Tom Clausen, though, an encouraging sign. Rhodes was in constant touch with Washington and felt confident that the cornerstone of Treasury Secretary Nicholas Brady's debt plan would be voluntary debt reduction.

Rhodes was under extraordinary pressure, for the rescheduling process was under heavy attack. Voices were growing strident for taking the debt crisis from the bankers' hands and putting it in the hands of an agency like the World Bank. There were cries for reducing debt by 50 percent rather than the 8 percent per year of Brazil's package and for imposing debt forgiveness on the banks. Writing it off. Although seven years of debt rescheduling had bought time for the banks, B of A's Coleman saw it becoming "less and less effective, as more and more players opt out of the process . . . Peru . . . regional banks."

Smaller banks had aggressively exited, swapping or selling their loans, purging their relatively small exposures of LDC debt from their portfolios, leaving some of the big banks as vulnerable as beached whales. When Paul Volcker had retired from the Fed, he had sent Rhodes a congratulatory letter, which Rhodes had framed and hung on his office wall; the letter could be read by anyone looking for signs as an elegy for debt restructuring: "Maybe you will be the last of that hardy band of warriors assembled in 1982 dedicated to fighting the debt crisis to victory. . . . Time passes and conditions change, but that can never be taken away." "We stepped up because the countries asked us to do it. We were filling a void," Rhodes reminded as the storm grew.

Rhodes had never intended the process to be permanent. "We hope the advisory committees will fade away as the countries work their way back," he said. But "the call for imposed debt forgiveness . . . would seriously retard the countries' return to the marketplace," he argued in the *Wall Street Journal* and in speeches in Berlin, Amsterdam, and New York. "Commercial banks, once losses are imposed on them, will stop or severely curtail lending to the countries . . . limiting their growth."

Yet even hard-line bankers like Tom Clausen knew that "genuine progress on solving the developing country debt problem has eluded our grasp. . . . The process . . . is spinning its wheels in the sand." He had held to the puritanical principles of the Baker Plan even as it crumbled. But on March 10, 1989, Clausen had stood before the Bretton Woods Committee at the Brookings Institution in Washington and bluntly declared to his fellow bankers that "the time has come to make the process more flexible." It was time for commercial banks to seize the initiative, and—the shocker—"to pay more attention to *debt service reduction*." To reducing the interest!

Just a year and a half earlier, at a hastily called secret summit meeting of major creditor banks during the September 1987 IMF/World Bank meetings in Washington, Clausen had been committed to the uncompromising posture that "we ask Brazil that they really put into place a strong program of economic reform" before rewarding it as a "deserving country" with new loans. All too often, Clausen warned, those loans were used by debtor nations as the "wherewithal to postpone addressing and stepping up to the difficult policy issues that it has to put into place." That meeting had ended with the chairman of France's Crédit Lyonnais affirming the banker's creed with the imperturbable faith of a fundamentalist preacher: "A debt is a debt. Interest is interest."

But now, at Bretton Woods, Clausen argued that new money alone—one of the cornerstones of the Baker Plan he had so ardently supported—"results in a build-up in the stock of debt, an increased, not lessened, burden." He proceeded to couch his bold proposal in quid pro quos, caveats, and "enhance-

ments" that would shield the banks from risk. He still invoked the catch-22 on
which solutions had foundered—the morally righteous demand that countries
reform themselves before qualifying for relief. But a seasoned Clausen watcher
thought that the speech revealed a new man. "He did a twist. His speech
changes the thinking to a more imaginative, flexible approach. . . . I think
MotherBank has finally cracked his shell."

That afternoon Nicholas Brady finally unleashed the bare bones of the
Brady Plan, the administration's solution. It was so closely aligned with
Clausen's that it might well have been worked out at Clausen's campfire at the
Bohemian Grove or at Brady's camp, Mandalay. It was satisfying to Rhodes;
voluntary debt reduction would be at the heart of it, along with continuing new
money flows to the countries. Negotiations on that reduction—how much,
how fast—would be worked out case by case between the countries and the
bank committees. The countries would use some of their borrowings from the
IMF and World Bank as collateral to protect the banks if the countries did not
honor their debt-reduced commitments. Japan, whose earlier debt initiatives
had been rejected by the United States, seized the moment to rise to its new
role as a global power, offering to carry a disproportionate share of the
financial burden by pledging billions of dollars.

There was caution on all sides, for the Brady Plan offered no neat "cookie
cutter." But a new era—the beginning of the end of the third world debt
crisis—seemed to have begun. The end of the petrodollar debacle and of the
conventional thinking that had permitted it. Through the spring, Rhodes and
the negotiating teams sat down again in New York with Mexico and Venezuela,
with the Philippines and Costa Rica in an attempt to implement the new
philosophy. Pulling themselves up from debt fatigue, the negotiators found
new energy in the marathon that might, this time, put to rest the agonizing
crisis and set the turbulent economies of Africa, Latin America, India, and
Eastern Europe on the path to stability and growth. It was a race to star in a
moment of history. "Venezuela says it wants to be first. But all eyes are on
Mexico," Rhodes said. It would end, apparently, where it had all begun in
1982. Euphemistically calling the guarantees "enhancements," the word
Clausen had used in his speech, the teams negotiated and drove for completion
of the first Brady Plan package by July 31, 1989, when Mexico's new president, Carlos Salinas de Gortari, wanted to present a foreign debt agreement as
the country's wage, price, and inflation control pact expired. As the bankers sat
down with Venezuela on May 5, a creditor banker said, "We may not have to
meet again with Chile. It may have had its last meeting."

But bankers had not been transmuted overnight into enlightened humanists.
Under Secretary of the Treasury David Mulford was forced to tell the Senate

Finance Committee in May that the Mexican talks were moving slowly. The Brady Plan's goals as to the size of debt reduction were still unclear; Mexico was asking 55 percent cuts in interest and in the value of loans; the banks' first counteroffer was 15 percent. Bankers still balked.

Brady went empty-handed to the summit of industrialized democracies in Paris in mid-July, his much-hyped Brady Plan still nothing more than promises.

ON THE WEEKEND of July 23, 1989, Tom Clausen, John Reed, Bill Rhodes, Angel Gurria, now under secretary of Mexico's Ministry of Finance, his boss Pedro Aspe, minister of finance, Swiss Bank Corp.'s Tony Spicijaric, and a handful of powerful bankers and government officials converged on Washington. They would not leave until an agreement in principle had been struck. Embarrassed by the delay and impatient that heads of state should be so urgently focused on the issue while commercial bankers left the job to their negotiators, Treasury Secretary Brady had called to the capital the chairmen of the two banks that had the largest Latin American debt exposure—Reed and Clausen, cochairs of the Mexican Advisory Committee.

At marathon meetings Saturday and Sunday in a third-floor conference room at the Treasury, New York Fed chief Gerald Corrigan orchestrated a "very tough give and take," as Rhodes described it, as the bankers battled through the stubborn obstacles to reach an accord. On both nights, just before midnight, Clausen, Reed, and Rhodes returned to the Bankers Association for Foreign Trade—the same room, Rhodes noted with a pang of déjà vu, where they had met with Mexico in '86 and Brazil in '87—to report to bankers representing the fifteen banks on the committee as well as the four hundred–plus commercial banks that held Mexican debt. On Sunday night the exhausted group reported their job done. They had compromised on the sticking points and forged an agreement in principle. Mexico would get both reduced interest and reduced principal, new money, the protection of thirty years' fixed interest, and an assurance that bankers would not lay claim to the lion's share of any oil bonanza that might come from a rise in oil prices—potentially Mexico's life blood, even though its economy relied less on oil now than it had during the early 1980s. Forty-eight billion dollars of its debt would be boldly reduced in value. The bankers had won a choice of options that would at least let them name their poison. They could swap their loans for guaranteed bonds at reduced face value (principal) or reduced interest, taking a loss of 35 percent on the loans' value either way. Or they could lend the new money still seen as the key to revitalizing Mexico's growth. The guarantees or "enhancements," should Mexico falter, would be paid by a multibillion-dollar consortium of funds from the IMF, World Bank, Japan, and Mexico itself.

Aspe called his president, Salinas, in Mexico City, and at midnight Salinas announced the news to his nation. Now the "term sheet" must be beaten out. Gurria and Rhodes, scarred veterans of all the Mexican crises, moved the marathon to Shearman and Sterling's offices in New York, where the endless dance of debt went on through August. The odd couple—Gurria, black-bearded and passionate, and Rhodes, bespectacled and unflappable—struck the final agreement in early September and rushed to send their document, a three hundred-page term sheet, to all the banks, then mount the global road show that would try to win the banks' support. As Rhodes sped direct to JFK Airport and caught Pan Am's last flight of the day to Paris to begin the wooing process, he was at the blazing white-hot center of the world. This time it was not just a Mexican "save," it seemed, but a save for the world's developing nations. A save that could help bring equilibrium to the global economic balance, thrown off by this prolonged agony. The process was holding. Although restructuring would still, Rhodes stressed, be "country by country, case by case, no cookie cutters," Mexico's groundbreaking debt agreement held hope for all those nations waiting in line for an inoculation of the Brady Plan.

Although some bankers complained that they had been forced to take losses and would never lend to Mexico again, there were widespread sighs of relief. Bush and Brady had regained for themselves and the United States the initiative in this most urgent of all global economic issues. Largely an American show, "Mexico" had stolen some of the thunder back from Japan, while giving Japan a chance to play the statesman's role in which its financial power cast it. Salinas had an offering with which to appease an anguished nation, reinforcing the image of leader that had begun to cloak him over the previous several months. Gurria the Turbulent would return home as one of Mexico's leading economic architects. Rhodes, soon to be promoted by Reed to a newly created job as senior executive, international, was moving into the role of banker-statesman as he and Paul Volcker, now chairman of the New York investment bank James D. Wolfensohn Inc., flew to Poland in December to advise on its new economic program. Commercial bankers had been bailed out, their losses contained well this side of the disaster they had faced and, many observers thought, earned. The community of debtor nations felt hope that the magic of debt reduction would rub off on them all.

And Tom Clausen, born-again banker, was again a star. Granted, his prospects for billion-dollar-plus profits for 1989 risked being swept away if he was forced to follow the lead of his peer banks—Chase, Morgan, Citi, and the

British banks Barclays and Midland—and raise his LDC reserves boldly, a prelude to those banks taking their losses and perhaps getting out of the foreign debt mess altogether. In the Washington meetings on Mexico, though, Rhodes had observed that "although John Reed had been the most forceful of the bankers, Tom was a key player, acting as a statesman throughout the negotiations." "He *has* learned from the World Bank experience," a former colleague said. If Clausen retired tomorrow, he would be leaving a bank, and a banking industry, that seemed, with the Mexican debt accord, to have weathered its worst trials. Stronger and wiser, the industry was armed with more sophisticated weapons with which to fight the remaining battles of the war that continued to revolutionize banks and bankers.

But as Gurria, Rhodes, and Clausen marched toward the high point of their careers, Carlos Fuentes, Mexico's greatest living novelist, released his new book, *Christopher Unborn*. In it he painted a doomsday scenario for Mexico in 1992, a Mexico in mayhem with "colossal debt, appalling scandal, environmental pollution and a huge gap between rich and poor," as the *New York Times* paraphrased Fuentes's searing vision. "He wrote it *before* we'd achieved the debt agreement," joked an international banker. But if artists are prophets, Fuentes's book forces the question: Have bankers learned from the past fifteen years? Or is the ritual of debt restructuring that cloaked the petrodollar era with psychic buffers from reality still cloaking bankers' failure to stretch beyond short-term self-interest to their own, and the globe's, larger good?

Regardless of Rhodes's personal sacrifice and belief that "the system would have gone down" had the commercial banks not filled the void, keeping debt negotiating within their hands had also been in the banks' self-interest, critics felt. But Rhodes was a realist. "The debt crisis is not behind us," he said. The Brady Plan was still a work in progress. It needed a better balance between debt reduction and new money; more incentives for the banks to lend, as well as exit; more of the flexibility from the IMF and World Bank that he genuinely believed the commercial banks and the countries were beginning to show; and, crucial to success, the kind of cooperation—*the will to make it work*—that had so often been lost in posturing and pride. But the new strategy had finally brought them to "a turning point," he sensed as he joined the international debt club in Montreal for meetings of the Inter-American Development Bank in April 1990. Since the near-panic over Mexico in Toronto in 1982 the mood had been depressed by "debt, debt, debt." Banks had tried to close the doors and run from involvement with Latin America. Now there was a gathering consensus—from B of A's senior debt negotiator Peter MacPherson, from Canada's finance minister Michael Wilson—that the doors must reopen. Brazil and Argentina had halted interest again. But Mexico seemed to be holding to its economic reforms. All the vital signs showed that confidence in Mexico was beginning to pulse again, within and without the country. Perhaps Gurria's joke that there was "life after debt" would come true. "But if not managed carefully, the strategy could undermine the progress to date," said Rhodes.

Yogi Berra's immortal "It's déjà vu all over again" came to mind as Rhodes flew in late April to Managua to the inauguration—post-Sandinista, post-Contra—of Nicaragua's new government and the installation of his old friend Alfredo Cesar as secretary of the Congress; at the first anniversary of Sandinista power ten years earlier Rhodes had met Cesar—then the Sandinistas' chief debt negotiator, subsequently a Contra leader. International bankers went on forever.

If reduced to its essence, BankAmerica's, and American banking's, trauma of the 1980s has three root causes: bankers' frailty and misjudgments, an unresponsive regulatory system in a time of dynamic change, and global economic turmoil. Reform and correction of the second and third problems depend on change within the first, the human component.

Yes, the banker is evolving to a performance-driven salesman who can compete more effectively. But the moment calls for evolution to a higher form. It is a time when the international financial community, along with the world's political leaders, are recognizing the survival imperative of a higher level of accountability and sensitivity to their actions than ever in the past. The IMF/ World Bank annual meeting in Washington in late September 1989 named protection of the environment as its highest priority and declared that new loans made to developing nations must take environmental protection into consideration. Even the World Bank has been forced to see that the dams and industrial and agricultural projects it has funded have eroded the integrity of the environment and local cultures. This raised consciousness was given dramatic impetus by the global uproar over the *Exxon Valdez* oil spill in Alaska and the destruction of Brazil's rainforest; the World Bank canceled a loan to Brazil as a lever to force its leaders to see the Amazonian forests as the world's, not Brazil's, resource.

It is a time when American bankers must shake free of the temptation to protectionism that blocks the nation's interface with the world in other threatened industries. No matter how frustrated they are by the haphazard progress of regulatory reform at home, bankers must heed foreign cries for reciprocity in entering each other's markets and permit British and Germans to play by "our" rules here if American bankers enjoy the freedom of "their" rules abroad.

"Bankers really don't have to be very smart," Pinola once said of his colleagues of the 1950s, '60s, and '70s. That is no longer true. And yet it is not clear that they have evolved even the simplest survival tool: the reasoning powers to protect their own self-interest. Capital flight is the classic case in point. Although *The Economist* and the *Wall Street Journal* are talking about it, bankers will not. In his otherwise thoughtful lakeside talk at the Grove, Lew Coleman mentioned capital flight only in passing. Yet it offers the very essence of insight into the banker's mind.

While making loans to the third world in the 1970s and '80s, commercial banks were at the same time luring, from the rich of those same countries, even more billions than they were lending, as deposits in the safe and tax-free haven of American offshore bank accounts. Economist and attorney James S. Henry, a specialist in underground economies, claims that Citibank, B of A, and others "went after it actively. Set up conduits for it. Sheltered it. Managed it. All off the balance sheet." Citi's international private bankers (IPBs), he says, are active in Mexico City today. Citibank reportedly holds $20 billion of Latin American flight capital, more than twice its roughly $9 billion in loans to the region. If the same ratios hold, Bank of America may hold roughly $15 billion from Latin America. Henry and a former Mexico City–based Citibank lending officer both confirm that B of A's extravagantly well connected "Mr. Mexico," Pepe Carral, was invaluable in sending money both ways: loans in, flight capital out. "He became untouchable. Clausen would protect him," says a former BankAmerican. "But bankers didn't see that if the money hadn't left, they wouldn't have had the bad loans. They hurt themselves."

It is the same failure as B of A's costly mismatch, the failure to grasp the connection between the two sides of the basic banking equation, funding and lending. Economist Milton Friedman sees this failure to connect cause and effect confirmed by bankers' initial *resistance* to deregulation, then their eager *embrace* of it as they saw regulators begin to aggressively invade the realm of decisions that had been the bankers' sacred turf. By that early resistance, Friedman suggests, bankers brought on themselves the money market funds that continue to strip banks' deposits.

The massive hemorrhaging of flight capital represents the money that might have paid bankers their interest and financed growth and exports. "It is the dirty little secret behind the third world 'debt crisis,' " claims Henry. If repatriated today, that money could solve the debt crisis far faster than the Brady Plan. For all the exquisite financial engineering and ceremonial signing in Mexico City on February 4, 1990, the celebrated agreement will reduce Mexico's interest payments by only $1.7 billion a year and bring only a modest flow of the new money needed to assure growth, interest payments, and "enhancements" for the banks.

The banks' role in facilitating capital flight could be condemned as moral failure, for it places the burden of servicing the debts on the backs of "some of the poorest people in the world, while the tax-free assets belong to a transnational elite. The effect has been that of a massive milking carried out by foreign bankers who should have known better," says Henry, who claims that capital flight is only "the tip of the iceberg" in a sea of fraudulent banking activity in the financial underground. Bankers, on the other hand, can claim to be little more than passive instruments in the irresistible movement of capital toward the safest havens and highest returns. They can say "It is a long-standing pattern. What can we do if people lack confidence in their country?" They can point—just as they point to laws requiring banks to reveal results every ninety days as the root cause of their quarterly-mindedness—to U.S. tax laws that encourage the foreign investment that funds the American deficit by *not taxing* interest earned on nonresident foreigners' bank deposits held in offshore branches of U.S. banks. Lending officers can say, piously and often accurately, that they never touched flight capital; elite squads of IPBs did that. Bankers might even justify in their minds the billions of dollars in flight capital sitting in their deposit accounts as some vague kind of backup collateral should their third world loans default, even though it could be used in that way only in very rare cases.

But beyond any moral lapse, flight capital, like B of A's mismatch, is really a symbol of the failure to learn the lessons of the past and to project them to the future. Mexico now proposes an amnesty for the return of its "prodigal sums," as *The Economist* wryly dubbed flight capital. Henry proposes that the United States and other creditor countries coordinate to levy an anonymous 10 to 15 percent tax on offshore assets, an extension of the tax treaty being proposed by the European Economic Community for 1992, and send the money to Mexico to retire its debts. The issue cries out for creative solutions—solutions that may be *forced* on bankers as federal prosecutors lift the lid on commercial banks' highly profitable practice of laundering Latin American drug money, the ugliest side of flight capital. But bankers are not seizing leadership.

There is hope that the 1980s, which saw the precipitous decline of the world's biggest bank, were a roller coaster ride so scary, a crucible so violent, that from that wrenching decade may be forged bankers smart enough to carry banking through the 1990s as a vital and independent industry, one that will serve the world as well as B of A once served California. There is hope that product-hustling retail bankers will learn that survival lies in scanning the larger landscape and in thinking—if not with the daring vision of A. P. Giannini, who sixty years ago projected the national banking system that still slouches toward Washington to be born—at least as citizens of a world far beyond Visalia. Historically, bankers have been flexible and responsive, riding the winds of change. Gradually casting off the image of the usurer rubbing his hands with avaricious glee, commercial banks forged from the *banca*—the moneychanger's booth set up at Europe's medieval trade fairs—a vital function as the pumping bloodstream of the West's commerce, trade, growth, and power. Clausen's B of A rose as swiftly to help and reassure a shaken state after 1989's devastating earthquake as did Giannini's infant Bank of Italy on the San Francisco docks after the great quake of 1906. But as a luxuriant growth of new financial forms spikes up through the corroding American bank, as foreign banks usurp its power, as the *"too big to fail"* doctrine falls before market forces, the future of The Bank, the institution symbolized by Bank of America, is as uncertain as the future of the powerful culture it has served.

As the final decade of the twentieth century begins, Tom Clausen rides the soaring numbers and accolades like a victorious coach hoisted to the shoulders of his team. The respect of the international financial elite cloaks him like a club jacket. Using the metaphors of war and sports that are the Esperanto of business, Clausen says proudly, "My whole career is winning," as his cheerleaders—analysts, shareholders, the media—chant buzzwords to win by: globalization, securitization, core business, shareholder value. Through mindless repetition these words already risk becoming mere mantras that may lull bankers into the same sheeplike complacency that caused Clausen and his colleagues to miss some vital signals in the 1970s.

Can bankers hear, as Clausen is carried gloriously off the field, the ironic echo of the cheers that were raised to his record-shattering triumphs of ten years ago? Do they recall his words as he led the seventy-five-year-old Mother-Bank, well upholstered in quadrupled assets and earnings, into the 1980s after a decade "of extraordinary progress," a decade that had concluded "on a strong footing" and been used "to prepare for the future"? If they do remember, if they can resist the complacency and hubris that masked profound frailties and that will doom bankers of the Information Age, the institution can survive. America is banking on it.

ON FEBRUARY 5, 1990, BankAmerica Corporation issued a news release:

> A. W. Clausen, chairman and chief executive officer of BankAmerica Corporation and its wholly owned subsidiary, Bank of America NT&SA, announced today that he will retire from those posts effective at the end of the corporation's annual meeting on May 24, 1990. He will be succeeded by Richard M. Rosenberg, presently vice chairman of the boards of directors and head of Bank of America's California Banking Group. . . . Rosenberg . . . has been the architect of the bank's profit resurgence in retail banking, real estate, and commercial

banking in California which, in turn, has been the key to the corporation's recovery. . . .

In addition to Rosenberg's election as president, Lewis W. Coleman, vice chairman and head of the World Banking Group, Frank N. Newman, vice chairman and Chief Financial Officer, and Glenhall E. Taylor, Jr., vice chairman and head of Credit Policy, were elected to the corporation's and the bank's boards of directors today.

"The job I was called back to do, and which I came back to do, is done," Clausen said. "The recovery has been completed."

SELECTED BIBLIOGRAPHY
·
ACKNOWLEDGMENTS
·
INDEX

Selected Bibliography

CALIFORNIA BANKING AND CULTURE

Bean, Walton Elbert. *California: An Interpretive History*. New York: McGraw-Hill, 1973.

Caughey, John Walton. *California*. Englewood Cliffs, N.J.: Prentice-Hall, 1953.

Cross, Ira B. *Financing an Empire: History of Banking in California*. Los Angeles: S. J. Clarke, 1927.

James, Marquis, and Bessie James. *Biography of a Bank: The Story of Bank of America, NT & SA*. New York: Harper and Brothers, 1954.

Kotkin, Joel, and Paul Grabowicz. *California, Inc*. New York: Rawson, Wade, 1982.

McWilliams, Carey. *California, The Great Exception*. New York: A. A. Wyn, 1949.

———. *The California Revolution*. New York: Grossman, 1968.

Minsky, Hyman P., ed. *California Banking in a Growing Economy, 1946–1975*. Berkeley: Institute of Business and Economic Research, University of California, Berkeley, 1965.

Wernette, John Philip. *Branch Banking in California*. Ph.D. thesis, Harvard University, 1932.
Yeates, Fred. *The Gentle Giant*. San Francisco: Wallace Kibbee and Son, 1954.

AMERICAN BANKING AND ECONOMICS

Cargill, Thomas F., and Gillian G. Garcia. *Financial Reform in the 1980s*. Stanford University: Hoover Institution Press, 1985.
Cleveland, Harold van B., and Thomas F. Huertas. *Citibank 1812–1970*. Cambridge, Mass.: Harvard University Press, 1985.
Corrigan, E. Gerald. *Financial Market Structure: A Longer View*. Federal Reserve Bank of New York Annual Report, 1987.
Dillard, Dudley. *The Economics of John Maynard Keynes: The Theory of a Monetary Economy*. New York: Prentice-Hall, 1948.
Friedman, Milton, and Anna Jacobson Schwartz. *A Monetary History of the United States, 1867–1960*. Princeton: Princeton University Press, 1963.
Gart, Alan. *Banks, Thrifts, and Insurance Companies: Surviving the 1980s*. Lexington, Mass.: D.C. Heath, 1985.
Greider, William. *Secrets of the Temple: How the Federal Reserve Runs the Country*. New York: Simon and Schuster, 1987.
Mayer, Martin. *The Bankers*. New York: Weybright and Talley, 1974.
———. *The Money Bazaars: Understanding the Banking Revolution Around Us*. New York: E. P. Dutton, 1984.
Reich, Robert B. *Tales of a New America*. New York: Times Books, 1987.
Triffin, Robert. *Gold and the Dollar Crisis: Yesterday and Tomorrow*. Essays in International Finance no. 132–145. Princeton: Princeton University Department of Economics, 1978.

HISTORY

Center for Medieval and Renaissance Studies, University of California, Los Angeles, ed. *The Dawn of Modern Banking*. New Haven: Yale University Press 1979.
De Roover, Raymond. *Money, Banking and Credit in Mediaeval Bruges*. Cambridge, Mass.: Medieval Academy of America, 1948.
———. *The Rise and Decline of the Medici Bank 1397–1494*. Cambridge, Mass.: Harvard University Press, 1963.
Ehrenberg, Richard. *Capital and Finance in the Age of the Renaissance: A Study of the Fuggers and Their Connections*. New York: Harcourt Brace, 1928.
Usher, Abbott P. *The Early History of Deposit Banking in Mediterranean Europe*. New York: Russell & Russell, 1943.

INTERNATIONAL BANKING AND THIRD WORLD DEBT

Aho, C. Michael, and Marc Levinson. *After Reagan: Confronting the Changed World Economy*. New York: Council on Foreign Relations, 1988.

Cline, William R. *Mobilizing Bank Lending to Debtor Countries*. Washington: Institute for International Economics, 1987.

Feldstein, Martin, ed. *The United States in the World Economy*. Cambridge, Mass.: National Bureau of Economic Research, 1987.

Frieden, Jeffry A. *Banking on the World: The Politics of American International Finance*. New York: Harper & Row, 1987.

Gwynne, S. C. *Selling Money*. New York: Weidenfeld & Nicolson, 1986.

International Banking Study Group of the Group of Thirty. *Risks in International Bank Lending*. New York: Group of Thirty, 1982.

Kraft, Joseph. *The Mexican Rescue*. New York: Group of Thirty, 1984.

Study Group of the Central Banks of the Group of Ten Countries. *Recent Innovations in International Banking*. Bank for International Settlements, 1986.

Task Force Report to the Trilateral Commission. *Restoring Growth in the Debt-Laden Third World*. Triangle Papers no. 33. Trilateral Commission, 1987.

Acknowledgments

The story of the Bank of America is told principally through the eyes of those who participated, within and without the bank. I conducted more than 250 hours of personal taped interviews that form a living chain of experience and insight stretching back to, and beyond, the legendary Transamerica proxy fight in the early 1930s that threatened the bank's survival as surely as did the events of the 1980s. It was particularly gratifying to win the trust and stories of the men and women, now in their late eighties to mid-nineties, who were there with A. P. Giannini: Claire Hoffman, his daughter; Russ Smith, his first international banker; Angelo Scampini, the firebrand orator of the Transamerica battle; and Salvatore Reina, one of A.P.'s troops in that fight.

A number of people who gave generously of their time and thoughts appear only briefly, if at all, in the book, but their "background" has contributed richly to the soundness of the book's economic, political, and historical underpinnings. They include such people as Federal Reserve Board Governor Martha Seger and former Fed Governor Dr. H. Robert Heller; economic adviser to the president of the Bank of Tokyo, Koei Narusawa; former Comptroller of the Currency John G. Heimann; attorney Robert Carswell, who served as deputy secretary of the Treasury through the Iran hostage, New York

City, and Chrysler crises; attorneys William M. Friedrich and Mark A. Walker; Daniel F. Adams of the World Bank's International Finance Corporation; investment banker Anthony M. Solomon, former head of the New York Fed; Dr. John Gilbert, British member of Parliament and former BankAmerican; Senator William Proxmire, as chairman of the Senate's banking committee; Carl J. Schmitt, former California superintendent of banks; and John F. Lee of the New York Clearing House. Mario Giannini's daughter, Anne McWilliams, was most generous and helpful. And others. I thank them all. I also wish to thank the many dozens of bankers, economists, and political scientists at think tanks and universities, the bank customers, lawyers, staffs of congressional committees and regulatory agencies, the journalists, librarians, corporate communications and public relations officers, the industry associations, and financial services corporations for their unsung but invaluable help.

Several scholars and economists whose work has been helpful are Professor Albert Fishlow, University of California, Berkeley; Jeffrey A. Frankel, Visiting Professor, John F. Kennedy School of Government, Harvard University; Alan Stoga, Kissinger Associates; Professor Jeffrey D. Sachs, Harvard University; and James S. Henry.

Vital to the book's balance and authenticity were personal interviews with the two men who ran the bank through the critical decades, the 1970s and '80s—Tom Clausen and Sam Armacost. My twenty-plus hours of interviews with Mr. Armacost constitute the only extended interviews he has given since leaving the bank in 1986. The Clausen and Armacost interviews permitted me to gain a fully rounded view of the bank's recovery. Ron Rhody, John Keane, and Peter Magnani of Bank of America's corporate communications staff kept doors to the bank open during the tensest of times, providing access to key players and to archival materials during the months when a beleaguered bank would have preferred to bleed and heal out of sight of journalists.

Every word of dialogue is drawn accurately from my own personal interviews or from reliable printed sources. In cases where the comments of a participant are the best recollection of another participant in a conversation, they are identified as such.

I am blessed to have worked with two of the finest professionals in New York publishing. The editorial skills of John Herman, editorial director of Ticknor & Fields, show on every page. Even under extraordinary publishing pressures, he steadily reassured me to hold to the ambitious vision we shared for the book. My agent at William Morris, Michael Carlisle, shepherded me through the three-and-a-half-year project with the unique combination of market astuteness, literary sensibilities, and sustained excitement over his writers' projects that makes me proud to be part of his distinguished "stable." He was there

MOIRA JOHNSTON

at that electric moment on the Belvedere lagoon when my former editor, John Dodds, gathered up his failing energies into one last fervent editorial directive: "Go *write* the Bank of America book."

I can never adequately thank "the team": my sister Sheilagh Simpson, researcher Shelley Tantau, my mother, author Christie Harris, and my children, Christie and Don, who have always brought humor and perspective to the stress and tumult of their mother's work. To this book they also brought fact-checking, research, and transcribing skills.

Finally, I thank the friends to whom this book is dedicated: Judge Tom and Lorrain Kongsgaard, Phyllis and Lewis Sarasy, Suzanne Simpson and Lewis Litzky, Joan and Bob Blum, Sheila and Arthur Hailey, Michael and Sande Marston, Margrit and Robert Mondavi, Veronica and Rene DiRosa, David Myrick, Diane Perry, Jonathan Rice, Clara Denman, Joseph Phelps, and Bob Devlin. You all know how you have strengthened me in this project. Also, the loving, inspiring, and stabilizing role of Dr. Alvin Lee Block in my life through this and future books deserves the deepest tribute.

Index

www.ingramcontent.com/pod-product-compliance
Lightning Source LLC
Chambersburg PA
CBHW021545210326
41599CB00010B/319